D1552668

America's Forgotten Holiday

AMERICAN HISTORY AND CULTURE

General Editors: Neil Foley, Kevin Gaines,
Martha Hodes, and Scott Sandage

America's Forgotten Holiday

*May Day and
Nationalism,
1867–1960*

Donna T. Haverty-Stacke

NEW YORK UNIVERSITY PRESS
New York and London

HD
7791
. H38
2009

NEW YORK UNIVERSITY PRESS
New York and London
www.nyupress.org

© 2009 by New York University
All rights reserved

Library of Congress Cataloging-in-Publication Data
Haverty-Stacke, Donna T.
America's forgotten holiday : May Day and nationalism, 1867–1960 /
Donna T. Haverty-Stacke.
p. cm.
Includes bibliographical references and index.
ISBN-13: 978-0-8147-3705-7 (cl : alk. paper)
ISBN-10: 0-8147-3705-6 (cl : alk. paper)
1. May Day (Labor holiday)—United States—History.
2. Nationalism—United States—History. I. Title.
HD7791.H38   2008
394.26270973'09041—dc22   2008025482

New York University Press books are printed on acid-free paper,
and their binding materials are chosen for strength and durability.
We strive to use environmentally responsible suppliers and materials
to the greatest extent possible in publishing our books.

Manufactured in the United States of America
10 9 8 7 6 5 4 3 2 1

Contents

University Libraries
Carnegie Mellon University
Pittsburgh, PA 15213-3890

Acknowledgments

Although only my name dons the cover of this work, I could not have completed it without the love and support of a great many people. I am most grateful to Michael Kammen, whose advice and support have been indispensable and much appreciated both during my time at Cornell and since I have begun my career as a young historian. As most people in this profession would agree, Michael's scholarly productivity is a marvel and an inspiration. He is a true and much-loved mentor.

I also would like to thank Isabel Hull and Richard Polenberg for their suggestions and criticisms as readers of my work. Their insights served to strengthen the earliest revisions of the manuscript. And I am grateful to the Cornell Graduate School and Department of History for supporting my research during my time there with the Sage Fellowship, Gates Award, DAR Fellowship, Farr Fellowship, Ihlder Fellowship, and Mellon Completion Fellowship. I would also like to thank the New-York Historical Society for awarding me an N-YHS Research Fellowship in January 2002.

As I began the long process of working on the book, Leon Fink provided tremendous support. He generously read the entire manuscript and provided sage advice at that early stage of revisions. Several other historians graciously took time out of their busy schedules to read and comment on portions of the work, including three of my colleagues from Hunter College, Benjamin Hett, Karen Kern, and Jonathan Rosenberg. I am particularly grateful to Jon for his "fine-tooth comb" reading of almost the entire manuscript.

I extend a special thank you to everyone who attended the February 2007 meeting of New York University's Center for the United States and the Cold War seminar for reading and discussing my chapter on May Day during the Cold War. I especially thank Michael Nash and Marilyn Young for inviting me to present my work, Richard Greenwald for his extremely helpful comments, and Jennifer Luff for her insights. I would also like to thank Richard Ellis and Kevin Gaines, who as commentator and chair of a panel I participated in during the April 2007 Organization of American Historians meeting offered helpful suggestions for my chapter on May Day in the 1920s. Thanks, too, to Nunzio Pernicone, who generously provided copies of some hard-to-track-down works by Pietro Gori. I am also deeply grateful to Ken Fones-Wolf, Danny Walkowitz, and the anonymous reader for their detailed and thoughtful reports to NYU Press that helped me reshape the entire manuscript into its final form. My editor at NYU Press, Eric Zinner, along with Emily Park, Ciara McLaughlin, and the Press staff skillfully oversaw its transformation into the book. Special thanks to Eric, who from our first meeting was enthusiastic about the project and remained committed to it throughout the entire publishing process.

I also must express my appreciation to Barbara Welter. As chair of the History Department at Hunter she has provided unswerving support for my professional development. Thanks to her sponsorship, I participated in City University of New York's Faculty Fellowship Publications Program during the spring 2006 semester. Not only did the course release provide me with time vital to the final preparations of the book, but the feedback I received there from my fellow CUNY colleagues also helped see the work to conclusion. And I would like to thank CUNY for sponsoring this innovative program for its junior faculty. I am also grateful to the CUNY Research Foundation for awarding me a PSC-CUNY Faculty Research Grant, which enabled me to travel to Chicago a third time and to cover the cost for the wonderful illustrations in the book. And I am deeply thankful to the provost of Hunter College, Vita Rabinowitz, for the grant that helped defray the cost of my publication subvention.

Many archivists and librarians assisted me in my years of research. In particular, I want to thank Patrizia Sione and Richard Strassberg at the Kheel Center for Labor-Management Documentation and Archives, M.P. Catherwood Library, Cornell University; Lesley Martin and Bryan Mc-Daniel at the Chicago History Museum; Itty Matthew and the Research Library staff at the New-York Historical Society; the staff of the Prints and Photographs Division of the Library of Congress; and Gail Malmgreen, Peter Filardo, Donna Davey, and Erika Gottfried at the Tamiment Library/ Robert F. Wagner Labor Archives at New York University. I am especially grateful to Erika, who worked with me to locate nonprint sources on May Day when this project was in its early stages of development, then rolled out the red carpet for me again as I prepared the manuscript for publication. This book would have been greatly diminished without all their help.

Portions of this work have appeared, in somewhat different form, in three of my previously published articles: "Creative Opposition to Radical America: 1920s Anti-May Day Demonstrations," *Labor: Studies in Working-Class History of the Americas* 4, 3 (Fall 2007): 59–80; "May Day in Urban America," in *Encyclopedia of American Holidays and National Days*, ed. Len Travers (Westport, Conn.: Greenwood Press, 2006), 177–190; and "'Boys Are the Backbone of Our Nation': The Cultural Politics of Youth Parades in Urban America," *Prospects: An Annual of American Cultural Studies* 29 (December 2004): 563–594. I would like to thank *Labor*, Greenwood Press, and Cambridge University Press for permission to reprint this material.

In addition to colleagues, friends and family have played a special role in helping this book take shape. Michelle Lucey Roper and Mary Bennis have given me support over the years via phone calls and email. Closer to home, my buddies Andrew Horgan, George Ganat, Vincent Cicarelli, Jason St. Germain, Suzanne Adler, Jon Rosenberg, Ben Hett, and Corinna Andiel have been loyal coconspirators in all sorts of adventures, most involving copious amounts of good food and even better drink. Without such reprieves from the *sturm und drang* of academic life, this book would not have been written. Vinny's sudden death this spring reminded us all how precious are these ties of friendship.

Finally, I want to express my gratitude to my family for their love and support. My uncle and aunt, Peter and Donna Salerno, generously opened their home to me for my research trips to Chicago. I am most grateful to them for their warm hospitality, the drives to and from the train station, and the laughs we shared. My parents, Mario and Rose Truglio, have long been a source of support, expressing their pride and faith in me in quiet ways over the years. They instilled in me the importance of a good education and sacrificed many years to provide me with one. My sister, Maria, has become one of my closest friends in adulthood, as we bond over our mutual love (and occasional hate) of academic life. For all the proofreading you have done for me and all the phone conversations in which we have shared our weekly ups and downs, I thank you. My brother, Joseph, the "real" doctor in the family, I thank for all the free medical advice. And my nephews, Anthony and Thomas, who have brought humor into everything we do as a family, have been a great force for keeping me grounded. Most of all I want to thank my husband, Dylan. He is the most centered person I know and has been a constant source of strength for me ever since our eyes met across that smoky pub in Brighton all those years ago.

He stayed with me as I returned to the United States to graduate from Georgetown, visited me during my years at Oxford, and even traveled back and forth to Ithaca during the depths of winter when I was at Cornell. He has tolerated my dashing into archives "just for a few hours" on our vacations and has come to accept the weekends of grading that take over our lives during the semester, learning what it means to live with an academic. For his steadfastness, loyalty, love, humor, and patience, I extend my greatest thanks, and, as always, all my love.

Introduction

On May 1, 2006, for the first time in decades, May Day became a rallying point for hundreds of thousands of Americans. Immigrant workers and their supporters coordinated a nationwide protest of America's immigration policy. Their plan was to stage an economic boycott "under the banner 'Day Without an Immigrant'" to draw attention to the tremendous contribution those workers make to the American economy. While this remained the official focus, "the day evolved into a sweeping round of protests intended to influence the debates in Congress over granting legal status to all or most of the estimated 11 million illegal immigrants in the country."[1] Demanding more lenient immigration laws, some 400,000 people turned out for mass marches in Chicago and more than a half million in New York. Shops and restaurants in these cities and in Los Angeles closed for the day as workers left their posts to march in the large, peaceful demonstrations. Throughout California, produce went unpicked and goods were not shipped, as those workers took to the streets as well. And throughout the Midwest, major meatpacking companies like Tyson Foods and Cargill shut down operations as they faced the reality of the temporary work disruption.[2] The mostly Latino demonstrators made their political point as they demonstrated their impact on the nation's economy.

One of the more notable characteristics of the May 1, 2006, protests was the overwhelming presence of American flags. The marchers also carried Mexican and other national standards during the march, but they were fewer in number. In part, this was in response to criticisms voiced by those opposed to immigration reform, who had labeled the protestors "un-American" for displaying pride in their home countries during smaller demonstrations staged earlier that year. Immigrants and their supporters then emphasized their commitment and claim to the Stars and Stripes on May 1 by making sure American flags outnumbered all other national symbols.[3] The politics (and cultural politics) of immigration reform that lay at the heart of this flag debate were central to the demonstration.

Yet, even as the demonstrators struggled to show their American patriotism, the organizers of the boycotts and marches chose *May 1* as the rallying point for their larger movement. Interestingly, according to news reports, for most immigrant and native-born workers and reform advocates, May 1 was known as International Workers' Day—not as an American May Day with roots in the U.S. labor movement.[4] Workers and radicals around the globe had taken up that holiday over the course of its one-hundred-plus-year history. Now immigrant workers brought it back to the land of its birth as a focal point for recognizing their contribution to America's economy. May Day would have this brief renaissance on U.S. soil in 2006, but most people would experience it as an imported tradition. Perhaps some remembered May Day's history in America, and saw the added significance that gave to the immigrants' cause as a patriotic, national one, but it is likely they would have been few and far between.[5]

Celebrated for centuries as a rite of spring, May Day took on new meaning in the United States during the late nineteenth century. The American labor movement initially set aside May 1 to make a nationwide demand for the eight-hour workday in 1886. From that moment on, May Day became known as something other than just the herald of spring: it became an annual event for labor's push for the shorter workday. In time, new agendas were added to this secular holiday. Most notably, anarchists, socialists, and communists claimed May Day as their own. It was to be more than a day to usher in the eight-hour demand; it would be the harbinger of the new international socialist order, a new world that would emerge after the anticipated demise of capitalism.

As the example of the 2006 May 1 demonstrations shows, most Americans are unaware of this history. For them, the term "May Day" is more likely to conjure up images of thousands of Russian troops marching in lockstep, accompanied by innumerable tanks, arrayed before Communist Party leaders gathered in Moscow's Red Square. The holiday is typically seen as a Soviet relic of the Cold War. For many in post–Cold War America, where the union movement has shrunk to an all-time low and most citizens downplay the existence of class divisions, the very idea that May Day originated in the United States is unbelievable. Yet, the holiday was created in the United States. Its history is the focus of this book.

First widely observed in 1886, May Day was created in a period that witnessed several efforts intended to reunite America, politically and culturally, after the Civil War. Most of these attempts embraced a process that sublimated regional, racial, and class divisions for an imagined nationalism of white unity in a promised land of industrial progress and consumer plenty.[6] For many of its advocates, especially in the North, American national identity was made manifest in overt displays of patriotism defined by a quasi-religious veneration of the American flag. It was celebrated in the creation of the Memorial Day, Flag Day, and, later, Armistice Day holidays. And it was literally taught to the community through the special observance of these new holidays in the nation's public schools and through neighborhood Fourth of July events beginning in the late 1870s.[7] It was in this changing landscape of popular political culture that May Day found an uneasy home.

Although May Day developed in this same period and existed alongside these patriotic events, it challenged their message. May Day's creators either offered alternative interpretations of American nationalism or articulated more purely internationalist visions for the future. These challenges would contribute to May Day's eventual eclipse, in both practice and memory. Recalling its existence and eventual decline in this context, however, is informative. The history of this now-forgotten holiday sheds new light on the nature of American national identity. It reveals the limits of acceptable political expression in a multicultural society that treasures shared political ideas as a binding force for the nation. And as this study shows, although the creators of May Day advocated different political ideas, many of their ideas were just as partisan as those touted in the culture's mainstream patriotic events.

Central to the history of May Day in America, then, is the relationship that has existed between this holiday and the cultural construction of American national identity. For both the individual participant and the wider American community, May Day provided a forum where alternative definitions of the American experience could be presented in a period otherwise marked by vehement assertions of nationalism. By organizing and participating in the holiday, its celebrants contributed to the construction of their own radical American identities.[8] At the same time, they also publicized alternative social and political models for the nation and for the world. Investigating this dual development will be one of the chief aims of this book.[9]

To understand this process, my research draws on the methods and insights of both labor history and cultural history. This approach helps us better understand the history of the working-class and radical worlds out of which May Day was created and sustained for more than six decades. Equally important, it illuminates the role that class-based concerns and political contestation played in the creation of this unique holiday.[10] Ultimately, the study adds a missing yet significant chapter to the broader history of American political culture. Specifically, it analyzes the manner in which adherents of internationalist Marxism either drew from or challenged contemporary definitions of American nationalism in creating their own radical identities and their plans for a new society. In recognizing the alternative political possibilities for the nation that were created on May Day from 1886 to 1960, this study rounds out the story of mainstream American nationalism's construction, which developed in dialogue with the dissent given voice on May Day.

Those who organized and participated in annual May Day events therefore not only constructed their own radical identities, but also formulated different definitions of Americanism, which can be understood as "a language of popular or vernacular nationalism." As Gary Gerstle has noted in his study of working-class Americanism, this "flexible language of politics" was "necessarily unstable": it changed over time, had many sources, and was implemented by distinct groups for particular reasons.[11] The "other" Americanisms that the radical supporters of May Day defined each May 1 were informed by the diversity of "multiple cross-border connections" found in their social profiles, the political ideas they espoused, the organizations they belonged to, and the cultural traditions they celebrated on the day.[12] In this sense, the study of May Day helps "contextualize the nation," a task that Thomas Bender and others seek to undertake as they "rethink" American history in a global perspective. This approach to the May Day holiday considers the "spectrum of social scales, both larger and smaller than the nation and not excluding the nation," as they were culturally created in annual celebration.[13]

Examining the history of May Day in America not only addresses this missing component of American cultural history, but also helps us to rethink the history of political radicalism in the United States. More specifically, it allows us to appreciate the historical importance of socialism, anarchism, and communism in America in a new way. While the history of the May Day holiday follows the familiar trajectory of the rise and fall of the left in the United States, it can also take us beyond that well-known story. My research is not intended to rehash old debates over the failure of these ideologies as viable political movements.[14] What it illuminates instead is the way in which political radicals left a deeper mark on American political culture than has heretofore been recognized. Much of the shape of American nationalism from the late nineteenth to the mid-twentieth centuries was forged around the rejection of left-wing radicalism. It was created, in large part, in opposition to the presence of these radicals and their political agenda. May Day offered an alternative to the martial, masculine, assimilationist, and, sometimes, reactionary definition of American nationalism forged between the late 1880s and the mid-twentieth century. To use Eric Foner's terms, it provided a "counterexample" to that nationalism, acting as an "opposite" or "negation" of the ideas sustaining that mainstream political vision.[15]

The story of the relationship between political radicalism and American political culture is, however, more complex than this reactionary one, for not all radicals defined their political identities in opposition to their American national identity. Most moderate socialists believed that their political agenda offered hope for the true fulfillment of American democracy and equality. They proudly carried the Stars and Stripes along with the red flag in their May Day demonstrations. This commitment to the American flag, and to the democratic values for which it stood, was shared not only by those in the Socialist Party of Eugene Debs, but also by those in radical corners where such support would least be expected. This study of May Day uncovers such commitments among those in the Socialist Labor Party during the 1890s, as well as in the Communist Party of the mid-1930s. The precise nature and reasons for these displays were complex, sometimes contributing to divisions within the parties in question. This support for the American flag, and for certain political values identified as uniquely American, speaks to the tension that existed in the hearts and minds of the event's organizers between their nationalist commitments (as Americans who cherished their nation's democratic promise) and their internationalist aspirations (as members of global socialist movements). It also shows how the emblematic meaning of the Stars and Stripes was not static or one-dimensional, despite the efforts of those who would seek to confine it to the more traditionally patriotic displays of Flag Day and the Fourth of July. The flag, like the nation's ceremonial calendar, was open to various uses and was invested with divergent meanings. This openness became a part of the contestation that surrounded May Day, not only between those on the left and the right, but also within the left itself.

Those who participated in this process included the leaders of radical political parties and progressive unions, as well as tens (or sometimes hundreds) of thousands of their members and supporters. Exploring the history of May Day is especially helpful in illuminating the self-images of these rank-and-file radicals. They were less likely than prominent public figures to have left a written record of how they understood their place in society. Instead, the public arena of urban American political culture was where they defined the meaning of their left-wing political affiliations and aspirations. An investigation into the history of May Day therefore does not simply provide an understanding of the official definitions of American radicalism that party and union leaders advanced. It can also uncover the many vernacular expressions that existed within the membership of radical organizations and among those who traveled on the margins of such insurgent institutions.

Addressing how these official and vernacular expressions coalesced or conflicted in the specific context of two urban centers will better illuminate the social complexity of this cultural process.[16] Because New York City and Chicago housed two of the largest populations of anarchists, socialists, and communists in the nation from the late nineteenth through the mid-twentieth centuries, and because these cities hosted some of the most visible and diverse May Day celebrations, evidence is drawn largely from these two locations. The specific contours of the radical self-images created in those celebrations were unique to each city and, in part, reflected the density and diversity of their respective urban populations. Yet, demonstrations held on May 1 in other cities, though smaller in scale, also followed a pattern common to the events staged in New York and Chicago, embracing similar themes, protests, and concerns from year to year.[17] Focusing on these two large cities thus allows us to gauge the main contours of the May Day experience in America.

Even as May Day began to take on a life of its own by the turn of the twentieth century, as an event that was clearly dominated by radicals and marked by its own traditions, it never became static or reified. Instead, it was a malleable medium for the definition of radicalism in America. As May Day became identified as a foundational moment for modern radical political movements, taking on an almost mythic quality, its meaning and use became linked to the contested concerns of those movements in the present. As Geneviève Fabre and Jürgen Heideking have argued, "public celebrations do not just 'reflect' social practices and reality, but they possess the power to 'construct' political concepts and create cultural meaning. Festive culture [including, I would argue, May Day celebrations] must therefore be seen as an integral part of the historical process which shapes and transforms power relations, social structures and popular mentalities."[18] The memory of May Day that was recalled and retold each year, both in celebration and in the popular radical press, supported the changing priorities of the holiday's supporters or detractors. That memory became a part of the process of both individual and political identity formation. For those on the political left, for example, this often meant recalling the uniquely American origins of the day. For those on the right, who vehemently opposed the event, that memory was often sharply cast in the light of the holiday's various foreign influences. How May Day was remembered and invoked was a cultural construction, but one that carried weight in shaping and advancing the different political agendas of the holiday's supporters or opponents.[19] My work is thus concerned not merely with May Day as an annual event but also as a culturally constructed icon that influenced contested political ideas and the communities that supported them.

Because of its dynamic quality, May Day became a platform from which particular trade unions and political groups annually voiced their central concerns. Over time, the increasing number of participating organizations adjusted the parade's style to encompass their changing cultural tastes, as well as their evolving political agendas. The basic political party and union parades of the 1890s came to include more elaborate floats, banners, costumes, and bands by the 1930s. This change, adopted most successfully by the Communist Party, showed a savvy trade in what was then the valuable tender of proto-mass- and mass-cultural styles. Some of May Day's creators thus incorporated both the changing technology and tastes of an emerging mass culture when they designed demonstrations to voice their radical political demands.

In their May Day demonstrations from 1886 to 1960, radicals joined the political conversation of the streets in a pidgin language that merged changing popular cultural styles of demonstration with particular radical symbols, metaphors, and messages.[20] This combination affected not just the manner but also the content of these demonstrations. Many of May Day's creators blended their Marxist beliefs in the emergence of a socialist commonwealth with their optimistic faith in America's democratic heritage, something they hoped to tap into and to "rescue" from the corruption of capitalism and oligarchy. In so doing, socialists, and some communists, created a new vocabulary for speaking in public, one that was neither wholly international nor national in its commitments, but rather comprised a new expression of radical Americanism.[21] Over the course of May Day's history, socialists and communists would infuse this expression with divergent meanings, according to their specific partisan beliefs. But in general, they voiced in radical Americanism a desire to see America's revolutionary promise of democracy birth a Marxist vision of equality within the nation's industrial sector, and they looked to global socialist or communist movements to further aid or inspire such a transformation.

Entering into the politics of the street with such discourse was not an easy task, nor did it go unchallenged. The civic elite, middle-class voluntary organizations, more moderate craft unions, and, later, progressive reformers, veterans' groups, and religious organizations opposed radicals and their May Day demonstrations at different moments in the holiday's history. In several instances, employers, the business community, and the state, through legal sanctions and sometimes with physical force, repressed May Day celebrations and the radical demands their supporters voiced.

Disdain for the insurgent political content that came to define the holiday, however, did not completely explain this opposition. Neither did the ethnicity of those who came to champion May Day, although the exaggerated middle-class fears of wild-eyed, bearded Bohemian and Italian anarchists played a part, especially prior to 1930.[22] Those who disliked May Day also deemed it a threat because it was an occasion when radicals publicly defined their character and offered alternative political and economic models for society. What they proposed differed from, and at times defied, the political identifications of most Americans. That majority included most laborers, who created their own version of working-class Americanism on the Fourth of July, Labor Day, and other public holidays from 1886 to 1960. It was therefore not just who political radicals were or what ideas they espoused, but also how they presented their ideas that triggered such strong opposition. Their holiday was one of protest, which did not fit comfortably within the spectrum of popular celebratory rites. The history of this reaction—of May Day's effect on the broader American political culture—has not been fully told. This book tells that story.

The history of May Day celebrations also reveals the presence of women and children in much more active roles than those offered in traditional national fêtes. Women did not just present flags to the men who engaged in the main events, as was so often the case on Memorial Day or the Fourth of July. Nor did they stand on the sidelines waving handkerchiefs in support of the activities taking place in the streets.[23] Instead, there is evidence that working-class women joined the ranks of those marching in May Day parades as early as 1895. By marching and singing, children also participated in the celebrations. The precise nature of this participation was complicated and changed over time. In some ways, it was related to the greater public activity of working-class women and their progressive supporters, as they fought for workplace protections and the vote in the early decades of the twentieth century. It was also tied to the changing position of women (and children) within the Socialist and Communist parties that organized the May Day events.[24] In addition to its other concerns, then, this study traces the role of women and children in public May Day events, considering the exact quality of and reasons for that greater participation. In so doing, it reveals an unfamiliar page in the history of American holidays and further complicates our understanding of the nation's political culture in these decades.

Even though African Americans and Hispanics never made up more than a small percentage[25] of the radical political groups of New York City and Chicago, which are at the heart of this study, this exploration of May Day also touches on the issue of race. Because African-American workers entered into the industrial workforce of both cities in significant numbers, particularly during and after World War I, it considers their place within the larger movement of organized labor during the 1910s and 1920s that was reacting against radical May Day demonstrations. The study grapples with the participation of some people of color in May Day events none-theless, particularly once the Communist Party embraced the issue of African-American civil rights during the 1930s. And it explores how non-radical workers laid claim to whiteness as they constructed the paradigm of the laborer-citizen in their parades during the 1890s. Ultimately this study considers the significance of what essentially amounted to radicals' prioritizing issues of class over those of race throughout May Day's history. In particular, the study addresses the consequences of these priorities after World War II, when concerns over issues of race moved to the fore of the progressive struggle in America.

Because of its radical nature, in terms of both its social profile and its political messages, May Day never became a national holiday. It is now virtually unknown in the land of its birth. Organizing the event as an annual protest against the characteristics of the existing economic and political system, May Day's supporters never sought the legitimacy of government recognition. For the most radical among them, May Day strikes and parades were to bring about the birth of a socialist order; they looked beyond the imagined community of the nation itself, envisioning a global socialist transformation. Most Americans had no desire to embrace an event laden with such insurgent meaning.

Despite the fact that for much of its history May Day was celebrated by only the most politically radical in America, it remains historically significant for at least two reasons. First, it illuminates the cultural creation of individual and collective political identities. And second, it shows the specific negotiation between radical political commitments and American national affiliations in the period from 1867 to 1960. Its history reveals the complex interaction of alternative political values within a public sphere that hosted the reassertion of a narrowly construed nationalist culture. The story of May Day thus provides the missing half of the story of that period's patriotic imaginings, and enables us to recognize the unexpected influence of political radicalism on American political culture.

In researching this study, I have consulted a variety of sources. The extensive radical political and union collections at both New York University's Tamiment Library and Robert F. Wagner Labor Archives and Cornell University's Kheel Center for Labor-Management Documentation and Archives formed the core of this research, along with materials from the Chicago History Museum and the New-York Historical Society. Particularly informative were the Files of the Communist Party of the USA in the Comintern Archives. I was able to consult the microfilm reproduction (fond 515, opis 1) of the records of the CPUSA from the Russian Center for the Preservation and Study of Documents of Recent History, held at Tamiment. These files, made available to scholars in the 1990s, reveal that in some instances the intentions of party leaders conformed to their public pronouncements about the purpose of the May Day parades, but in other cases there was a clear discrepancy between the two. Such sources help pierce the rhetoric of the party press, uncovering, for example, the true motives for the party's embrace of the united front in 1934. While there seems to have been genuine support for cooperation with noncommunist antifascist forces among the party's rank and file and fellow travelers, those higher up in the Communist Party (CP) clearly intended the joint efforts to be controlled by the party and used as a recruiting tool. This source reminds us, then, of the significance of distinguishing between the official and vernacular meanings imposed on May Day each year.[26]

Disputes over the purpose of May Day therefore existed not just between the socialists and communists, but also within each radical organization. Internal debates over the meaning of May Day and the reasons for participating in it were present in the minutes from meetings of various union locals and party assemblies, and occasionally from rank-and-file correspondence. Nonprint sources revealed the final outcome of these debates, disclosing how the symbolic economies of participating groups were mobilized in the parades. Photos and moving pictures showed these groups in the unfolding process of their own cultural and political definition in the streets of the city. Oral history collections further contributed to the understanding of why individuals participated in the parades, what that meant to them, and what it was like to be a part of such vibrant events. Samples from the mainstream American press, select government committees, and patriotic organizations rounded out the material explored, and provided a sense of how those radical definitions were received by America's evolving mainstream civic culture.

To keep the many questions and aims of this study in focus, I present the story of May Day along a fairly straightforward chronological pattern. After explaining the origins of the holiday as an event and icon during the 1880s in chapter 1, I move on in chapter 2 to explore the contestation within organized labor over the purpose and usefulness of May Day to the eight-hour cause during the 1890s, particularly in light of the internationalist meanings the holiday took on after it was adopted by the Second International in 1890 and in the wake of the Haymarket tragedy of 1886. In chapter 3, I discuss how in the early years of the twentieth century labor leaders like Samuel Gompers and John Fitzpatrick supported Labor Day, which they believed was both more respectable and more American than the socialist- and anarchist-dominated May Day. At the same time, I note how many workers still turned out for both days, ignoring radical leaders' demands for an adherence to political orthodoxy on May 1, as well as their union bosses' calls for leisure reform on Labor Day. Chapter 4 tackles the fate of May Day during the politically chilly decade of the 1920s. After considering the role of the emerging Communist Party on May Day and the opposition that all radicals faced from self-defined patriotic groups, like the American Defense Society, I look at the untold story of children's participation both in May Day events and in a range of alternative "patriotic" events, like Loyalty Day and National Child Health Day, which adults in the Boy Scouts, Rotary Club, and other organizations staged to draw the youngsters' attention away from international socialism.

Chapter 5 focuses on the partisan contestation that existed between socialists and communists during the Depression era as they fought to dominate the streets each May 1. In that struggle, the Communist Party emerged victorious. It staged some of the largest parades in the holiday's history by the late 1930s, including that of 1939, which drew 700,000 participants and spectators in New York. Yet, because of the reaction against the communist dominance of these Popular Front May Day parades, this success would be short-lived. With the announcement of the Nazi-Soviet Pact in August 1939 and the reversal in the CP's stand on the war against fascism, Old Guard socialists and most nonradical workers had their suspicions confirmed: it would seem that the communist leadership were the stooges of Moscow. That event reinforced the existing fissures on the left, and also caused many socialists and their union allies to vilify May Day as foreign and un-American. As I demonstrate in this chapter, the alienation of May Day in the United States began well before the opening salvos of the Cold War.

In chapter 6, I explore how during World War II many workers turned away from May Day and embraced revived Labor Day and Flag Day celebrations. There, and in the newly created "I Am an American Day," they created a distinctly working-class version of their American identity. Also evident in these patriotic events, especially in the "American Day" gatherings of citizens from all walks of life, were expressions of national unity and loyalty in wartime, as well as a progressive faith in the benefits of America's democratic and capitalist system. By the end of the war, these public definitions of Americanism filled the landscape of the nation's popular political culture. Communists, socialists, and progressive workers who sought to revive May Day would face a significant challenge, particularly as the Cold War began to heat up.

In chapter 7, I track this final decline of May Day during the Cold War years. Here I argue that there has been a deeper significance to the popular forgetting of May Day's past in America. Most Americans know nothing of the holiday's roots in the United States, not just because it is no longer celebrated in any significant fashion here, but also because those who opposed it, like the Veterans of Foreign Wars, New York City's Fourteenth Street Association, and the American Federation of Labor, intentionally obscured its history. May Day—and its "purposeful forgetting"— were a part of the mechanism through which these groups accomplished the naturalization of the Americanism that emerged by the mid-twentieth century. Their definition of America, as a staunchly anticommunist defender of the free world and the free market, became so reified and standardized during the Cold War that it obscured its own making.

As I argue in *America's Forgotten Holiday*, the history of May Day reveals the complex interaction of alternative political values within a public sphere that hosted the reassertion of such a narrowly construed nationalist culture. May Day's less well-known history in the land of its birth demonstrates the indirect influence political radicalism has had on the shape of American nationalism, illuminating the vibrancy and changing nature of American political culture from the late nineteenth to the mid-twentieth centuries.

1

Out of America's Urban, Industrial Cauldron

The Origins of May Day as Event and Icon, 1867–1890

On May 1, 1867, workers paraded in Chicago in celebration of a new state law that had established the eight-hour workday.[1] Several dozen trade associations marched to demonstrate their approval of the legislation, which went into effect that day. That morning, "thousands of local workers set out to the accompaniment of bands" carrying banners that announced: "Eight Hours and No Concession," "To the Advantage of the Coming Generation," and "United We Stand, Divided We Fall."[2] Cited by some historians as the first modern May Day demonstration, this event was really an important social, political, and cultural precursor to what would become an annual holiday later in the century.[3]

The parade, "more than a mile long," formed on Lake Street, "set out at ten [o'clock]," and made its way to the lakeshore. According to a newspaper account, "all along the procession route, the stairways and doorways, even roofs, were jammed with curious spectators."[4] In addition to the many banners proclaiming the importance of the eight-hour day, these spectators would have seen the city's workers organized according to their particular craft and wearing the uniforms of their trade. Many workers also demonstrated their skills and displayed the results of their work as they rode on floats through the streets. The "tanners. . . . had a wagon on which two men were working intently on a beam," and "ship carpenters and caulkers had erected a completely rigged ship on which the caulkers were working" for the duration of the parade.[5] In its most basic manifestation, then, this was a celebration of labor by workers proud of their skills and the contributions they made to the development of their city. As they marched, they ritually defined and reinforced their identity as hard-working and productive members of their community.

Demonstrations like these were not new to the 1867 celebration. Workers had long taken part in civic processions organized along the lines of their trade. In those parades they proudly displayed the badges, tools, processes, and products of their trade to celebrate publicly their identity as craftsmen and show support for particular political causes.[6] What was new in this parade was the assertion of that identity in support of the eight-hour day, a uniquely working-class concern. Chicago's laborers manifested their working-class consciousness again in the days following this celebration of the eight-hour law, when they went on strike to enforce the shorter day against their employers' opposition. In 1867, however, the workers' efforts were unsuccessful: under the mayor's orders, the local police and the militia had broken the laborers' militant stand for shorter hours.[7]

Although the movement for the eight-hour day would be sidetracked for much of the 1870s, a revived trade unionist movement in Chicago and in New York took up the cause again in the 1880s. These cities' nascent socialist and anarchist communities joined it in a massive demonstration on May 1, 1886. By then, craft unions, like those of the tanners, no longer dominated the ceremonial expressions of this public debate. Instead, they became part of a broader, if tenuous and short-lived, coalition that reflected the economic, social, and political changes of the intervening two decades. The 1886 event was marked not only by traditional laborite rituals, but also by demonstrations of politically radical sensibilities, echoing the agenda of anarchists and socialists who joined the line of march. These different constituencies, coming to the May 1 demonstrations with their overlapping yet distinct concerns, forged a precarious alliance that year. That alliance, however, quickly fell apart, too weak to sustain the weight of its differences.

In turn, as trade unionists, anarchists, and socialists forged separate paths for their economic and political activities, they vied for control of May Day as both an event and an icon. This annual holiday, particularly once it became an international workers' day, became a focal point in the contestation among these groups. The debate among trade unionists and radicals over the meaning and use of May Day was more than just a reflection of their different political positions. That argument contributed to their public self-definition; the way these groups observed May Day became a part of their creation as distinct movements in a turbulent, urban industrial landscape.

One of the main components of this turbulent landscape was the struggle that laborers waged for reduced working hours. Although the demonstration in support of the eight-hour day on May 1, 1886, was unique in its massive scale and reach, it was not the first time workers expressed their desire for the shorter workday. As far back as the early national period, when changes in merchant capital resulted in a reduction in work breaks and an increase in hours, a ten-hour movement emerged in city workshops. The desire for a shorter workday soon spread, as more and more trades encountered similar changes in their work rhythms and work patterns during the nineteenth century. In their study of American labor and the working day, David Roediger and Philip Foner chart the history of this shorter-hours movement.[8] By the 1860s, workers across the country had formed groups to support the implementation of reduced working hours.[9] By 1867, the eight-hour laws passed in Illinois and New York seemed initially to have secured important victories for workers in those two states. But when it soon became evident that employers were regularly flouting these new regulations, workers realized they needed to continue their struggle.[10]

Throughout the late 1860s and early 1870s, carpenters, bricklayers, and painters in the "mostly English-speaking building trades" and German-American furniture makers in New York spearheaded small-scale, local campaigns.[11] While these workers met with some success because their demands could be made against small employers, members of other trades encountered greater resistance from larger manufacturers.[12] This resistance was strengthened in New York, for example, when "an alliance of very wealthy businessmen and middle-class reformers" displaced the political machine of Tammany Hall in 1872 and took over the reins of city government. They now had the police and the militia at their disposal and did not shy away from using them to break up eight-hour strikes and demonstrations.[13] Chicago's strikers met with similar resistance.

The movement for shorter hours was derailed temporarily by the depression that lasted from approximately 1873 to 1879. Workers faced other concerns in these years, including unemployment and hunger. While these issues were not new to the 1870s, they were exacerbated by the economic downturn. The events of these years changed the social and economic landscapes of New York City and Chicago. Out of the struggles waged against hunger and unemployment during the 1870s, some laborers turned to more aggressive trade union organizing. Others welcomed more radical solutions. Organized labor's fight for the eight-hour day instigated the first urban May Day demonstration of 1886, but anarchist and socialist political agendas would also come to characterize the holiday as it evolved during the 1890s.

The roots of this holiday, then, sank deeply into the social and economic soil from which both the modern American trade union movement and the socialist and anarchist movements grew. Beginning in the decade or so after the Civil War, New York City and Chicago became the epicenters for all three groups, as intense demographic and economic change altered these urban communities. The 1870s witnessed rapid population growth in New York and especially in Chicago, mostly from immigration. By 1880 "four-fifths of New York's 1.2 million population were either first generation immigrants (foreign born) or their offspring (second generation)."[14] Chicago's population grew by 69 percent between 1870 and 1880.[15] Many of those who came to these cities were able to find work in the expanding industrial sectors, but their jobs were not necessarily secure. In Chicago, the slaughterhouses and lumberyards became neighbors to iron and steel foundries and machine shops, as the city's economy shifted from one dominated by commerce to one dominated by manufacturing in the years after the Great Fire of 1871.[16] In New York, the garment, printing and publishing, cigar-making, and furniture-making industries continued to grow. But the quick and uneven expansion of the manufacturing base in Chicago and the intensely competitive and mainly decentralized nature of the industries in New York did not make for secure employment, particularly for those workers who filled unskilled or semiskilled positions.[17] The widening employment pool that resulted from rapid population growth made workers who held those positions easily replaceable as well. Economic insecurity became something most workers had in common.

In both cities, these workers came to understand their circumstances in different ways. Socialism, anarchism, and trade unionism offered laborers distinct means with which to make sense of their experiences in the rapidly developing industrial metropolis. Newly organized socialist and anarchist associations and recently established or reorganized trade unions provided them with resources to work for different kinds of change. The history of how the ethnically, racially, and religiously diverse American working class was drawn to one or another of these movements is vast and complex. One way to make sense of this is to follow the paths taken by

Albert Parsons in Chicago and by Samuel Gompers in New York. Taken together, their journeys in 1870s and 1880s urban America illuminate the working-class and radical worlds out of which May Day originated.

Albert Parsons, who arrived in Chicago from Texas in 1872, became a member of the city's Typographical Union 16. He soon found work at the *Chicago Times*, remaining in the newspaper trade that he had become familiar with as a young man in the South.[18] As a new resident of the Northern industrial city, he quickly became aware of the great disparity that existed between Chicago's very wealthy and very poor citizens. Specifically, Parsons witnessed the neglect that the Relief and Aid Society showed to those who were most in need of help after the Great Fire. When the poor attempted to protest this neglect during the winter of 1872, the police beat them in the streets. After hearing about this tragedy, Parsons quickly became attracted to the city's growing socialist community.[19] In his view, neither municipal charities nor trade unions provided an adequate response to the economic deprivation and "its collateral evils" that he witnessed in his city. Only the socialists seemed to have "made any protest or offered any remedy for the enforced poverty" of the modern industrial city.[20]

His interest in socialism piqued, Parsons soon entered the movement wholeheartedly. He became an active member of the Workingmen's Party of the United States (WPUS), formed at a congress in Pittsburgh in 1876, then, when the WPUS changed its name in 1877, of the Socialist Labor Party (SLP).[21] Although Parsons was a native-born American of English descent, the SLP in Chicago had its strongest base of support among the city's German workers. The traditions of republicanism and free thought that many brought with them from their experiences in the revolutions of 1848, and the "dense network of social organizations" they transplanted into their new neighborhoods, contributed to the shape of Chicago's socialist movement.[22] In addition to the affiliation of certain trade associations in the city with the SLP, much of the party's strength came from these German members. They blended their social activities in the workingmen's halls and clubs of their North Chicago neighborhoods into a socialist political culture of meetings, parades, picnics, dances, and shooting competitions, and used that "as a base for recruiting and maintaining socialist membership."[23]

The SLP initially favored electoral socialism with a platform that dealt with issues of concern to the city's workers. It called for the eight-hour workday, the repeal of prison labor, conspiracy and vagrancy laws, the abolition of child labor, and the institution of municipal ownership of streetcars and gas works.[24] Viewing the nationwide protest for the eight-hour day on May 1, 1886, as part of this larger program, the SLP's membership and affiliated unions gave it their support. Parsons eventually embraced the eight-hour demand as well, seeing it as the first step toward the broader socialist program for state control of the means of production.[25]

In advocating this program, socialists went far beyond the demands of most trade unionists, who were focused on the issues of hours, pay, and working conditions, not grand schemes of revolution. Yet, socialists who hoped to achieve state control of the means of production planned to use the ballot, not the bullet, to do so. While their goals were quite radical, then, the means they used to reach them were not. Despite this fact, and the fact that socialists only made up a small percentage of Chicago's population, employers, the middle class and the urban elite disdained them, seeing them as threats to the existing order. Even more feared were anarchists who were willing to embrace direct action (including violence) to bring down capitalism. Although they, too, constituted only a small segment of the population in Chicago, the anarchists' radical tactics and rhetoric brought them considerable negative attention.[26]

As he became increasingly disillusioned with the slowness of political change, Parsons was soon to be found among these more radical Chicagoans. As a worker in the city, he had seen how the long hours that men worked left them with little or no time to participate in politics. As a political activist, Parsons also witnessed the "intimidation, duplicity, corruption & bull-dozing" that met laborers at the urban ballot box. Both pressures, he believed, had virtually disenfranchised workers. Parsons therefore decided to turn his attention "toward an effort to reduce the hours of labor," as many within the trade union movement were doing.[27] Yet, he also gravitated toward the emerging American anarchist movement and its tactics of direct action, embracing what has been termed the "Chicago idea" of revolutionary unionism.[28] In 1880, the left wing of the SLP split off to form the International Revolutionary Socialists, and Parsons went with it. He was elected as a delegate to its convention in Pittsburgh in 1883, where the American branch of Johann Most's anarchist International Working People's Association (IWPA) was founded.[29] Active in Chicago's IWPA, Parsons became editor of its main English-language newspaper, *The Alarm*.

While Parsons argued that "anarchism nor anarchists either [sic] advises, abets nor encourages the working people to the use of force or a resort to violence," he did not shy away from armed resistance as a form of self-defense. He argued that anarchists did not have to encourage direct action because they knew workers "will be driven to use it in self-defense in self-preservation against those who are degrading, enslaving and destroying them."[30] This understanding of workers as the enslaved of the capitalists initially placed most anarchists in opposition to the demand for the eight-hour day in 1886 because they thought it was too limited a goal. Instead, they favored more thorough, systemic change, which they tried to instigate through public demonstrations.

Consequently, anarchist agitation in the early 1880s did not rely on violence so much as it did on direct confrontation. In November 1884, for example, Parsons, along with August Spies, editor of the German-language anarchist Chicago paper, the *Arbeiter Zeitung*, and Samuel Fielden, treasurer of the IWPA, coordinated and spoke at a gathering of more than 3,000 poor and unemployed in Market Square on Thanksgiving Day. They then led the crowd in a procession behind black and red flags through the city's well-to-do neighborhoods, where they shouted anarchist slogans, demanded jobs, and drew attention to the disparity between their hunger and the "turkeys and champagne" that graced the tables of the rich.[31] Through such public and symbolic confrontation, a tactic that was used again in the 1885 march toward the Board of Trade, Parsons, Spies, Fielden, and the anarchists and workers who participated identified their support for direct action and for change that was to be instigated outside the voting booth.[32]

In such public displays, Chicago's anarchists also created a symbolic arsenal of flags, slogans, banners, and songs with which they defined their movement and broadcast their demands. The black flag of hunger and the red flag of international solidarity became the standards of American anarchism. The display of these flags in future May Day demonstrations signified anarchist support for the event. It also became a visible sign of their interpretation of the day's meaning as a harbinger of the end of capitalism, a goal that went well beyond the call for the eight-hour workday. Anarchists' ability to participate in May Day (especially after the post-Haymarket crackdown on radicals in Chicago) signified their resolve to continue their crusade. And their invocation of the day, which they would wed to the history of the Haymarket martyrs, provided them with a kind of spiritual and symbolic sustenance for their daily struggles, as well as a focal point for their self-definition as a politically persecuted minority.

If anarchism had become the face of political radicalism in Chicago, a thousand miles to the east socialism dominated the radical landscape in New York. Its presence exerted a strong influence on Samuel Gompers and his understanding of the trade union movement. After arriving in New York from London in 1863, Gompers found work first in a tenement shop and later in a factory, where he continued in his trade as a cigarmaker. At the factory, he quickly affiliated himself with an informal discussion group of skilled immigrant workers, most of whom came from Germany and were members of the Marxist wing of the International Workingmen's Association (IWA) in America.[33] The IWA, or First International, founded by Karl Marx in London in 1863, was dominated in New York by German-American unionists, who quickly moved it to the fore of the city's labor movement. They joined with the English-speaking workers of the National Labor Union in their campaign for the eight-hour day in the late 1860s. By the early 1870s, the German-American unions of the IWA took the lead in the wave of eight-hour strikes waged in their city.[34]

From his experience in the cigar factory and his interaction with Marxists in the IWA, Gompers came to understand that the labor movement was best served by economic organization. Strong trade unions could win concessions in the workplace, like the eight-hour day, to improve workers' lives.[35] He applied this conviction to his work when building the Cigarmakers International Union (CMIU) Local 144 with Adolph Strasser and when he became president of that local in 1875.[36]

Partly because of the influence of German Marxists on his thinking in these years, Gompers rejected what he considered to be the utopian political hopes of many other socialists. His skepticism of radical reformers was reinforced by the Tompkins Square Riot of 1874. What started out as a meeting of the city's unemployed, which had been organized by the IWA and the local Workingmen's Council, turned into a riot when club-wielding police charged the crowd. According to Gompers, it was "an orgy of brutality" from which he "barely saved [his] head from being cracked by jumping down a cellarway."[37] The "attacks of the police kept up all day long," he recalled, and in subsequent days, the police raided and closed down indoor meetings in their "reign of terror" against what they believed was a nascent communist uprising.[38]

Although there had been some miscommunication between the meeting's organizers and the police over the status of the permit for the demonstration, Gompers believed that the root of the discrepancy and the cause of the authorities' heavy-handed reaction to the gathering were the fault of political radicals. In the days before the meeting, the so-called Spring Street faction of radical reformers and communists who dominated

Section 12 of the IWA had issued inflammatory circulars. Gompers faulted their action for instigating the riot.[39] And he came to believe that the public's fear of radical demands, and the police repression of radicals in response to that fear, could lead both to a disruption in the organizing capabilities of the labor movement and to the death of its members in the streets.[40]

But Gompers also realized that "many of those radical, revolutionary impatient group were of the labor movement and just as sincere as many of those whose judgment was more dependable." Although he disliked the ideas and did not fully trust the motives of radicals, Gompers admitted that the overall welfare of the labor movement, "made up of men and women of all sorts of natures and experiences," depended on "solidarity" and on all doing "what they can for mutual protection."[41] Gompers recognized that, much like the complex landscape of local and national trade union associations in Chicago, New York City's trades were characterized by a web of overlapping political and organizational affiliations. A cigarmaker, for example, could be a member of his CMIU local and the local Knights of Labor assembly. Some of these locals were dominated by Marxist socialists and others were not; some were influenced by radical reformers and others were not. In the expanding garment industry, the Yiddish United Hebrew Trades, founded in 1888, was affiliated with the SLP, while the United Garment Workers, a predominantly Irish and German union, did not have socialist ties; instead, its members tended to support the Democratic Party.[42] In Gompers' mind, these divisions could pose a threat to united action and to the stability and achievements of the labor movement as a whole.

In particular, Gompers believed the Knights of Labor's mixed assemblies were in competition with local branches of trade unions for membership and support. The Knights of Labor was established in 1869 as a secret labor organization, grew slowly during the 1870s, and opened up into "more aggressive public organizing" in 1879, after Terence V. Powderly became its leader. One of its distinctive features was the mixed local assembly: a union local composed of workers from different trades. Although Gompers favored national coordination of the labor movement, he wanted it to be based on the craft union, not the mixed assembly. He hoped it would be voluntary and maintain the autonomy of the individual unions.[43] And while he clearly desired this kind of united labor movement, Gompers did not shy away from leaving out of his plans those who he felt undermined that solidarity, including unskilled workers, the Chinese, and new immigrants from Southern and Eastern Europe. The racism and exclusionary impulses he shared with most others active in craft unionism during the late nineteenth century, therefore, also shaped his vision.[44]

Beginning in the early 1880s, Gompers and other like-minded trade union leaders worked to "create a national labor association to promote the common interests of the national craft unions." At an 1881 meeting in Pittsburgh, they founded the Federation of Organized Trades and Labor Unions (FOTLU). Initially many individual Knights participated in this new national body, but by the next year the FOTLU would become dominated by "only those workers who held membership in the national union of their craft."[45] Members from this organization were responsible for planning the first workers' May Day in 1886.

By 1886, the milieu of New York City's and Chicago's labor and radical movements had become a complex web of diverse affiliations, including those of trade, skill level, ethnicity, and political allegiance. The protest for the eight-hour day would temporarily bring many different camps together in a common cause. Instead of the local strikes of the early 1870s, the May 1, 1886, demonstration would make the demand by "a single simultaneous mass act" against employers across the country.[46] In itself, this would be a watershed moment in the history American labor. May Day developed out of both an ongoing eight-hour campaign and the diverse working-class and radical movements that were particularly strong in New York City and Chicago. Its organization brought a new harmony, albeit a fragile and temporary one, to the relationship among these movements. In the years and decades to come, those diverse groups would give May Day a number of often-contradictory meanings, as they used the holiday to construct publicly their different identities as radical and working-class Americans.

Although socialists and anarchists eventually would infuse May Day with their own radical political messages, trade unionists (socialists and anarchists among them) originally called for the massive demonstration of May 1, 1886, to demand the eight-hour day. In the early 1880s, representatives from local assemblies within the Knights of Labor first proposed setting aside a specific day each year to agitate for the shorter workday. In 1881, for example, Theodore Cuno, a painter from New York, suggested the Knights choose a day to issue an address "setting forth the necessity of the Emancipation of Labor, the said address to be a second *Declaration of Independence*." It was to be read "at a certain day from all parts of the country where the Order is established."[47] Although members voted that action on the resolution be "indefinitely postponed," Cuno's suggestion demonstrates that there was an interest among some of the Knights for a coordinated, nationwide demonstration of labor solidarity in assertion of labor's worth and its need for independence from the deepening slavery of long hours.[48]

That same year, John Elliot, a Baltimore painter, suggested the Knights recognize the first Monday in September as labor's day to make a general demand for the eight-hour day. His resolution was rejected as "inexpedient on account of [the Knights'] numerical weakness."[49] The following year Elliot tried again, this time suggesting the first Monday in May 1883 as the target date. In 1883, another representative from Maryland, Conrad Kraft, forwarded a similar resolution; he wanted the demand to be made on May 1, 1884. The motions were discussed but no action was taken.[50] Because the records of the General Assembly do not detail the debates within committee, there is no account of why Elliot initially chose a September date then changed it to May, or why Kraft suggested that May 1 be the focus for labor's demand. It is also unclear why, beyond concerns over "numerical weakness," the committee rejected each of these motions. Given the experiences of many workers in the early 1870s, whose efforts had been met with physical intimidation and violence from employers and police when they last struck or demonstrated for the eight-hour day, it is understandable why they opposed new action.

In addition, there was the possibility that some Knights may have shared the attitudes of their national leader regarding such direct action. As Grand Master Workman of the Order, Terence Powderly generally opposed strikes, considering them risky tools for change, especially when assemblies were too weak numerically to sustain them. In his "Address of the Grand Master Workman" in 1880, for example, Powderly argued that "the remedy for the redress of the wrongs we complain of does not lie in the suicidal strike." Instead, he advocated "effective organization" that, once perfected, would lead to the creation of a "system of cooperation which will eventually make every man his own master—every man his own employer; a system which would give the laborer a fair proportion of the products of his toil."[51] Although organization work may not be as dramatic as striking, Powderly hoped that ultimately it would effect broader and longer-lasting change.

Despite Powderly's views and the failure of the General Assembly to act on the resolutions, it is clear that at least some Knights were interested in coordinating a broad push for shorter hours by the early 1880s. These members, along with veterans of the eight-hour drives of the early 1870s, favored a bold strike over the gradual organization that Powderly advocated. As leader of CMIU Local 144, Gompers was willing to embrace the strike when necessary, as were many national trade union leaders who joined with him in forming the FOTLU in 1881. This new labor organization, rather than the Knights, became the locus from which the nationwide strike campaign for the eight-hour day was launched.

During FOTLU's October 1884 meeting in Chicago, Gabriel Edmonston of the Brotherhood of Carpenters and Joiners made the proposal for shorter hours that would finally be acted on. Gompers claimed in his autobiography that he "helped to draft the resolution" in which they called for "the workers [to] obtain contracts for the establishment of the eight-hour day in all industry."[52] At the meeting, Edmonston submitted the following: "that eight hours shall constitute a legal day's labor from and after May 1, 1886, and that we recommend to labor organizations throughout this jurisdiction that they so direct their laws as to conform to this resolution by the time named."[53] Because May 1 marked the beginning of the contract year in the building trades, Edmonston chose it to be the focus of this united demand. It would be a practical rallying point for workers around the nation.

Aside from this tactical benefit, Edmonston would also have been aware of the commemorative power of this date: on May 1, 1867, workers in Chicago had celebrated a victory for their shorter-hour campaign, but it was one that did not last. Now, Edmonston hoped, they could fight to make the eight-hour day a permanent reality. He, like all nineteenth-century urbanites, also would have recognized the transformative associations of May 1, known as May Moving Day, when housing leases expired and were renewed, sending thousands of residents into the streets with their belongings as they moved from old abode to new.[54] And while he most likely also knew that the centuries-old traditions of maypole dancing and flower-gathering rites were still associated with May 1 (most prominently maintained by students at women's colleges and by young girls in public parks around the nation), it is unlikely that Edmonston or his fellow workmen would have been directly concerned with these cultural implications.[55] The practical association of the day with the renewal of contracts was the original deciding factor; any rhetorical or iconographic associations with spring rebirth (what Italian anarchists would call *la Pasqua dei lavoratori* (the workers' Easter), for example) came later in the development of the workers' May Day, once it became an annual event where tradesmen could tap into such ancient cultural associations to voice their demands. In so doing, these workers carried on what had been the rebellious side of the medieval spring rite tradition—the associations of May Day with "the mythical Robin Hood, for whom people gathered in the greenwood," and with social revolt and popular banditry—rather than the original court-sanctioned a-Maying, intended to celebrate the regeneration of the existing social order.[56] The latter, more conservative tradition could be found reemerging in the late nineteenth century in the maypole dancing and flower-gathering rites organized in parks and playgrounds by reformers concerned with assimilating a diversifying nation into an Anglo-American cultural identity. But the former, more rebellious tradition was the one workers could have comfortably embraced as they reinvented May Day in the context of the 1880s urban industrial world.[57] Edmonston's call for May 1 to be the rallying point for the eight-hour day did not consciously embrace this connection, but it set in motion its creation. The American trade union would thus leave its mark on what would eventually become an important holiday for workers and radicals around the world.

Edmonston's resolution passed by a vote of 23 to 2 in the convention and was sent out to the member unions for a vote. At the next national meeting, in December 1885, the returns were noted: 69 of the 78 affiliated unions approved. Among those organizations that rejected the proposal, some feared they were not prepared to take the necessary action, while others, like those from California, which had the nine-hour day, were satisfied with what they had already achieved.[58]

Most affiliates, however, believed that action had to be taken. Henry Emrich, a New York delegate from the International Furniture Workers Union, one of the leading trades in the eight-hour strikes of the early 1870s, submitted a resolution in 1885 reiterating Edmonston's calls for the May 1, 1886, demand. Emrich made clear his belief that strike action was necessary given the failure of the existing eight-hour legislation. It is not surprising that he supported this demand. Not only had Emrich's union participated in the strikes of the previous decades, but as a *craft* union, it also shared in a tradition of enforcing its own rules, both with employers and among its own membership.[59] Emrich insisted on the importance of a "united demand," making March 1, 1886, the deadline for the individual unions to report back their decision to join and their plan of action. He suggested that unions preparing to turn out on May 1 should initially notify their employers. His hope was that workers could elicit an agreement on eight hours just by threatening a strike.[60]

A number of groups supported Emrich's resolution. These included individuals and unions that favored the primacy of economic action, such as Gompers, the CMIU, and the Brotherhood of Carpenters and Joiners. But there were also the predominantly Irish Knights of Labor local assemblies and the Anglo-American-dominated Trades and Labor Assembly in Chicago, along with the Chicago Typographical Union 16. Thus it was not just the German Marxist IWA veterans of the 1870s' eight-hour drives who favored such national action. Despite the official opposition of the Knights to strikes, these different trade organizations came together in 1885 to organize and prepare for mass action in favor of the eight-hour day on May 1, 1886.[61]

Even Chicago's Central Labor Union (CLU), whose leadership was dominated by German and Bohemian anarchists, eventually decided to support FOTLU plans. Yet, this support came after months of criticism and only after the CLU leadership changed its position. In August 1885, *The Alarm* published the circular sent out by the federation announcing Edmonston's resolution and asking for local union support. In a short editorial that followed, Albert Parsons explained the anarchists' initial opposition to the shorter-hours movement. He argued that "the hours of labor can not [sic] be reduced by working people so long as the machinery which displaces us and forces us into compulsory idleness, and a destructive competition, *is held as private property.*" In his opinion, even mass action for the eight-hour day was useless, for true liberation of workers would not occur until they combined "to remove [this] *cause* which makes labor the slave of capital."[62] An article printed in September repeated this essential rejection of the eight-hour movement as a distraction from the "real" issues and as a waste of time and energy for anarchists.[63]

It was not until the following month that the leadership of the CLU decided to support the May 1, 1886, eight-hour drive. By then, popular support for the shorter-hours movement had grown, even among many anarchists. CLU leaders now believed it was important for both the integrity and the development of their organization to seize this momentum.[64] By supporting the FOTLU resolution, they hoped to direct this enthusiasm among CLU members into continued support for the anarchist agenda of fundamental economic and political change.

After releasing a circular announcing their plans and calling for a meeting of the eleven member unions, CLU leaders met with approximately

600 workers who turned out to hear their explanation of the change in policy. August Spies offered the resolution, which, after a brief discussion, was "carried with only a few dissents." It stated:

> That while we are skeptical in regard to the benefits that will accrue to the wage workers from an introduction of an eight-hour work day, we nevertheless pledge ourselves to aid and assist our brethren in this class struggle with all that lies in our power as long as they show an open and defiant front to our common enemy, the labor devouring class of aristocratic vagabonds.[65]

The need for solidarity, in what was understood as one step in the larger class struggle, overrode the anarchists' doubts about the eight-hour movement and justified their leading the CLU into coalition with the FOTLU affiliates on May 1, 1886. If a mass demonstration were going to take place in their city, the anarchist leaders believed it was better to join it on their own terms than to be left out altogether.

Consequently, as a precaution against the police opposition they expected to face during the strike and demonstration, the IWPA leadership of the CLU also added a resolution advocating that workers arm themselves for self-defense.[66] They repeated this call and encouraged workers to join unions and the IWPA during the eight-hour meetings they organized throughout January 1886.[67] Within a few short months, then, Chicago anarchists had shaped the May 1 event into a rallying point for the development of their movement. As part of the great demonstration for the eight-hour day, these political radicals would add a distinctly anticapitalist and internationalist agenda to the event. Because of that, what would be a watershed event in the history of American labor would also become a vital touchstone for the cultural and political identification of radicals in the United States and around the world for decades to come.

At 10 A.M. on May 1, 1886, the parade in Chicago stepped off from its assembly point at Haymarket Square. With his wife, Lucy, and their two children, Albert Parsons marched near the front. The procession made its way through the center of the city to Michigan Avenue and then to the lakefront. Once there, the nearly 80,000 marchers gathered for a mass meeting at which Spies and Parsons were scheduled to speak.[68] Although the day's events were peaceful, they took place under tense circumstances. These laborers and anarchists demonstrated their strength and resolve in a city that had for so long denied them their demands and feared their public presence. In addition to joining in the parade and mass meeting, several unions in the city were on strike. The May 1 demonstration thus wed both a celebratory and a militant tone. Workers marched proudly to protest their employers' failure to meet their demand for reduced hours without a cut in pay. Nearly 40,000 laborers had walked out, disrupting the railroads and shutting down factories.[69] As with previous demonstrations of workers in Chicago, the police feared a possible outbreak of violence and stationed themselves quite visibly around the city. Officers were poised on the city's rooftops "with Gatling guns awaiting orders." More than 1,000 National Guard troops stood by in the armories.[70] Yet, all the day's events were peaceful.

Across the country, the same was true. At the "monster demonstration" held in New York's Union Square, nearly 30,000 people gathered, many of whom wore red and blue ribbons. Transparencies calling for the eight-hour day illuminated the buildings surrounding the square. Approximately 600 policemen were on hand with another 200 to 300 ready for deployment in the surrounding side streets, but they were not needed.[71] The English-language speakers at the meeting included John Swinton, who stressed the practical reasons why employers should support the eight-hour day. From the German-language speaker's stand on Broadway came more radical rhetoric. S. E. Schevitsch denounced capital, while others argued that if employers would not recognize the eight-hour rule, then workers might not follow any law at all.[72] Across the city, unions also held their own meetings where they "reported progress of the [eight-hour] movement in their trades."[73] Like Chicago, there was a temporary alliance among workers and radicals on the first May Day.

Throughout New York City, various constituencies gathered on this day to voice their particular concerns as they demanded shorter work hours. As the example of Union Square shows, sometimes these different groups came together in the same ritual space. Trade unionists, socialists, and anarchists may have differed in their estimation of the type and degree of action necessary to improve their circumstances. Yet, they all agreed on the need for this massive display of strength and unity on May 1, through which they demanded the attention of their employers and the public. This type of concerted action would gradually become more difficult in the coming decade, as trade unionists and radicals of various stripes broke with one another, politically and ritually, in the wake of Haymarket and the European embrace of May Day.

But for the time being, on May 1, 1886, the coalition held. The joint demonstrations and strikes in New York and Chicago were accompanied by similar actions in St. Louis, Minneapolis, Indianapolis, Akron, Boston, Baltimore, and Milwaukee. May Day had flowered in nineteenth-century urban America, and as Gompers later asserted, "never before, in the history of the country, was there such a general upheaval noticed among the industrial masses." The first nationwide general strike and accompanying demonstrations gave a "stimulus and impetus" to the labor movement.[74] He and the other leaders of the national trade unions affiliated with the FOTLU, along with local urban Trades and Labor Assemblies (TLAs) and CLUs, and many of the Knights assemblies, had come together in a nationwide demonstration for the eight-hour day. They directed the attention of their employers and the public to the issue of the shorter-hours law, and they reinvigorated workers' faith in the labor movement after the struggles and defeats of the previous decade. In these ways, the event was a resounding triumph.

However, in terms of the actual number of trades that managed to secure the guarantee of the eight-hour day without a reduction in pay, the first May Day was only a partial success. Even Samuel Gompers noted in his report to the first annual meeting of the American Federation of Labor (AFL) in December 1886 that it was "painful to acknowledge that more was not accomplished."[75] While nearly 200,000 strikers were able to secure promises of the eight-hour day from their employers in May, many of them found themselves pressured back into working longer hours by the end of the year.[76] Gompers attributed the erosion of results not only to employer opposition, but also to Powderly's lack of support. He later insisted that the workers would have been successful if the strikers' "efforts [had] been met with the co-operation of the Knights of Labor" rather than with its "hostility."[77] In fact, many unions affiliated with the Knights did strike, but the official position of the Order, voiced by Powderly, was opposition to the May Day strikes.[78]

In a secret circular released on March 13, 1886, to unions affiliated with the Knights, Powderly made his opposition to the May 1 strikes clear, and cautioned his members against participating in them.[79] For Powderly, a strike should always be the last resort because it drained the resources of the unions and, if it failed, devastated both their ranks and their bargaining position with employers. Consequently, his opposition was based, in part, on his practical desire to lead the Knights cautiously in its demands for economic change.[80]

Powderly's resistance to the May 1, 1886, strike, however, may also have been rooted in his desire to control the expanding and unwieldy ranks of his organization, which were tempted by the FOTLU's call to take more immediate action under its leadership. He was especially concerned with the wave of new members who "rushed into the Order so rapidly, and with such slight preparation" once the movement for the nationwide eight-hour push began that they did not seem to know where the Knights stood on the issue. In his circular, he cautioned these workers that if they joined the walkout, they would not be able to receive any financial support from the Knights, which, under his leadership, had not officially endorsed the strike.[81] Both his general discomfort with the strike as a useful tool for labor and his fear of losing control of his organization's locals to the nascent AFL explain Powderly's opposition to the 1886 walkout.

Whether Powderly's circular actually undermined the May Day strikes is unclear, but Gompers made political hay out of it anyway. His accusation that it did weaken the effort seems to have come from his desire to undermine Powderly and the Knights while winning adherents to the newly created American Federation of Labor. Gompers voiced his criticism at the AFL's first convention in December 1886 during the portion of his address that focused on labor's struggles over the past year. He cast the Knights as obstacles to labor's progress in his speech and promoted the new federation as the workers' better choice.[82]

Despite the uneven success of the first May Day, under Gompers' presidency the AFL did not abandon the eight-hour demand. Through the late 1880s and into the early 1890s, the AFL restructured the eight-hour drives to avoid interference by the Knights. More importantly, as time progressed, it also moved to distance its work from May Day's association with socialism and anarchism, a link that was first intensified by political fallout from the events that became known as the Haymarket tragedy.

The story of the Haymarket tragedy has become a familiar one in labor and radical political history.[83] The event took on special significance both for the socialists and the anarchists who came to dominate May Day in the 1890s, and for those more conventional trade unionists who gradually distanced themselves from the annual demonstration in those same years. For the latter group, the violence of May 4 and the ensuing Red Scare reinforced their ideological and tactical disagreements with socialist and anarchist organizers. The AFL worked diligently in the years following the bombing to differentiate its demonstrations for the eight-hour day on

May 1 from the anniversary of Haymarket. For the radicals, the political repression that followed in the wake of May 4, and the arrest, unfair trial, and execution of the convicted anarchists, reinforced their conviction that there was no justice in a capitalist system. The memory of this martyrdom informed the way anarchists constructed their political and cultural identities on May Day in succeeding decades. In the shadow of this urban act of terror came a divided memory of May Day.

Although no one knows precisely who threw the bomb into the crowd of workers and police in Haymarket Square on the night of May 4, 1886, contemporary law enforcement officials and most nervous middle-class and elite Chicagoans quickly blamed the anarchist leaders who had organized the protest meeting. Anxious to mete out justice for the seven policemen who died as a result of the wounds inflicted that night, the state's attorney general, Julius Grinnell, prosecuted the eight defendants—Albert Parsons, August Spies, Samuel Fielden, Louis Lingg, George Engel, Adolph Fischer, Michael Schwab, and Oscar Neebe—in one of the nineteenth century's most sensational and infamous trials. Ultimately, Fielden, Neebe, and Schwab were given life sentences, Lingg died in jail before his execution, and the remaining four, including Parsons and Spies, died on the gallows on November 11, 1887. In his last moments, Parsons tried to deliver one final speech. Behind the mask that had been placed over his face, standing on the scaffold with the noose hung loosely around his neck, he addressed those who had gathered to watch. "Oh, men of America! May I be allowed the privilege of speech even at the last moment? Harken to the voice of the people." Parsons' final words were drowned out by the sound of the trap door opening, his speech cut off, as he and the other three anarchists met their grim fate.[84]

The Haymarket bombing not only led to the silencing of Parsons and his fellow defendants on that November day, but also brought about the near destruction of the anarchist movement in Chicago. With its presses and meeting halls in disarray, its followers intimidated and beaten by police in the raids following the bombing, and some of its most influential leaders executed, the movement was severely weakened. It was as if Chicago's urban elite had finally removed the anarchist thorn that had caused it such discomfort since the 1870s.[85] Parsons certainly believed this to be the case, and went further, seeing a different kind of conspiracy than that advanced by Grinnell. Before his execution, Parsons wrote that he believed the bomb was thrown by an agent of the "monopolistic corporations & privileged class" sent from New York in a plot "engineered by the

Pinkerton thugs" to derail the eight-hour drive and to destroy the labor movement. Because the anarchist and the labor movements in Chicago had been growing in size and strength, and because the concerted demand for the eight-hour day had been so well organized, Parsons believed that the May 1 strikes in his city were obvious targets for such a reactionary conspiracy.[86]

Although Parsons' accusations cannot be proven, his reflections on the consequences of the Haymarket tragedy cannot be disputed. While New York and Chicago monopolists and Pinkerton thugs were probably not responsible for the bomb, they did use it to their advantage. As Parsons noted, it provided a "golden opportunity to make a horrible example of the Anarchists, & by 'the deep damnation of their taking off' give the discontented American workingmen a terrible warning!"[87] Aside from the near dismantling of the anarchist movement in the months after May 1886, additional restrictions on the organizational capacity and public activity of radical groups and labor organizations were put into place in the aftermath of Haymarket. On July 23, the city council passed an ordinance forbidding any parades, processions, or open-air meetings in the city's streets or squares without a police permit.[88] For the first time in the city's history, anyone wishing to organize a public demonstration or meeting needed police permission. Now the public activities of workers and radicals were under even closer scrutiny and the constant threat of police interference.

Haymarket contributed not only to the intensification of police oversight of public assemblies, but also to the reworking of the public memory of the first May Day. Chicago's mainstream press presented the May 1 strikes and the Haymarket tragedy as comparable examples of radical extremism in the city.[89] It conflated the bloodshed of the May 4 bombing with the demonstrations of May 1, and criticized both as having been the thin end of an anarchist revolutionary wedge. While Samuel Gompers and most AFL-affiliated trade union leaders quickly refuted this association in the hope of salvaging their crusade for shorter working hours, anarchists in Chicago and New York embraced it. They defined the meaning of May Day as something that went beyond its original and, as they believed, limited demand for the eight-hour day. These anarchists touted the expressions of worker solidarity on May 1 as evidence of the holiday's revolutionary and transnational potential. They celebrated this radical vision both in the pages of their newspapers and in their May Day demonstrations during the late 1880s, constructing their unique public memory of the events of 1886 in a way that served their immediate political needs.

The anarchists' transnational aspirations, and the belief that May Day contained the potential to bring them to fruition, had existed within their political communities even before the first nationwide eight-hour demonstrations of 1886. The resolution that Chicago's anarchist-dominated CLU passed in October 1885 voiced the hope that the May 1 strikes would signify more than just the call for a shorter workday. August Spies, who expressed the CLU's position, believed that the events of May 1, 1886, would offer the initial manifestation of worker solidarity that would be necessary for the ultimate realization of economic and political self-rule.[90] He and his fellow Chicago anarchists agreed to participate in the demonstrations, but only because they believed that engagement would help hasten the demise of capitalism.

In an assessment of the first May Day published in 1887, the *Vorbote*, the Sunday edition of the *Arbeiter Zeitung*, echoed the belief that the exhibition of labor solidarity on May 1, 1886, portended revolution. The German-American anarchists who authored the piece defined the day as a turning point in history, the "beginning of a new era." They believed that from then on, May 1 should be considered the "anniversary of the modern labor movement and the modern struggle for freedom."[91] They compared May Day's radical newness, its meaning as a point of departure from the past and as a herald of liberty, to the French Revolution. These German-American anarchists deemed it a moment so significant as to command the creation of a new calendar, a new delineation of time itself.[92]

It may seem unlikely that this community, which had been so devastated after the post-Haymarket raids and prosecutions, would entertain such an optimistic vision. Although that repression initially weakened the infrastructure of the anarchist movement in Chicago, the trial of the accused conspirators and the death sentence that the court handed down to five of them also fueled a campaign of resistance.[93] Because the anarchists believed that the Haymarket martyrs did not conspire in the May 4 bombing, their execution signified both a heroic sacrifice and a miscarriage of justice. It signaled to anarchists the need for redoubled protest against the capitalist order that perpetuated such abuses. Dyer Lum, as the new editor of *The Alarm*, urged his anarchist compatriots to venerate the martyrs' faith in anarchy by carrying on their fight. He called on his readers to vindicate the men's deaths by speeding the birth of anarchy.[94]

One way anarchists responded to this call was by participating in May Day demonstrations. Many anarchists remembered the solidarity of laborers and radicals in the demonstrations of May 1, 1886, and during the general strikes in the days that followed, as evidence of the *possibility* of achieving the abolition of class rule.[95] Although the real revolutionary promise of this annual day of labor unity was held in check by post-Haymarket political repression (as well as by the desire of most organized workers not to go beyond the demand for the eight-hour day), anarchists continued to support that potential into the 1890s.

As the optimistic language of the *Vorbote* article evidenced, anarchists believed that the holiday provided an annual opportunity for workers and radicals to join together in protest. In the years following Haymarket, annual May Day parades became a favorite police target because of this increased socialist and anarchist affiliation. Police and city officials feared such gatherings of the city's radicals, which contributed to the construction of the annual event as one marked by rebellion and outlaw status. They used the permit law to justify their oversight of public displays, deciding what would and would not be tolerated.

In 1892, for example, Chicago's City Corporation Counsel advised Mayor Washburne and Police Chief McClaughry that any man "displaying a red flag could be legally arrested, as could any one uttering anarchistic ideas from the public platform" during the city's May Day events.[96] Based on this briefing, Assistant Police Chief Hubbard directed his men to search the parade for any "sanguinary" banners. From the many red flags that were carried in the parade that year, the police seized the three with the most direct representations of socialist and anarchist sentiments: those of the German Debattir Club, the Socialistiche Arbeiter Partei, and the anarchist *Arbeiter Zeitung*. After they seized the banners from the marchers, the police placed them in the office of the Superintendent of Police. While the capture and display of the red flags signaled a victory of the law over its violators, such acts may also have been intended as a symbolic imprisonment of the political sentiments the banners represented.[97] Like a victorious general on the battlefield, the police superintendent could gloat over having captured the enemy's standard. Even workers not affiliated with the radical movements in question recognized the significance of the act. A contributor to the *Journal of the Knights of Labor* warned how "gradually, but not slowly either, the police are arrogating to themselves the right to say and determine what men may and may not do." The police were "becoming the judges of the law—aye, and makers of it."[98] Part of the allure of gathering on May Day now became the risk of protesting against this kind of tyranny. Some workers and radicals embraced such rebelliousness as they defined themselves and their political position through public ritual each year.

Not all workers shared this sentiment. Once the mainstream press condemned the May 1 demonstration as a contributing factor in the May 4 riot, the fragile coalition that had come together on May Day began to crack. Not everyone who marched on May 1 wanted to embrace the outlaw status the police and press had thrust on them. The ethnic, religious, and political divisions that already ran deep between Chicago's TLA and CLU before the nationwide push for the eight-hour day in 1886 reemerged with renewed vigor after Haymarket.[99] The heightened antiradical sentiment of the police, the employers, the business elite, and the city's middle-class public raised the stakes for both the German and Bohemian anarchists and socialists in the CLU and the Irish and Anglo trade unionists in the TLA. The radicals had to deal with the increased and persistent criticism, harassment, and legal restrictions placed on them by the mainstream press, public opinion, and the city's authorities. But the trade unionists confronted this political fallout, too. Many in the Chicago TLA and in AFL affiliates throughout the country attempted to sever their relations with the political radicals among them as a result.[100]

In a symbolic step in this direction, the Chicago TLA decided in 1887 to ban the display of red flags in its Labor Day parades. That year the organization resolved to "extend an invitation to all labor organizations in Chicago and vicinity to participate in the demonstration on Labor National Holiday with the stipulation however that no flag but the American flag, or the flag of the organization be allowed in the procession." It insisted that "the red flag of revolution be regidly [sic] excluded."[101] TLA members defined their separation from the radicals in their midst, as well as their devotion to the American nation, not only by including a literal waving of the Stars and Stripes, but also by excluding the banner of radical revolution and international brotherhood.

On the national level, Gompers worked to distance the AFL officially from the socialist and anarchist agendas that were starting to dominate May Day by focusing the federation's efforts on the eight-hour demand alone, in a newly structured, "patriotic" campaign. Although Gompers admitted that political fallout from the Haymarket tragedy was a "catastrophe" for the eight-hour program, the AFL did not give up on this important goal.[102] National organization for the eight-hour day was temporarily suspended in 1887, but at the federation's meeting in St. Louis in 1888, Gompers suggested the use of a holiday, "probably February 22, 1889," for mass meetings to discuss the campaign's future.[103] His plan to hold "simultaneous eight-hour meetings throughout the country" on Washington's Birthday demonstrated Gompers' realization that to salvage the respectability of the shorter-hours movement, it would be necessary to associate it with a well-established patriotic holiday.[104] The AFL's Special Committee on the Eight-Hour Day adopted the proposal. It resolved to support member unions' participation in a "period of agitation" that was to take place on Washington's Birthday, the Fourth of July, and the first Monday in September 1889.[105] The meetings were to continue on Washington's Birthday 1890, and culminate in strikes on May 1, 1890.[106]

This choice revealed Gompers' and the Special Committee's savvy in guiding their organization within the broader context of American popular culture. During the late nineteenth century, many Americans became preoccupied with exploring and celebrating their national heritage. As Michael Kammen and Matthew Dennis have shown, there was a near obsession with demonstrations of patriotism and nostalgia for America's past, especially its revolutionary past, in the closing decades of the century. Much of this came from the ranks of native-born Americans, many of whom were among the nation's well-to-do. They created organizations like the Daughters of the American Revolution to celebrate their ties to the past, and to distinguish themselves from the millions of new immigrants arriving at the nation's shores each year.[107] The AFL's decision to turn to the patriotic touchstones of Washington's Birthday and the Fourth of July suggests more than its desire to gain access to displays of national pride. It also had to do with tapping into expressions of loyalty and associations of respectability and nativism.[108] It was thus not only elites who maneuvered in this way during the 1890s, but labor leaders as well. Concerning the meaning and purpose of May Day, Gompers also hoped that by establishing this ritual link, he could underscore his desire to keep the event focused narrowly on the achievement of the eight-hour day. That in itself was quite ambitious, but it fell well shy of the rebellion touted by the anarchists or the political revolution advocated by the socialists.

Gompers gave his full support to the AFL's sponsorship of pamphlets to "concentrate thought and activity on eight hours" among its affiliated unions. He also "wrote to practically every labor organization urging agitation for the eight-hour day," with the intention of "creat[ing] sympathetic understanding for the eight-hour movement and to forestall any association of the movement with anarchistic influences."[109] Gompers and his supporters in the AFL hoped to sever this association by moving the focus of the eight-hour campaign away from May Day alone, which, in the minds of employers and the public, had become conflated with the Haymarket anarchists. By linking labor's agitation for shorter hours to the Father of the Country and the Declaration of Independence, they hoped to foster a more positive association of the movement with the patriotism represented by those holidays, and to appropriate that patriotism for their cause. Implicit in this link between the trade unionist fight for shorter hours and the patriotism constructed in these late-nineteenth-century holidays was the celebration of "white" male skilled craftsmen from Northern European backgrounds, not those seen as "swarthy" immigrant radicals; it was a national pride circumscribed by the AFL's deepening labor nativism.[110] By December 1889, Gompers reported the success of the initial round of meetings in spreading the word of the eight-hour movement, reviving active membership in many of the unions, and, most importantly, calming the general public's fear of May Day by situating it within the broad context of a year-long, peaceful, and patriotic eight-hour campaign.[111]

In addition to attempts to secure favorable, or at least not hostile, public opinion for the eight-hour movement, Gompers employed a two-pronged approach to improve the trade unions' chances of achieving this goal. First, he tried to secure the support of the Knights' national leadership, or at least ensure that Powderly would not interfere again with another denunciation of strikes, as he had done in 1886. He corresponded with Powderly throughout 1889 through the general secretary of the AFL, P. J. McGuire.[112] Officers from both unions met twice that year to iron out grievances over working cards, labels, and expulsions. Powderly and his officers could not guarantee that the Knights' member unions would turn out on May 1, 1890, but they did not openly oppose the movement this time.[113]

Gompers then supported the AFL in its shift away from the tactic of the general strike as had been attempted in 1886. Instead of multiple walkouts, one trade per year would make the demand. It was hoped that this approach would quell employers' accusations that the unions were trying to stage a nationwide economic upheaval as a possible precursor to anarchist or socialist revolution. It also was a more practical plan because the AFL could support the one trade that was best able and most ready to make the demand in a given year.

As Gompers later recalled, "of the several organizations that made application, the Carpenters were designated to be the standard-bearers for

1890."[114] Throughout the country on May 1, 1890, the carpenters put down their tools.[115] P. J. McGuire, general secretary of the AFL and one of the founders of the United Brotherhood of Carpenters and Joiners, later reported success in 137 cities, benefiting "46,197 workmen in that trade, and countless others in every branch of the building trades."[116] This more focused approach seemed to produce tangible and lasting effects. Gompers noted that by 1891, after the United Mine Workers made a concerted demand, "it was no longer necessary for the national labor movement to sponsor specific eight-hour movements." He insisted that the AFL's "educational work had been sufficiently thorough to enable each national union to carry forward the shorter hours movement in its own industry."[117] During the early 1890s, then, the AFL supported its member unions as they organized strikes on May Day that focused on the specific fight for the eight-hour day. Unlike the anarchists and socialists, who would use May 1 to define their radical identities and to assert their anticapitalist agenda, trade unionists tried to sustain the event as a weapon in their bread-and-butter struggle for shorter hours within the capitalist system.

Paradoxically, it would be trade unionists who encouraged the use of May Day abroad, where socialists turned it into an annual rallying point for their radical political agenda. Part of the AFL's work in fighting for the shorter workday in the United States included its consideration of Europe's influence on the labor market. Gompers later noted how he and other leaders in the federation realized they "could widen [their] purpose" as they developed their plans for the eight-hour demand in 1889 if they reached out across the Atlantic. At the same time that he was fostering links between the eight-hour movement and patriotic holidays in America, Gompers was also seeking support from workers in Europe meeting at the two International Workingmen's Congresses in Paris. Although it may at first seem as though Gompers was working at cross purposes (by establishing ties to European socialists while working to distance the AFL from political radicals at home), he was, in fact, carefully maneuvering to assure the ultimate security of the eight-hour movement in the United States. The constant influx of cheap immigrant labor from Europe had begun to undermine many of the advances made by unions in their negotiations with employers over hours and pay. Gompers believed that this was an issue that needed to be addressed if the eight-hour demand were to be truly secure in America.[118] It should be recalled, therefore, that his concern for advancing the eight-hour day in Europe was quite self-serving.

His desire for protectionism at home was wedded to a nativist vision of excluding the cheap competition of "undesirables" from abroad.[119]

Gompers wanted a congress between the AFL and European labor leaders, but he was wary of the political approach most Europeans took to their shared concerns. Gompers favored instead, as he always had, "strictly trade-unionist" economic strategies.[120] When the European Marxist and Possibilist factions held their separate conferences in Paris in July 1889, Gompers hoped they "could aid our movement by an expression of world-wide sympathy."[121] However, the AFL would not condone the dispatch of official delegates to Paris, perhaps because of the political nature of the conferences. Instead, it "instructed Gompers to send a 'letter of fraternal good will,'" which he released to Hugh McGregor "as a personal envoy, without official mandate."[122] While the letter has not survived, minutes from the separate congresses report McGregor's having read it aloud at each meeting.

According to the research of Hubert Perrier and Michel Cordillot, these minutes, along with reports from American delegates from the SLP and United Hebrew Trades who were in attendance at the Paris meetings, substantiate the contents of Gompers' letter as having brought "the attention of both congresses to the ongoing struggle for the eight-hour day" in America, and to the demand that was planned among the carpenters for May 1, 1890.[123] The Possibilist congress passed a resolution wishing success for the AFL's campaign, while the Marxist congress, the Second International, called for the organization in each country of "an international eight hour demonstration on May 1st [sic]."[124] Henceforth, May Day would be celebrated throughout Europe by socialists, anarchists, and trade unionists. Rather quickly, word of this new reality echoed across the Atlantic to the United States and began to influence the choices American workers and radicals faced over whether or not to support what was now an international labor day.

For at least a year and a half after the Paris meetings, both the AFL and the European Marxists embraced the unity and promise of a symbolic workers' front represented by the new international May Day. But soon the ideological differences that separated the two groups, expressed in the different tactics they employed during their separate May Day demonstrations, overwhelmed this initial wave of cordiality. As Perrier and Cordillot have argued, the AFL and the American trade unions "believed in workers confronting employers directly with the shorter-workday demand," whereas French Marxists "believed in mass demonstrations on a fixed date in order to make a formal demand to the 'public authorities'—i.e., the state at its various levels."[125] By the mid-1890s, the French Marxists (Guesdists) began to downplay the role of the AFL in May Day's origin, partly because of their ideological disagreements with the American trade unionists' focus on economic strategy. Their denial that the AFL had given any inspiration other than just the date of May 1 for the May Day holiday was part of a wider internal process of the Guesdists' creating their own cultural identity in 1890s France. They wanted to take credit for what they now defined as an international Marxist worker holiday.[126] This in itself made any gestures of unity or even cordiality from Gompers much less likely.

In addition, the hostility that developed at home between the AFL and the SLP in the mid-1890s widened the separation between American trade unionists and May Day, which was being celebrated in Europe and among American socialists as an international workers' holiday.[127] By 1891, the AFL was no longer coordinating the eight-hour demands on May 1, leaving that instead to individual national unions. Increasingly, the federation and many of its local affiliates began to pull away from participating in May Day parades and demonstrations, as anarchists, socialists, and their affiliated unions came to dominate those events. The same two developments, which encouraged the retreat of the AFL from the observation of the workers' holiday it had created, provided grist for the cultural mill of America's socialists and anarchists. These groups would embrace both the radical implications of Haymarket's heritage and the international Marxist associations that had become ascribed to May Day as they made the holiday their own during the 1890s.

Conceived in response to the economic upheaval wrought by the processes of industrialization in America's great cities during the 1870s and early 1880s, and midwifed by the growing trade union, anarchist, and socialist movements, May Day was born on May 1, 1886, as a child of protest in one of the greatest demonstrations of labor's strength in American history. Although trade unionists and political radicals managed to sustain their alliance for this historic moment, the aftershock of the Haymarket tragedy and the European socialists' adoption of May Day would undermine that cooperation. As the AFL tried to maintain the focus of this new holiday on workers' push for the eight-hour day, anarchists and socialists took up the more radical implications that Haymarket and the new international reach of May Day offered them.

In the closing decade of the nineteenth century, these anarchists and socialists would create their own iconography and rhetoric for the new, modern, urban May Day. They wove elements from their particular ethnic and religious heritages with their concerns as workers in a rapidly industrializing America, all within a Marxist or anarchist philosophical framework. They deployed this new combination on May Day to voice their immediate concerns as immigrant and American radicals in 1890s New York and Chicago. At the same time, more moderate trade unionists struggled over the decision of whether or not to participate in the May Day event, as it became more radicalized and internationalized during the 1890s. Many began to support a September Labor Day holiday instead, and to define for themselves a more traditional symbolism and rhetoric that celebrated the skilled laborer and his contributions to the nation, even as its workforce became much more diverse in terms of ethnicity, race, and skill level. The ideological, strategic, and tactical political differences among New York's and Chicago's socialists, anarchists, and trade unionists were now competing on the playing field of the nation's civic culture. Here, each group would find the means to define publicly its political identities as they developed in the 1890s. As the next chapter will demonstrate, sometimes that definition included a distinctly working-class or radical Americanism: May Day became an unexpected part of the process of what James Barrett has called "Americanization from the bottom up."[128] At the same time, it was on May Day that workers and radicals contributed to the debate over the public and ritual definition of American nationalism, offering hybrid alternatives to the well-known official versions sustained in other, more mainstream public holidays.

2

Revolutionary Dreams
and Practical Action
May Day and Labor Day, 1890–1903

In November 1903, the American Federation of Labor (AFL) held its thirty-third annual convention in Boston. During the morning session on the fifth day, Maurice Mikol, a delegate from New York City's radical-dominated United Cloth Hat, Cap and Millinery Workers Union, stood up and proposed a fiery resolution. He called on the federation to adopt May 1 as a "day of protest against the present obnoxious system of exploitation and the dawn of emancipation of the Proletariat." Mikol argued that May 1 was "recognized by all class-conscious workers of the world as a day not only for the edification of the eight-hour work day, but for a day where the capitalistic yoke shall be shaken off forever."[1] Indeed, by 1903, May Day had become more closely associated with such radical politics. During the 1890s, socialists and anarchists had made the event their own, observing it with impressive parades and mass meetings. The Socialist Labor Party (SLP) shared Mikol's support for May Day as an international labor day that heralded the demise of capitalism. As a result, the AFL's Committee on Resolutions voted against his proposal, for while support for May 1 was contested within the AFL, by 1903 it had become a decidedly minority position. Instead, the federation had officially sanctioned the September Labor Day as the holiday for American workers.

The rejection of Mikol's resolution in 1903 indicated a shift that had taken place in the AFL's perception of May Day over the previous decade. The federation had continued to support its member unions when they fought for the eight-hour day on May 1 during the 1890s. But by the early twentieth century, the AFL began to distance itself from what had become a holiday dominated by anarchists, socialists, and their union allies. Anarchist groups, in their newspapers and annual May Day gatherings, defined the day as offering hope for the realization of a transnational order. The Socialist Labor Party recognized the holiday's internationalism, too, celebrating its promise as the harbinger of global socialism. Both socialists and anarchists forged the symbolic status of May Day in this radical cast during the 1890s and early 1900s. In addition, socialists developed the holiday into a political organizing tool. They used their May Day parades and demonstrations to reinforce and increase their party ranks, especially among the working class.

Given these iconic and practical associations of radicalism with May Day, the politically moderate trade unionists who dominated the leadership of the AFL found it difficult to keep the annual event focused on the eight-hour movement alone. Instead, by 1903, they, along with many trade unions within the federation, supported the celebration of respectable unionism that characterized the September Labor Day holiday. The distinct aesthetic of worker's pride that characterized this holiday distinguished it from the transnational socialism that had come to dominate May Day. How workers and radicals created and promoted these two very different holidays in the United States reveals the growing political fissures within the working class during these years. It illuminates the unique creation of a militant, but not politically radical, trade unionism in America at the turn of the last century. And it also demonstrates how that development took place not only in the convention halls and offices of the growing labor movement, but also in the streets, in the realm of popular political culture.

In addition, the history of the evolution of these two holidays reveals the tensions within the ranks of the nation's craft unions. As the example of Mikol's resolution demonstrates, the official political position of the AFL was not necessarily representative of all its members; different opinions were held within individual trade unions. Such diversity was especially visible in the cultural politics that existed at the grassroots level. There, workers constructed a sense of their own place within both the union movement and the nation. They did so, in part, by choosing which holiday to support and which elements of their world as workers and Americans to celebrate or protest.

Grassroots diversity could also be seen within the SLP and anarchist associations. Their members came from a number of neighborhoods characterized by different ethnic and religious ties. These affiliations often influenced the translation of radical ideas and their communication in the May Day displays. In the case of many anarchists, this communication often resulted in expressions of desire for a new transnational social and political order. There was really no room for embracing any form of American identification: the focus was purely international and Marxist. Yet, sometimes the translation of radical ideas resulted in a demonstration of their compatibility with American democracy. This certainly was the case with some socialists.

Interestingly, not only did those whom we may think of as orthodox internationalists appeal to the ideas and ceremonial trappings of American democracy in certain May Day events. Skilled trade unionists also found ways to voice their adherence to more radical political visions by marching in *both* Labor Day and May Day processions, to the dismay of the AFL's national leadership. The history of May Day and Labor Day during the 1890s and early 1900s thus illuminates these more complex, hybrid identifications among radicals and workers created within American popular political culture. And that, in turn, indicates how there was a good deal of cross-pollination at the grass roots between conceptions now thought to be opposites: nationalism and internationalist socialism.

Such cross-pollination and hybrid identities were least visible within anarchist communities. Unlike some socialists, who would find ways to blend American nationalist identifications with their internationalist Marxist beliefs, anarchists constructed more purely radical and transnational representations of themselves. During the 1890s, Haymarket became one of the more important touchstones for anarchists as they constructed such public identities. These radicals embraced the symbolic confluence of the May 1 and May 4 events, celebrating the rebellious potential of May Day to protest the entire capitalist system.

Anarchists used May Day to construct publicly their identity as radicals who, unlike most of the laborers with whom they marched, sought more than the implementation of the eight-hour day. From within their local trade unions, social clubs, and political party assemblies, anarchists turned out to strike, parade, and join mass meetings on May Day during the 1890s, to voice their desire for economic and political self-rule, and to try to bring that new order into being. They proudly marched with their red and black banners through the streets of Chicago and New York, despite police opposition, in the hopes of realizing what they believed was the holiday's nascent revolutionary possibility.[2] Although that potential was never realized, the anarchists' presence at May Day demonstrations in the 1890s reinforced the popular assessment that the event was a holiday for political radicals who hoped to transform, rather than merely reform, the economic and political status quo.

In part because it was a holiday of dissent, most native-born Americans, be they working-class, middle-class, or elite, considered May Day "un-American." The event's changing social profile during the 1890s reinforced this perception, and thus further marginalized its adherents. The vision of May Day's revolutionary potential, voiced first among Chicago's German-American anarchists, was shared among those in the growing Italian-American anarchist communities there and in New York. Although they were a minority within the massive wave of Italian immigrants that began arriving in America in the late 1890s, these anarchists and their refugee leaders contributed to the character of May Day celebrations.[3] Along with radical immigrants from other ethnic backgrounds, they sustained these celebrations at the turn of the century, because by then most politically moderate native-born and immigrant laborers had begun to abandon May Day demonstrations altogether.[4] Through their celebration of the holiday in American cities, immigrant anarchists (and socialists) contributed to May Day's growing internationalist flavor and constructed their own hybrid identities as radical immigrants.

In large cities like New York and Chicago, foreign-born anarchists and socialists had the opportunity to join with insurgents from other ethnic backgrounds on May Day, experiencing, as it were, the internationalism of the radical ideology they professed.[5] Public May 1 celebrations were one place where this fraternity was encountered. By the mid- to late 1890s, for example, a joint May Day gathering of New York's Italian, German, Jewish, and native-born socialists was held in Union Square, where speeches were delivered in many different languages.[6] Through their intermingling and their public show of unity in support of revolution, they both momentarily experienced and symbolically achieved a version of international worker solidarity. The May Day gathering was one place were they actively created this unity. The annual demonstration did not merely reflect the existing social and political world. Instead, it was an important forum where ethnically diverse working-class radicals expressed the idea of transnational proletarian cooperation and attempted to put that concept into action, temporarily creating a new social reality.

Augmenting the expanding "foreign" social profile of May Day supporters was one particularly influential Italian anarchist leader. Pietro Gori was an important contributor to the creation of May Day's radical and international character. One of many anarchists the Italian government imprisoned during its widespread crackdown on political radicals in the mid-1890s, Gori was deported from Italy to Germany in 1895. He left for America soon thereafter.[7] Gori remained in the United States for only one year but left an indelible mark on anarchist culture there, organizing nearly 400 meetings around the nation and founding the anarchist periodical *La Questione Sociale* in Paterson, New Jersey.[8] A poet and a playwright, Gori also contributed to the tone and content of May Day celebrations held among Italian-American radicals at the turn of the century. He brought a romantic vision of transnationalism to anarchist political culture, both in the language and with the religious references familiar to his fellow Italians.

Gori expressed this romantic vision in his one-act play, *Primo Maggio*, which he wrote while jailed in Italy in 1890.[9] This short drama was originally published in 1896. An anarchist drama group in Paterson first performed it that same year with Gori in the cast.[10] Anarchist communities throughout America and Italy quickly adopted the play as a principal element of their May Day festivities, staging their own performances annually.[11] One of Gori's poems, also entitled "Primo Maggio," became a central part of these yearly festivities after he put the words to music. The new song became the unofficial May Day anthem that Italian-American anarchists sang at their demonstrations from the late 1890s into the early years of the twentieth century.[12] It suggests the kind of plural identity that these anarchists may have constructed for themselves as Italian immigrant radicals confronting the challenges of their new urban, industrial American surroundings.

In the song "Primo Maggio," Gori called for the coming of May, the "Sweet Easter" of the laborers that would release them from their earthly toil. He called on radical workers—who, when singing the lyrics, called on each other—to "join together in a growing force" to "redeem [their] world." Workers in solidarity, not the Son of God, were hailed as the temporal, rather than the transcendent, savior.[13] In his work, then, Gori used religious references that would have been familiar to the audience of Italian anarchists who, although they were most likely atheists, had come from a cultural milieu steeped in Catholic Christianity. Gori tapped into the familiarity of such sacred themes to support his secular, anarchist message of temporal change. He used the same technique in *Primo Maggio* the play. The character of the wandering stranger, Lo Straniero, for example, functions as a Christ figure who brings the "gospel" of socialism to the small Italian village through which he is passing. He gathers as his apostolic followers Ida, a young farm girl, as well as a worker and a sailor on his pilgrimage to the promised land of equality and freedom.[14]

In addition to these religious references, Gori's play clearly included a story of migration, which would have been familiar to him as a political exile and to his Italian-American immigrant audiences. It is clear that for Gori, anarchism, the ultimate state of freedom, was his ideal final destination. It was the "homeland" he longed for as a radical who, like many other advocates of labor internationalism during the 1890s, had felt the wrath of the young Italian nation-state.[15] For his audiences, however, this message could have been translated in complex ways, casting Gori in the role of a "radical ethnic broker," to use Elisabetta Vezzosi's term.[16] As such, immigrant audiences may have interpreted Gori's appeal to a promised land of equality and freedom to mean America, the land they had just crossed an ocean to settle. Gori may have thus aided immigrants' accommodation to their new home as Americans. But if his work fostered this kind of adjustment, it did so from a radical political perspective: it called for that new home to be a seedbed of anarchism. Gori's work advocates the creation of a socialist order and serves as a vehicle of protest against capitalism. And only political radicals performed *Primo Maggio* on May Day. To complicate things further, Gori's play is written in the language and steeped in the melodramatic culture of his fellow Italians, even as it calls for aspirations to a state of international brotherhood that would reach beyond Italy. Those who performed and watched this play could therefore partake in it as way to define themselves as political radicals, who were Italian, but who were also trying to find their footing in their new American homeland as internationally minded anarchists.

These multiple identifications are also held in tension in Gori's anarchist hymn, "Primo Maggio." Such tension can be sensed in the meaning associated with the melody as opposed to that found in the lyrics. Gori set the words of his poem "Primo Maggio" to the melody of "Va, Pensiero!," Giuseppe Verdi's well-known chorus from his 1842 opera *Nabucco*. "Va Pensiero!" was a "lament of the Hebrews by the river Jordan for a home of their own"; it echoed the desire of a wandering people for a nation. Verdi's chorus became well known to Italians later in the nineteenth century because it was adopted as the unofficial anthem of the Italian state after unification in 1870. Despite this clear association with nationalism, or perhaps because of it, Gori chose to use Verdi's famous melody for the "Primo Maggio" hymn. Rather than celebrating a traditional nation-state, however, Gori extolled the "Green May of humankind," which would flower across the globe in the form of worker solidarity. In his lyrics, Gori proposed that the ideal homeland be one that embodied the political freedom and economic equality promised in anarchism, turning the more popular nationalist use of the song on its head.[17] Once this freedom was realized, the "vaganti," of whom Gori wrote in a second poem entitled "Primo Maggio," like the poor family in his play *Senza Patria* (who were forced to wander the earth in search of work and sustenance), would find a true home, *una vera patria*, in the brotherhood of mankind.[18]

As Italian-American anarchists sang "Primo Maggio" during their May Day celebrations, they called on each other to bring about a new order of transnational self-rule. The annual commemoration of the first nationwide expression of labor solidarity became a moment for anarchists to gather and publicly express their identity as radicals who shared this desire for the triumph of the "Green May of humankind." They paused to reflect on and to extol this vision for the future, which they might then work to achieve, be it through political and economic organization or direct acts of violence, during the rest of the year.[19]

In their May Day celebrations, these anarchists constructed identities for themselves that celebrated their ethnic roots and their radical political visions for the future. These were rather romantic self-images that were focused on the goal of global economic and political transformation. Although Gori played with representations of nationalism in his adoption of Verdi's melody for the "Primo Maggio" hymn, it was Italian, not American, nationalism he refashioned. During the 1890s, New York's and Chicago's mostly immigrant anarchist communities defined themselves in public each May 1 as radicals within a transnational movement. And in so doing, they further imbued May Day with radical and internationalist meanings.

During the 1890s, the Socialist Labor Party also celebrated May Day as a rallying point for international worker solidarity. It used the holiday to focus its efforts on socialist economic and political organization. When Marxists meeting at the Second International in Paris in 1889 resolved that May 1 should become an annual day for workers to protest throughout Europe, they gave the labor holiday that was created in America a new international socialist context. European socialists quickly embraced the anniversary, staging parades and demonstrations.[20] And in the case of radical artists like Walter Crane, they memorialized the transnational potential of the holiday in lively iconography.[21]

Figure 2.1. A European representation of the transnational nature of May Day is evident in this Walter Crane cartoon, "International Solidarity of Labor," from 1889.

The Socialist Labor Party in New York City and Chicago also acknowledged this new context. Through its parades and meetings and in speeches and reports, the SLP officially defined May Day as the harbinger of socialism's global implementation. The party redefined May Day as International Labor Day, and used it to bolster its agenda of change through economic and political organization, organization intended to awaken the American worker to this "inevitable" birth of socialism around the world.

In the process of creating its May Day demonstrations, however, there were differences of opinion among the party's membership and among those in its affiliated organizations over the details of the May Day events. At the core of these differences lay conflicts among socialists over the precise nature of their political sympathies. Specifically, party members were in disagreement over what it meant to be a radical *and* an American within the international socialist order envisioned by the party during the 1890s. There is evidence that as early as 1898, some members of the party came to embrace a compound identity, championing the display of the American flag alongside the red flag. Others could not accommodate such displays and remained wholeheartedly focused on their understanding of themselves as international socialists.

Partly the SLP advocated this transnational character of May Day for ideological reasons. The party considered May Day a global day of protest. In their mass meetings in Union Square, for example, party members resolved to unite their voices with the workers of all countries, and to support the oneness of the laborer's cause around the world.[22] They were cognizant of the concerns of American workers, but saw them as part of this broader global struggle of "uniting our voices with the proletarians of all countries." Party members on the square that day vowed to "re-assert the demand. . . . that the reduction of the hours of labor to eight is of immediate necessity," and pledged their "sympathy and support for all efforts of labor to secure that end," including "the striking coke-workers of Pennsylvania." They "urge[d] our fellow workers and friends to assist [those striking coalminers] financially in their heroic struggle against hired assassins and capital's most powerful ally: hunger."[23] But they also argued that, "in order to resist the encroachments of consolidated capital, the wage-workers must immediately consolidate their forces for *political* as well economic action."[24] The SLP activists who supported these resolutions thus shaped May Day to fit their ideological commitment to international socialism.

The party also sought political ownership of the event not only so it could mobilize it to these global, socialist ends, but also so it could undermine the AFL's role in coordinating May Day demonstrations. Party leaders most strongly challenged the AFL's claim to May Day in the mid-1890s, when tensions between them and Samuel Gompers came to a head. After marshaling enough support to push Gompers out of the office of AFL president for a year in 1895, many socialists within the federation followed Daniel DeLeon's call to join the newly created Socialist Trades and Labor Alliance (ST&LA).[25] The SLP worked with the ST&LA to coordinate May Day demonstrations in New York, Chicago, and other cities around the nation. At those events, DeLeon, Lucien Sanial and other SLP leaders asserted the socialist paternity of the holiday. In speeches delivered each May 1, they retold the history of May Day. DeLeon, Sanial and other prominent party members formally referred to the annual event as *International Labor Day*, contributing both to the SLP's ideological position that the demonstrations were global in their composition and purpose and to its practical goal of supplanting the AFL.

In so doing, they made it clear that they did not want to chronicle the American roots of the event, or its links to the mainstream trade union movement. DeLeon, Sanial, and the other party leaders instead wanted to co-opt May Day to serve the party and international socialism. They crafted a new history of the holiday as international in its origins, nature, and purpose. In official party rhetoric, therefore, there was no desire to accommodate a hybrid radical Americanism: the eyes of the SLP's leaders were turned outward on the global socialist movement. DeLeon and Sanial argued that May Day had its beginnings not in resolutions supported by Gompers and passed by the AFL at St. Louis in 1888, but in the Marxist declaration issued by the Second International at Paris in 1889. They essentially reconstructed the story of May Day's founding, establishing a public memory that attributed the holiday's origins to socialists at the Second International instead of to trade unionists in the American Midwest.[26]

DeLeon and other party leaders sought not only representational but also organizational control of May Day. They mobilized the SLP's affiliated trade unions and its party infrastructure to use the holiday for its own ends. In particular, the party used the May 1 events to bring its message to potential members, especially those within the majority of the working class who did not support socialism. One way the SLP attempted to draw the attention of the laborer to the promise of socialism was through the production and distribution of leaflets, fly posters, and special-edition newspapers each May 1.[27] In 1895, for example, the SLP's May Day

Conference members reported that volunteers were busy hanging party leaflets along the streets and in the squares where the demonstration was to be held that year.[28] Conference members believed it was important not only to reinforce support for the SLP where it was strongest (among the progressive German trades and Jewish garment industries of the Lower East Side), but also to garner support in working-class districts where it was weakest, supporting a parade through the less-well-organized lower section of the west side.[29]

Tremendous energy was also devoted to perfecting the event's trappings. A special committee read and approved the mottoes for transparencies to make sure that they were spelled correctly and that only party slogans would appear.[30] The SLP wanted to present itself as strong in number, well organized, and articulate in its May Day demonstrations. It hoped that such attention to detail would not only stave off as much criticism as possible from the already hostile mainstream press, but also win the party the support of the city's workers. Party members were somewhat successful, coordinating parades and mass meetings in Union Square during the 1890s that drew close to 10,000 people each year, according to their own estimates.[31] Despite this impressive showing, the SLP never won over the majority of the working class in either New York or Chicago. But that did not stop them from striving to do just that.

Planning for the annual May Day event was one way the party carried out its organizing work. Local assemblies distributed circulars among its enrolled voters and members of its affiliated progressive unions and benefit societies to form organizing committees for May Day parades and mass meetings.[32] The minutes from these special conferences voiced concerns over both practical issues of logistics and funding and specific political concerns, such as the demonstration of party strength in particular neighborhoods. Yet, at times committee members also voiced differences of opinion over the public definition of their political identities as socialists and as Americans. These differences belie the hardened official position of the party that DeLeon, Sanial, and others expressed. In the leaders' speeches, and in official party resolutions, there was a single focus on the significance of May Day as an international labor day, as a harbinger of global socialism. The vernacular expressions found in the extant party records at the local level, however, reveal different interpretations. They demonstrate the definition of alternative Americanisms at the grassroots level.

At a February 26, 1898, meeting in New York, a motion was proposed calling for the Stars and Stripes to be displayed on the cottage-like

bandstand in Union Square. It also requested that the participating organizations carry the American flag along with the red flag as they marched
in the parade.[33] The proposal sparked a "lengthy discussion," the details of
which are not recorded. Despite objections, the motion ultimately passed.
In subsequent meetings, representatives voiced additional protests against
the resolution. Members from the Thirtieth Assembly District insisted
that they would not carry an American flag, arguing that the "Red flag
[was] good enough for them." The Socialist Frauenverein's delegates similarly registered their dissatisfaction with the motion.[34] At later meetings,
representatives from additional party branches and unions joined them in
their objection.[35]

It is not surprising that some of these socialist and progressive groups
objected to the idea of displaying the American flag on May Day. By
1898, the Stars and Stripes had come to signify a "law-and-order" patriotism that celebrated national unity, in both political and social terms,
under the rubric of "one country, one flag," and that extolled the virtue
of liberty under law. Many civic-minded businessmen and prominent
citizens, including members of the New York and Chicago Union League
Clubs, created this brand of patriotism in response to what they perceived to be a deepening crisis of urban order: a crisis that originated, in
part, from the public agitation of workers and radicals begun during the
Great Railroad Strike of 1877. In the subsequent two decades, members
of veterans' organizations and patriotic societies joined the businessmen
and Union Leaguers as they coordinated a series of programs for the
public schools and for local communities designed to teach such law-
and-order patriotism.[36] The American flag was at the center of these programs, which included the creation of the Pledge of Allegiance in 1892,
the schoolhouse flag movement sponsored by the Grand Army of the
Republic, the Daughters of the American Revolution and the Sons of the
American Revolution throughout the 1890s, and the founding of Flag
Day in 1893.[37]

Given the association of the Stars and Stripes with this more conservative definition of patriotism, it may seem surprising that some socialists
would favor displaying the flag on their revolutionary day. This is particularly interesting given the position of the party's national leadership,
which wanted the event to be focused on global socialism, not on demonstrations of national loyalty or on any recognition of May Day's American
roots. The call made by some New York socialists to display the American
flag on May 1, 1898, suggests that there were those within the party who

had values different from those of their party leaders, and who tried to find a way to forge a hybrid identity as radical Americans.

Ultimately, however, the question of whether or not to display the flag was moot when the police in New York revoked the SLP's parade permit on April 30.[38] Worried that the event would include "inflammatory speeches" that might spark a riot, Police Chief John McCullagh, a Republican and Mason "in high standing," had demanded to vet the resolutions that the socialists planned to present at their postparade meeting in Union Square.[39] When the SLP refused, arguing that America "was not an absolute monarchy," McCullagh revoked its permit. In response to the cancellation of their parade, party members held an "indignation meeting" at the Germania Assembly Rooms in the Bowery. There, Lucien Sanial roundly criticized McCullagh and, with reference to contemporary foreign affairs, denounced America's making such a "fuss over the Cubans when many thousands starved right here." Among the resolutions the party then passed enthusiastically were hearty greetings to socialists around the globe, including the SLP's socialist brethren in Spain.[40]

The *New York Times* cited this last resolution, and Sanial's criticism of America's support for Cuba, as evidence of the inflammatory speech that the party refused to have McCullagh vet. The paper also noted how the Federation of Hebrew Trades and the Debs Democracy (a socialist splinter group with a presence in some of the SLP's assembly districts) cooperated with the police, did not issue any controversial resolutions, and were allowed to march. Those groups paraded "through several east side streets to Twelfth Avenue, thence to Fifth Avenue, and down to Washington Square," carrying both American flags and Cuban flags. As they marched, the men and women of these two organizations cheered for Cuba and listened to their bands play "patriotic airs, including the 'Star-Spangled Banner,' 'The Red, White, and Blue,' and 'America.'" Because the Federation of Hebrew Trades and the Debs Democracy presented a more traditionally defined patriotic demonstration, and one that supported the nation's contemporary foreign policy, they were allowed to march. The police did not expect any riots or disturbances to surround such an event.[41]

This type of police oversight would remain a challenge for decades to come for political radicals who wanted to demonstrate on May 1. But here, in 1898, it added an interesting wrinkle to the story of those socialists within the SLP who wanted to carry the American flag on May Day. Clearly, antiradical sentiment in the city was running higher than usual that spring because of the rising jingoist support for the war that had just broken out with Spain. McCullagh's revocation of the SLP's permit was ostensibly intended to prevent a public disturbance, which included possible attacks on radicals for protesting the war. Yet, by preventing them from parading, the police chief also silenced the socialists' dissent. The delegates at the February 26 May Day conference who wanted to carry the American flag may have recognized the practical importance of making such a patriotic display. They may have decided to include the Stars and Stripes as a tactical maneuver to ensure the safety of the May Day celebrants in the context of the popular antiradical hostility that was then so palpable in their city. This may also have been the case with those who joined the ranks of the Debs Democracy, a group that was then peeling away members from several of the SLP's assemblies in New York.[42]

Yet, those socialists still within the ranks of the SLP who supported the display of the American flag on May 1 also may have done so because they thought this gesture would demonstrate what they believed was the standard's true symbolic meaning. Although they espoused a political ideology that officially prioritized the solidarity of an international working class, a position that was at odds with the nationalist "law-and-order" patriotism conservatives celebrated since the late 1870s, these socialist Americans rejected neither the democratic promise of their nation nor the flag that they believed symbolized that promise. Their desire to display the Stars and Stripes at Union Square and to carry it alongside the red flag on parade voiced their confidence in this alternative version of American patriotism: one that included their radical political aspirations for the future. Understood in this light, their decision to carry the flag is not that surprising. Indeed, there is evidence that SLP members had placed the American flag on display at Union Square during their May Day meetings in 1893 and in 1895, indicating a history of such radical American identification.[43]

This choice demonstrated that—despite the intentions of the Union Leaguers and patriotic society members to define a static and timeless law-and-order patriotism—the cultural meanings that could be attributed to the flag, and to the nationalism it represented, were much more fluid. The socialists who wanted to carry the Stars and Stripes in their May Day parade in 1898 bore witness to the fact that their American national identity, and the flag that represented it, could contain devotion to their country and to their radical political aspirations at the same time. This would have been particularly true for those members who were native-born and those who believed in the gradual achievement of socialism through democratic practices. But it could also be true for those immigrants in the party's ranks who may have been working through their own process of assimilation into their new homeland. By carrying the national standard in a May Day parade, they would have manifested their compound identity as radical Americans. They would have at once seized the flag to support this alternative political position and altered its meaning in the very same use.

As other celebrations suggest—ranging from Fourth of July observances to St. Patrick's Day and Columbus Day events organized in these same years—the creation and expression of plural loyalty was a fairly common practice in American political culture.[44] Yet, what was taking place on May Day was in many ways very different from the ethnic-Americanisms being created and celebrated in these other events. For radicals, claiming their identity as Americans consisted of more than latching on to a set of ideas about democracy and freedom. It entailed claiming those ideas and expanding them to include room for socialist revolution. These socialists did not need the Union League or the Daughters of the American Revolution to teach them what it meant to be an American. They decided to pick up the flag in the figurative classroom of the May Day parade and, there, tutor themselves in what it meant to be a radical American.[45]

The SLP-organized May Day parades of the 1890s and early 1900s also reveal the unexpected when it came to the participation of women. Unlike other contemporary civic holidays, where women were present only as spectators, or perhaps dressed as allegorical figures on floats, socialist-sponsored May Day parades offered an opportunity for women to participate more directly. Women did not merely applaud men's accomplishments in the public sphere from the sidelines, as they did on the Fourth of July or George Washington's Birthday.[46] Instead, women members of socialist clubs and those of some workers' associations had the opportunity to march in the streets as active participants.

As historians Nan Enstad and Annelise Orleck have demonstrated, despite their assumed absence from the traditional public sphere, women were indeed politically active in spaces like working-class tenement neighborhoods, the shop floor, and local markets through rent strikes, union activities, meat riots, and their interaction with consumer culture.[47] Yet, as this study of May Day reveals, many of these same women also were active in street parades as early as the mid-1890s. This was unusual for the time. Although some women did march in temperance parades during the nineteenth century, and the Salvation Army lassies also took to the streets during the late 1880s and 1890s, their participation in such demonstrations was deemed unseemly and inappropriate.[48] As May Day speakers, marchers, and organizers, working-class and radical women defied these conventions and carved out a place for themselves in the nation's otherwise manly politics of the street.

During the 1890s, women took their place in the SLP's May Day events as fellow socialists and laborers. In 1895, 1,000 working women, organized in six different garment unions and workers' benefit associations, walked in the second division of the SLP's New York May Day parade.[49] The Socialist Frauenverein joined two other socialist women's clubs and possibly some women representatives from participating garment unions as delegates to the 1898 May Day conference.[50] And during the indoor mass meeting they helped organize that year, Martha Moore Avery gave a memorable speech to the assembled crowd.[51] A native-born Yankee from a "respectable family," Avery had embraced radical political ideas and became a well-known speaker on the socialist lecture circuit. She succeeded in appealing to both the English-language members and the German-American core of the party.[52] Throughout the mid- to late 1890s, then, women played a visible and active part in May Day events as socialists and organized workers.[53]

This public participation of women in parades and mass meetings should not be taken as a sign of socialist support for women's rights per se. During this decade, the SLP remained officially committed to the priority of class solidarity over gender equality. Many radicals in the 1880s and 1890s, including women socialists, thought that gender equality would come with the arrival of the socialist commonwealth, and that working toward that latter goal was their main concern.[54] They believed that in the commonwealth, women would be freed from factory work because men would be able to provide enough for their families, and women would be liberated from the daily drudgery of housework, through the innovations of cooperative housing arrangements.[55] However radical their economic and political beliefs, these socialists clearly maintained traditional attitudes toward women. They still considered the female the fairer sex that needed protection from the harsh world of work. Even with their vision of the cooperative commonwealth, socialists continued to deem woman the natural arbiter of the home and family, be she in a nuclear or communal setting. Therefore, although the active presence of women in these public events was significant, it must be understood within the proper historical context of late-nineteenth-century socialist attitudes toward women.

Such attitudes were evident in the backroom planning of SLP May Day events. At the 1899 special May Day conference, a motion was adopted that "politely requested [the workingwomen's societies] not to participate in [the] parade, but instead to meet [the others] at Webster Hall at the social gathering and dance arranged by Section Greater New York."[56] While there is neither any explanation for this decision nor a record of any debate surrounding it, it may have been prompted by concerns for the women's safety. Given the cancellation of the parade by the police the year before because of the intense antiradical sentiment pulsing through the city, the delegates to the planning committee may have believed it best for the women's groups to be spared any rough street confrontations. Although they had ventured into those streets before, it would seem that their fellow male comrades in the party still believed they needed special care, despite orthodox socialist proclamations that women were partners in the broader class struggle.[57] Instead, the "delicate" females were politely asked to go straight to the indoor social and dance. There is no record of the women's response to this request, nor is there a record of their attending the parade.[58] Although many women members who proudly marched in 1895 may have protested this protectionism, others may have shared its assumptions and bypassed the 1899 parade without complaint. Due to the dearth of sources, it is difficult to know exactly how they responded.

As this incident demonstrates, women found more opportunities for participation in SLP-sponsored May Day demonstrations than in other civic events, yet they also still faced traditional assumptions about their gender and public roles that sometimes restricted their activities as equals with men in the public sphere. These tensions not only were evident in the records of May Day event planning, but also were depicted in the party's iconography of the holiday during the 1890s.[59] In an illustration produced for the front page of *The People* in May 1896, for example, a larger-than-life female figure dressed in a classical Greek or Roman gown is seated on a throne atop a pedestal in the center of the frame. With her right arm upraised, she clasps a torch with which she lights a banner above her head that proclaims, "May Day 1896." Surrounding this allegorical figure, who represents both May Day and its promise of socialism to come, are the means to the new dawn she heralds. There is the banner of the Socialist Labor Party on her left, representing the leading role that organization is to have in the process of uniting workers of all countries, a goal proclaimed in the banner to her right. Below her feet is an assembly of laborers from around the world. One of them places a laurel wreath

Figure 2.2. "May Day 1896" shows an early Socialist Labor Party representation of May Day as published in The People. *Negative 80119d. Collection of The New-York Historical Society.*

under a plaque that adorns the base of the pedestal and that reads, "labor produces all wealth." In this celebration of male producerism and international socialism, a life-sized figure of a woman is found in the foreground, kneeling with one arm wrapped around the shoulder of a small boy. With her other arm she directs the boy's attention up to the oversized May Day figure.[60] While she could embody the promise of socialism in allegorical form, woman, as she was represented in the official SLP press, was relegated in "real" life to a prostrate mother figure, among but not of the male worker-heroes.

Although the female members of the socialist clubs and workers' associations sometimes were able to march under their own banners in SLP-sponsored May Day parades in the 1890s, their presence should not be interpreted as denoting a devotion to gender equality within the party. The primary concern for the SLP in the late nineteenth century was carrying out the "greater deeds" of ending wage slavery and ushering in the socialist commonwealth. In the 1890s, May Day became an annual opportunity to work toward these goals through the didactic displays of the party on parade and in its mass meetings. The SLP redefined May Day as International Labor Day, and saw in those demonstrations both a harbinger and the temporary realization of their goal of international socialist brotherhood.

During the same years that the SLP organized celebrations and published newspaper accounts that defined May Day as International Labor Day, the AFL continued to keep the focus of its May 1 demonstrations on labor's demand for the eight-hour day. Gompers initially placed this campaign within a broader cultural context. He believed that the organization of eight-hour meetings on the Fourth of July, George Washington's Birthday, and the September Labor Day in 1890 and 1891 would connect the demand for shorter hours with the patriotism that had come to characterize these American holidays and thereby deradicalize its message.[61] The AFL supported similar campaigns into the early years of the twentieth century, as it continued to endorse strike action by its affiliated national unions. Even this use of May Day, however, became increasingly more difficult to sustain within the federation. Not only were there the competing anarchist and socialist definitions of May Day for the federation's unions to contend with, but also dissension within those unions over exactly what to do in response.

The AFL's commitment to the gradual achievement of the eight-hour day in all industries was made clear, nevertheless, as it backed up its member unions' demands in the 1890s. The pattern of an initial round of meetings scheduled on national holidays that culminated on May 1 was planned in aid of the carpenters' shorter-hours drive in 1890 and that of the miners' in 1891. During 1895 and 1896, the AFL supported a sustained buildup to the International Seaman's Union's making the eight-hour demand on May 1, 1898. Providing help with circulars, speakers, and funding, the federation sponsored a different trade every few years with its pattern of holiday meetings.[62] Consequently, when unions affiliated with the AFL turned out on May Day, they demonstrated as part of a chronologically broader and nationally based labor campaign for the shorter workday.

This official understanding of May Day was voiced repeatedly in the AFL's journal, the *American Federationist*. Unlike *The People*, which proclaimed May 1 an International Labor Day for the global implementation of socialism, the *Federationist* defined May Day as an annual event that provided a "golden opportunity. . . . for practical action" in enforcing the eight-hour day.[63] Refuting its international and socialist affiliations, the journal emphasized May Day's birth in St. Louis in 1888, where Gompers renewed Gabriel Edmonston's original resolution to have the day become the focus of a broader eight-hour campaign. While it recognized the adoption of the annual holiday abroad, the *Federationist* presented it as an example of the spread of organized and coordinated trade unionism based on the model of the federation, not as the herald of international socialism.[64] As it retold the history of May Day each year in its official newspaper, the AFL underscored the holiday's American roots and its purpose in advancing the cause of trade unionism. Under Gompers' direction, the AFL tried to cast May Day in a patriotic and pro-union light.

That agenda stood in direct contrast to the vision presented by Maurice Mikol in his resolution at the AFL's 1903 convention. The AFL's rejection of this resolution corresponded with the broader campaign that Gompers and like-minded craft union leaders launched against the socialists at the federation's meeting in Boston that year.[65] The AFL leader railed against the socialists and their political program, and oversaw the defeat of their agenda at this convention.[66] For Gompers, the rejection of Mikol's proposal was most likely as much a vote against the socialists' influence within the AFL's organization as it was a vote for the survival of trade unionism. His skepticism of radical political reformers, rooted in his earlier experience with the Spring Street faction of the International Workingmen's Association and the Tompkins Square Riot in 1874, grew in subsequent decades into the outright hostility he expressed at the 1903 convention. During the

1890s, a series of developments reinforced his conviction that trade union organization, with its focus on making economic demands on employers, was the only way forward for labor.

The first of these developments was the rapid rise in the "new" immigration. Beginning in the early 1890s and continuing through the turn of the century, millions of Italians, Poles, Slovaks, Hungarians, Russians, and others from Eastern and Southern Europe, who were mainly Catholic or Jewish, arrived in America. While Jewish bundists may have come from an industrial background, many of these other migrants had "no experience with factory work, industrial discipline, or trade unionism." They became the chief source of semi- and unskilled labor that fueled the growing industrial economy, itself being transformed by new technology. Many native-born workers and those who immigrated earlier in the century, like Gompers, saw these new arrivals through a nativist lens, considering them, and the new economy they supported, a threat to the survival of the skilled worker.[67] They believed that the only means of shoring up the economic and social position of that worker was through the trade union and the coordinated economic demands it could make on the employer.

It was precisely in these same years that organized labor experienced a series of major defeats, however, as many employers began to tap into the power of the state to dismantle unions. This destruction was achieved, in part, through the deployment of the National Guard, as was done at Homestead in 1892, and even of federal troops, as occurred during the Pullman strike in 1894.[68] It later was sanctified in the courts. The Danbury Hatters' case, for example, found the United Hatters responsible for $252,000 in damages to D. E. Lowe & Company of Danbury, Conn., for having launched a boycott in 1902. The courts upheld the company's charge that the union had conspired to restrain trade in violation of the Sherman Anti-Trust Act.[69] As Shelton Stromquist has argued, by the turn of the century, Gompers and his supporters in the AFL believed themselves caught between the threat from the new wave of unskilled, unorganized immigrant labor and the opposition of employers who were proving adept at invoking state power to weaken unions. Trade unionists needed allies, and found them "in an emerging network of middle-class social reformers and among groups of farsighted employers."[70]

It was in this context that Mikol's proposal for the AFL to celebrate May Day as a "day of protest against the present obnoxious system of exploitation and the dawn of emancipation of the Proletariat" was received and rejected. By 1903, given its experience in coordinating annual eight-

hour drives and its understanding of the social and economic developments of the 1890s that led it into a defensive craft unionism, the AFL's
national leadership could not advocate such a radical purpose for May 1.
Instead, the federation began to turn its attention completely away from
May Day, focusing its efforts on making impressive demonstrations of
union strength on Labor Day.

This other workers' holiday had been celebrated annually in America
on the first Monday in September since its initial observance in New York
in 1882. It became an official national holiday in 1894. For some radicals,
like Maurice Mikol, Labor Day undermined the radical purpose that had
come to define May Day in the 1890s. It frustrated the "aspiration of the
wage workers of the entire world as announced at the International Congress of Paris 1889, that the workers of both continents shall be in unison
in international solidarity."[71] The autumn holiday threatened this solidarity both literally and figuratively. It encouraged American workers to mobilize in September rather than in May with European laborers. And as a
national holiday, it was at odds with the international aspirations of many
radicals. By the late 1890s, however, this was exactly what Gompers and
craft union officials in the AFL wanted. Not only did they try to limit their
unions' participation in May Day events to mass meetings and strikes for
the eight-hour day, but they also quickly supported adopting September
Labor Day as a legally sanctioned holiday. It provided the perfect outlet
for labor to demonstrate publicly its respectability and patriotism. These
were two important characteristics the AFL wanted to cultivate and advance in its negotiation with employers and in its alliance-building with
middle-class reformers by the turn of the century.

The September Labor Day had not always been characterized by such
respectability and patriotism. In fact, the labor parade and mass meeting held in Manhattan in early September 1882 was organized as a day of
dissent by the more radical unions within the city's Central Labor Union
(CLU) and by socialist-affiliated Knights of Labor locals. It was the CLU's
secretary, Matthew Maguire, who first proposed that the city's unions
"make a public show of [their] organized strength" and unity that fall. A
socialist and machinist from Brooklyn, Maguire conceived this display of
labor's power as one of protest against monopolists.[72] William McCabe,
the grand marshal of the parade of some 20,000 workers, heralded it and
the postmarch gathering in Elm Park as having been like a "review before the battle," which he believed had "awakened the city" to the workman's concerns.[73] The success of the event, in terms of turnout and profits

raised for the unions, encouraged the CLU to resolve in 1884 that Labor Day, the first Monday in September, should become an annual holiday. The tradition was adopted in Chicago by its Trades and Labor Assembly, and spread to several other cities in subsequent years.[74]

Regardless of these radical origins, the temper of the new Labor Day changed rather quickly. Despite the presence of Maguire's radical Advanced Labor Club of Brooklyn, with its red badges and inflammatory antirent banners, records reveal that most of New York's laborers, who watched from their factory or shop windows, were baffled or bemused by the whole affair.[75] They were not necessarily awakened to the need for union organization or the radical demands voiced by the CLU and Knights' assemblies on parade. By the end of the 1880s, with the decline of the Knights of Labor and the contemporaneous growth of the AFL, the September Labor Day demonstrations took on a decidedly different tone. Rather than a day of protest, it became a day of celebration of and by traditional craft unions affiliated with the AFL. With the unions' sponsorship, the September event was organized in locales around the nation, becoming a recognized holiday, first on the state level, beginning with Oregon in 1887, then on the national level.[76]

On June 28, 1894, President Cleveland signed into law the act making the first Monday in September a national holiday. Representative Amos Cummings of New York was the sponsor of the bill in the House. Cummings was a former printer, and therefore may have sincerely believed in the need for a day to honor the nation's laborers.[77] Yet, he was also a Democrat like Cleveland. And both men realized the need to smooth over relations with the country's growing labor movement, which was riveted to the then ongoing convulsions surrounding the Pullman boycott.[78] Cleveland had already alienated the AFL when he "refused to enforce the anti-Chinese Geary Act even after the Supreme Court upheld the act in 1893."[79] And his administration did not seem to be doing much to alleviate the depression of these years either, a point sharpened by the carnevalesque display of Coxey's Army during April and May 1894. Even before this great march of the unemployed on Washington, the Republicans had made gains at the polls during the 1893 local elections.[80] Cummings' sponsorship and Cleveland's support for the Labor Day bill may have thus also stemmed, in part, from political expediency.

Because of the AFL's support for this law, Cummings gave the pen he received from Cleveland at the signing to Samuel Gompers. By then, because of P. J. McGuire's work as secretary of the AFL (organizing Labor

Day events, publicizing them, and lobbying for the day's recognition as a legal holiday since the mid-1880s), Matthew Maguire's role in founding the original event in 1882 was officially forgotten. P. J. McGuire literally rewrote the radical history of the original September Labor Day in the pages of the *American Federationist*, as he and the AFL claimed paternity of the holiday and shaped it to meet their political needs.[81]

From its very beginnings, then, Labor Day was cast to fit many different molds. While Cleveland and Cummings used the official sanctioning of the event to try to cement organized labor's commitment to the Democratic Party, the AFL saw Labor Day as an opportunity for labor's public demonstration of its organized strength, respectability, and patriotism. The legalization of the September holiday was a victory for the AFL. For McGuire and Gompers, a national Labor Day signaled the state's official acknowledgment of organized labor, with the AFL at its helm, as a legitimate contributor to and as a valid contending interest within national politics and the marketplace. Labor Day provided an ideal opportunity for organized trade unions to "celebrate and demonstrate" their strength and solidarity.[82] Union members turned out on parade and at mass meetings across the nation in early September to show the continued viability of their organizations, despite the threats of injunctions, antiunion court decisions, or the flood of unskilled and unorganized labor.[83] Yet, they did so on a national holiday, sanctioned by the state, that was characterized by a celebration of the worker. Such fêtes were intended to "mold public opinion" into recognizing the importance of organized labor, both for the benefit of the worker and for the well-being of the economy and society as a whole.[84]

The AFL and its affiliated trade unions tapped into this nationalist character both in the rhetoric they used to discuss Labor Day and in the details of the parades they organized to celebrate it. Chicago's Trades and Labor Assembly and the members of Typographical Union 16, for example, referred to the annual event as Labor's *National* Holiday in 1891 and 1893, even before it was legally sanctioned as such.[85] There was no international component to this yearly demonstration, as there had become with May Day. In the language used by the unions in discussing the event, the September Labor Day was presented as a day for celebrating *American* labor. For the union members who supported its recognition as a national holiday in 1894, the autumn fête was considered as significant a moment for the display of their patriotism as the Fourth of July, George Washington's Birthday, and Flag Day. American laborers would celebrate and be celebrated as producers and as citizens.

As a result, the details of their unions' trappings in the parade were given considerable attention. The particulars of paraphernalia were political; they transmitted the message of worker solidarity and national pride that gave physical manifestation to their identity as American laborer-citizens. Since the founding of the republic, workers had worn ceremonial versions of their work clothes when they marched in parades.[86] Those who came to celebrate Labor Day had this tradition of the craft procession from which to draw for inspiration. The German-American bricklayers who turned out to celebrate the eight-hour law in Chicago in 1867, for example, had worn aprons with the "organization's insignia—hammer and trowel embroidered in gold."[87] Such formal versions of workers' garb were a familiar sight in urban parades, from the white hats and aprons of the bakers' contingents to the neat stripes of the butchers' smocks. They continued to be part of the display on Labor Day during the 1890s. By wearing these clean, ceremonial uniforms, union members enhanced their display of pride, unity, order, and strength in numbers.

By the late nineteenth century, however, some laborers began to wear very different styles of dress for the Labor Day parade. For example, during many of its meetings in the 1890s, the United Brotherhood of Carpenters and Joiners adopted resolutions in favor of members donning hats and canes along with their union badges when they marched on Labor Day.[88] This version of the laborer's garb connoted a different kind respectability from that communicated by the ceremonial work clothes traditionally worn in parades.[89] Like the "Sunday best" many skilled workers began to wear in portraits taken during the late nineteenth century, the hat and cane may have signified the carpenter's pride in his place within the broader social order, as well as in his individual economic stability.[90] He was both a self-sufficient laborer, the foundation of a civilized society as understood within the labor theory of value, and a successful, "well-dressed breadwinner."[91] As someone who embodied both these things, he dressed in his best clothes to win the respect he believed he deserved from the wider community. By wearing this new "uniform" as he marched alongside dozens of his fellow unionists, he also demonstrated the strength of that communal body and defended its right to exist.

In addition, workers demonstrated their patriotism on Labor Day, manifesting their identity as good citizens and linking themselves to the wider national community. In part, the desire to create such dignified and patriotic public identities came out of a perceived need for unionists to win economic and political allies within the progressive middle class.[92]

Figure 2.3. Workers in a 1904 Chicago Labor Day parade, wearing the new "uniform" of bowler hats and canes. DN-0002298. Chicago Daily News negative collection, Chicago History Museum.

Yet, these expressions also seem to have been sincere and part of the laborers' own construction of a unique identity as an American worker. In 1888, for example, the United Carpenters Council adopted a motion calling for the color of its badge to be red, white, and blue.[93] In 1894, Chicago's Trades and Labor Assembly (TLA) presented the Carpenter's District Council with a bonus for turning out the largest percentage of their members on Labor Day that year. The prize included a grand American flag, "the largest silk stars-and-stripes in the city."[94] And two years later, the TLA's secretary, Lee M. Hart, asserted in a report to the *American Federationist* that the predominance of American flags in that year's Labor Day parade "demonstrated to the generous public that unionism was not only for law and order, but for love of country as well."[95] In the decade when Union League Club members, veterans' organizations, and patriotic societies were creating this same kind of conventional patriotism in schoolhouse flag rituals, this prominent display of the Stars and Stripes most likely did express the message Hart described. The trade unionist represented himself as a worker and a loyal, law-abiding American.

One way some workers also expressed this identity was to refuse to accommodate the symbols of political radicalism. Since 1887, the Chicago TLA had instituted a ban on the display of the red flag in its Labor Day demonstrations.[96] Although many of the delegates to the assembly shared an opposition to the anarchism and socialism represented by the red flag, the ban sparked divisions within many of the city's unions that lasted into the 1890s. Those organizations affiliated with the radical-dominated CLU held separate demonstrations where the display of the crimson banner was welcome.[97] A similar dispute took place in New York between the socialist-dominated Central Labor Federation (which included the United Hebrew Trades), and the more moderate Central Labor Union (which housed Typographical Union 6).[98]

Looking closely at how events like Labor Day and May Day played out at the local level is one way of uncovering these differences. Just as it is revealing to find that some members of the otherwise internationally focused SLP supported the display of the American flag on May Day in 1898, so, too, is it informative to recognize that some skilled unionists clamored to carry the red flag on Labor Day.[99] These realities remind us that the two events, however much they were becoming polar opposites, were not yet mutually exclusive, nor were their constituents able to choose easily between the radical and American parts of their hybrid sympathies.

While there was still some ideological diversity evident among those who observed Labor Day during the 1890s, the parades remained rather homogenous in their gendered composition. Although women workers were sometimes present in the processions, they did not walk in the streets with the men. Instead, they rode in carriages at the end of the line of march. Reports from a 1903 parade in Chicago also detail how most of the women participants wore white dresses.[100] Such demonstrations of women workers on Labor Day reinforced existing cultural definitions of gender, prioritizing a masculine representation of labor on parade. Women rode as pure and delicate objects in carriages behind the men, who strode as virile laborer-citizens up the main public streets of their city. Unlike May Day parades, where women marched in the streets in defiance of social and political conventions, in Labor Day parades they adhered more closely to those constraints by remaining sheltered in carriages.

During the 1890s, then, the AFL and its affiliated national unions turned Labor's National Day into an ideal forum where organized laborers could present themselves as upstanding, patriotic union workers. In their holiday parades, male laborers dominated, expressing a masculine standard for that identity. Labor Day provided an opportunity for trade union members to demonstrate the respectability and love of country they believed was necessary to help them deal with their employers and gain political allies in the middle class. It also allowed them to express their sincere feelings of pride in themselves and in the dignity of their work, as well as loyalty to their nation. While some workers also used Labor Day to demonstrate their politically radical sympathies, insisting on carrying the red flag alongside the Stars and Stripes in their parades during the 1890s, the official tone of the September holiday increasingly became more anti-socialist and anti-internationalist over time. The AFL's national leadership valued the opportunity that the autumn holiday provided workers to display their union militancy and national loyalty, considering it conducive to their emerging liberal agenda. They would thus maintain their support for Labor Day in subsequent decades.

One of the main reasons the AFL gradually embraced Labor Day as it distanced itself from May Day was the influence that anarchists and socialists had gained over the spring holiday during the last decade of the nineteenth century. Those radicals increasingly dominated the May 1 parades and mass meetings and embraced the holiday's radical internationalist potential during the 1890s. Anarchists, in particular, constructed an identity for themselves in their May Day demonstrations that embraced a romantic notion of transnationalism. New York's and Chicago's German and Italian anarchists brought an international flavor to the holiday with their songs, plays, and fiery foreign-language speeches touting the day's global meaning. As they celebrated this event as part of a bigger international socialist community, these immigrant anarchists presented themselves as members of a global radical movement. The SLP officially embraced a similar understanding of May Day as a focal point for international worker solidarity. Party leaders defined the day in their speeches and in the columns of the party press as a product of the Second International in Paris. They rejected May Day's American roots. Yet, at the same time SLP leaders engaged in this historical revisionism, rank-and-file members of this staunchly orthodox Marxist party laid claim to their American democratic heritage. One of the ways these party members constructed hybrid identities for themselves as radical Americans was by insisting on their right to carry the Stars and Stripes alongside the red flag on May Day. In so doing, they also challenged contemporary definitions of the flag as a symbol for law-and-order patriotism.

Despite this cross-pollination between nationalist symbols and international socialist beliefs within the SLP, more politically moderate trade unionists came to disdain May Day, seeing only its foreign social profile and radical political agenda. The national leadership of AFL tried to sustain May 1 as a rallying point in the fight for the eight-hour day during the 1890s, but by the early 1900s, it found such a strategy difficult and undesirable in the wake of May Day's radical transformation. Gompers and other AFL leaders believed it made more sense to focus trade unionists' efforts on the September Labor Day. The autumn holiday served workers' definition of themselves as respectable and patriotic Americans. Such a public representation was important to these laborers as they struggled for union recognition and against the forces of the new immigration and advanced industrialization that were changing their world. Yet, given the complexity of workers' political affiliations during the 1890s and early 1900s, even self-proclaimed socialists turned out on Labor Day, just as many radical trade unionists continued to support May Day, regardless of the opposition of their organizations' national leadership.

Because it was a legal national holiday that accepted the existing capitalist system, Labor Day increasingly came under a barrage of criticism from the political left. Gradually, it became more difficult for the autumn event to house the ranks of radical unionists. The SLP and, later, the Socialist Democratic Party sharply condemned the event. Echoing Mikol's rejection of the autumn holiday as an illegitimate day, the leaders of these radical parties continued to celebrate May Day instead, and more and more of their membership followed, leaving Labor Day behind. Yet, this embrace of the spring holiday was not without conflict. The two radical parties came to disagree over the true spirit of what had become identified as an international holiday during the 1890s. In the opening decades of the new century, their members came to dispute not only the nature of May Day. They would also debate whether through their celebration of it they could (or should) represent themselves as both radicals and Americans.

3

Working-Class Resistance and Accommodation
May Day and Labor Day, 1903–1916

On the morning of May 1, 1916, a total of approximately 100,000 men, women, and children marched in three May Day parades organized by the Socialist Party (SP) held on Manhattan's East Side and Yorkville and in Brownsville, Brooklyn. Dozens of unions joined various party locals and neighborhood working-class benevolent associations in a demonstration against the nation's preparedness campaign for the war in Europe. On the speakers' platform in Union Square, party notables like Joseph Cannon and Theresa Malkiel articulated this position and defended the SP's commitment to antimilitarism. Those gathered adopted a resolution in which they reaffirmed their "faith in the principle of international solidarity of the working class," and pledged themselves "to struggle for the overthrow of the capitalist system."[1]

Among those who participated in the giant march were thousands of the city's garment workers, including many women shirtwaist makers who had just won a bitter strike that January. They had decided to spend four hundred dollars on flowers for their division to make a good showing in the parade, despite the financial sacrifices needed to do so.[2] A photo taken by the Bain News Service shows another group of women garment workers, who posed for the camera while waving their special red "May Day" pennants. One of the women held aloft a giant blouse, festooned with flowers and ribbons.[3] Both the shirtwaist makers and the women captured in the news photo may have supported some, if not all, of the radical political sentiments expressed by Cannon, Malkiel, and the party's official resolution. Yet, it is also clear from their appearance that these workers came to the parade with their own interests and concerns.

Figure 3.1. Garment workers demonstrating support for May Day in New York, 1916. George Grantham Bain Collection, Library of Congress.

The shirtwaist makers prioritized the event, turning out en masse and in festive floral decoration to demonstrate their solidarity, strength, and endurance after a difficult winter strike. The garment workers, who smiled for the camera and displayed the specially crafted example of their wares, demonstrated their pride in their work and in themselves as workers.[4] They also showed good humor in enjoying a day away from their labors. Consequently, while the annual May Day celebration remained an important forum where those affiliated with the Socialist Party could construct their political identities, it allowed for the expression of various manifestations of those identities. The many vernacular voices, like those of the shirtwaist makers and the garment workers that were heard along the line of march, gave those demonstrations diversity and strength. The large number of participants in these May Day parades came not only from active party members marching with their locals, but also from union members. Workers may have turned out to show their solidarity with the SP, but also, as seen in the nature of their displays, they did so to address more specific local interests that happened to coincide with the party's contemporary radical program.

The women workers who turned out in the 1916 May Day parade also marched in the city's Labor Day parades. Since at least 1911, they turned out in force, carrying banners that expressed their desire for better working conditions.[5] This shift, from the limited presence of women in the autumn parade of the 1890s to these more active displays by the 1910s, corresponded to the growing strength of New York's garment unions, particularly those locals affiliated with the International Ladies' Garment Workers' Union (ILGWU). Since the turn of the century, these previously unorganized workers, including many semiskilled and unskilled hands, had built up a new union movement. Women organizers, like Pauline Newman, helped lead the way.[6] Unionized women workers came out on both May Day and Labor Day in these years to voice their demands, celebrate their victories, and demonstrate their pride as workers.

Socialists welcomed their presence in the May Day events, and cited it as evidence of the growing influence of radicalism among the working class. Samuel Gompers and other national and regional leaders in the American Federation of Labor (AFL), however, became increasingly hostile to the radical domination of the spring event and continued to push for a uniquely union-focused Labor Day to advance the cause of organized labor. During the early years of the new century, the competition of more popular amusements, such as boozy picnics, sporting events, and new forms of commercialized leisure, challenged such Labor Day demonstrations. Here, too, then, as in the spring May Day celebrations, grassroots interests and concerns coexisted with, and sometimes contested, official agendas. A tension between rebellion and accommodation characterized both holidays. Many workers rebelled against both the political orthodoxy of socialist organizers and the cultural propriety of trade union leaders as they constructed their own versions of these events. At the same time, socialists and their working-class allies continued to turn out on May Day and defended their right to carry both the red flag and the American flag in the streets of their cities. Against a variety of pressures to conform to certain standards of cultural and political orthodoxy, workers and radicals forged their own paths on May Day and Labor Day. Exploring this process brings to light the debate that existed in these years over the nature of public celebrations and their relationship to organized labor, commercial culture, radical politics, and contested concepts of patriotism.

By the early 1900s, the American Federation of Labor and its affiliated trade unions had turned the first Monday of September into a celebration of and by organized labor. Despite the AFL's continuing support for this demonstration of unity, it soon found itself confronted by different vernacular interpretations of the holiday. By the early years of the twentieth century, both dissension within local unions and the competition of popular and increasingly commercialized amusements began to alter the composition of Labor Day events. Alongside the image of the ideal American laborer-citizen celebrated in the trade union parades, there was now the figure of the American worker as a free consumer of leisure present at Labor Day picnics and sporting events. In response to these developments, the AFL at the national level, and the Chicago Federation of Labor (CFL) at the local level, attempted to streamline and make sacred Labor's National Day. In so doing, the leaders of these organizations refined the identity of the American laborer-citizen as one who was to be a disciplined and devout soldier in the trade union army.

Engaging in popular amusements on Labor Day was not unique to the early years of the twentieth century. The holiday's first celebration, held in New York City in 1882, included a postparade picnic.[7] The outdoor gathering combined time for the enjoyment of good food, plentiful beer, and the company of friends with opportunities for speeches and union fundraising.[8] Picnics remained a popular part of the Labor Day holiday through the 1890s, as several Knights of Labor local and district assemblies hosted them to raise money for their organizations.[9] Even after the AFL rose to national prominence and promoted the observation of the holiday across the country, large union parades were often followed by outdoor amusements.[10]

By the early 1900s, however, more and more local union members wanted to engage in the amusements without having to parade. At a meeting in September 1906, members of the New York Typographical

Society 6, who had been appointed to discuss the possibility of parading on Labor Day, reported that they did not think their union would make a good showing that year. They based their finding on the great number of negative responses they had received from the chapels, or local chapters of the union, which they had surveyed in the weeks before the September meeting.[11] The following year the members again decided to decline an invitation from the city's Central Federated Union (CFU) to join the Labor Day parade, deeming it "inexpedient to participate." While there was no explanation for the chapels' rejection of the parade in 1906, or of similar majority votes against the march that were recorded in 1910 and 1913, the minutes from 1907 revealed the committee members' concerns over this lack of enthusiasm among the general membership.[12] Although they were willing to donate one hundred dollars to the CFU "to help defray the expenses of the parade," the union delegates did not think there was enough support for the march among their members. Some suggested that special meetings be held to "induce interest in the parade," and others thought fines for nonattendance might help sustain the event.[13]

Perhaps the members' lack of ardor for the Labor Day parades was due to the amount of work that had to go into their planning, or to the time it took to march through the streets. The Chicago Federation of Labor's Labor Day Committee reported in 1908 that many of the unions with which they had corresponded about joining the city's holiday parade would not attend because the event took up too much of their day.[14] For other organizations, the issue was financing. The uniforms, bands, banners, and floats for the parade cost money, and many unions declined participation because their funds were low.[15] Consequently, although many local union members may have shared the AFL's and CFL's belief that the Labor Day parade was an important way to show their strength, they often found themselves concerned with its costs in terms of two things that were equally precious to them: their free time and their union's money.

For many unions, by the early 1900s, the fundraising picnic became a more attractive replacement for, rather than an accompaniment to, the Labor Day parade. Unlike the parade, those attending the picnic could be required to purchase tickets for admission to defray the costs of organizing the event and to help raise money for the union. To assure a good turnout, members organized races and baseball games and scheduled music and dancing in addition to the usual speeches.[16] These events were not just more economically feasible for many unions, they were also a lot of fun.

The gradual eclipse of the union parade was therefore also due to workers' changing tastes and desires. The old-style craft parade would not entirely disappear, but the rapid and widespread growth of other forms of amusements attracted workers who were eager to engage in them. New patterns of recreation that included more commercialized entertainments accelerated this shift.[17] Now that they had a legally sanctioned holiday on which to spend time away from work, and since that day had become a routine part of their calendar, many workers chose to spend it with family and friends enjoying time at one of their city's new amusement parks, penny arcades, or sporting events, rather than in a stodgy union parade or at an overcrowded and boring mass meeting.[18]

The inclusion of more popular amusements on Labor Day, sometimes to the exclusion of participation in the union parade, did not signal, as the leadership of the AFL and CFL feared, the erosion of skilled workers' commitment to their trade unions. Rather, it evidenced a different interpretation of what union membership meant.[19] In the debates that took place at the local level over the issue of joining the holiday parade, union members voiced their desire to represent themselves not only as producers, but also as independent workers in a democratic society. Attempts to make their participation in the march compulsory most often failed. Members of New York Typographical Society 6 considered the idea of fines for nonattendance a "violation of personal liberty," and struck down the resolution suggesting them.[20] If they were going to parade to demonstrate their solidarity, they would do so of their own accord.

Many local union members also voiced their desire to represent themselves on Labor Day as consumers of leisure. The trend among many unions to decline invitations to march in citywide parades and to host their own picnics instead was due not only to their members' practical concerns over the costs of joining the parade, but also to their understanding of the day as their own, to do with as they pleased. By 1916, for example, the Chicago Federation of Labor concluded that because Labor Day came "at the end of the vacation season and the half-holiday on Saturday, . . . a great many of the members of local unions find this their last chance to enjoy a vacation." It noted that these men tended to "take Saturday, Sunday and Monday—three days—off to enjoy themselves in their own way," with some attending the picnics and games that their local unions organized.[21] These men were in fact articulating a new understanding of themselves as laborers: they expressed a more modern "consumerist class consciousness."[22] They made Labor Day a time to enjoy the fruits of their labor, rather than an explicit celebration of their work. The traditional parade, so prevalent in the nineteenth century, in which union men marched in their uniforms and performed the tasks of their labor on floats in celebration of producerism, was losing its place in the emerging consumer culture. Workingmen, who now demanded the higher wages necessary to support a comfortable lifestyle for themselves and their families as male breadwinner (the living wage), celebrated what they understood to be their right to leisure in these extended vacations.[23] Labor Day for many workers, even the most committed of union men, became a day on which they could do as they pleased, or do nothing at all.

They asserted that right not only against attempts by their local unions to compel their participation in the parades through fines for nonattendance, but also against the rhetoric of their regional and national union leaders who worked to reform Labor Day. By enjoying their holiday as a day of rest and play, which often included their partaking in "cheap amusements," workers rebelled against the leisure reform of elite and middle-class do-gooders in their communities, who engaged in things like playground and library extension movements.[24] And they also rejected the specific attempts of their union leaders to organize more disciplined and respectable Labor Day demonstrations.[25]

This attitude, along with the declining number and size of Labor Day parades it fostered, troubled Samuel Gompers and the leadership of the AFL. They believed it threatened to atomize organized workers into the position of individual consumers of leisure, thereby undermining the strength and purpose of the union movement. During the first two decades of the new century, Gompers and the AFL's Executive Council repeatedly argued that Labor's National Day was "not a time for merry-making," but was a day that should be set aside for the serious consideration of issues important to the fate of organized labor.[26] Gompers insisted that the short-term expenses required for union parades were not wasteful when their long-term benefits were considered. In his annual reports to the federation's convention, and in yearly Labor Day editorials in the *American Federationist*, Gompers tried to disabuse the local unions of their belief that the parades were too costly. He insisted that no price could be put on the publicity gained by a solid display of union strength. Gompers believed that by marching through their city streets each year, workers would impress spectators and the press with their unity, discipline, and respectability as labor-citizens, thus gaining support for the cause of trade unionism.[27]

Figure 3.2. Trade unionists demonstrating strength in numbers and pride in their status as American workers as they carry American flags in their 1904 Labor Day parade along Michigan Avenue in Chicago. DN-002297. Chicago Daily News negative collection, Chicago History Museum.

John Fitzpatrick and other leaders of the Chicago Federation of Labor shared this understanding of Labor Day's purpose. They believed that the holiday was a time for disciplined and militant displays of organized labor's strength. They also wanted the parade specifically to represent labor's unity against the "hostile influence of the Employers' Association" in Chicago, which had been using injunctions to undermine the ability of the unions to organize there. In 1908, CFL President Fitzpatrick and Secretary E. N. Nockels called on the federation's affiliated locals to turn out and march in unity like a "steam-roller" down Jackson Boulevard to Michigan Avenue, demonstrating their might before their employers and the public.[28] Following the Stars and Stripes and the banners of their trades, the uniformed men who turned out for the parade strode down the streets of Chicago with military precision in defense of their right to organize.[29] They were the soldiers in what Gompers termed the "holy and noble cause of Labor's uplift."[30]

Yet, as his annual editorials and reports lamented, by 1908, there were not enough unionists turning out each year in the Labor Day parade to fight effectively for this cause. Even though some 40,000 workers turned out in 1908 for the parade down Fifth Avenue from Fifty-ninth Street to the Washington Arch in Manhattan, labor leaders worried that this was insufficient.[31] In addition to the dissension of local union members, who were concerned with financing such displays, "outings, picnics, and excursions, gotten up purely for private profit" were luring workers away from the parades.[32] To outside observers like Gompers and the AFL's national leadership, their local celebrations, which often focused within particular ethnic neighborhoods on drinking, dancing, and general "merry-making," seemed undisciplined and undignified.

Recognizing this, Gompers and the AFL leadership sought to make Labor Day an almost sacred occasion in the hopes of restoring its focus on the demonstration of organized labor's might. In 1909, the federation approved a resolution recommending that the Sunday preceding the first Monday in September be known as Labor Sunday, on which everyone would be encouraged to contemplate issues of concern to workers. It called on ministers to devote part of their church services on the day to this task.[33]

Gompers argued that by turning the church-going public's attention to labor issues, Labor Sunday would increase support for the "proper" observance of Labor Day that the AFL favored. The federation advertised the special religious services with leaflets and circulars in advance. It hoped to benefit from the association with Christian respectability that such church gatherings brought.[34] The AFL intended Labor Sunday to set the tone for the orderly Labor Day parades and meetings that were to follow the next day. Together these events were to provide a public affirmation of "the significance, the honor, the pride of trade unionism."[35]

Although many local union members asserted their understanding of the laborer-citizen as one who had a right to relax and enjoy the fruits of his labor on his special holiday, Gompers stridently rejected the inclusion of popular amusements on Labor's National Day. With the creation of the new Labor Sunday, he instead attempted to advance the image of the laborer-citizen as the disciplined and devout union member, who still had to fight for and defend his right to organize. Despite Gompers' attempts to shore up the respectable union parade, during the early decades of the twentieth century more workers preferred to attend picnics and other popular amusements on Labor Day. As they came to appreciate this autumn holiday as their own, workers increasingly chose to enjoy themselves by flocking to sporting events and amusement parks, rather than to celebrate their role as producers in traditional craft union processions. Although those parades still drew workers to their ranks, by the early 1920s, the lure of cheap entertainments proved to be quite strong competition.

To the objection of their union leaders, many workers not only enjoyed commercial entertainments on Labor Day, but some of them also continued to support May Day. During the first two decades of the twentieth century, many members of the nation's new industrial unions gave their support to May 1 events organized by the young Socialist Party of America. The workers who turned out for these parades and mass meetings constructed their own identity as radical, working-class Americans. And they did this during a time when significant pressure was placed on them to conform to a particular version of Americanism manifested through English-speaking demonstrations of loyalty to the nation state. These displays were most often held in schools for children and in workplaces for adults, particularly during World War I.[36] Yet, these radicals and workers found their own way to define who they were and what they believed, including a unique version of what it meant to be an American. May Day may not have been the only place they did this, but it was one of the more significant and visible ones.[37]

As such, it acted as a countertradition in a political culture awash with more conventional expressions of nationalism. The individuals who celebrated May Day offered an alternative vision not just for themselves, but also for the wider national community. Because of the growing hostility to the radical politics associated with the day, the dissent voiced each May 1 generally resonated only within the communities that expressed it. But, when that dissent received attention from the mainstream, it was negative and intense. The impact of the alternative definitions of Americanism on the wider national community, then, was surprisingly powerful: it fueled reactionary shifts in the popular construction of American nationalism, including, by 1919, a quite vehement demand for public demonstrations of single-minded allegiance to the state.

Part of the reason for this reaction was the fact that the radical discourse surrounding May Day intensified in this period. In the first two decades of the twentieth century, political radicals began to define May Day as an important socialist tradition with its own history. Both the Socialist Labor Party (SLP) and the newly created Socialist Party of America attempted to lay claim to that heritage to validate themselves as the one, true party of socialism. Articles in both the Socialist Labor Party and the Socialist Party press detailed celebrations taking place in "time-honored" ways. They shared party members' "reminiscences" of the great parades of the 1890s.[38] Party calls to previous May Day demonstrations were reprinted, and distinguished party members who had attended those original parades graced the platform at meetings in Union Square.[39] By recalling and fostering such links to the past, socialists from both parties ceremoniously defined their May 1 observance as an historic anniversary. They celebrated the event not just to foster workers' solidarity, but also because they had come to appreciate it as a radical custom. Each political party, then, asserted its own authority over that custom, insisting that its observance was the most "authentic" and, by implication, that it was the true voice of socialism in America.

As the older of these two parties, the SLP should have been able to lay claim to May Day's heritage because it was the one that had sustained the event during the 1890s. As its numbers declined due to the schism that led to the creation of the SP in July 1901, however, the SLP began to focus its energies not so much on large-scale parades on May 1, but on indoor mass meetings.[40] Such gatherings were less costly and could be more easily organized within the remaining SLP strongholds in each city: the radical German, Jewish, and growing Italian communities of New York's Lower East Side and the German and Scandinavian neighborhoods of Chicago's North Side. Party branches, mostly organized along the lines of local ethnic communities, assembled in New York at Cooper Union or Webster Hall, with anywhere from 1,000 to 3,000 attendees. Those in Chicago gathered in Ulrich Hall or Clifton Hall, and managed to attract from 200 to 400 participants.[41]

At these annual May Day mass meetings and in special holiday editions of *The People*, party leaders asserted that the SLP was the true workers' party. They insisted that it alone could carry out the full promise of May Day: the social and economic equality and justice that was to come after the revolution. They argued that this new world order was to be brought to fruition only through the industrial unionism of the Socialist Trades and Labor Alliance and, after its formation in 1905, the Industrial Workers of the World (IWW) in concert with the revolutionary socialism of the SLP.[42]

Despite the confidence of its pronouncements, the SLP could not draw more than a few hundred followers to its annual demonstrations by the late 1910s. Partly this may have been due to its intense political dogmatism, which alienated most workers and contributed to the schism that gave birth to the Socialist Party. The SP rose to greater popularity because its leaders, including Eugene Debs and Morris Hillquit, melded their radical politics with America's democratic heritage. This newer party also had a fairly solid base, both in former populist strongholds across the country and in industrial urban centers.[43]

In New York City and Chicago, the SP embraced May Day's potential as a tool for building up its organization. It unashamedly advanced its official party position at its May 1 demonstrations, yet also eagerly accommodated calls for intermediate reforms that enabled it to coordinate broader coalitions than those formed by the flagging SLP. Particularly in New York City, where it rather quickly developed a solid infrastructure, the SP organized impressive May Day displays during the first two decades of the twentieth century. For these socialists, May 1 was not a day for invoking bloody revolution but rather a celebration of the "sweet heyday of democracy." The holiday was an opportunity for them to "organize and educate" themselves along with prospective party members.[44] It was a time for party leaders, in what was considered one of many out-of-doors campaign meetings, to advocate the importance of the ballot as the weapon of choice in bringing about change.[45]

By the 1910s, one of the ways the SP built up support among workers was to use May 1 demonstrations to "voice protest against wrongs."[46] Each year, party members and their trade union allies focused on a different social evil. They targeted, among other things, the tragedy of the Triangle shirtwaist factory fire in 1911, the arrests of Joseph Ettor and Arturo Giovannitti during the Lawrence strike in 1912, and the horror of the Ludlow Massacre in 1914.[47] Clearly the party locals that organized such protests were tapping into the concerns of their newly affiliated unions, particularly the ILGWU. Much of the party's energy, particularly in New York and Chicago, was now linked to the interests of these left-led unions, especially in the garment trades. Those unions had made tremendous strides in organizing workers in the industry since the 1909 shirtwaist makers' strike.[48] On May Day, SP leaders and members numbering in the tens of thousands did not just call for the ultimate creation of the socialist order, as did those in the SLP. They also expressed their desire to affect current political, economic, and social conditions in the meantime. These included concerns over working conditions and standards in the trades, the right of unions to organize, and the heavy-handed tactics used by employers and the state to quash strikes and quell free speech. By addressing these issues, the SP made room for its new union allies.[49]

The structure of these alliances was visible in the makeup of annual May Day parades. Party members in Chicago, for example, coordinated marches with divisions from around the city, including the German and Scandinavian North Side, the Jewish North West Side, and the Bohemian South West Side neighborhoods, drawing a total of nearly 10,000 people.[50] SP branches were supported by local ethnically based socialist clubs and unions. These groups joined in the parades and held separate mass gatherings in their respective community meeting halls. Each May Day, at least a half dozen or so such assemblies took place throughout Chicago, as these different clubs met in the evening to hear speakers and sing songs in their particular native tongue.[51] In addition, the party also sometimes hosted a central meeting, open to those from all neighborhoods, including the English-speaking branches.[52]

The Socialist Party's ties to these local unions and progressive clubs not only contributed to the growing institutional strength of the Socialist Party in Chicago, but also further enhanced the transnational flavor of its annual May Day celebrations. As had been the case among immigrant anarchists and members of the SLP during the 1890s, those who came together on May 1 during the 1910s under the auspices of the SP did so from within their distinct working-class and ethnic associations. In so doing, they created a kind of transnational solidarity among German, Bohemian, Scandinavian, Italian, Jewish, and native-born workers. In their united parade and during their mass meetings, these radical workers temporarily manifested this utopian socialist vision in Chicago's streets.

In New York City, between 30,000 to 50,000 people marched each May 1 during the early years of the twentieth century.[53] A significant number were SP members. Those from different party branches generally paraded around their own neighborhoods, where they would find sympathetic and supportive crowds. They forged large, separate lines of march in Manhattan's uptown and downtown eastside districts, in Brooklyn (mainly in Brownsville), and in the Bronx.[54] In each borough, party members also marched with those from local and ethnically diverse progressive unions and benevolent societies. The memberships of these different organizations sometimes overlapped, contributing to the large size of the parade.

In Manhattan, the party's uptown branches, based in the German neighborhoods of the Upper East Side, formed their line of march along with an array of German and Hungarian butcher, baker, building trades, and furniture craft unions. They processed downtown from the Labor Temple at Eighty-fourth Street and Second Avenue, crisscrossing every ten blocks or so over to First Avenue, then to Third Avenue, and finally to Eighth Avenue, until they reached Seventeenth Street and entered Union

Square. The downtown party branches, housed in the Lower East Side, marched with the Jewish, Russian, and Italian members of the United Hebrew Trades. They were also joined by members from International Ladies' Garment Workers' Union locals and, after 1914, by the Amalgamated Clothing Workers of America. This division usually stepped off from outside of the *Jewish Daily Forward* offices on Rutgers Square and made its way, via East Broadway, Canal Street, Grand Street, and Waverly Place, over to Union Square, where it joined the uptown contingent for an outdoor mass meeting.[55]

Once in the square, the SP hosted a program of speakers in English, Italian, Russian, and Yiddish for the ethnically diverse audience. Those gathered to celebrate May Day created this moment of transnational unity around their shared concerns as radicals and workers. The speakers addressed the particular reform issues that the party and its union supporters held in common, be it the call for sweatshop reforms or for the release of Ettor and Giovannitti. Even though SP leaders structured the May Day mass meeting to advocate the beliefs of the party and to win it electoral support, it was able to emphasize issues that had the widest appeal among the more radical elements in the city's working class. In the party press, Socialist Party leaders interpreted the participation of the different trade unions and benevolent organizations at the Union Square gathering as evidence of partisan support.[56]

Of course, while the members of these unions agreed with many of the party's policies, they also had their own reasons for celebrating May Day.[57] Consider the contingent of Jewish bakers, who were among the many unions that joined the downtown line of march in 1911. The *New York Call* reported that some 2,500 of them turned out wearing white shirts with red badges and white hats with red bands. The men were on strike that year for higher wages and came out in large numbers to show their united strength and determination. Some of them marched alongside a wagon, decorated in red, which carried an oversized loaf of bread. The bakers' wives and children, demonstrating their support for the strike, accompanied them in the procession.[58] While the bakers may have decided to parade on May 1 to support the Socialist Party, they most likely came out primarily to demonstrate continued unity in their ongoing strike. They adorned themselves and their float with the red color of socialism's fraternity, but also wore the white uniform of their trade and marched alongside a sample product of their labor. The giant loaf of bread represented not only the bakers' handiwork, but also that which

Figure 3.3. Striking Jewish bakers in solidarity on May Day in New York, 1909. George Grantham Bain Collection, Library of Congress.

they wanted to be able to provide for their families, who marched with them in solidarity.[59]

These workers were not an industrial proletariat, raging against far-away capitalist owners in protest of the mechanization of their industry. Instead, the bakers were calling for what they believed was a fairer distribution of the profits in a highly competitive craft. Although sections of the baking industry, particularly the biscuit and cracker industry, had become centralized into partially mechanized factories by the early 1900s, bread-baking in urban areas was still largely carried out in small shops in tenement basements with one to four bakers.[60] These strikers were demonstrating against their bosses who owned those shops, and who may have still worked alongside them. Their reliance on the old-style craft parade communicated this relationship, harkening back to the ideal world of the artisan, in an otherwise politically radical May Day parade. The bakers presented themselves as craftsmen who demanded the right to enjoy the fruits of their labor: not the crumbs, not part of the loaf, but the whole, great product that they celebrated on parade.

The 1911 parade witnessed some 30,000 participants in the downtown section alone. The *Call* reported that approximately 60,000 people came out in the neighborhoods to watch, as almost the whole Lower East Side was decorated in red flags and banners. As the example of the Jewish bakers indicated, not all of this support was expressed directly for the SP, even if party leaders later interpreted it that way in the party press. Instead, many participants demonstrated their basic concerns for wages and bread. They used this holiday, which had become associated more with protest than the celebration that characterized Labor Day, to advance their cause as organized workers. Even though union leaders like Gompers and Fitzpatrick could not see the use of May Day for the American worker, laborers like these bakers could, and they turned out in large numbers each spring.

Workers in the city's garment trades joined them in the May Day parade. The great "rising of the 20,000" garment workers in 1909 and the subsequent strikes carried out between 1910 and 1913 against the long hours, horrible working conditions, and falling piece rates of the sweated labor system did not just strengthen the ranks of the International Ladies' Garment Workers' Union and usher in the Amalgamated Clothing Workers in 1914. They also motivated many of these unions and their members to participate in the annual May Day parades in greater numbers. There they could demonstrate their united strength and carry out their protests against injustices in the workplace in a peaceful, public display of unity. Like the Jewish bakers, some of these garment workers carried representations of the products of their labor, such as the steam-iron workers who displayed a "monster shirt."[61] Others carried their union banners and placards, with which they expressed their specific demands for better wages and shorter hours.[62]

These men and women turned out on May Day to represent themselves as supporters of their city's Socialist Party and as unionized workers who wanted to make immediate changes to improve their everyday lives. The large-scale parades that the SP and radical-dominated trades organized in these years, reaching a reported 125,000 marchers in 1917, provided the opportunity for them to construct their complex social and political identities.[63] Both the official transcript constructed by the party leaders and the vernacular messages delivered by the diverse participants existed in a delicately balanced tension each year.

This tension was also evidenced in the different ways women took part in May Day parades and in how the SP represented that participation. Women walked as members of their particular union or as members of the Socialist Party's local branches, language associations, and special committees. Although the party represented their presence in a way that advanced its agenda, these women also had their own concerns that led them to join the march on May 1.

For the party, the women's presence signified the cosmopolitan and democratic nature of the May Day holiday in general and of the SP's parade in particular.[64] However, although the party celebrated this coming together of men and women, it did not fully embrace a vision of gender equality much before 1915. In the same edition of the *Call* that touted May Day's populism, for example, its iconographic representations of labor were still "male": a brawny man with hammer in hand.[65] Women were celebrated as contributing to the holiday's display, but they were not yet considered integral to the day's overall struggle, perhaps because they did not yet have the vote. To be sure, many socialists did believe that true democracy could only be achieved once women had the vote and could be real political equals with men. But, as socialists, many of them also sublimated their acting toward that equality to achieving solidarity among the working class first. This was especially true in the SLP, which was dominated by stricter Marxist thinking. Such a position was less entrenched in the SP, which had a larger contingent of native-born male and female members who drew from among various American reform movements and favored women's suffrage and equality.[66]

By 1915, party members fashioned support for these rights in their May Day demonstration. That year, the SP's Socialist Suffrage Campaign became a major component of New York's uptown parade division. The party had organized the holiday not just in support of the industrial freedom sought by the participating ILGWU locals, but also to demand women's suffrage. The work of the party's female members within the Suffrage Committee ensured this focus, which was backed by the growing number of the city's women workers in the garment trades. It became one of the main rallying points of the day, proclaimed in banners and pennants throughout the parade. The male and female members of the Rand School, the city's socialist-founded workers' school, sported sashes demanding "Votes for Women" as they marched down the street. In addition, 500 women garment workers wearing similar regalia walked behind the "women's suffrage auto," making their call for the vote known through their choice to march in this division rather than with their union. Pro-suffrage speakers made their case both from the open back of the slow-moving car along the parade route and on the stands in Union Square during the postprocession mass meeting.[67]

Throughout the day, then, the speakers presented their arguments for the legal institution of the vote for women. In 1913, the New York State Legislature had agreed to place a referendum on women's suffrage on the ballot for November 1915. The prosuffrage demonstrations in the 1915 May Day parade were part of a broader campaign that the party waged to support this referendum. Theresa Malkiel, member of the party's Suffrage Campaign Committee, who had been actively organizing open-air meetings, building up neighborhood suffrage committees, and coordinating leafleting campaigns, was a prominent figure in the May 1 event.[68] She argued that if they had the vote, women could become true comrades with men, supporting them in their backing of the Socialist Party at the polls. She wanted to "put the vote in the service of Socialism."[69] Pauline Newman, former organizer of ILGWU Local 25 and member of the Women's Trade Union League, also had been quite active in the suffrage movement and agreed with Malkiel, who was her mentor. Yet, Newman insisted that women also needed the vote to defend themselves as workers against the politicians and their employer allies who oppressed them.[70] Malkiel emphasized the partisan gains that would result from suffrage, while Newman saw the vote as another arrow in the organized worker's quiver of union protest tactics. Both voiced the support that the SP gave to the women's suffrage campaign in these years.

Figure 3.4. Members of the Women's Auxiliary Typographical Union riding in a Labor Day float in the 1909 New York parade. George Grantham Bain Collection, Library of Congress.

Figure 3.5. Women marching in the streets during a May Day parade, New York 1910. George Grantham Bain Collection, Library of Congress.

In this way, the May 1 parades did embody the "sweet heyday of democracy" that the SP celebrated in its press. Unlike the contemporary Labor Day parades, in which many women workers still rode on floats or in carriages at the end of the line of march, in the socialist May Day parades of the 1910s, women walked proudly alongside men demanding both economic freedom and political equality.[71] Whereas they had once marched as socialists and workers first, and women second, these activists and their female supporters now presented themselves as women who deserved equal rights, so they could be more effective socialists and better-organized workers. The change corresponded not only to the shift in the SP's official position on women socialists, but also to the real-life experiences of individuals like Malkiel and Newman who wanted to strike down the barriers of political inequality that were obstructing their organizing work in the party and the union.[72]

In addition to the participation of women in May Day parades, there were also many children who joined in the day's events. The city's Socialist Sunday schools, loosely affiliated with the party, began organizing separate children's processions on May 1 in 1911. There were fourteen of these schools in New York where staff members encouraged children to think independently, while also presenting them with basic socialist tenets, during two-hour sessions once a week.[73] In their May Day parades, the children marched through the streets surrounding the schools in their Yorkville and Brownsville neighborhoods. Anywhere from 1,000 to 3,000 children paraded in a given year. They also attended the postprocession exercises held in their community meeting halls that included speeches, songs, recitations, and short plays.[74]

For many radicals, these "little parades," as they were called, demonstrated the growing strength of socialism in their city. In its press, the Socialist Party represented the children as the literal future of the socialist movement; they paraded in support of the radical politics that they learned each week in their special schools. In 1912, the *Call* reported that the children's processions were intended "to show that there are thousands of children in this city who are imbued with the spirit that they belong to the working class." Their parades were a public statement about the literal viability of the Socialist Party in New York. The *Call* characterized the children as "part of the big progressive movement" and insisted "that they have reason to be proud of it and not to be ashamed of showing it openly."[75]

As "little parades," these children's processions were held separately from the main parade. The route was shorter for the youngsters and confined to the neighborhood immediately surrounding the socialist school. In 1912, for example, the children marched from the Labor Temple on Eighty-fourth Street, crisscrossing through the Upper East Side neighborhood to Eighty-seventh Street, down to Sixty-eighth Street, and finally to Sokol Hall on Seventy-second Street. They remained within these twenty blocks, unlike the adult May Day parade, which consisted of one contingent from the Upper East Side and one from the Lower East Side that eventually converged on Union Square.[76] For the younger children, the "little parades" provided them with a comfortable and safe route in familiar surroundings as they ventured forth in public as young socialists for the first time. The circumscribed nature of the route functioned much like the socialist schools: it gave the children a controlled space in which to learn about and experiment with radical ideas and sympathies.

While these "little parades" were a unique addition to the holiday, they were not the only way socialist youth participated. As they had done for several years, some of the older children in the radical neighborhoods marched in the main May Day parade instead of in the special Sunday school processions. In 1915, 200 Boy Pioneers, ranging in age from seven to fourteen, walked the entire route with the adults. The Education Club of the Young People's Socialist League, made up of teens and young adults, followed closely behind. By joining with mature party members in the main parade, these youths demonstrated their deepening commitment to socialism. Their presence also signified their promise as the future of the movement.

SP leaders made it clear in their reports on May Day that they believed these young people, along with the children in the "little parades," marched as living representations of the next generation of American socialists.[77] The *Call* reported how "that army" of 5,000 children who marched in the Socialist Sunday school parade of 1915 "was a sight to move the most indifferent observer." It noted how "the simple red flag that each [child] carried formed an endless stream of cheers that bobbed up and down with the stride of each kiddie," in a display that was "gripping in its effect." The "women watching the children from the curb wept with the pride and joy of them," and "men waved their hats as [the children] passed them" carrying banners that condemned ignorance and proclaimed socialism as the only hope for humanity. The *Call* observed how "one realized it meant something to have all those children already awaken to the grim realities about them": they were becoming the next generation of socialist leaders.[78]

While the Socialist Party made its understanding of the significance of the children's participation in both the adult May Day procession and the "little parades" clear in its press, what all this meant to the children was less evident. No doubt many of them went along as a matter of course, treating the outing like any other special school event. Some of the children probably also enjoyed the experience of marching through their city's streets and of singing and dancing at the postparade programs for their teachers and parents.[79] Surely others may have been bored by the whole affair, particularly by the speeches that their instructors delivered on the benefits of socialist education, which were more likely aimed at their parents.[80] Because some of them became members of the Pioneers, and when they were older the Young People's Socialist League (YPSL), at least a few of the children who marched must have sincerely meant their cries of "Are we in it? Well, I guess. Socialists, Socialists, yes, yes, yes!"[81] Others may have simply enjoyed the day free from school or work, indulging themselves in the ice cream and games provided after the official ceremonies concluded.[82]

Many of these children were most likely pleased not to have to attend school on May Day. They were also very fortunate not to have to go to work. Those who were able to attend school full time were not

representative of the majority of working-class children in the city. As David MacLeod has argued in his history of American children at the turn
of the century, the concept of sheltered childhood, as it has since become
known, was just emerging in the first two decades of the twentieth century. It embraced the desire for children to be reared and cared for in
protective environments, where nurture and self-development were ends
in themselves. It sustained the movement for children to be educated in
age-graded classrooms, allowed to explore in safe playgrounds, and sheltered from the harsh conditions of the factory and the city streets. The
shift to this perspective was a result of a complex combination of efforts
by middle-class social reformers and the social and demographic effects of
declining birthrates and urbanization.[83] In the 1910s, the effects of this new
understanding of childhood were limited, realized first in the urban middle class. Most children, including those who took part in the socialist-
sponsored May Day parades, either worked full time contributing to the
family economy of their working-class homes or perhaps balanced some
part-time schooling with their jobs in the city. Like the Boy Pioneers who
marched in the main holiday parade each May 1, many of these children
were an integral part of the urban adult world on an everyday basis.

This was particularly true for working children. In the 1913 May Day
procession, child garment workers walked alongside adult members in the
delegation of the United Hebrew Trades.[84] The youngsters, mainly white-
goods workers, publicly demonstrated their identity as laborers first, before their status as children. Their experience in the May Day celebration,
and in the city year-round, was thus different from their counterparts in
the school processions. In its coverage of the event, the SP press made
the distinction clear: the child workers were understood to represent the
current conditions of the family economy, straining under the pressures
of capitalism, whereas the schoolchildren were seen as representatives of
the possibilities of the freedom and education for youth that could come
with socialism. The presence of working children in the May Day parade
and socialist students in the "little parades" reflected the social reality of
the former group's hardships and the latter's privilege. In its press, the SP
drew attention to this disparity to advance its political agenda.

For the Socialist Party members who organized the "little parades"
through the Sunday schools, the existence of child labor was thus considered yet another abomination of capitalism that had to be brought
to an end. As they marched through the streets of their neighborhoods,
the schoolchildren were encouraged not only to shout their affirmation

Figure 3.6. Children protesting child labor during a May Day parade in New York, 1909. George Grantham Bain Collection, Library of Congress.

of socialism, but also to voice their denunciation of child labor, just like their older comrades did in the main holiday parade.[85] The Sunday school instructors who organized the youth parades intended them to be a didactic experience both for the children participating in them and for the spectators who lined the streets or watched from their windows.

Not everyone was willing to witness the socialization of these children into radical politics or to hear their insurgent chants, however. In 1912, as the parade passed by St. Monica's High School on East Eightieth Street, teachers drew the shades in silent protest.[86] The teachers' reaction is not surprising. For most Catholic immigrants, their local parish and the parish school were central parts of their everyday lives. The Socialist Sunday school parade would have been considered an intrusion into their community, which was defined by their shared faith, the parish itself, and the surrounding streets of the local neighborhood.[87] It may also have been deemed disrespectful, given many socialists' rejection of religion. Among the banners the radical youngsters carried was one that read, "We Don't Want to Believe, We Want to Know."[88] No doubt the teachers at St. Monica's would have taken offense at such a provocative proclamation. While

they pulled down the shades, other Catholic school leaders held May Day
processions of their own, in which students (usually girls) marched with
flowers to crown the statue of the Virgin Mary in their church.[89] They thus
not only turned a blind eye to the socialists' demonstrations, but also carried on their own traditions in direct opposition. Both events, and the
contestation that surrounded them, were part of the grassroots ritual life
of urban working-class neighborhoods. Those streets were host to the patriotic and the holy as well as to the radical and the profane.

Despite the existence of local hostility to the May 1 events, the Socialist Sunday school parades continued through the 1910s. The SP sustained
these little May Day parades despite, or perhaps because of, alternative
May 1 activities. In addition to Catholic crownings of the Blessed Mother,
there were other events that social reformers coordinated in the city's playgrounds to offset the socialist activities. These rites, which included maypole dancing and the crowning of a May queen, celebrated May 1 in its traditional European mode as a holiday that heralded the coming of spring.[90]
As David Glassberg has argued, educators and social workers came to favor
such exercises in the first decade of the twentieth century, in part because
the revival of Renaissance and medieval traditions of the maypole dance
and flower-gathering rituals seemed to have the "aesthetic richness" they felt
was absent in America's modern, commercialized leisure. In addition, these
reformers believed that the maypole dance could teach all nationalities to
come together "within the framework of a white, Anglo-Saxon Protestant
nation." For some, particularly playground reformers and social workers,
this coming together was understood as a progressive, democratic exchange
of immigrant traditions. For others, especially those in the city's patriotic
and hereditary societies, the old English May Day rituals were thought of as
one way, in a more broadly conceived use of historical pageantry, to preserve
and promote the dominance of Anglo-American culture.[91]

This supremacy was aimed not just at the cultural traditions being
brought to America by newly arriving Southern and Eastern European
immigrants, but also at what had become the specifically socialist and anarchist political tradition of May Day. As the little May Day parades suggest, that holiday was observed by both native-born and immigrant children in the Socialist Sunday schools.[92] Although the city's public schools
actively tried to undermine this inculcation of radical politics, both in the
classroom and now on the playground, the SP's youth continued to sustain
their own traditions. Sometimes this included the use of the same springtime themes and performance genres that the social reformers deployed

Figure 3.7. Children celebrating the rites of spring on May Day in Central Park, 1908, George Grantham Bain Collection, Library of Congress.

to undermine them. The significant difference, of course, was the political content. At one of their Sunday schools in the Bronx, socialists organized a tableau in which the dance of the poppies was accompanied by the dance of the workers. Flowerchildren crowned the May Queen, who was then surrounded by children carrying the flags of twenty nations, symbolizing international unity. One girl, carrying the red flag, strode to the center of the stage and signaled all the "nations" to salute the crimson standard and sing "Hurrah for the Red."[93] The children had mobilized the springtime motif and the tradition of the May Queen in a concerted celebration of socialism. The socialist instructors at the Bronx school did not reject the "aesthetic richness" of the spring pageant tradition; they just adopted it as another way to proclaim their radical politics.

The Socialist Party engaged in a similar reinterpretation of symbolic meaning when it laid claim to the nation's flag. During their May Day parades and at their mass meetings, SP members displayed the American flag and declared that the equality, liberty, and democracy it represented would be most fully realized in a socialist order. They did not shy away from carrying the Stars and Stripes alongside their party's red banner each May 1. Like those members of the SLP in New York who wanted to carry the American flag on parade in 1898, the SP members who defended their right to do the same in the 1910s shaped their identity as Americans. They, too, defined the hybridity of being a radical American.

Morris Hillquit, a prominent party leader in New York, articulated what this symbolic unity meant to socialists in an editorial printed in the *Call* in 1912, entitled "The Red Flag and Stars and Stripes."[94] His argument was intended both to dispel the popular sentiment that the two flags were incompatible and to assert socialism's claim to America's democratic heritage. Hillquit disagreed with opponents of socialism who considered the red flag to be a symbol of "carnage and bloodshed" that should not be carried beside the American flag. He insisted that the crimson banner really stood for "world-wide peace, harmony and brotherhood" and was the "standard in the great international fight against corruption, exploitation and oppression." Consequently, Hillquit argued, the red flag supplemented the Stars and Stripes, the "emblem of American independence and democratic justice." Furthermore, he believed that socialists had a better claim to this national flag because they fought to "re-establish equality, democracy and social justice" in their country, qualities that had been undermined by the same wealthy industrialists and politicians who considered themselves patriots for denouncing radicals. Hillquit denied these self-appointed patriots' ownership of the American flag, asserting that they had "long pawned the stars to the trusts and monopolies" and that their "stripes [were] the stripes of prison garb." Instead, he thought the "black flag of the pirate" was a more appropriate emblem for them. Only socialists, Hillquit insisted, held true to the democratic promise symbolized by the Stars and Stripes, and therefore they had every right to carry it alongside their red flag on parade.[95]

As Hillquit described it, this was a patriotism that appreciated the nation's political heritage of democratic promise, but one that envisioned socialism as the way to its fulfillment. In the SP May Day parades, this understanding that American liberty could midwife true equality was defined in the prominent display of the Stars and Stripes alongside party banners and placards demanding change. When party members carried the American flag at the head of their marching delegations and used it to decorate their speaker's stands and reviewing platforms, they constructed this composite message.[96] Such demonstrations did not indicate an unquestioning approval of the status quo of the nation-state, for which the flag also stood. Instead, they were expressions of support for what the nation could become.

For these socialists, the red flag symbolized the path to that future: the international brotherhood of socialism. Although the opposition of the general public and the hostility of the police often challenged their display of red flags, socialists paraded their banners each May 1 anyway, and fought for their right to do so. Arguing in defense of Edward Wladzilinski, a socialist who had been arrested in Chicago for carrying a red flag in the 1906 May Day parade, party leader Thomas Morgan insisted that the crimson banner was "in no sense an emblem of anarchy, but [was] the emblem of an orderly legal political party."[97] Despite such appeals to free speech, Chicago police continued to interrupt socialist parades and confiscate party banners as they had done since the 1890s.[98]

Although there would be no official ban on the display of red flags in New York City until 1918, socialists also faced similar challenges there in the early 1900s.[99] During the 1909 May Day procession in Brooklyn, the police confronted Louis Goldberg, a twenty-four-year-old cloakmaker, financial secretary of Branch Two of the SP's Twenty-Third Assembly District, and member of Local 11 of the ILGWU. Goldberg had refused to furl the red flag that he was carrying and was ultimately arrested for leading the procession down a street not included in the party's parade permit. Many of those who were marching with Goldberg accompanied him to the police station and awaited his release the next morning, after he had been arraigned. Once the owner of a local furniture store bailed him out, Goldberg's fellow socialists rallied around him on the steps of the precinct in protest of the entire affair.[100]

Goldberg's arrest demonstrated the continued hostility socialists faced for carrying their red flags in public on May Day, as well as the closeness with which the police watched them during their public gatherings. Although the police did not initially interfere with the socialists' demonstration, and allowed the parade to carry on for fifteen blocks before taking any action, they eventually stopped the procession when it strayed beyond the boundaries granted it in the parade permit. Under the authority of enforcing this ordinance, the police took issue with the socialists' display of the red flag. Their disdain for the banner was evident in the action taken by one of the junior arresting officers on the scene: he trod on the six-by-nine-foot flag that had been confiscated from Goldberg.[101]

Despite this harassment, the Socialist Party used the incident to tout the courage of its members and to claim a victory in what it described as a grassroots battle for respect and free speech that included the right to wave the red flag in public. The report in the *Call* cast Goldberg as an unassuming hero and the Brooklyn socialists who rallied around him as fellow fighters in a struggle for political freedom. Many of the socialists who marched with Goldberg in the May Day parade accompanied him to the station upon his arrest in a show of support for him and of solidarity against the police. After he was bailed out, emerging from the station with the red flag under his arm, the supporters escorted him along the streets to the place where he was arrested and defiantly carried on the parade that had been interrupted the day before. Afterward, they assembled in a local meeting hall, where Goldberg was met with cheers and where prominent party members delivered "fiery speeches" on the significance of the red flag as a symbol of international brotherhood.[102]

Perhaps the futility of confiscating the red flags contributed to the police's decision to allow the Socialist Party to carry its standard during its May Day parade the following year. At the April 18, 1910, meeting of the party's City Executive Committee, the organizer reported that as a result of his negotiations, socialists would be allowed to march with their red banner. Police Captain Schmittberger had "ordered the city supply of permits, across the face of which the legend 'No red flags to be carried' has customarily appeared, to be destroyed."[103] Despite this change, the general hostility that surrounded the display of the red flag in the city did not disappear. Hillquit's defense of the red flag in his 1912 editorial is evidence of this persistent popular disdain. Although the restriction printed on the permit may have been temporarily lifted, the police and many citizens still held the banner in contempt.

All this wrangling over the presence of red flags illuminated the popular hostility toward socialists and the discomfort many politically moderate and conservative citizens experienced when they witnessed the *public expression* of commitment to socialism. They objected to the unfurling and waving of the radical banner because they perceived it as being incompatible with the Stars and Stripes and an affront to everything they believed that national standard stood for. Such local culture wars reveal just how heavily demarcated and policed the boundaries of acceptable displays of patriotism were, and how those who opposed alternatives to those displays either repressed them or endured them quite uneasily. After taking the red flag ban off the permits in 1910, city authorities maintained a strained tolerance for the Socialist Party's May Day demonstrations.

That tolerance, as well as the SP's devotion to defending the American flag, was put to the test in 1912 after a controversial incident at the party's May Day meeting in Union Square. Party leaders and guest speakers were assembled on the platform at one end of the square. A large crowd had formed around them, many people having just come from the successfully completed parade. A group that had gathered near the front of the crowd, just below the podium, demanded that the American flag be removed from the stage. After the standard bearer refused to comply, some of the men from the small, vocal group rushed the platform and tried to tear down the flag. They were unsuccessful. The dignitaries gathered onstage repelled the protestors and restored order. Jacob Panken, one of the invited speakers, then quickly argued that the Stars and Stripes should remain onstage because it represented the freedoms that those gathered, as socialists, wanted to win back for the people.[104]

Despite Panken's words, the mainstream press pointed to the attempt to tear down the American flag as evidence of the disloyal and anarchistic elements within the city's socialist community. The *New York Times* reported the incident as a "socialist riot" during which the flag was "trampled on."[105] Once again, the mainstream press portrayed radicals as unpatriotic and out to destroy the nation, here represented by the flag. Such official pronouncements and popular reactions became part of the parallel construction of mainstream nationalism, in which there was no room for any kind of radical dissent. The annual May Day event provided fodder for this process, especially when there was a controversial episode like the one that took place in Union Square in 1912.

In response to both the event and its negative press coverage, the SP's Central Committee quickly called for action from its own May Day Demonstration Conference. The Conference recommended that the streets be closed for next year's meeting and that the police be asked to maintain tighter security, especially around the platform in the square.[106] That same month the party's Executive Committee passed a resolution denouncing the attempt to remove the Stars and Stripes as a "malicious and vicious act of irresponsible individuals" whom they insisted were not members of the SP and had not been invited to the meeting. The resolution repeated Hillquit's and Panken's sentiments that the Socialist Party harbored no hostility toward the American flag, despite what its opponents may have thought, and that it could not be responsible for the actions of a few fanatical outsiders.[107] As one editorialist argued, although socialists were not jingoes, neither were they fools. They recognized that "it is more important to hand a workingman a Socialist leaflet or paper than it is to wave a red flag in front of him, and that it is a ridiculous proceeding to snatch an American flag out of his hands just because it had been misused by the capitalist class."[108]

In its reaction to the controversy, the SP not only identified its members as patriotic Americans, but also specifically dissociated them from the "fanatics" it charged with nearly causing a riot during their meeting. The insurgents to whom the party referred were most likely some of the city's anarchists, who may have joined the meeting of their own accord. The *New York Times* reported that the men who rushed the stage were members of the Italian Socialist Federation allied with members of the Industrial Workers of the World.[109] Although the Socialist Party's May Day parade and mass meeting in Union Square tended to dominate the city's public spaces each year, other socialist and anarchist groups also observed the day. Some of the anarchists did indeed favor the use of violent tactics in the pursuit of their political ideas, especially the Italian followers of Luigi Galleani, who organized cells in Harlem.[110] Others may not have been as ready to use bombs to achieve their goals, but they also might not have been averse to instigating disturbances like the one surrounding the display of the American flag. In the same years the SP coordinated its large-scale May Day events, several hundred anarchists also came out for the day and gathered in Mulberry Bend Park, just south of Canal Street on the city's East Side, to hear Alexander Berkman speak. In their demonstrations there were no American flags, only anarchism's standards: the red flag of solidarity and the black flag of hunger.[111]

Socialists and anarchists coexisted uneasily in the city's public space, each group espousing a different political agenda and using different tactics. During the 1910s, Socialist Party leaders asserted the right of their members to assemble peacefully on May Day. Like Hillquit, they also insisted on their right to display both the red flag and the Stars and Stripes during those demonstrations. Unlike the anarchists who gathered on the Lower East Side under red and black banners rejecting any claim to national sympathies, these socialists constructed a hybrid identity for themselves as radicals and Americans each May 1. As they marched through the city streets, they proudly carried the standards of their party and their country, defying public hostility and police opposition. In so doing, these radical Americans offered an alternative Americanism to the more conventional expressions found elsewhere in the popular culture. Those mainstream definitions of what it meant to be an American had been forged in public celebrations, like Independence Day and Washington's

Figure 3.8. An IWW gathering at Mulberry Square in New York on May Day 1914. Alexander Berkman addresses the crowd. George Grantham Bain Collection, Library of Congress.

Birthday, for decades. Reformers had touted them in the public schools and workplaces since the turn of the century, and by World War I they had become increasingly jingoist and more deeply nativist. Socialists offered a very different vision for the nation and for themselves. In their May Day celebrations of transnational solidarity, these radicals envisioned a world in which the exploitations of capitalism would come to an end through the power of American democracy, which would then usher in the full flowering of the equality and liberty promised in 1776. In advocating such ideas, symbolized in their carrying both the red flag and the Stars and Stripes, these socialists created a truly radical composite identity for themselves and posed a dramatic alternative for the nation. It was not warmly received, and during the next decade such radical offerings would be strongly, and sometimes violently, rejected.[112]

During the early decades of the twentieth century, both socialists and their union allies exhibited boldness in constructing their hybrid political sympathies. Even though SP leaders interpreted the presence of unionists in the May Day parades as evidence of their support for the party line, workers came to those events with their own concerns. Craft unionists, like the striking bakers in 1911, and industrial unionists, like the garment workers in 1916, chose to march on May 1 to demonstrate their unity and pride as workers, to manifest their commitment to their unions, and to voice their demands for better wages and working conditions. A similar pattern of grassroots divergence from official plans could be found on Labor Day in these same decades. While the national and regional leadership of the AFL and CFL encouraged their members to turn out en masse in respectable trade union parades, many of the rank and file increasingly preferred to attend various popular amusements instead. There, they constructed their own identity as workers who took pride in their hard work, but also believed they had earned the right to enjoy the fruits of their labors by having fun on their own time. Yet, such vernacular constructions did not stop union and party leaders from defending their respective positions. Gompers and Fitzpatrick continued to advocate the need to demonstrate trade union strength on Labor Day. Hillquit and Panken persisted in their defense of socialists' orderly and patriotic May Day events.

The SP leaders' concerns with public order and their defense of the American flag became increasingly important currency in the public exchange of urban politics during and after World War I. In those years, the SP continued to distance itself from anarchists during its May Day meetings, and its members persisted in asserting their hybrid radical American identities.[113] By the early 1920s, despite these displays, the party and its May 1 demonstrations faced intense opposition. The impact of the Sedition Act of 1918 and of the Palmer Raids of 1920 on the infrastructure and membership of the party would be felt for many years. In its May Day demonstrations, many driven off the streets and into the meeting hall, the Socialist Party would no longer celebrate the "sweet heyday of democracy," but would protest its political persecution. At the same time, mainstream American nationalism would take on one of its most virulent and intolerant forms. During the 1920s, both adults and children supported events purposefully designed to display their loyalty to the state and to a nation defined in opposition to the aspirations that radicals had once expressed on May Day.

4

Defining Americanism in the Shadow of Reaction

*May Day and the Cultural Politics
of Urban Celebrations, 1917–1935*

In 1925, the Workers (Communist) Party (W(C)P) and its allied labor unions in New York held their May Day meeting at the city's Metropolitan Opera House. As the *New York Times* reported, that day "Reds who cheered for Soviet Russia and a dictatorship of the proletariat replaced those who ordinarily occupy the boxes in the 'diamond horseshoe.'"[1] The choice of venue may have been intended to evoke this sense of carnival: to symbolize the world turned upside down in proletarian revolution. Yet, the radical display came as a surprise to the management of the Opera House, who thought the hall had been rented for a musical and educational program, not a political rally. Nathan Franko, the orchestra's conductor, also expressed his dismay over the communist program. In what the *New York Times* described as a bitter backstage quarrel with the event's organizers, Franko at first refused to begin the program. He argued that as "a native-born American," he would "not have anything to do with this meeting unless the national anthem is played first."[2] After party and union leaders finally agreed to his demand, Franko led his orchestra in "The Star-Spangled Banner." The assembled crowd stood in silence.

The Freiheit Chorus, made up of seventy-five girls and fifty boys, did not sing along either. Just as Franko was determined to demonstrate his brand of patriotic Americanism, so, too, were the crowd and chorus firm in displaying their political radicalism. Only when the orchestra began "The Internationale" did they sing out and cheer. Franko then cut the prepared number of classical pieces that were to follow from ten to two. He and his musicians "left the stage before the revolutionary speeches were made."[3]

About a thousand miles away in Chicago on that same evening of May 1, 1925, more than 2,000 people crowded into the city's Temple Hall for the annual Workers (Communist) Party's May Day celebration. Once the majority of the crowd had made its way into the hall, the meeting opened with the singing of "The Internationale." A contingent from the party's Junior Section of the Young Workers League, made up of young boys and girls ranging in age from seven to fourteen, marched up the center aisle and joined their adult comrades in song. Wearing red neckerchiefs and carrying red banners, the Juniors walked onstage and continued to lead the assembly in revolutionary hymns, helping to set the tone for the fiery speeches that were to follow.[4]

Albert Galatsky, a twelve-year-old boy, delivered the first address of the evening. Speaking about himself and his fellow Juniors, he declared that they represented "more than the children of the working class"; that they were "the Communist children of the working class" who were prepared to join with workers in Europe "in the struggle for the overthrow of capitalism." Galatsky then noted how, despite the laws against child labor in Illinois, many youngsters still found it necessary to work to survive, including newsboys, boot blacks, and store clerks who were in the hall with them that night. The young communist declared that because of their daily struggles under capitalism, these children were committed to supporting the establishment of workers' protections like those instituted in Soviet Russia. Galatsky brought the cheering audience to its feet.[5]

The confrontation that took place at the Metropolitan Opera and the colorful display that party youth presented at Chicago's Temple Hall demonstrate three notable characteristics of May Day during the politically chilly 1920s, when labor and the left confronted the Red Scare and its aftereffects. Both episodes reveal the arrival of a new political movement on the scene of American public life: the Communist Party (CP) would become an increasingly more influential player in annual May Day celebrations beginning in this decade. The story of Nathan Franko's opposition to the communist celebration in New York in 1925 exemplifies the heightened antagonism that May Day demonstrations faced during the 1920s. And the events in Chicago indicate the more widespread and visible presence of children in such demonstrations, a participation that would trigger heated opposition from both political moderates and conservatives.

Those, like Franko, who were offended or frightened by May Day's radical displays, sought to assert their own definition of Americanism during the 1920s. Many of them chose to ignore these demonstrations, just as

Franko and his orchestra did by walking offstage. Others, including many veterans recently returned from the Great War, decided to attack May Day supporters physically. And still others, organized in self-defined patriotic associations like the American Defense Society, tried to create new public events that celebrated a different, more conservative, and martial Americanism to compete with, and hopefully replace, the radical interpretations expressed on May Day.

Despite this opposition, socialists and communists continued to voice their radical political aspirations during May 1 celebrations. Because of the legal restrictions on their ability to assemble and speak out that were enforced during the Red Scare, radicals struggled to maintain their annual observance of May Day against the threat of arrests and deportations. For most of the decade they took their demonstrations behind closed doors into mass meetings, temporarily abandoning the great street parades of previous years. In the process, the holiday's significance as a sign of their solidarity deepened. During the Red Scare and in the years immediately following, this process of radical American self-definition and the May Day holiday on which it took place became part of the larger cultural debate in the 1920s over who should rightfully be considered an American. It was not just in the familiar forums of legal persecution and vigilante violence that such conflict took place then, but also in the realm of the nation's festive culture.

By the 1920s, as the episode in Chicago demonstrates, children and teens had taken on a greater role in that festive culture. May Day celebrations, in particular, became host not only to the unions and political organizations of adults, but also to their youth auxiliaries, like the Junior section of the Young Workers League. While adults staged these events with their own particular political program in mind, children and teens became the special focus of them and participated in large numbers. Like Galatsky, some even seemed to accept the politics of their elders in the process. Although it is difficult to discern precisely how much political awareness or commitment the children embraced, the memoirs of Peggy Dennis, Robert Schrank, and others attest that participation in such celebrations was often a defining moment in their political awakening. Others may have shared in some of the official Communist Party doctrine, too, but mainly turned out to enjoy the festivity and sociability of the occasion with friends and family.

No matter how deeply the children internalized official party doctrine, those outside the political left were disturbed by the mere fact that youngsters were present during these radical demonstrations each May. While members of the American Defense Society organized alternative civic events in the 1920s to draw the attention of adults away from radical May Day displays, other groups considered the place of children in public life. Beginning in 1920, the Rotary Club and the Boy Scouts organized elaborate Loyalty Day parades in both Chicago and New York, in part to counter the left-leaning May Day celebrations in their cities. A diverse coalition of politicians, public school officials, social workers, and unionists supported the creation of National Child Health Day events in these years as well, partly to undermine the significance of what had become a largely socialist and communist May 1 holiday. These urban parades and festivals were important not only for the children participating in them, but also for the agendas of their parents and elders who saw the events as battlegrounds for the political consciousness of the next generation.

Despite such efforts to derail radical May Day demonstrations and the participation of youths in them, the Communist and Socialist parties maintained the presence of youngsters in their indoor celebrations. For many children of radicals who filled the ranks of the party's junior organizations, these May Day events became defining political moments in their young lives. The reactionary cultural politics of the 1920s, then, may have temporarily driven elaborate May 1 parades off the streets, but they also contributed to the radical identities of many children of socialists and communists, who came of age in this period of repression through the struggle to defend May Day.

Although antiradical sentiment in America did not originate in the twentieth century, as the wave of political repression that followed the Haymarket bombing in 1886 suggests, it achieved a more heightened pitch and a more thoroughly national reach during the Red Scare of 1919 and 1920.[6] Building gradually soon after U.S. entry into the Great War in Europe in April 1917, this intense nativist sentiment gained momentum and took on concrete expression in the legal restrictions, including the infamous Espionage Act of June 1917 and the Sedition Act of 1918, that were enforced against radicals and their organizations in subsequent years.[7]

Congress passed such draconian legislation, in part, because of the perceived need for the nation to defend itself against spies and traitors in wartime. Yet, the Espionage Act has remained in effect and the Sedition Act was not repealed until 1921, reflecting the continued existence of antiradical and antiforeign sentiment after the war. In effect, these laws provided justification for the repression of socialists, anarchists, and communists in America, many of whom were foreign-born immigrants critical of the war effort. With the outbreak of the Bolshevik Revolution in Russia in November 1917, fear of socialist and communist organizing power abroad and at home increased in the United States. The great strike wave that hit America in 1919 exacerbated these concerns.[8] And the exposure of an anarchist bomb plot planned for May 1919 only heightened popular fears. The plot targeted officials at the Department of Justice, Congress, and the courts who had passed or were enforcing restrictive immigration acts that allowed for the deportation of anarchists. A group of Italian anarchists, angered at the arrest and pending deportation of their leader, Luigi Galleani, had mailed explosives timed to arrive on May 1, 1919, to thirty public officials and industrialists, including Attorney General A. Mitchell Palmer. Fortunately for the intended victims, vigilant postal employees intercepted all but one of the bombs and no one was killed.[9] Nevertheless, the incident frightened the public and further deepened popular antiradical sentiment.

Beginning in May 1919 but accelerating in November, law enforcement officials on both the local and the national levels stepped up their raids on the homes and offices of known radicals and radical groups, shutting down presses, disrupting party organizations, and rounding up hundreds of individuals.[10] In December, 249 Russian- and foreign-born aliens were deported, including the anarchist feminist Emma Goldman.[11] By the spring of 1920, anarchist communities in America were greatly weakened, and Socialist and Communist party factions were under siege in the shadow of reaction. With many of their leaders in jail, their presses raided or closed, and their elected politicians ousted from office, these radicals still found ways to continue their observance of May Day.[12] In these commemorations, they both protested their political persecution and heralded what they hoped would be their eventual redemption through a socialist order brought about by their continued organization.

For the Socialist Party of Eugene Debs, the May Day celebrations of 1919 were rallies of resistance at which those gathered were to demand "Open Jails for Political Prisoners!"[13] Because of the nation's new sedition laws, many of the party's leading figures had been imprisoned for speaking out or writing against the war and the government. Debs' address at Canton, Ohio, in June 1918 resulted in his receiving a ten-year sentence in the Atlanta Penitentiary, which he began in Moundsville, West Virginia, in April 1919. Kate Richards O'Hare, a prominent party organizer and speaker, entered the Jefferson City, Missouri, jail that same month and began a five-year sentence. Rose Pastor Stokes, a supporter of the party's left wing and a writer for its press, also was sentenced to the same prison for a ten-year term.[14] William Kruse, director of the Young People's Socialist League, and Adolph Germer, the party's executive secretary, were each sentenced to twenty years in Leavenworth.[15] For most of these socialists, May 1, 1919, was spent behind bars, but they worked to see that the day did not pass in vain. Not only did they support each other through their correspondence in jail, but they also welcomed the "letters from comrades all over the country with May Day greetings."[16] They maintained their spirit of defiance against what they believed were the unjust laws that placed them in jail, and fostered a spirit of unity in the wider community of socialists around their separate but simultaneous observances of the radical holiday.

Most of the imprisoned Socialist Party (SP) leaders commemorated May Day by releasing special messages to the party. SP members, who met behind closed doors during these trying times, would read such messages aloud at local May Day meetings around the nation. In the process, they remained connected to their imprisoned leaders, and those leaders maintained a link to the socialist community beyond the prison gates. In 1919, the SP's Department of Organization and Propaganda in Chicago gathered these dispatches into a program it published along with a guide to coordinating a "successful holiday meeting." It sent the booklet out to party locals across the country.[17]

In each of their separate addresses, party leaders such as Eugene Debs and William Kruse lamented the state of their political persecution, casting themselves and their party as martyrs to the cause of justice. They also voiced hope for the restoration of that justice through the full realization of what they understood to be the true promise of 1776: the achievement of socialism. These radical leaders thus laid claim to an American identity by voicing their unique interpretation of the nation's democratic heritage and revolutionary history. Just as other political movements drew on certain aspects of the Revolution to create their own story about 1776, socialists expressed support for that heritage at the same time as they rewrote its history. Men like Debs and Kruse located the class struggle at that history's center, arguing that their party would complete the *economic* revolution that they believed was necessary to make America a truly free nation. Using the materials of ritual and memory, these socialist leaders advanced their new definition of Americanism in the speeches the party printed and distributed on May Day.[18]

While these socialists claimed the heritage of 1776 in their demand for the reestablishment of their basic American rights, others in the party invoked international fellowship. Rose Pastor Stokes, for example, heralded May Day as the annual reaffirmation of socialists' "solidarity with our brothers in revolutionary lands."[19] Indeed, by 1919, May Day had become an important annual holiday in Bolshevik Russia, where its supporters stood in solidarity with socialists and communists around the world.[20] The 1917 Revolution had become another touchstone in radical political discourse for rebellion against tyranny, and the Soviet state was looked to as a living example of radical change. Some American socialists incorporated these new realities into their rhetoric. They characterized the sedition laws and the Federal Bureau of Investigation not only as manifestations of autocracy or of the Prussianism recently defeated in the Great War, but also of the czarism overthrown by the Russian revolutionaries and the "White Terror" that then threatened the nascent Soviet state.[21]

Associations between American socialists and the new Bolshevik order in Russia were not limited to the rhetorical. Personal connections were also forged among the more internationally minded members of the SP, like Stokes, who left it to form the new Workers (Communist) Party in 1919, and among those in the Russian branches who established their own Communist Party faction. Consequently, although the SP may not have forged such links to Soviet Russia, the popular association of Bolshevism with all things politically left of center deepened in these years of reaction at home. Even when Debs, Kruse, and other socialists invoked the tradition of the American Revolution and its political heritage of freedom and rights on May Day, most Americans quickly painted them with the same antiradical brush as they did the communists. They considered them all the domestic advocates of the more recent Bolshevik Revolution instead, and thought of May Day as the celebration of a dangerous and foreign political creed.

As a result, by 1919, May Day demonstrations were met with both official and popular opposition. In terms of the official repression, the parades became the special focus of police restrictions that were ostensibly intended to suppress violent outbreaks, but which actually suggested the persistence of antiradical sentiment in the wake of the Red Scare. In 1919, for example, the Chicago police denied local Industrial Workers of the World (IWW) organizations parade permits and banned all other processions on May Day throughout the city. Because of the recent imprisonment of the IWW's leadership under the sedition laws, the police were more concerned than usual that radicals might stage an unruly protest.[22] Police went so far as to station rifle squads and federal agents at "strategic points" and to organize "larger numbers" of men at police headquarters and various substations "for quick movement to any part of the city."[23] When twenty-five people tried to hold a parade, they were quickly arrested.[24] For the time being, then, the police were able to push Chicago's radical May Day observations off the streets and behind closed doors.

State-sanctioned opposition to May Day also had reached a new height in New York between 1919 and 1921. In those years, parade permits were denied, the ban on the public display of the red flag remained in effect, and radicals were arrested for distributing May Day literature.[25] But, in New York, radicals also confronted popular opposition: the challenge of intense vigilante violence during the early days of the Red Scare. All through the day and into the evening of May 1, 1919, a group of approximately 100 uniformed military men and recent war veterans roamed the streets harassing and beating radicals who had gathered to celebrate May Day. The group came together around Louis Kulke, a Victory Loan speaker, who was addressing the crowds at Grand Central Station. After whipping the men into an antiradical frenzy, Kulke led them over to the Rand School, where they broke in and forced a man there to kiss the American flag. They then continued down to East Fifteenth Street, where the Russian branch of the SP regularly held its meetings and, as Kulke later described it, they found "15 or 20 men and we beat 'em up pretty badly."[26] After this initial round of assaults, the men headed for the new offices of the *Call*, where they broke in and attacked a group of some 400 men, women, and children who had gathered in an upstairs room to hear party speakers praise the new press facility. Kulke later noted that they "kicked hell out of the men there."[27]

Despite the persistence of these forms of hostility, socialists continued to observe May Day. The grand parades of the 1890s and 1900s may not have been possible, but the many different SP foreign-language and neighborhood branches, including an African-American assembly in Harlem, held their own separate indoor rallies throughout New York and Chicago.[28] In addition, in New York, some 200,000 men and women represented by the Amalgamated Clothing Workers of America, the International Ladies' Garment Workers' Union, and the International Fur Workers began to take the day off as an official union-recognized holiday. They coordinated their own indoor gatherings with speeches and musical entertainment each year.[29] May Day thus remained important as a labor day for the union locals allied with the Socialist Party. They continued to observe it, albeit in these more subdued ways, even during this period of heightened opposition.

The nascent Workers (Communist) Party of America, which remained underground and divided among its multiple factions for the first four years of its existence, also organized May Day demonstrations in the early 1920s.[30] In its press, the W(C)P proclaimed May 1's potency as an annual rallying point for workers around the world. And it also constructed a revised memory of the holiday in which it designated itself as the party at the vanguard of that international worker solidarity. It used this newly minted memory to assert itself as the leader of the revolution and new world order that the spring holiday heralded. In so doing, the W(C)P clearly embraced the transnational potential of May Day, ignoring the holiday's roots in America. It chose to look outward to a global communist community rather than to forge, as Socialist Party members and their union allies had, any form of hybrid radical American identity at this time.

Such an international communist focus was evident in the party's iconographic representations of May Day throughout the 1920s, as seen in a 1929 illustration from the *New Masses*, where a disciplined line of mostly faceless marchers follows a red flag with the hammer and sickle insignia of Soviet Russia, not the Stars and Stripes of the United States.[31] This focus was also clearly articulated in speeches delivered at communist May 1 celebrations and in articles party leaders published in the *Daily Worker*. These W(C)P leaders insisted that May Day originated in Paris at the Second International in 1889, not in America in 1886.[32] Influenced by their contemporary concern to support the fledgling Soviet state, these communists also asserted that the holiday had reached a new historical turning point in Russia since 1917.[33] With the Bolshevik Revolution, the first workers' state was established, and May Day soon became one of its most important holidays. Harrison George, an editorialist at the *Daily Worker*, eagerly proclaimed in 1924 that the "voice of the proletariat is raised today in every land and every clime—in the chant of 'The Internationale.' The flags they march under are red, my comrade, and—led by the Communist International, they march to victory!"[34] The party, which at this point was made up mostly of new immigrants, including an entire branch of Russians, was clearly distancing itself from the American associations that May Day had taken on since its origins in 1886. Instead,

Figure 4.1. This May Day issue cover of the New Masses *from May 1929 shows the Communist (Workers) Party's iconographic representation of May Day as an event that had its focus on the Soviet Union and the party's disciplined ranks, rather than on the holiday's American roots. Courtesy of the Tamiment Library and Robert F. Wagner Labor Archives, New York University.*

these communists had their political eyes on Russia, evoking 1917, not 1776, as their revolutionary touchstone. May Day still functioned as a forum where radicals could create and express their political identities but, for these immigrant communists, the process resulted in a heightened version of internationalism, with almost no American connection.

Many Americans found such an agenda far too radical to embrace. By touting this cause on May Day, which they defined as an international holiday, these communists further alienated themselves and the May 1 event from the American public. During the 1920s, the W(C)P and its internationalist May Day became the foil for much more conservative definitions of nationalism. In particular, the urban business elite, the Rotary Club, the Boy Scouts, and an array of progressive reformers concerned with the fate of the nation's children quickly cast communists as an object of scorn. As these groups came to define the meaning of Americanism for themselves, they did so in opposition to the "un-American" communist May Day.

The American Defense Society (ADS), an association established among prominent business leaders in New York City during the Great War, was one such group that opposed May Day. The ADS originally carried out its mission to "Serve at Home" by compiling proposals for Congress that included the internment of alien enemies and pro-German sympathizers and the banning of German-language publications.[35] After the war, the organization continued its propaganda campaign, shifting its focus to the Americanization of immigrants and the political repression of radicals under its new slogan, "Eternal Vigilance Is STILL the Price of Liberty."[36] One of its main targets became the May 1 holiday.

Beginning in 1920, the ADS attempted to rename and reclaim May 1 as "American Day." This would be the first of many attempts by those who disdained socialism and communism to redefine May Day as something other than a day for radicals and workers. Working in conjunction with the National Security League, the ADS planned patriotic-themed parades and mass meetings around the nation, similar to those that had been coordinated for the preparedness campaign in 1916.[37] Richard Hurd, president of the Lawyer's Mortgage Company and chairman of the ADS Committee on Revolutionary Movements, oversaw the coordination of the American Day meetings by 1921.[38]

Hurd argued that by organizing the "American Day" events, "May 1st [could] thus be most advantageously utilized as the occasion of a program of public activities as well [as] to show how we can preserve our

Americanism against the sinister infiltration of anarchy and lawlessness." The new holiday would "also. . . . afford an opportunity for all patriotic citizens to re-consecrate themselves to the ideals and institutions of all those things that have made us a great and united people." Hurd insisted that this rededication of loyal Americans would have the greatest effect if it were to take place on what had become the radicals' holiday. A direct attack on the "forces which threaten our Government today," as Hurd described "communism, IWW'ism or Bolshevism," was believed necessary to counter their "deep-seated conspiracy against civilization." He and his committee of arrangements at the ADS argued "that a mobilization of patriotic Americans on May 1st will be a great discouragement to the disloyal propaganda with which the Communists now strive to destroy our free and independent nation."[39]

According to one of the American Day meeting programs, the celebration would give all patriotic citizens a chance to take such action: "to re-consecrate themselves to the duty of preserving Americanism" against the influence of socialists and communists.[40] In both the details of the celebration and the rhetoric of the printed program, the ADS placed those political radicals beyond the pale of "patriotic citizens," grouping them all as lawless anarchists instead. Even the *New York Times* reported the gathering at Carnegie Hall as a "meeting of protest against the 'reds.'"[41] The organizers purposefully coordinated the events of the day to celebrate such nativist patriotism. ADS members voiced this sentiment, along with their xenophobia and isolationism, when they sang along to Grace Hawthorne's hymn, "March on America!" Together they praised their nation as the "land of truth," where Americans teach "the children of [their] Saxon race" to honor the Stars and Stripes, the great flag that waved over a nation whose "future is thine own!"[42] In addition to this meeting in New York, the ADS coordinated similar gatherings in more than 800 cities throughout the continental United States, Hawaii, Puerto Rico, and Alaska in its "campaign against anarchy and Bolshevism."[43] Through such public demonstrations, these patriotic citizens celebrated their own version of a socially and politically exclusive America.

Central to this definition, and to the American Day program, was the American flag. The ADS meeting opened with a salute to the Stars and Stripes, the singing of the national anthem, and the recitation of the Pledge of Allegiance. These acts not only symbolized how those gathered publicly rededicated themselves to their nation, but also signified their rejection of other allegiances, be they to another country or to alternative political values. The ADS reinforced this point in its published program when it reprinted "The Last Public Message of Theodore Roosevelt." The former U.S. president, who was also honorary president of the ADS, asserted that in the battle to Americanize the immigrant there could be "no divided allegiance." He insisted that, "we have room but for one flag, the American flag, and this excludes the red flag, which symbolizes all wars against liberty and civilization, just as much as it excludes any foreign flag of a nation to which we are hostile."[44]

The ADS's interpretation of the American flag, then, was one-dimensional. For Hurd and others in the society, the flag stood for undivided loyalty to and an unquestioning faith in the nation and left no room for political dissenters. This position differed greatly from the dynamic meaning socialists had given to the flag, and to the nation, since the 1890s. What members of the SLP had advanced in 1898, what Hillquit defended in 1912, and what Debs adhered to as late as 1919 were different versions of a hybrid radical Americanism: they cherished the Stars and Stripes as a symbol of democracy and freedom, which they believed was necessary and complementary to the development of socialism. The conservatives in the ADS rejected such interpretations of the nation's political heritage. They also clearly objected to the forthright internationalism the communists advocated on May Day as equally dangerous.

ADS members instead constructed a reactionary event during which they imbued the American flag with conservative, nativist meaning. Their definition of Americanism was shaped by their rejection of the dissenting political visions that radicals had tried to assert on May Day in the recent past. Rather than a democracy that would bring socialism to fruition, the ADS understood America to be a nation of assimilated citizens who were loyal to the state and its system of free enterprise. In their annual celebration of American Day from 1919 to 1921, this voluntary organization of self-defined patriotic citizens temporarily challenged the dominance of radical demonstrations on May Day in New York. Through the creation of a competing public festival, they also tried to restrict symbolically the definition of those whom they believed could and could not rightfully be considered American.

Loyalty Day parades held on May 1 during the early 1920s were another of the alternative civic events that had the effect of displacing radical May Day demonstrations, but they were specifically concerned with the participation of children and provided a more progressive definition of

Americanism than that which the ADS offered. The Rotary Club organized these parades in New York City from 1920 to 1925 and in Chicago from 1921 to 1924.[45] The event marked the beginning of seven days of special programs held throughout each city for the "United Boys' Week," which the Rotary Clubs sponsored as part of their general service work with children.[46] In place of the "red-bannered parades of orators counseling sedition" on May Day, there was to be a march of loyal boys, America's rising generation.[47] This substitution took place in Manhattan in 1920, for example, where, because of the heightened state of alert caused by fears of a possible recurrence of the 1919 anarchist bomb plot, municipal authorities in Manhattan denied parade permits to both the Socialist and Communist parties.[48] The Rotary Club and its allied supporters secured a permit for their demonstration, however, because they had no radical ties or aspirations. Loyalty Day supporters were able to capture this political space partly because the state's repression of communists and socialists had cleared the way for them.

Needless to say, the city's socialist community was angered by this turn of events. The *New York Call* reported that "the parade was announced to be an antidote for Socialism," recognizing the significance of the Rotary's having chosen May Day for its event's debut.[49] The Loyalty Day supporters had gained access to the city's streets on the most important day in the radical celebratory calendar. Socialists interpreted this choice as a direct attack on their organizational work, especially among the city's working-class youth. The socialists and communists who organized May Day demonstrations were already under heightened pressure from the legal restrictions and popular vigilantism of the Red Scare. Now the radicals had to contend with politically conservative activists and their competing civic event. The Rotary organizers had captured the public space and reclaimed May 1 to set forth their own vision for the nation and for the place of children within it.

In the New York Loyalty Day parade of May 1920, for example, some 25,000 boys participated, led by military veteran General George W. Wingate. Organized into eight divisions, and "subdivided into brigades, regiments, companies and platoons," each with its own "boy officer" in the lead, the young men were accompanied by uniformed bands and several fife and drum corps. They marched downtown from Sixty-ninth Street and Fifth Avenue to the Washington Square Arch. It took nearly three hours for the entire line to pass. Both working-class and middle-class boys were represented, walking with their fellows from the city's public and parochial schools, welfare clubs, or settlement houses. Many of them carried American flags and waved to Mayor John Hylan and Governor Al Smith as they passed by the reviewing stand at Madison Square.[50]

The Rotary Club in New York was joined by the city's Henry Street Settlement, the local Child Health Organization, and the Boy Scouts in its sponsorship of the Loyalty Day parade.[51] In Chicago, the Rotary united with a variety of youth organizations, including the Chicago Commons, the Boy Scouts, the Boys' Brotherhood Republic, and the Jewish Club. In 1921, 50,000 boys marched down Michigan Avenue demonstrating "their loyalty, their courage, and their spirit of Americanism."[52] Beginning in 1921, the Scouts became a central feature of the demonstration. With their military-style uniforms and disciplined ranks, they fit easily into the overall martial structure and tone of the parade. They also sponsored colorful floats that represented the celebration of loyal boy citizens, the central theme of the new civic event. For example, in the 1923 New York parade, the Scouts enacted a scene on a flatbed truck, entitled "Gang Rule vs. Boy Scout Rule." A young boy, sitting on a fence "in a state of indecision first reclined one way and then the other" over a "gang of street urchins" shooting a game of craps on one side and a gathering of Scouts sitting before a campfire telling stories on the other.[53]

The message promoting wholesome citizenship over urban vice could also be seen on the placards that many of the marchers carried in the parade, which heralded: "Boys Are the Backbone of Our Nation" and "The Boys of Today Will Be the Men of Tomorrow."[54] Discipline and self-control were demonstrated in the military-style organization of the parade itself and by the neat uniforms of the Scouts and some of the schoolboys. Habits of health and good hygiene were celebrated in the theatrical displays on the floats sponsored by the Child Health Organization. For example, in 1921 it sponsored a float on which a boy, dressed as a bottle of milk, chased away two other boys dressed as a cup of tea and a mug of coffee, the caffeine-laden "enemies" of healthy childhood development.[55] The importance of wholesome and physically challenging recreation was expressed through the presence of some school-affiliated baseball teams, which marched in their uniforms, as well as the Scouts' display of camping.[56] Moral uprightness was promoted, too, in the production of the "Gang Rule vs. Boy Scout Rule" float, and in the drama of the parade itself. The Loyalty Day organizers intended the precise marching of thousands of the city's boys, carrying American flags and waving in salute to the municipal and state authorities on the reviewing stand, to be a physical manifestation of the boys' loyalty to the city and the nation. It was to be a celebration of their potential as the next generation of leaders and responsible citizens.

The decision to hold this celebration on May 1 was most likely intentional. For the Rotary Club and the Boy Scouts, at least, the disciplined activities celebrated in the Loyalty Day parades would teach boys good citizenship and draw their attention away from the activities of socialist and communist youth groups on May Day. Inaugurating the "Boys' Week" activities on May 1 with a "Loyalty Day" parade, instead of with a public hygiene seminar or an educational forum on any other day of the year, underscored the Rotary's desire to demonstrate publicly its definition of patriotism in direct opposition to that which the radicals offered. The SP criticized this effort as an attempt to pull boys away from socialism, chiding it as "dozens of psychological tricks [that were] planned for directing the interests, developments and reactions of boys in the way they should go so that when they are old they will not depart therefrom."[57] Of course, the SP did not object to working toward improved health and hygiene or safe and wholesome recreation for children, which the Loyalty Day parades advocated.[58] What it did object to, and what the SP criticized as the cheap "tricks" of this new event, was its overtly martial structure and its celebration of patriotism as defined by loyalty to the nation-state above all else. That precluded the more fluid identification that socialists had created for themselves on May Day as radical Americans. The Rotary Club's and Boy Scouts' public assertion of a more rigid version of patriotism on May 1 intensified radical opposition to Loyalty Day.

The dominant presence of the Boy Scouts in Loyalty Day parades reinforced these radical objections. American socialists had criticized the Scouts since the organization took root in the United States in 1910 for the way it trained boys in military-style exercises and crowd-control techniques. They also railed against the loyalty oaths that Scouts were obliged to take to their parents, their country, and their employers. Radicals believed such oaths undermined the individual boy's ability to think for himself and to question authority. That several wealthy businessmen made substantial donations to the Scouts also became grist for the mill of radical criticism.[59] One socialist even accused the organization of being "a capitalist school for developing scabs and military murder machines for the profit and protection of the capitalist class."[60]

While these accusations exaggerated the power of the Boy Scouts in American society, the SP and the CP were right to be wary of the organization for its basic opposition to political radicalism, which was also evident in its support for Loyalty Day over May Day. This antisocialist and anticommunist sentiment was not always expressed overtly, however, nor was it the only motivation for the public displays of loyalty on May 1. Instead, the antiradical presumptions of the latter were intertwined with an earnest desire to protect America's children, especially its working-class boys, from being lost to the perceived immorality and dangers of urban street life. This concern was particularly evident in the Scouts' "Gang Rule" float in the 1923 parade. There was also the desire to rescue middle-class boys from the effeminacy many feared would follow from a combination of too much mothering and the sedentary routines of modern urban life. In addition, these concerns were intensified by the nation's recent experience in the Great War, which had resulted in the deaths of thousands of young men to the guns and gas of the Western Front.[61] Consequently, Loyalty Day expressed both the more general, and mostly middle-class, anxieties over the challenges of urban existence that had been common since the turn of the century, and the more specific and recent preoccupations with the fate of the nation's future and security, represented in the lives, and quality of life, of its men.[62]

By 1920, these anxieties were expressed more specifically in terms of support for displays of military-style strength and discipline. There was a championing of the qualities of the dutiful and heroic soldier, yet without the hawkish desire for war. The nation had added Armistice Day to its calendar of events as a holiday ostensibly established to commemorate peace. Yet, its strongest supporter, the American Legion, quickly dominated the event during the 1920s, turning it into a celebration of military discipline and strength and a denunciation of radicalism and pacifism.[63] During this period, other men played the role of the loyal and skilled soldier, but, significantly, without the reality of battle, by becoming Boy Scout troop leaders. As Scouts, their sons embraced this martial mimicry.[64] Working-class men may also have shared in this brand of patriotic sentiment, especially those who had recently returned from fighting in the war. Not only could they have embraced the martial elements of this national pride, but also the antiradical, participating in acts of vigilante violence that targeted "reds" in the city and around the nation,[65] as their boys marched in the Loyalty Day parades with their school or settlement house groups.

As the placards in the Loyalty Day parades proclaimed, it was the sons, not the daughters, who were considered the backbone of the nation. They were its future citizens: its leaders, voters, and defenders. Even by the mid-1920s, after national women's suffrage had been achieved, the ideal citizen was generally considered, and celebrated in these new parades on May 1, as male. Girls were present, but not in the line of march. Instead, they stood on the sidelines as spectators, or, in some years, assembled on the steps of the New York Public Library and sang to the marching young men as they passed by on Fifth Avenue.[66] Females were relegated to the role of cheering supporters of the male citizen's activities in the public sphere, a role reminiscent of the limited public activity of women in the late eighteenth and early nineteenth centuries and not reflective of the reality of their place in 1920s public life.[67] The organizers of Loyalty Day thus also struck a reactionary note when it came to the cultural construction of gender: they placed the active male citizen at the center of public life, while relegating women to the periphery.

Consequently, these parades brought together a broad range of contemporary cultural concerns. Begun in the midst of the Red Scare, Loyalty Day in New York and Chicago officially promoted a socially and politically specific definition of Americanism for its young participants. It is difficult to know to what degree the boys who took part in the parade internalized these values, especially since no firsthand accounts have been uncovered. Of course, many of the children joined in the celebration because it was compulsory, a required part of their school day. Newspaper reports also note how some broke free from the rigidly structured demands of the organizers, leaving their appointed divisions to ride down the avenue on roller skates or bicycles, enjoying the day out of the classroom, the colorful flags, and the festive music.[68]

This annual parade of boys was organized for only a few years in each city, even though the Rotary continued to coordinate the other Boys' Week activities for decades.[69] One of the main reasons for the parade's eclipse was that it was soon overshadowed by other patriotic events. The new National Child Health Day parades and pageants on May 1 became the focus of children's activities in the schools by the mid- and late 1920s. Local patriotic civic societies and the Veterans of Foreign Wars revived Loyalty Day celebrations on May Day during the late 1920s and 1930s, but geared them toward adult participants with their own mass meetings and parades.[70] Yet, this transition did not diminish the contemporary importance of the original children's Loyalty Day of the early 1920s. The Rotary Club, the Scouts, and other major sponsors organized the event as an alternative public demonstration to the May Day parades that had filled the streets of New York and Chicago for decades before. They succeeded, with the aid of the state, in displacing the radical holiday's outdoor presence for several years, and their efforts revealed the deep concerns they held for the fate of their sons and for their sons' place in American public life. If boys were the future of the nation, these middle- and working-class parents, Scout leaders, reformers, and fraternal association members sought to provide what they thought were properly defined values of loyalty, discipline, and patriotism: values they believed were incompatible with the political radicalism they sought to displace from their city's streets.

A different coalition of reform-minded groups came together in the early 1920s to promote the improvement of children's health. Like those who coordinated the Loyalty Day parades in New York and Chicago, these politicians, businessmen, unionists, and social workers ultimately directed their campaign against public assertions of political radicalism each May Day. In its place they proposed that May 1 become known as National Child Health Day.

The original impetus for focusing national attention on the issue of child health in America came from Herbert Hoover, who had been the director of Belgium Relief abroad and of the Food Administration at home during the Great War. During the late 1910s and early 1920s, Hoover became attuned to the concern shared by many American reformers for the welfare of the nation's children.[71] Well-known child-study expert Dr. L. Emmett Holt informed Hoover of the high infant mortality rate that still plagued America.[72] Hoover was disturbed by this reality and in 1923, after meeting with leading child specialists, directed the creation of the American Child Health Association (ACHA). It was to function as an umbrella group for existing scientific and educational organizations already dedicated to child welfare.[73]

Part of the ACHA's work was to gather information on the status of children's health in America. The surveys it conducted in its first year of existence revealed some startling statistics. In Hoover's words, the findings determined that Americans were "far behind what a national conscience should demand for the public protection of the well-being of our children." He argued that even with "all the enlightenment and all the prosperity of our great people," the Association had found "that in five other nations there is a lower death rate among infants." In addition, Hoover cited ACHA's findings drawn from recent medical exams of young men drafted into the military, noting that "something like eighty percent of the men examined were deficient in some particular or another."[74] In his memoirs, Hoover would explain that while "military service is not the purpose of the nation," the draft had provided "a cross-section that must give us national concern, for the physical and moral well-being of the nation marches forward on the feet of healthy children."[75]

Hoover's reflections on the health status of the nation's youth reveals that he understood the problem not merely as a moral issue, but also as a political one for the entire nation. The failing health of America's children and young adults was related to America's reputation as a civilized society that could provide for the basic needs of its people, as well as to its security as a population that was inadequately prepared to defend itself physically. Along with his newly created association, Hoover argued that the best remedy for the deficient state of children's health was to encourage more community-based health programs and public education initiatives, as well as the better coordination of both on a national scale each year.

One of the association's ardent supporters, Aida de Acosta Root (the philanthropist wife of Elihu Root's nephew, Oren Root), is credited with suggesting that May Day become the rallying point for this new annual, national campaign.[76] She believed that teachers and parents could use the traditional spring rites of May to advance the message of children's health. The maypole dance, the gathering of flowers, and other customary games could be celebrated by schoolchildren with the appropriate lessons of proper nutrition, hygiene, and exercise worked into the amusements.[77] Beginning in 1924, May Day as Child Health Day became a focus of the ACHA's publicity for the health campaign. The daisy and the maypole became two of its symbols.[78]

Various state boards of health quickly adopted this campaign. Their Child Hygiene Divisions organized immunization, safe-milk, sanitation, and normal-weight campaigns on May 1. These local boards became the driving force behind the May Day activities in most states, each with its own May Day chairman and committee. Local schools also joined the crusade, organizing special parades, pageants, and field days to focus on and celebrate child health, appropriating existing May Day spring fêtes to serve the new Health Day cause.[79] In New York City, 500 schoolchildren joined in a 1928 celebration in Central Park, where "two of the healthiest preschool children in the city were crowned King and Queen of Health." Others distributed flowers to sick children in area hospitals, and one "healthy New York boy" was appointed City Health Commissioner for the day.[80]

Initially, the ACHA's main impetus for selecting May 1 as the focus of its national campaign was the date's traditional cultural associations with

springtime rebirth and renewal. As suggested by the activities they carried out on Child Health Day, reformers found this theme easy to apply
in their campaigns for the improvement of child health. But Hoover was
not blind to the political implications of the choice of May 1. He noted
in his memoirs that, while "the Communists had previously appropriated
[this] ancient festival of May Day for their demonstrations," he "took special satisfaction in giving them this particular competition."[81] The American Federation of Labor (AFL) shared in this satisfaction, too. It gave its
support to the ACHA campaign and specifically sought to focus it on this
antiradical purpose.

In terms of sharing the general concern over the physical welfare of
the nation's children, the AFL's position was clear. In March 1924, Samuel
Gompers wrote to the Child Health Association expressing his support
for its goals.[82] At its Forty-Seventh Annual Convention in Los Angeles in
October 1927, the AFL's Executive Council recommended that the federation present a joint resolution to Congress "similar to that which created
Mother's Day," which would request that May 1 be declared Child Health
Day. It was hoped that this measure would "attract nation-wide attention"
to the cause and campaign already being carried out by local schools and
health boards with the support of the ACHA.[83] The Executive Council justified its support for this measure by noting how organized labor had long
been an advocate for child safety and welfare, opposing the evil of child
labor and supporting compulsory education.[84]

In terms of sharing Hoover's antiradical agenda, the AFL also made
its position clear in the language of the joint resolution it proposed. It
believed that the Child Health Day initiative could be used to safeguard
more than just the physical well-being of the nation's youth. It also implied that a rejection of political radicalism was essential to the welfare
of children and, by extension, the future of the nation. The original resolution that the federation proposed to Congress reflected these assumptions. Asserting first that "the quality of the adult citizenry of a country
depends upon the opportunities for wholesome development provided in
childhood," the federation argued that it was "essential that provisions be
made for a year-round child health program." It insisted that this would
be "effectively achieved by setting aside one day for this purpose as 'child
health day.'"[85] The original resolution then called on Congress to authorize and request the president "to issue a proclamation calling upon the
Government officials to display the United States flag on all Government
buildings, and the people of the United States to display the flag at their

homes or other suitable places, on May 1 of each year."[86] Lastly, the resolution asserted that "May 1 shall hereafter be designated and known as
May day [sic] child health day and it shall be the duty of the President to
request its observance as provided in this resolution."[87] It would seem that
the federation hoped an overt display of American patriotism and an official redefinition of May 1 as Child Health Day would symbolically purge
the date of its socialist and communist meaning. The federation clearly
understood the Stars and Stripes to be indicative of the type of patriotism
it cherished, one that encompassed a loyalty to American democracy and
freedom, while disavowing international Marxist commitments. The AFL's
call for the display of the American flag on May 1 as part of the Child
Health Day program was a manifestation of its broader antiradical political agenda, and a new addition to the ACHA campaign. It became the
focus of discussion at the congressional hearings held on the joint resolution in the spring of 1928.

The Senate had already passed the original version of the resolution
when the hearings were held before the House Committee on Education
on April 13 and 20, 1928.[88] Representative A. H. Greenwood of Indiana
introduced the proposal there. Echoing the sentiment of its AFL sponsors,
he stated that the intention of the resolution was to place the full "influence and prestige" of the federal government behind the Child Health
Day movement already taking place in many states. Greenwood reassured
some of his fellow congressmen, who had expressed doubt about the
measure in their questions, that the resolution would lead neither to any
formal centralization nor to compulsory activities for the local schools.
He reiterated that the purpose of the measure was solely to create a focal
point on May 1 for all the existing child health activities by granting them
the recognition of the Congress and the president. It would make the day
an annual rallying point for the other year-round activities, the details of
which would remain based in local communities.[89] He argued that the
federal government had a duty to support the issue of child health in this
way because the children were the future and security of the nation.[90]

Despite such reassurances, some committee members remained uncomfortable with the flag-raising stipulation and with Greenwood's argument for congressional and presidential recognition of the day, especially
since the grassroots health programs were already proceeding apace on
May 1. The question of why there was such an *urgent* need for this was
finally answered when the AFL's representative at the hearings, Edward
McGrady, testified. He acknowledged that the federation had drafted the

resolution and had "hoped to get it adopted by this 1st of May." Ultimately, McGrady admitted that the federation was "very anxious to have this put on May 1" because it was "confronted every year with the fact that May 1 had been generally recognized as a radical day when all the radicals of the world get together and talk world revolution." He argued that "on May 1 for the last 15 or 18 years there have been anywhere from 1,500 to 2,000 meetings held in this country by the radicals," who were "calling for a revolutionary program, denouncing the Government, asking for a change of Government, and rule by the proletariat." McGrady emphasized how "they have always centered upon May 1."[91] The AFL hoped to change the meaning of this day.

When asked by one congressman if the AFL were "inspired by a desire to neutralize" the radical May Day, McGrady said yes. He argued that the federation wanted "to get the workers thinking not of world revolution," but of "the most valuable thing the Government has, the health of the children." Choosing May 1 and displaying the American flag on that day would aid this shift in focus. Everyone would then know that "the day had been dedicated to the health of the children of our country."[92] McGrady admitted the antiradical agenda of the federation in supporting the original resolution.

Although some of the representatives responded favorably to McGrady's defense of the measure, what passed in the House later that spring was a significantly altered version. Due to the concern of many in Congress over the mandated display of the American flag, that stipulation was dropped. Instead, Congress resolved to authorize and request that the president issue an annual proclamation "setting apart May 1 of each year as Child Health Day" and inviting "all agencies and organizations interested in child welfare" to coordinate their educational activities on that day.[93] President Coolidge followed suit, issuing a proclamation that echoed the language in the congressional resolution, setting aside May 1 and inviting all the local organizations to observe the new National Child Health Day.[94]

The American Child Health Association celebrated this national recognition with special publications that detailed the history of Child Health Day and suggested ways that the new national May 1 holiday could be used to advance the many existing yearlong health campaigns. The association noted how different state-based boards of health could continue their immunization drives, safe-milk campaigns, and child weigh-ins.[95] It also proposed that schools should conduct special "May Day as Child

Health Day" pageants and how the Boy Scouts could become involved, integrating their camping and hiking activities more closely with lessons on proper physical exercise.[96] In another report, the ACHA described how the National Child Health Day effort had already received commercial support. Department stores, like J.C. Penney, decorated their shop windows with sunsuits for children, designed to encourage healthful outdoor play, and the A&P market advertised specials on food products deemed especially nutritious.[97]

Although the president's proclamation and the final congressional resolution did not stipulate the display of the American flag in these Child Health Day observances, the AFL still claimed victory for its antiradical cause. In its report to the federation's 1928 convention in New Orleans, the Executive Council celebrated the significance of recognizing May 1 as National Child Health Day by contextualizing the redefinition within a revised history of the May Day holiday. Noting how May 1 traditionally had been the day when many union contracts were renewed (and was, therefore, a time when many strikes occurred), the council argued that this practice of striking gradually had died down by the turn of the century as unions increasingly changed the dates for making their agreements. Denying the role of the predecessor of the AFL in creating the first labor May Day in America in 1886, it attributed the birth of the spring holiday to the European labor movement in 1890. The Executive Council insisted that the "American trade union movement" had chosen to observe the September Labor Day instead beginning in 1884 and had remained dedicated solely to it ever since. In this revised history, the council essentially denied the presence of AFL affiliates in May Day celebrations during the 1890s and early twentieth century. The federation not only sought to purge the radical holiday from the nation's streets by supporting the competing National Child Health Day in its stead, but also aimed to erase May Day from American history through its revised version of the past. The AFL's Executive Council reinterpreted the past under the weight of contemporary values in a way that serviced its current political agenda of presenting itself as the moderate, loyal, and respectable face of organized labor.[98]

The un-American quality that the federation attributed to May Day by the 1920s was thereby cast back in time to the event's founding in this revision of its history. The council claimed that the May 1 holiday was and always had been an event for Europeans and radicals, effectively denying the annual celebration's rich history in America. It noted how "the communists still maintain May 1 as Labor Day." Now, with the presidential proclamation that "May 1 will be known as Child Health Day," the council celebrated what it hoped would be May Day's final transformation in America: "May 1 no longer will be known as either a strike day or a Communist Labor Day," but a time to focus on the protection and health of America's children.[99]

Of course, while the president's proclamation asserted this designation, and although many local and national organizations observed National Child Health Day on May 1, the socialist and communist May Day holiday did not suddenly disappear. Instead, these radicals continued to hold their separate observances. But now they also focused much of their criticism of American capitalism on what they believed was the fundamentally misguided effort of National Child Health Day.

As the ACHA's campaign to define May 1 as National Child Health Day gained support in the mid-1920s, members of the Communist Party protested. Alongside the usual articles in the *Daily Worker* celebrating the international solidarity of the party's annual May Day demonstrations, there were now editorials criticizing efforts to remake the radical holiday into a didactic campaign for children's health. In 1927, one communist noted how in some states this campaign included "prizes for the best fed children," and sarcastically remarked that the "children of the great masses, who are compelled to go to work before they are physically developed" were unlikely to be among the winners.[100] As far as the Communist Party was concerned, Child Health Day was a misguided idea at best, and an obstruction to revolution at worst.[101] In line with their Marxist ideology, CP leaders argued in the party press that the only way to truly ensure the health of all the nation's children was to overthrow the capitalist system, which they deemed the root cause of poverty and its associated social and physical ills.[102] By choosing May 1 as its focal point, the health campaign reinforced the survival of capitalism by distracting workers from the "real" significance of May Day: the demonstration of international worker solidarity that would eventually overthrow capitalism and establish the communist order.[103]

Like much of the Communist Party rhetoric from the late 1920s and early 1930s, this criticism of the palliative effects of reform was intense. If taken literally, it also sacrificed the intermediary benefits of such reform for the sake of ideological purity. The rejection of Child Health Day as a capitalist sham was based on an interpretation of Marxist-Leninist ideology that assumed revolution would result from the Great Depression that began in 1929. The Comintern's Sixth Congress believed that the Depression was evidence of the collapse of capitalism after its so-called third and final period of expansion. It argued that revolution would be the inevitable next stage of development. The party's official position was that it had to lead this revolutionary movement by winning the support of a majority of the working class.[104] Especially from the late 1920s until the slow shift to the "united front from above," beginning in 1933, party leaders in America defended this doctrinal orthodoxy. This position isolated them from officially supporting intermediate reforms, like those represented in the child health initiative.

Instead, the CP leadership tried to assert the party's authority as a protector of child welfare in both the present and the future, by arguing that only workers' solidarity and revolution could truly eradicate the problems of poverty and poor health. Consequently, they deemed the continued organization of communist May Day demonstrations essential to resist the expansion of Child Health Day. Yet, even during the so-called third period, when the party's official rhetoric was intensely orthodox, local party branches actively engaged in work that would help improve the lot of workers' children as well as advance the cause of revolution. From 1929 to 1933, these branches not only agitated on the shop floor for stronger unions, but also led hunger marches and demonstrations against evictions, high rents, and poor housing in New York, Chicago, and other major cities.[105] Recent research by historians like Randi Storch has uncovered such complex relationships within the CP at the city and neighborhood level. Storch has identified this central "tension that existed at the party's local level between independent action (and sometimes resistance), on the one hand, and party leaders' efforts to rein in the rank and file, on the other," noting how the ranks "followed their minds, sometimes broke the rules, and created the diversity that characterized the local Communist experience."[106] So, even while CP leaders continued to condemn National Child Health Day as misguided and limited in its palliative purpose, its members carried out reforms at the grassroots level to improve the lot of children and their families.

Officially, however, the CP remained committed to its belief that only revolutionary change would effect such lasting improvements, and thus it sustained its rejection of the holiday. In 1935, the party's affiliated benevolent organization, the International Workers Order (IWO), published a play that dramatized this criticism.[107] It included Sam Pevzner's drama, *The Gang Learns About May Day*, in a volume of "true to life" productions designed for children.[108] The IWO intended the play to be an educational and recreational tool for its local IWO Juniors, the fraternal association's youth section.[109] At the center of the play were an expression of the party's objection to Child Health Day and its celebration of May Day as the "real" workers' holiday.

"The Gang" in the play's title comprises of a group of working-class friends: Spike, Marty, Pinky, Skinny, and Anna. As the curtain rises, they are found playing on the stoop of their tenement. Their neighbor, Mr. Morris, returns to his apartment, explaining to the children as he passes them on the stairs that he is on strike against his employer, the Finchley Wire Works Company. In the distance, the boys and Anna hear the voices of some older neighborhood kids who are members of the Young Pioneers, the CP youth group. Butch, one of the Pioneers who is admired by Skinny but disliked by Spike, urges the gang to follow him and his friends to the park, where the mayor is officiating over the Child Health Day activities. Butch and his fellow Pioneers tell the gang that they plan to demonstrate for unemployment insurance instead of joining in the maypole dance.[110]

Scene Two opens with the youngsters in the park, standing to the side of a large, festooned maypole that J. B. Finchley, owner of the wire works company, has donated to the city. After the mayor dedicates the pole for the occasion, the local schoolteacher, Miss Milhooey, begins to lead all the children who have special tickets in the maypole dance. Because Spike has intimidated a fat rich boy out of his ticket, Elsie Morris, the gang's neighbor and friend, is able to join in the promenade. When Miss Milhooey discovers this breach, she at first moves to notify the police, but is interrupted by screams from the crowd as the young, delicate Elsie suddenly collapses to the ground by the side of the maypole.[111]

The Gang then reaches its didactic climax when Butch rallies his fellow Pioneers to Elsie's side. Although Mr. Finchley quickly tries to quiet the crowd by explaining Elsie's collapse as an accident, Butch climbs on the shoulders of Spike and Skinny and delivers his interpretation of the event as a young communist. He argues that Elsie had collapsed because she has not eaten that day, and that she has not eaten because her father, Mr. Morris, is on strike against Mr. Finchley's company. Butch explains that Morris had to go on strike because Finchley pays him "such lousy wages." As the mouthpiece within the play for the CP's position, the Young Pioneer then asks the crowd, "If Mr. Finchley loves us kids so much, why don't he give our fathers enough pay to live decently so that we don't drop from starvation."[112]

Butch ends his speech by praising the Young Pioneers and the "real" May Day, which he and his comrades observe by fighting for unemployment insurance so that children like Elsie will not starve. His words prove powerful enough to sway even the originally skeptical Spike, who stands up next and declares that he is "going to the May First demonstration." Asking the assembled crowd in the play, and, by extension, the audience, "who's with me?," Spike leads the children away from the shamble that has become the Child Health Day party in the park to the "real" May Day march on the streets of the city.[113]

Butch, the Young Pioneer hero, exemplifies the active, politically engaged youth that the Communist Party hoped to cultivate in its children's programs. With the support of his comrades, he not only exposes the hypocrisy of Child Health Day, but also wins over the local working-class kids for the radical May Day celebration in the city. The play taught other lessons, too: to question authority figures, like Milhooey, Finchley, and the mayor, and to view society as divided fundamentally by class. The working-class gang is set apart from the fat rich kids with their special mayoral tickets for the maypole dance. The play also advanced a masculine militancy in the character of Butch and in the banners and chants of his Pioneer brethren. They were poised in opposition to the florally festooned maypole, the effeminate and weak fat boy whom Spike intimidates, and the maypole dance, which Skinny mocks as girlish. Here the political left characterizes the wealthy as unmanly in their idleness (the fat boy) and their indifference (Finchley), while casting itself as the virile, young working-class boys, Butch and Spike. Communists thus also presented a masculine figure as the ideal political agent, just as the organizers of the Loyalty Day parade had done in the previous decade. Although women may have marched in the streets of May Day parades when they were held outdoors again in the 1930s, they were still not represented in much of the literature of the left as central players.[114] The same was true in leftist iconography, as Figure 4.2 shows.[115] As in Pevzner's play, the *ideal* representation was still one of men and boys taking the lead.

In some instances, real-life Butches did rise to the occasion, speaking out at May Day demonstrations in favor of the party line. During the mid- to late 1920s and into the 1930s, radical working-class children and teens took increasingly active roles in communist May Day celebrations. Despite the attempts of Hoover, the AFL, and the real-world Milhooeys, not all youngsters were drawn away from the radical displays. Instead, a

Figure 4.2. Although women marched in May Day parades, the brawny male worker was still the favored iconographic representation of labor for the left, as seen in this William Gropper cartoon from the New Masses, May 4, 1937. Courtesy of the Tamiment Library and Robert F. Wagner Labor Archives, New York University.

new generation of native-born, working-class American radicals came of age politically in the annual real-life dramas each May 1.

Youngsters had participated in these radical May Day demonstrations since the early years of the twentieth century. During the 1910s, for example, there were the lively "little parades" of the Socialist Party's Sunday schoolchildren held in Manhattan and Brooklyn each May 1.[116] During the early to mid-1920s, and continuing into the 1930s, the Socialist Party and the Communist Party created additional special youth groups for the children of their party members.[117] Through these clubs many youngsters joined in annual May Day demonstrations for the first time, thereby both enlivening those celebrations and gaining direct exposure to radical politics in action. For some who looked back on these events in their memoirs, they remembered the experience as a politically defining moment in their young lives.

One of the most active of the radical youth groups was the Communist Party's Young Pioneers (YP), to which the character Butch belonged in Pevzner's play. Founded in 1922 as the Junior Section of the Young Workers League, the YP took its new name in 1926 when the Workers (Communist) Party came fully above ground and changed its name to the Communist Party, USA (CPUSA). The Pioneers were originally "intended to include working-class children whose parents were not Communists": children who were to be recruited from the neighborhoods and the schools. The hope was that these children, like the fictitious Spike and his gang, would become active in the YP, join the Young Communist League (YCL) as teens, and ultimately enter the party as young adults. However, "in reality, most Young Pioneers were children of Communist Party members and sympathizers."[118] Working-class children of parents who were not radical were educated by the city's public schools or Catholic parish schools, and socialized within neighborhood networks dominated by these antiradical institutions. They generally did not enter the ranks of the party.[119]

For the children of radicals who generally did join the party's youth organizations, the activities they participated in educated them in their parents' politics. YP groups held their own meetings, usually supervised by a member from the YCL. They contributed to the organization's magazine, the *Young Pioneer*, and participated in local campaigns for issues that were of interest to them as radical children. Through leafleting their schools and attending demonstrations, for example, they both protested what they believed was the imperialist propaganda of the public school curriculum and fought against child labor.[120]

Like Butch, the fictional Pioneer, most YPs also came out to demonstrate on May 1. Not only did they march in the May Day parades, but they also distributed party literature on the streets and, like Albert Galatsky, the twelve-year-old communist orator, spoke during the party's mass meetings.[121] A year after Galatsky's speech in Chicago, another Pioneer took the stage at the party's annual rally in 1926. Before a crowd of 8,000 in the Coliseum, Jack Cohen warned working-class parents of the dangers inherent in the public schools, which, he argued, were really capitalist educational institutions. He urged them to send their children to the Pioneers, where they would be taught to recognize such dangers and how to protest them.[122] In 1927, at the party's May Day meeting in New York, the fifteen-year-old "boy communist," Irving Lifschitz, voiced a similar charge against the Boy Scouts. In a fiery speech, he argued that the Scouts was an "organ of the capitalist class used to poison the minds of the children" with its martial aesthetic and its required loyalty oath.[123]

Lifschitz's sharp rhetoric, and the logic espoused by Cohen in his speech, echoed the official language of the party and may not have been penned independently by the boys. In part, they were probably mouthing the party line that they had learned from adult communists. Lifschitz's words also might have been exaggerated by the report in the *New York Times* that portrayed him as a young zealot. While it is unclear if Lifschitz and Cohen took to heart what they said at these meetings, it is clear that their presence was of value to adult party members. They supported this public demonstration of the children's politicization. It is also clear that this same politicization (however deep it ran) unsettled those outside the radical political left, who heard the words of the "boy communists" as evidence of their indoctrination into a dangerous orthodoxy.

To reach working-class children whose parents were not affiliated with the CP, and who were not in the meeting halls to hear the speeches of Galatsky, Cohen, or Lifschitz directly, the Pioneers coordinated school boycott campaigns each May 1. Party leaders helped the Pioneers organize the annual walkouts and described them as "school strikes," akin to the strikes many working-class radical adults waged against their employers on May Day. While the children of political moderates and conservatives mimicked the soldier as their masculine hero during Loyalty Day parades, those of political radicals modeled themselves on the brawny, striking factory hand in their May 1 boycotts. It was hoped that such action would set an example for the other working-class children in the schools, but more often than not, the Pioneers left the classrooms on their own.[124] Some even ended the day at the police station, arrested for distributing party leaflets on the streets outside their schools.[125] From such accounts, a certain amount of commitment to the cause on the part of the youths themselves seems evident. Despite these difficulties, the Pioneers carried on their demonstrations each year from the late 1920s into the 1930s.

During these same years, children of SP members carried out similar activities each May Day. The Socialist Pioneer Youth, like the Communist YP, was a youth club organized along neighborhood lines that socialized children into the workings of the party. It also ran summer camps outside New York City as politically alternative recreational facilities for radical families.[126] Perhaps because the Pioneer Youth emphasized the social and recreational elements of its programs more than direct political activism, its members were less directly involved in May Day celebrations than the CP's Young Pioneers. Instead, within the SP it was the older members of the Young People's Socialist League, or "Yipsels," who enthusiastically joined in the annual May 1 demonstrations.[127] They coordinated annual meetings at the Rand School with guest speakers from the party and from local unions, and distributed thousands of leaflets at SP May Day gatherings, which they also helped to organize.[128]

The literal and symbolic significance of the Yipsels within the SP was made manifest at these May Day meetings. Not only did the young radicals perform the physical tasks of coordinating displays and handing out party literature, the basic trench work of party organization, but they also signified the viability of the next generation of the party. The Yipsels were the base of the party's young, and increasingly more militant, membership. Within the CP, the Young Pioneers and the YCL filled similar roles. In their demonstrations, they both represented the party's future and actively touted the party's political line in speeches, dramatic presentations, and the school-strike campaign. Through their May Day activities, these youths publicly asserted their affiliation with the CPUSA and its agenda, and physically engaged in the practice of political action on the streets of their cities.

This political socialization of its youth was precisely what each radical party wanted. It was the motivation for the organization of these junior groups and for the encouragement of children's participation in annual May Day events. Yet, in addition to this official version of the meaning of the youngsters' role in the May 1 demonstrations, there was, of course, a range of vernacular interpretations held among the youths themselves. For all the individuals who later recorded their childhood memories, the connection of their family to either the SP or the CP was cited as the primary determinant of their own politics.[129] But their participation in May Day celebrations became their first public assertion of this nascent political identity.

Memoirs provide insight into what these events meant to the children when they first experienced them. Peggy Dennis recalled how she and her sister "stayed out of school on May First, International Workers' Day of Solidarity and Struggle." From her parents, Dennis argued, she learned at the time that "it was important to make it clear to teacher and classmates the socially significant reason for [their] absence that day," and noted how "neither [they] nor [their] parents would use the easy 'she was sick excuse.'"[130] Raised in a community of left-wing immigrants in Los Angeles, Dennis learned the meaning of May Day from her Russian-Jewish socialist parents, who guided her and her sister in the etiquette of radical civil disobedience. For Dennis, staying out of school on May 1 was initially not the result of her affiliation with the party, which came later as a pre-teen when she joined the Young Pioneers. Instead, it came from her family's politics—what she defined as their "belligerently atheist, internationalist, and anti-imperialist" position—which led her into the activities of the party. Her sense of belonging to this radical tradition, first within her family and later within the party, gave Dennis the courage to boycott school on May Day, against the regulations of the district and the objection of her teacher and classmates. She noted how her political values, reinforced by her family and later by the party, made her feel "special and superior" to what she then believed was the "narrow-mindedness of [her] block, [her] school, and [her] community" as she walked out of the classroom as a young child.[131]

Not all children of politically radical parents felt so special when they boycotted school each May 1. In his autobiography, Robert Schrank recalls feeling somewhat "embarrassed" at having "to stand alone against the authority of the school."[132] Like Dennis, Schrank was raised in a home steeped in socialist thinking. His father was a Jewish radical who "leaned toward the Wobbly or anarcho-syndicalist position that the world ought to be run by workers' councils."[133] As a young boy in the late 1920s, Schrank was "kept out of school" by his father "to participate in the parade and celebration of the workers' holiday."[134] His recollection of these annual school boycotts underscored his early recognition of the political differences between himself and the other children in his school. But un-like Dennis, Schrank did not exalt in a sense of superiority or pride in this separation. Instead, he remembers how he tried to organize a "little gang of boys to join him in the fooling around" that landed him in still more trouble with school authorities.[135] As a young child, Schrank's radical political affiliation set him apart in ways that made him feel uncomfortable and isolated.

For other children, May Day was a fond memory of a spirited, fun occasion. Ruth Pinkson, also raised in a Jewish socialist home, attended a Yiddish-language shule in Harlem. There she learned about and came to cherish both her ethnic heritage and the radical political ideas of her parents.[136] She recalls how "marching in New York City's annual May Day parade with [her] friends and teachers was the highlight of [her] shule experience." Perhaps because she had the support of her extended community and shule classmates, Pinkson remembered May 1 as a "great event." She noted how she and her parents "arose early in the morning, dressed in special attire, and got into a spirit that none of the other holidays evoked."[137] The camaraderie of her family and friends marked the center of her experience as a radical child, which she celebrated on May Day as a young girl.

Although Robert Schrank may not have enjoyed the May Day school boycotts of his early childhood, he, too, came to embrace the carnival quality of the holiday as he grew into a young teen. Spurred by a concern for the unemployment that both he and his father faced in the early years of the Great Depression, already familiar with much of the radical ideology espoused by the CP, and attracted by the friendships promised by the communist youth organization, Schrank was drawn into the YCL. It was then that he began to support actively the party's annual May Day demonstrations.[138]

As a teen, the holiday took on a different meaning from what he experienced as a small child. As young adults, Schrank and his YCL comrades appreciated more fully the political demands they voiced as they marched. They also contributed more actively to the formation of those demands when they met and discussed them in the local cafeteria and designed the placards they would carry in the parade. The experience of gathering and planning for the demonstration became their schooling in political activism. That experience also simultaneously fulfilled a vital social function. Schrank had fun meeting up with his fellow YCL members, and made many new friends through the organization, including a few girlfriends over the years. He noted in his autobiography, for example, how his attraction to a young woman named Miriam occupied much of his attention the night before the 1936 May Day parade in New York. Although they had only met once before, he claimed that he and Miriam "felt the immediate intimacy of being members of the same crusading army," and observed that "the excitement of a cause can be quite an aphrodisiac."[139]

Schrank's experiences in the YCL were similar to many other young radicals, who, as the native-born sons and daughters of radical immigrants, came of political age in the late 1920s and became the backbone of the CP's membership during the 1930s.[140] The combination of discussing radical political ideology and participating in public demonstrations while forming friendships and attending parties characterized the experience of many of these second-generation American ethnic radicals in the YCL. In the words of one former member, the league became for him "Leninist-Marxist theory all mixed up with baseball, screwing, dancing, selling the *Daily Worker*, bullshitting, and living the American-Jewish street life."[141] This milieu was common for many young radicals in these years, and the childhood stories of those like Dennis, Pinkson, and Schrank are familiar to those acquainted with the literature on such "red diaper babies."[142] Their recollections of May Day are significant, however, because they show how this holiday became a ritual focal point for the public definition and display of their complex social and political affiliations. Particularly for secular Jews, who cast off religious rituals, May 1 became the center of this display. As one radical later recalled of May Day: "*that* was our election day, our Fourth of July, our Hanukkah, and our Christmas."[143]

As small children in the early to mid-1920s, these sons and daughters of radical immigrants experienced the May Day school boycotts as one of the more important initial declarations of their political difference from their fellow native-born classmates. It was a moment of political awakening for Dennis, a youthful embarrassment for Schrank, and a cherished time of celebration for Pinkson. By the time these youngsters matured into teens and young adults in the early 1930s, they embraced May Day's radical potential, taking on a more self-conscious political identity as they actively planned and participated in the CP's demonstrations. By then, May Day had also become a familiar part of the local cultural landscape, especially for those who lived in radical ethnic enclaves within New York and Chicago. Each year, the youthful members of the YCL publicly defined their difference from those who did not share their political beliefs, as they also reaffirmed their ties to their local neighborhoods and communities of fellow league and party members. Through their participation in the May Day demonstrations, they became both radicals and Americans, a complex identity they would articulate more clearly during the Popular Front May Day parades and mass meetings of the mid- to late 1930s.

As the experiences of these young radicals demonstrate, radical political youth groups like the YP and the YCL rarely drew their members from among boys in nonradical communities. Instead, children of party members and sympathizers filled the ranks of these organizations. Even among the working class, the Pioneers and YCL tended to draw their support from the sons and daughters of those who already espoused radical ideology, or who at least did not have an alternative belief system with which to inculcate their children in opposition to radicalism.[144] In the same way, the Boy Scouts did not draw much, if any, support from among the second-generation ethnic radical Americans. Loyalty Day and Child Health Day offered opportunities not for conversion, but for "reconsecration." For those who opposed the presence of socialists and communists in their city streets each May 1, these new holidays provided an effective way to reclaim the public space. Neither socialist nor communist May Day parades took place in the early 1920s.

The presence of thousands of working-class children from nonradical communities in Loyalty Day and Child Health Day events raises some interesting questions. These reform-oriented celebrations were linked to the public schools and, with their more benign assertions of patriotism, could have provided a vehicle for these children and their parents to assert their own version of working-class Americanism. In the early 1920s, that Americanism clearly included the rejection of political radicalism. Yet, it is also evident, from the rather quick disappearance of these anti–May Days, that there were limits to this opposition. There were more than just assertions of loyalty to the nation and rejections of socialism in the working-class Americanism that found expression in these events. There were also claims to healthy citizenship and participation in campaigns against urban vice and the ills that plagued workers' neighborhoods. By looking beyond the well-known legal and political history of the Red Scare to that of public celebrations like Loyalty Day and National Child Health Day, these parallel priorities within 1920s working-class culture are illuminated, and the contours of that decade's antiradicalism better understood.

Despite the effectiveness of those antiradical campaigns in displacing May Day parades from the streets during the 1920s, the SP and the CP sustained a range of youth groups for the politicization of their members' children and teens. The two parties drew young people into more active roles during their annual indoor May Day celebrations, which they continued to observe defiantly, despite the many attempts that had been launched since the Red Scare to quash the holiday. In those demonstrations, some of the youngsters found their political voices for the first time, speaking to the party faithful at indoor gatherings. Others would also publicly assert their radical identities through participation in school strikes and the revived parades on May Day during the early 1930s. If not all of the nation's children were drawn into the politics of the left, as conservative and mainstream political adherents feared, neither were they all attracted to the alternative offerings of National Child Health Day and Loyalty Day. Instead, a minority of children within existing urban radical communities asserted their affiliation with the left as second-generation ethnic Americans. They would bring their youthful experiences to bear as leaders and members of the CP and the SP in the mid- to late 1930s, integrating their complex social and political affiliations into the radical American May Day demonstrations of the Popular Front years.

5

May Day's Heyday

The Promises and Perils of the Depression Era and the Popular Front, 1929–1939

During the 1930s, after nearly a decade of small indoor demonstrations, lively May Day celebrations filled city streets again. By early in the decade, the continued activity of the Communist Party (CP) in urban working-class neighborhoods and the Socialist Party (SP) within trade unions resulted in increased support for both parties. Given the extent of the Great Depression, both socialist and communist political agendas, which demanded economic equality, resonated more deeply and across a broader audience for the first time. In an unexpected but promising turn of events for those on the left, both the SP and the CP experienced an increase in membership during these years.[1] Although both parties still represented radical political opinions and remained on the margins of American politics, their public activities were tolerated because of this popular Depression-era support.

Yet, along with such promising growth came internal strife. In the early 1930s, May Day celebrations became embroiled in dramatic partisan contestation. Many in the SP and its affiliated unions distrusted communists. And, officially, the CP regarded socialists as reformers who slowed the progress of revolution. In their May Day demonstrations the two parties competed for access to favored public spaces, like Union Square, and for the support of working-class spectators. This political contestation spilled over into unions, dividing locals and fracturing the ranks over the question of whether to attend socialist-led or communist-organized events. Even after the creation of a united-front May Day in 1934, each party continued to use the holiday as an opportunity to augment its ranks and advance its political agenda.

This partisan contestation, however, had significance beyond the internal workings of the political left. As socialists and communists vied for control of May Day celebrations, they appealed to particular definitions of Americanism to make their case. In so doing, they created unique, hybrid radical American identities for themselves. But they also contextualized this creative process within a larger debate that took place during the New Deal era—a debate over what kind of nation America should be and how it should address its unprecedented economic crisis. These radicals experienced their left-wing partisan struggles within this broader reconstruction of American nationalism taking place during the 1930s and, in turn, contributed to the shape of that reconstruction.

Once the Communist Party supported the creation of a Popular Front in 1936, welcoming a broad coalition of progressive reform groups, it hosted some of the largest May Day parades in the event's history. From then on, it would be the communists who claimed public ownership of the holiday. In these grand parades of some quarter of a million participants, May Day reached its climax in numerical terms and in popular cultural resonance. It appeared to its supporters that the May 1 holiday had at last found a welcome place within American political culture, providing an outlet for the creation and expression of Popular Front concerns, like antifascism and support for labor rights and civil rights. May Day celebrants asserted that such progressive values were consonant with America's democratic heritage. Overt displays of American patriotism filled the ranks of marching party and union members. May Day became Popular Front America's greatest public celebration.

But deciphering just what those displays meant to the participants and why May Day organizers encouraged them reveals a more complex relationship between the holiday and the nation's popular political culture. For some, these were genuine expressions of support and admiration for America's democratic heritage, which they believed would achieve its full flowering under communism. But for others, particularly those in the CP leadership, the prominent display of the American flag, the invocation of the Founding Fathers, and the claims made to the freedom born in 1776 were merely instrumental maneuvers intended to implement Moscow's order to strengthen the party and maintain control of May Day.

In the minds of some outside observers, the Communist Party leaders' more instrumental motives (rather than the sincere belief of rank-and-file participants in the vitality of a unique radical Americanism) came to characterize May Day. While by the end of the 1930s the CP was responsible for some of May Day's largest demonstrations, the party's ties to the Soviet Union would ultimately undermine the holiday's usefulness in the

United States because of a growing anticommunist consensus within and outside the left. May Day celebrations had long been important rallying points for socialists and workers to define publicly their radical American-ism. The communists' ties to Moscow undermined this function; it made them, and the holiday, vulnerable to America's growing anticommunist hysteria. As early as the mid-1930s, Socialist Party members believed this to be the case. Many socialist leaders would never trust their communist counterparts and refused to join them in the Popular Front parades. This was especially true after the declaration of the Nazi-Soviet Pact in August 1939, under which Stalin agreed to keep his nation out of the fight if Hit-ler chose to advance in Europe. Immediately after the announcement of the pact, the Communist Party ceased its antifascist protests and called for neutrality when war erupted in September. Even once the CP took up the antifascist crusade again and supported the allied war effort after the German invasion of the Soviet Union in June 1941, the damage had been done. Old Guard socialists and their union supporters could not bring themselves to stand with the communists on May Day.

Despite the attempts of socialists and other progressives to assert the American roots of the holiday during the late 1930s, for them, and those outside the left, the Communist Party's dominance over May Day raised the specter of foreign interference in the shape of Stalinist control. That influence rendered the holiday a problematic addition to the nation's cel-ebratory calendar once again. And so, May Day's heyday in 1930s America was significant, troubled, and fleeting.

Much of the strife surrounding May Day in the 1930s resulted from in-tense partisan contestation, which characterized the revival of the holi-day in this period. When socialists and communists once again began to organize open-air meetings on May Day, they focused their energies on two goals. Both parties sought to encourage more workers to turn out on May Day, and in this endeavor each party aimed to outdo the other. What was at stake was the organization and representation of the working class' political presence. Both the CP and the SP wanted to move and speak for the masses. Both parties wanted to claim the power and legitimacy of that role. And from such a position, the dominant party hoped to influ-ence the direction of urban policy and, ultimately, national politics. Dur-ing the 1930s, the Communist Party would emerge as the more influential of the two political movements. As the greater visible and vocal force at the grassroots level (through their domination of public events like May

Day), communists added a heightened radical dimension to the character of America's working class and its demands during the New Deal years.

As communists vied with socialists for this dominant position during the early 1930s, one of the few things both groups agreed on was that too few American workers were celebrating May Day. The AFL had repudiated the spring holiday as an un-American display of radical political aspirations harmful to the interests of labor. Since the turn of the century, the federation and many of its constituent unions had supported Labor Day demonstrations instead. With the added chill of the first Red Scare of 1919, more workers stayed away from May Day because they found it difficult to see beyond its radical political associations to its origins as a day for American labor. By the late 1920s, many unions had abandoned the May 1 holiday, which had become almost the sole preserve of the socialists and communists.

Socialist Party leaders wanted to change this pattern and woo more laborers to their cause by drawing attention to their support for workers' issues. May Day became a focus for the party's fight to end company unions and the open shop, as well as its call for the shorter working week, unemployment insurance, and social insurance.[2] In its special May Day publications, the party emphasized the roots of the holiday in the American labor movement's fight for the eight-hour day, casting it as the predecessor to workers' current struggle for the shorter working week. The SP presented itself as the one organization that had maintained what it called a noble tradition: the demonstration of worker solidarity and the continued fight for issues that mattered to the American laborer.[3]

The Communist Party also wanted to win the support of the American worker, but from the late 1920s through the early 1930s it took a different approach from the socialists. In these years, the CP officially adhered to the strict revolutionary orthodoxy of third-period analysis. It regarded both the SP and the AFL as equally dangerous "social fascists" that, with their respective reform agendas, threatened to derail revolution and delay the supposed inevitable destruction of capitalism.[4] Instead of using May Day to call for immediate changes, like shorter hours and better working conditions, the CP officially emphasized the goal of revolution and touted the Soviet model. In speeches that party leaders delivered, as well as in written descriptions and visual representations of the holiday found in its press, the CP celebrated May Day for its international working-class character.[5] From 1928 until 1933, the party continued to criticize sharply the SP and undermined any attempts at united action.[6]

Figure 5.1. *The Communist Party's celebration of May Day's international working-class character is represented in this May Day issue cover from the* New Masses, *May 1930. Courtesy of the Tamiment Library and Robert F. Wagner Labor Archives, New York University.*

Communist criticism of the SP softened *somewhat* in 1933, when for a third time certain constituencies within the party advocated the creation of a united-front May Day demonstration. The fledgling Workers (Communist) Party had attempted in 1925 and 1927 to convert union members and socialists to its cause on May Day.[7] In 1933, the CP tried for a united front once more, intending to strengthen the party by infiltrating the SP and its affiliated unions. This motive of building up the CP ranks was not declared publicly. Confidential reports from the Comintern to the Anglo-American Secretariat reveal party leaders' concerns over the CP's poor showing in the 1932 election, its underestimation of SP organization, and its need to ally more closely with unions, especially industrial unions with socialist ties.[8] The Executive Committee of the Communist International considered the development of a united front a good way to expand the party's "work of political education" that would "contribute to the winning over of those workers to the Communist Party."[9]

Many party members sincerely embraced the need for unity among all progressives, even if their leaders professed it for purely tactical reasons. The broader context of the Depression and the growing threat of fascism abroad influenced them to support a united front. With the appointment of Adolf Hitler to the position of Germany's chancellor in January 1933 and his seizure of dictatorial power in March, some intellectuals affiliated with the CPUSA, along with many of the party's younger members, came to see fascism as their greatest and most immediate threat.[10] They feared that such right-wing dictatorships, instead of proletarian revolution, might become the end result of the contemporary worldwide economic crisis. The need to unite with other radical and progressive forces in society to oppose this development was driven home as they learned what had befallen their German comrades, who, adhering to the party's strict third-period analysis, did not create a formidable opposition to fascism's rise. The new Nazi regime in Germany quickly rounded up known left-wing political figures, many of whom were beaten and arrested. It then outlawed communism and ousted the party's parliamentary representatives.[11] Fearful that such fascism might take root in the soil of economically depressed America, the intellectuals and youth in the CPUSA favored progressive unity over partisan isolation.[12] Their call for joint May Day demonstrations with the socialists was made as early as 1933 and echoed this concern. It also predated by several years the CP's official shift in policy to the Popular Front.

The transformation away from third-period orthodoxy, however, was gradual and uneven. As the Comintern documents show, Communist Party leaders maintained a sense of doctrinal supremacy; for them, the united front was intended ultimately to pull more workers and progressives into the communist fold. Persistent, sharp criticism came from the CP's leaders when attempts to coordinate these united May Day celebrations from 1933 to 1935 failed.[13] While the CP extended invitations to the SP and to the city's many unions for a united demonstration on May 1, it did so in a way that clearly expressed its determination to take a leading role in the celebration. Party directives instructed affiliated organizations to "cooperate with each other and with the sections of the Communist Party" and to distribute May Day literature prepared by the party, including issues of the *Daily Worker*.[14] Other internal documents reveal how CP leaders instructed members to use the united-front May Day to win at least one new member to the revolutionary movement. They also suggest that the organization of the day's events was to be controlled by communist branches in each neighborhood or shop that would take the lead in a "systematic ideological campaign" to win workers to the united front.[15]

When SP leaders officially refused to join this united front because they did not want to subject themselves to such obvious communist control, CP leaders used the rejection to criticize the socialists and to support their claim to be at the helm of the genuine party of the worker. They had set up a win-win situation. If the socialists complied with the invitation to the united-front May Day, CP leaders would organize it in such a way that only they could be in control. If the socialists refused (which they did), communist leaders could claim (and they did) that despite their best efforts to arrange a united front against war and fascism, the socialists had proven to be an obstacle.[16] Between 1933 and 1935, the communists pursued this course, presenting themselves as the true defenders of workers' interests each May Day.

Although the SP officially rejected the CP's calls for a united front before 1936, the communists did not always meet complete resistance. Instead, the overtures for unity flowed through the channels that were already working to divide the SP. The younger generations within the Socialist Party, who were politically progressive, well represented in the Young People's Socialist League (YPSL), and supportive of Norman Thomas, favored the call for united action on May Day. The party's older generations, and many of those affiliated with it in the New York garment unions, favored a united front of SP branches and unions only, with no

CP participation. The animus the Old Guard felt for the communists ran deep and was based on more than mere partisan bickering. Disdaining the Communist Party for ideological and moral reasons, they believed an oppressive and autocratic Stalinism dominated its inner workings.[17] Not surprisingly, then, in 1933, after four members of the Young People's Socialist League in New York City suggested that the SP accept the CP's call for a united May Day demonstration, the Old Guard leadership expelled them from the party. After YPSL and party members around the country protested, the SP National Committee overrode the local's ruling and reinstated the four members. Yet, the controversy in New York revealed a growing divide within the SP, which the question of a united May Day only served to deepen.[18]

The rebirth of the outdoor May Day celebrations in the early 1930s was thus accompanied by intense partisan conflict as each group tried to assert its domination over this important annual demonstration. In the end, the CP proved to be savvier than the SP in maneuvering itself into the top position. Its attempts to create a united front lured some socialist militants into its camp beginning in 1933. And in the following year, communists took aim at the remainder of the SP, challenging its ability to dominate New York's public spaces on May 1. In 1934, communists and their supporters made Union Square the focus of their celebration, successfully undermining their socialist rivals' ability to dominate this symbolically important gathering place on May Day. Using the power of the committed number of followers it had on its side, the CP had pressured the LaGuardia administration into granting it a permit for the more favorable (and longer) time slot in the square. In response to the preference given to the CP, socialists decided to hold their meeting elsewhere. The only other time the socialists had been so displaced was during the dark days of the reactionary Red Scare. The communists' victory, then, was more than symbolic. They had taken control of New York's historic May Day gathering place, and in so doing had demonstrated their party's growing strength and influence among many of the city's working class.[19]

In Chicago, such partisan infighting on May Day took a back seat as both the CP and the SP had to deal with a ban on parades, which the city had enacted in 1934. The municipal government implemented the ban in reaction to a series of bombings that had occurred on May Day in 1933. On May 1 at 2:30 A.M., an explosion tore through the warehouse of the Hibbard-Spencer-Bartlett Hardware Company on East North Water Street. Less than three minutes later, a bomb went off two blocks north at the Willet Bus and Teaming Company on East Grand Avenue. Within the next five minutes, the final three explosions occurred in the offices and plant of the Illinois Bell Telephone Company on West Washington Street, the Stratford Building on South Wells Street, and a wholesale grocery on West Erie Street. As the *Chicago Daily Tribune* headline screamed, "5 May Day Bombs Jar City." The *Tribune* reported that fifty thousand dollars in damages had occurred "in what police believe to have been a communistic attempt at May day terrorism." Miraculously, no one was killed, but a night watchman was injured by the blast at the Willet barns.[20]

The initial reaction of public authorities and the local press was to assume that radicals were to blame. As the *Tribune* reported, "an utter absence of ordinary motives for any one of the bombings led investigators to the belief that a communistic plot as a May day demonstration was behind them."[21] The intense, closely timed explosions—which blew out windows of adjacent buildings in the Loop, including the Tribune tower, destroyed the first and second floors of the Willet stables, and started a "smoldering fire" at each site—struck fear into the hearts of the city's residents. As an act of urban terror, the bombings were frightening enough, but because they had occurred on May Day, many feared they were part of some broader revolutionary agenda. Once the police commissioner received word of the early-morning events, he posted police guards at all public buildings and issued an "informal warning to industrial executives to protect their plants against possible attack."[22] In addition to bringing in the head of Chicago's bomb squad, John Tracy, to assist in the investigation, the police called on Mike Mills, "the former chief of the bomb squad and the department expert on radicals." Mills was "drafted hurriedly to lead an inquiry into the possible communistic angle of the outrages."[23]

Given the infamous nationwide bomb plot of May Day 1919 and the ghost of the Haymarket bombing that still haunted Chicagoans' public memory, such assumptions were not that far-fetched. Haymarket, in particular, still struck a nerve among the city's residents. But that historic event was recalled in two very different ways. There was the "subversive" memory of martyrdom that workers and radicals in the United States and around the world sustained on May Day and through their creation of the monument at Waldheim Cemetery. But there was also the "official" public memory in Chicago, supported by the editors of the *Tribune* (first Joseph Medill and later Robert R. McCormick), that recalled the event as a riot and cast the police responders as heroes. The latter lent support to the building of the police monument in Haymarket Square in 1889.[24] By the late 1920s, this more conservative version still had traction and may well have informed the reaction to the 1933 bombings. With the help of the mainstream press in constructing and sustaining this official memory, it became the hegemonic, not necessarily the popular, view of the original May 4 events. Because of this interpretation of Haymarket, May Day and violence had become so deeply linked in the minds of many of the city's residents that an event like the 1933 explosions was inevitably blamed on the local socialist or communist community. Even though radicals were not at fault, the association of communists with the damage that had taken place on May Day was hard to refute. It was only after two more bombs went off on May 2 and 3 that police expanded their investigation.[25] Rather than a "communistic" May Day plot, they gradually discovered that the violence was part of an ongoing struggle for control of the local Chicago Teamsters Union and was the handiwork of labor racketeers.[26]

On the day of the initial explosions, when all fingers were pointing at the communists, the CP had protested its innocence and tried to direct attention to the racketeers in the craft unions instead. But until the police investigation uncovered this link, many Chicagoans remained firmly convinced this was yet another May Day plot. Even after the truth came out, the antiradical sentiment remained strong enough to support the city's ban on May Day parades in 1934. As a result, contestation over the holiday in Chicago did not focus so much on disputes between the CP and the SP as between each of the radical parties and the city administration.[27] Unlike in New York, there was less opportunity for impressive May Day displays or the political competition that accompanied it. In the two years following the 1933 bombings, communists and socialists in Chicago busied themselves by trying to regain their right to march on May 1.

May Day parades were staged again in 1935, but only after the CP's May Day committee struggled for more than a month to get the necessary permit. The city council and the mayor at first did not answer the party's repeated requests. It was only after a sustained campaign of telegrams and resolutions that permission was granted at the eleventh hour, on April 29.[28] As was the case in New York, the CP came to dominate the large May Day demonstrations that reemerged in Chicago and expanded its influence among the working class by the mid-1930s.

One of the reasons the Communist Party began to coordinate bigger May Day events than those hosted by the socialists in both New York City and Chicago was the CP's success in appealing to the urban working class during the depression decade. In 1934, for example, the *Daily Worker* claimed that some 200,000 men, women, and children, from the ranks of the party, several industrial unions, the International Workers Order (IWO), and other communist-affiliated fraternal organizations, turned out for New York's May Day parade and joined in the party's mass meeting in Union Square. There they demanded an increase in wages and an end to relief cuts, war, and fascism.[29]

In addition to representing the CP's traditional constituents, the party's 1934 and 1935 May Day parades reflected the fruits of communist efforts to organize within the garment trades and mass industries, as well as within urban African-American communities. The celebration in New York included many members of progressive union locals who had defied the rulings of their internationals not to march, choosing instead to heed the communists' call for a united front. Joining the CP-led parade were members of the Steel and Metal Workers Industrial Union, the Local 499 Painters and Decorators Union, four locals from the AFL-affiliated Bakers Union, the Painters' and Paperhangers' Local 121, the United Textile Workers Union, the Carpenters' Union Local 2090, and the International Ladies' Garment Workers' Union (ILGWU) Local 20.[30] Even though black membership in the party also remained low, there were several predominantly African-American organizations in the ranks that evidenced the CP's participation in the mobilizations against unemployment and high rents in Harlem. These organizations, unofficially affiliated with the party, included the Cafeteria Workers Union, neighborhood Unemployed Councils, and community civil rights leagues.[31]

Some of the progressive union locals that turned out for the CP-led May Day parades in these years were among those whose parent unions founded the Committee for Industrial Organization in 1935. Inspired, in part, by the legal protections afforded unions under the New Deal's Wagner Act, eight international unions, including the United Mine Workers (UMW), the Amalgamated Clothing Workers of America (ACWA), and the ILGWU, formed the Committee for Industrial Organization in November 1935 within the AFL in an effort to unionize mass-production workers in basic industries, including steel, auto, rubber, and textiles. After winning recognition for the new unions in the steel and auto industries in 1937, the Committee for Industrial Organization broke with the AFL in May 1938 and became the Congress of Industrial Organizations (CIO), with more than three million members in thirty-two unions.[32] Communist organizers had been active in developing the CIO from the start. Despite the anticommunist sentiments of John L. Lewis, president of the UMW, and David Dubinsky, president of the ILGWU, those communists initially were welcomed for their hard work and dedication to building up the unions. They were also a strong presence within some AFL affiliates, including the New York City locals of the Painters Union, the Cafeteria, Hotel, and Restaurant Employees Union, and Local 5 of the Federation of Teachers.[33] These locals joined the others in the CP-led May Day parades during the mid-1930s.

In addition to the sympathy the CP was winning from left-led union locals, it had increased its public presence in the nation's cities in a number of ways during the late 1920s and early 1930s. Through its grassroots activism fighting against hunger, unemployment, and evictions, the party became a familiar sight in many working-class neighborhoods. This work, carried out on the local level and often mostly by women members, began during the party's third period, despite contradictory official pronouncements.[34] Such neighborhood work awakened many urban workers to the relevance of the party in their communities. In its May Day parades, the CP increased its profile further, dramatically broadcasting its political agenda while accommodating a host of supporters. Its popular appeal grew among a wide range of social reformers who, although they may never have officially become members of the party, were interested in linking their struggle for civil rights, jobs, peace, and social justice to the organizing activity of the communists. Those activities included May 1 demonstrations as an annual rallying point.[35] These reformers consisted of a broad and loose coalition of unions fighting for jobs and better wages, neighborhood and tenant leagues fighting against evictions and police brutality, civil rights organizations, and fraternal organizations voicing opposition to fascism. Some groups, like the International Labor Defense and the John Reed Clubs, were tied tightly to CP leadership. Others, like the Federation of German Workers' Clubs and a delegation from Father Divine's congregation, were not.[36] Most had some followers who were CP members, and many who never joined the party. In working with these different groups in New York and Chicago, the Communist Party gradually increased its influence among the working class in both cities.

Thus, out of the partisan wrangling of the early 1930s, the CP emerged on solid footing with strong ties to more progressive unions and neighborhood organizations, ready to take the lead in organizing the May Day events of the Popular Front years. Nevertheless, the CP would still face opposition from Old Guard socialists and their union allies, who endured schisms within their organizations over the question of whether to unite with communists on May Day. The annual holiday, long a rallying point for radicals, became a very public test of political loyalties for both Socialist Party and union members.

The act of choosing whether to join with the communists on May Day was of particular concern to those on the left. Yet, because those socialists and unionists who grappled with this choice appealed to particular definitions of Americanism in the process of asserting their position, they broadened the meaning of this debate beyond the narrow confines of the political left. Their actions laid bare the ways that such radicals publicly defined their understanding of themselves as socialists and as Americans, or as progressive workers and as Americans. Communists, too, contributed to the construction of radical Americanism during the Popular Front years, offering their own version of this identity. Each group at once worked within, pushed against, and forged new dimensions to public definitions of Americanism in the depression and New Deal era. So while much of the history of May Day during the latter part of the 1930s was caught up in continued partisan infighting, the fact that the struggle was contextualized within a larger debate about national identity—a debate that was then, in turn, influenced by these left-wing struggles—makes it relevant to the broader story of the construction of American nationalism.

During the mid- to late 1930s, several left-led unions in New York were caught up in this debate. As American workers, members of these unions confronted the question of whether to join with the communists on May Day. Although the Communist Party had gained the support of many locals, particularly those affiliated with the young CIO, many unionists continued to distrust communists in the labor movement. They believed that communist organizers took their orders from Moscow. Max Zaritsky, the socialist president of the United Cloth Hat, Cap and Millinery Workers, felt that they were "misleading our honest boys and girls." Zaritsky believed that CP policy, not the best interest of union members, dictated the organizers' actions. He vowed that he would "not entrust any responsible work [in his union] to any one who is a member of the Communist party."[37] For many in the labor movement, this distrust of the Communist Party did not fade away by the mid-1930s, when the calls for united-front May Day celebrations increased.[38]

For others, the idea of forming a united May Day with the CP-dominated United Front May Day Committee was appealing, and consistent with their understanding of themselves as radical Americans. In 1936, Charles Zimmerman, manager of Local 22, ILGWU in New York, took the initiative and set up a Provisional United Labor May Day Conference. This new committee included Zimmerman, A. Philip Randolph, president of the Brotherhood of Sleeping Car Porters, and managers from the city's pocketbook workers', meat cutters', bakery workers', and painters' unions.[39] It proposed that there be one united May Day parade that year to demonstrate labor's solidarity, especially in light of fascism's growing power abroad and of the continued rise of unemployment and wage cuts at home.[40] Taking a strong stand on these issues in public was deemed more important than maintaining their distance from the communists; it was seen as not only a desirable protest, but also a necessary one for those who considered themselves radical Americans. Zimmerman's Local 22 responded positively to the committee's call and sent five delegates to the meeting at the Hotel Delano, where future plans were to be arranged. It also pledged two hundred fifty dollars for the arrangements.[41] Within Local 155, a "Knitgoods Workers May Day Initiative Committee" was formed to organize support for the united effort among its union's members.[42]

Upon hearing about this call for united action, ILGWU President David Dubinsky reprimanded Zimmerman for his efforts. Writing to Zimmerman that March, Dubinsky chided him for calling the united May Day conference. He argued that Zimmerman had broken the union's disciplinary rules by taking such action without first securing approval from the International, and that in so doing he had risked the unity of the International.[43] Dubinsky was worried about the fissures within the garment unions between the Old Guard and militants over how to relate to the CP, especially on May Day.[44] He wanted union members to know that the only May Day event they should attend was the mass meeting that the union and the SP were planning to hold on the Polo Grounds, not the united parade promoted by Zimmerman and his supporters. In an open letter issued that spring, Dubinsky directed his union members to proceed directly to the sporting facility on 157th Street for the authorized May Day meeting, not to Union Square where the communists were planning to rally after their parade.[45] For Dubinsky, ensuring ILGWU unity at the Polo Grounds and keeping its members away from the United May Day parade was essential to maintaining discipline within the union and the legitimacy of his leadership. He believed that Zimmerman's organizing the Provisional May Day committee was a direct attack on his authority as president and another manifestation of the CP's attempt to reach into the ILGWU and the SP by appealing to the noncommunist militants among them.[46]

Dubinsky's fears were well founded. The push for the United Front May Day did come from within the ILGWU locals, but was not necessarily cultivated by the CP as directly as he thought. Local 22 was a stronghold for so-called Lovestonites, the right-opposition communists who were officially expelled from the CP in 1929 for criticizing the Comintern's analysis of capitalism and the coming revolution. Jay Lovestone, leader of this right-opposition, believed in the distinctiveness of American capitalism and rejected Moscow's predictions for its speedy collapse.[47] Zimmerman had once been closely aligned with Lovestone. Although he had cast off his communist affiliation in the late 1920s and had become an ally of Dubinsky's by the 1930s, Zimmerman and his fellow members of Local 22 believed so strongly in the need for a united front on May Day in 1936 that they were willing to cooperate with the CP. By 1936, many on the left considered the threat of fascism and reaction to be so great that only united action among radicals, progressives, and labor could stop it.

Norman Thomas, national leader of the Socialist Party, agreed with the argument for unity and supported efforts to construct a "harmonious May Day." In a letter to Luigi Antonini, manager of Local 89 of the ILGWU, he argued that "the danger of reaction, even of Fascism, in America is so great that labor ought to be able to get together on one day on the basis of labor issues without committing itself to a program of political action." According to Thomas, "if Communists are included in unions they can be included in the line of March [sic]."[48] He applauded the plans that were made for the meeting at the Polo Grounds but also encouraged participation among SP members in the united parade.[49] In Chicago, the Cook County SP supported united action as well, and decided to join with the CP for a single demonstration of labor unity. In its display of labor and radical solidarity on May Day, the party there also sought the support of the city's progressive labor unions that were affiliated with the AFL.[50]

These efforts at united action among the CP, the SP, and progressive unions, no matter how informal or temporary, were met with criticism from dissenters within the SP and some unions. Many doubted the communists' intentions and were hostile to attempts to create a joint event.[51] In Chicago, the Northwest Verband and German Branches of the SP protested the party district's decision to join the united May Day,[52] while in New York, the SP's right wing made its disapproval known, stating that it would withdraw its membership if the party went ahead with the united parade. Harry Laidler, chairman of the Public Affairs Committee of the SP, responded to this threat, arguing that the united action was limited and that those who favored cooperation with communists on May Day were still "opposed to organic unity" with the CP. Despite Laidler's attempts to justify the need for the socialists to work occasionally with communists "in the fight against specific evils such as war and suppression of civil rights," the right wing seceded from the SP that year and formed the Social Democratic Federation (SDF).[53] As American socialists, these dissenters could not see themselves allied with those they believed were beholden to Moscow, no matter how many progressive concerns they may have shared.

For those who remained in the SP and who did not balk at the idea of temporarily cooperating with the communists, the united May Day parades of 1936 and 1937 were a success. Thousands of communists, socialists, and trade unionists turned out for the celebration. Nearly 300,000 took to the streets in Manhattan and some 15,000 marched in Chicago. The Socialist Party sound truck was a popular feature in the Chicago parade, while colorful contingents from the IWO and the lively CP-sponsored floats drew attention in New York.[54]

Even as each group was united in celebrating May Day, it carried its own banners and marched in distinct delegations. As Harry Laidler noted, the unity for action on specific causes (including the fight against war and fascism and the struggle for civil rights and social insurance) did not equal ideological or organizational uniformity among the loose coalition of unions, party locals, neighborhood leagues, and ethnic and fraternal clubs that joined the May Day parade. Although the hundreds of thousands who marched in New York and the several thousand who came out in Chicago made an impressive display of their solidarity on these core issues, each of the different progressive and radical groups that demonstrated on May Day maintained its ideological, political, and organizational autonomy.

For some socialists and communists, however, even this degree of united action was problematic. The absence of the Old Guard of the SP, which had reorganized itself into the SDF, exemplified how the persistence of ideological divisions prevented certain groups from joining the united May Day parade. At times, communists within the CPUSA also expressed hesitation over working with those who had been expelled from their ranks but who continued to organize and work within the city's unions. In Chicago, for example, the CP's District 18 refused to work with one of the delegates at the united May Day Conference in 1937 because it claimed he was a Trotskyist and a counter-revolutionary.[55] The mainstream CP applied such labels freely to anyone who did not adhere strictly to the official Stalinist party line, not just to those who had been expelled from the CP in 1928 for supporting Leon Trotsky and who later formed a left-opposition to the party.[56]

Such intellectual rigidity made united action difficult and suggests how some communists sought to defend their political identities in narrow, orthodox terms. In one case, this intolerance resulted in a violent encounter during the 1937 united parade in Chicago. The Revolutionary Workers League, with only seventeen members in line, carried banners that apparently "were obnoxious to the Stalinates [sic]." Four times during the march, they "were assailed by [the communists] with sticks." One YPSL member who "attempted to defend [the Revolutionary Workers League members] was sent to the hospital" with two missing teeth and a severely injured face. Clearly, the experience of these parades at the grassroots level belied the niceties of progressive harmony that the official party presses projected. As one socialist who witnessed the event acidly commented, "that is a united front for you."[57]

It was not only socialists who were cynical about the ability of communists to carry out united May Day demonstrations with those they had otherwise and for so long disdained. Richard Wright, who would become one of America's leading black literary figures, recalled what he believed was the hypocrisy of the CP's claim to facilitate working-class and radical unity on May 1 when he remembered his experience in the 1936 Chicago parade. Wright, who was a member of the party at that time, had fallen afoul of the local CP leadership. As a writer, freethinker, and friend of another party member who had been tried as a counter-revolutionary, Wright had been branded an intellectual Trotskyist and was no longer on good terms with local party leaders.[58] On May 1, 1936, he tried to join the parade anyway but discovered on his arrival downtown that his union local had already left the staging area. An old party friend in the CP's South Side delegation invited Wright to join the Communist Party section in the parade, reassuring him that because it was May Day, everyone was welcome.[59]

No sooner had Wright hesitatingly heeded the advice of his friend than Cy Perry, the white district leader of the CP in Chicago, shouted at him to "get out of our ranks!"[60] Although Wright protested, Perry continued to demand that he be removed. No one came to Wright's aid. Finally, Perry grabbed Wright, lifted him up, and threw him out of the ranks onto the curb across the road. Wright, having been cast out of the party for his ideological "fault," had been literally tossed aside as his former fellow communists looked on "with cold eyes of non-recognition."[61] His former comrades had rendered him a nonperson.

The united May Day parade then surged forward, as the "vast ranks of the Communist Party began to move." As Wright remembered it, the "scarlet banners with the hammer and sickle emblem of world revolution were lifted, and they fluttered in the May breeze. Drums beat. Voices were chanting. The tramp of many feet shook the earth. A long line of set-faced men and women, white and black, flowed past me."[62] Wright's eerie description of the disciplined and closed ranks of the communist marchers suggests the ideological rigidity, the "darkness" he believed characterized the party's suppression of free thought, which had resulted in his expulsion. It indicated, moreover, one of the ways these "united" May Day demonstrations functioned at the grassroots level: to reinforce the uniformity of official communist doctrine and the party's authority among its followers.

It was this kind of ideological rigidity that Wright disdained and later criticized. Writing as a former communist during the height of the Cold War in 1950, he offered an indictment of the party's suppression of free thought, explaining that this oppression was one of the main reasons why he eventually left the CP in 1944. As an intellectual and freethinker, he found it impossible to be associated with such an inflexible movement. Yet, he also explains how his original involvement with the party in the 1930s stemmed from his admiration of its activist struggle for workers' rights and civil rights.[63] His attraction to communism was something many socially conscious young liberals shared during the depression decade.

One such young liberal was Wendell Carroll. Like Wright, Carroll admired the CP's civil rights activism. But unlike Wright, Carroll never joined the Communist Party, only briefly flirting with it as a member of the American Youth for Democracy (AYD). Yet, he, like Wright, felt the fury of the CP's sectarianism when as an AYD member he came to the defense of three Socialist Workers Party representatives. Communist Party members in the AYD accused him of being a Trotskyist and a counterrevolutionary. In an oral history recorded in 1983, Carroll recalled being stunned by this attack. He remembered how he had become the object of rumors and the subject of "subtle threats of violence." Carroll's brief encounter with the hardcore sectarians of the CP reinforced his assessment that the party was at heart authoritarian, even totalitarian.[64] As Wright experienced it, this ugly face of the party exposed its fangs even during what was meant to be a day of radical unity. But as the official tactics behind the CP's call for the united May Day have shown, the event always was intended, by the party leadership at least, to be turned to such sectarian purposes.

As Wright's former friend in the South Side Section demonstrated before his district leader intimidated him, the *rank and file* of the CP did not always see the united May Day demonstrations in the same rigid fashion as their leaders. Some progressives and unionists, especially those outside the Communist Party, did call for genuinely united action that reached beyond their leadership's ideological and partisan barriers. One ILGWU member in New York expressed this desire in 1936. L. Barkin penned his message on the back of a letter that David Dubinsky had sent out to the union membership directing them not to attend the CP-led united May Day parade but to go instead to the socialist and union gathering at the Polo Grounds. Barkin protested by returning the letter and asking in his scrawled hand, "do we ever expect to reach a happy medium when we are divided into groups—instead of one solid block?" Concluding, he asserted that "since the United Front May Day Committee has a broader base and a wider united front—Im [sic] afraid I shall have to be a 'disloyal' union member & march on Fifth Ave. where 'unity' is a sincere slogan & not a farce."[65]

For Barkin, the United Front May Day was more impressive and it attracted him to its ranks. The Old Guard of the ILGWU and the SP seemed a greater threat to working-class unity than the CP's dogmatism that Wright and Carroll had confronted. Over the next few years, working-class and progressive groups in New York and Chicago would have to decide whose side they were on. Many followed Barkin into the CP-led united May Day demonstrations during the Popular Front years beginning in 1938. But others, who either maintained their skepticism of the CP or became disillusioned with what they saw as the party's authoritarianism, continued to organize separate May Day celebrations.

By the late 1930s, May Day thus continued to be a forum for and object of left-wing political struggles. At the same time, the holiday remained caught up in the larger debate about radical and working-class Americanism. On the one hand, the CP and its supporters came to articulate one version of this Americanism in their May Day parades during the Popular Front years that drew the support of large numbers of people in New York and Chicago. On the other hand, the SP and its union supporters (including even the militants who split from their united front with the communists after 1939) continued to defend their understanding of radical and working-class Americanism, which they believed was truly democratic and had no ties to Moscow. As the CP came to dominate May Day in the closing years of the 1930s, socialists and workers who found the political gap between themselves and the communists too great to cross continued to defend their own distinct brand of Americanism; and, they came to reject May Day as a Soviet-dominated event that they now considered useless as a site for the expression of true American political sympathies.

Although Old Guard socialists and many workers would not support the communist-dominated Popular Front May Day celebrations, those events had implications beyond such internal left-wing strife. The holiday's parades became a forum where CP members and supporters could construct their understanding of themselves as radical Americans. May Day enabled them to push for an even more inclusive and democratic Americanism, in terms of race and class, than that found in the broader political culture of the New Deal. While that culture embraced the idea of industrial democracy (as seen in the Wagner Act of 1935), and the administrative and regulatory state (as evidenced in programs like the Tennessee Valley Authority, the Works Progress Administration, and in laws like the Glass-Steagall Act), it did not prioritize the fight for African-American civil rights, nor did it seek to usher in a socialist commonwealth, despite the fears of its conservative critics. On May Day, communists, radical reformers, and left-leaning unionists called for the New Deal order to embrace these broader concerns and challenged the nation to transform itself in the process.[66]

The progressive groups that marched in CP-led Popular Front May Day parades called for an America that would support a broad array of labor and civil rights and that would stand up to all forms of fascist aggression. Central to achieving these goals was working-class unity, which many, like Barkin, believed was best achieved by turning out on May Day with the CP. By 1938, the party managed to win the support of many labor unions and progressive organizations for its united May Day demonstrations. In New York, not only had several locals in the ILGWU broken with their national leadership to join the united CP May Day, but also some AFL affiliates did the same, such as District Council 9 of the Painters Union. They took to the streets on May 1 with the city's CP branches, the Young Communist League, and the IWO. In Chicago, new CIO affiliates, such as the

Figure 5.2. Despite objections from the AFL, DC 9 of the Painters Union in New York participated in the 1936 May Day parade. Tamiment Library, New York University. Photograph by John Albok.

Steelworkers Organizing Committee and Typographical Union 16, joined with the Workmen's Circles to march for "jobs, security, and peace."[67]

From 1938 to 1941, between 50,000 and 70,000 men, women, and children paraded in Chicago, and some 200,000 marched in New York, where up to 500,000 people lined the streets as spectators each May 1.[68] Party and union members were joined by local branches of progressive community groups, including Unemployed Councils, tenants' leagues, and youth organizations, and members of the more recently created unions of artists, writers, accountants, and other professionals.⁶⁹ Such celebrations marked May Day's high point in the United States. Despite the absence of the Old Guard socialists and their union allies, these Popular Front May Day events comprised the largest demonstration of radical and working-class strength in the holiday's history.

In many ways, such events indicated how May Day became Popular Front America's greatest public holiday, resonating with the depression and New Deal era's concern for labor rights and other progressive reforms. Workers, socialists, and communists had struggled for decades to secure union recognition and the right to bargain collectively, for safer working conditions, shorter working hours, better wages, and unemployment insurance. These goals had been the rallying cries of many a May Day parade. Now, during the Roosevelt administration's period of "bold experimentation" in the face of the unprecedented crisis of the Great Depression, New Deal programs met many of these goals. With the Wagner Act, the Fair Labor Standards Act, and the Social Security Act, the federal government moved workers' rights to the center of its reform agenda. This more hospitable environment for labor activism enabled those workers and radicals who wanted to tap into the broader New Deal reform ethos to do so with relative ease. While workers and radicals would keep up their fight to make union recognition a reality in the face of continued

Figure 5.3. Teachers Union Local 5, AFL marched in New York's 1937 May Day parade, despite the objections of the AFL. Tamiment Library, New York University. Photograph by Daniel Nilva.

employer opposition, their May Day celebrations now fit more comfortably within the broader culture of reform that characterized America during the New Deal era. From this position radicals pushed for even greater social and economic change, challenging America to address the persistence of class-based and racial inequality, ultimately, for some, through the establishment of a communist order.

CP members housed this more radical political agenda within a growing and more Americanized movement. May Day's deeper cultural resonance during the 1930s was also partly due to this change in the social profile of its organizers and participants. By the late 1930s, a majority of the CP's members were no longer immigrants or the unemployed; more were unionized, and most new recruits were working, white-collar professionals who were mainly native-born children of immigrant parents.[70] The turn to more overt demonstrations of American patriotism in the May Day parades of these years was partly a reflection of the Americanization of the party's membership. It also was the result of the party's official abandonment of its third-period analysis. Instead, it now embraced an array of progressive groups as it pursued a Popular Front policy against fascism and for labor and civil rights. In addition to the support that individual party members and supporters lent to these issues, presenting them on May Day as indicators of their identities as radical Americans, the party used the May Day demonstrations in these years in a more instrumental way to pursue its political agenda. Both the vernacular concerns of the rank and file and the official interests of the party leadership are suggested in the details of the May Day displays.

One of the most notable features of communist Popular Front May Day demonstrations was their celebration of America and American democracy. The CP had made symbolic nods to the nation and its democratic heritage in previous May Day events, but not to the extent visible later in the Popular Front years. During the third period, communists emphasized May Day's international scope and history, and only marginally tapped into the symbols of America's *revolutionary* heritage. Before 1938, some American flags were carried alongside the party's red flag in the parades, for example, and the IWO constructed a float that referred to the heritage of 1776 in its fight for a social insurance bill in 1936. But until 1938, the Socialist Party parades were where purposeful attention was given to the totemic use of the Stars and Stripes as a signifier of the SP's particular adherence to the nation's democratic heritage.[71] It was not until the Communist Party officially included the amalgamation of this heritage with its political plan in 1938 that it brought out these symbols so overtly each May Day. During the late Popular Front period, the party heavily emphasized U.S. *democratic* traditions more than it praised the Soviet model.[72]

Partly, then, this celebration of American democracy resulted from the grassroots patriotism of its more socially diverse party members and progressive supporters who made up a new Popular Front coalition, many of whom had been born in America and sincerely held such vernacular beliefs. This coalition "became a radical historical bloc uniting industrial unionists, communists, independent socialists, community activists, and émigré anti-fascists around laborist social democracy, anti-fascism, and anti-lynching," and was, therefore, broader than and distinct from the official Popular Front policy of the CP.[73] Yet, the exalting of America and its democratic heritage on May Day also reflected the party's latest official position, which Earl Browder pronounced at Carnegie Hall during the Tenth National Convention of the CPUSA in 1938. Outlining the party's commitment to both the democratic front and the continued push for the realization of socialism, Browder described this new approach as being built on an "amalgamation" of the political philosophies of Jefferson, Marx, Engels, Lenin, and Stalin. He asserted that in its fight for the "full Communist program," the CPUSA was "carrying on the work of Jefferson, Paine, Jackson and Lincoln." The party, Browder argued, would see to the full realization of the nation's democratic promise in the birth of socialism through democracy, understood as an extension of America's heritage of freedom from 1776 and 1865. "Communism," Browder declared, "is twentieth-century Americanism."[74]

In the months and years that followed this proclamation, the party focused its policies and organizational activities on methods that better engaged with the American political environment, specifically America's tradition of democracy represented in its revolutionary founding (1776) and the transformative experience of emancipation (1865). If they could win a majority of Americans over to communism, party leaders argued, the transformation to a workers' state would be democratically fostered.[75] Attention to this tradition, and its "amalgamation" with communism, was symbolically achieved in the CP's May Day parades in a number of ways.

One of the most notable visible expressions of this reference to the nation's democratic tradition was the overwhelming presence of American flags that marchers carried along with red flags during the parade. John Albok, a tailor and amateur photographer, captured such displays in the photographs and rare film footage he took of these May Day parades.[76]

Figure 5.4. With raised fists and American flags these May Day marchers demonstrate their hybrid radical American identities during a 1938 May Day parade in New York. Tamiment Library, New York University. Photograph by John Albok.

For example, in 1938, almost every contingent in the parade was headed by a color guard of men and women carrying the American flag who marched along with others carrying the red flag and the banner of their organization.[77] Many flag bearers held the Stars and Stripes in one hand and lifted their other fist in salute, further integrating symbols from the two political traditions.[78] In so doing, they made visible their support for a militant American democracy they believed would be based on strong worker and radical solidarity. Such displays suggest both the individual identifications of the parade's participants and the official agenda of the party, which coordinated the events.

This melding of Marxist and American political traditions was also represented in one of the parade floats used in Chicago. It depicted the images of Lincoln, Washington, and Jefferson off to one side and those of Marx, Lenin, and Stalin to the other. Above the slogan "For Progress Democracy Peace & Socialism" was the image of Earl Browder. By visual implication, Browder was presented as the man to lead the party—and the nation—into achieving these goals by drawing from the best traditions that were represented by both sets of "founding fathers." Browder would combine America's democratic and revolutionary heritage with the teachings of leading socialist and communist figures to create a social democracy of peace and plenty.[79]

The party's desire to represent the compatibility of communism with American democracy also inspired its written accounts of May 1. These touted May Day's birth in America as evidence of the radical holiday's relevance in the United States. A *Daily Worker* article heralded May Day as "the symbol of labor's march to freedom, peace and Socialism." It deemed the holiday "as American as July Fourth, as American as baseball, or the Star-Spangled Banner," arguing that "fifty years of May Days have made this tradition part of the marrow of American life."[80] Here the CP again proclaimed the American roots of the holiday, even though for so long it had ignored this history in favor of May Day's international resonance. In the new era of the Popular Front, Communist Party leaders deemed this claim to a national identification better suited to building a broad-based progressive, antifascist movement. But, of course, as these leaders understood it, the party would direct that movement. The dramatic transformation from the earlier, third-period written accounts of May Day to these Popular Front interpretations is stark evidence of the instrumental nature of the party's embrace of American democracy.

Beyond this newly honed focus on the importance of America's democratic heritage, the Communist Party expressed renewed recognition of the power and value of distinct ethnic traditions within American society. This notion had emerged slowly from the experiences of the party at the grassroots level since the early 1930s. To organize successfully within the nation's diverse urban communities, the CP found it beneficial to establish party branches there and to work within existing community organizations, which were often ethnically or racially based. The party also encouraged the formation of foreign-language federations within its fraternal organization, the IWO, including the IWO's Junior Division for children, which paralleled, and sometimes replaced, these neighborhood ethnic or national associations.[81] A celebration of this democratic ethnic pluralism, understood as intrinsic to the American experience, became a defining characteristic of the Communist Popular Front May Day demonstrations.[82] Again, both official party motives and sincerely felt individual reasons drove such demonstrations. For the party, embracing ethnic pluralism would help swell the ranks; for the individual member or fellow traveler, it indicated the value they placed on social diversity and multiethnic harmony, which they celebrated as uniquely American.

On May 1, 1939, several sections of the IWO paraded in New York under a banner proclaiming "Immigrants All—Americans All," in what they called a "March of All Nations." The younger members of the group's Junior Section walked in costumes intended to represent the garb native to their particular ancestral homeland.[83] The celebration of American pluralism, and ostensibly the democracy that allowed it to flourish, served as a poignant repudiation of the fascist regimes in Europe, where such diversity was not tolerated. Behind the IWO sections marched other groups, such as the Italian May Day Committee, the United Ukrainian Organizations, the Russian May Day Committee, and the Federation of German-American Clubs.[84] Those who turned out in their ethnic dress might have sincerely entered into the event as a celebration of the pluralism and freedom that characterized American society.

This exalting of diversity within the CP-led May Day parade was quite striking, however, given the experiences of many national groups abroad under the Soviet communist regime. During the late 1930s, Soviet xenophobia fueled a concern over the security of the borderlands and the loyalty of its residents, resulting in a "national operations" policy of forced migration, arrests, deportations, and executions of hundreds of thousands of Poles, Germans, Ukrainians, and others. This policy was responsible for nearly one-fifth of all arrests and one-third of all executions during the Great Terror of 1937–1938.[85] CPUSA members and those progressives who joined them in the Popular Front May Day parades either chose to ignore these events or were unaware of them. Instead of acknowledging the existence of such "hard line" policies in the Soviet Union, they celebrated the "soft line" tactics of ethnic boosting that had existed in the borderlands before the implementation of the national operations policy.[86] Whether out of ignorance or denial, American communists did not protest the evils taking place in the Soviet Union. Along with members of the city's many ethnic benevolent organizations, they instead celebrated the beauty of American pluralism in their May Day parades. Many may have genuinely exalted this aspect of American culture as a sign of their nation's strength and freedom; it became another way to construct a radical *American* identity for themselves. Others, especially those higher up in the party, may have also recognized how they could appropriate this celebration of diversity to represent their partisan cause. The "March of All Nations" thus visually suggested the international harmony that could emerge once communism took root around the globe.

Figure 5.5. The Ukrainian IWO on parade in New York on May Day, 1938. Tamiment Library, New York University. Photograph by John Albok.

At the same time, by presenting themselves as a political party that embraced such diversity, the CP also contributed to the pluralist and populist trends that marked America's New Deal–era Popular Front culture. Emerging within a political climate that favored the idea of industrial democracy, this culture celebrated the average American worker and heralded American pluralism as intrinsic to the nation's greatness. The blue-collar, working-class hero became a familiar presence in the art and literature of the period, often represented in the exaggerated form of a brawny male factory worker. Other artistic representations produced in this decade, including Earl Robinson and John LaTouche's "Ballad for Americans" (a popular labor cantata that was also played during CP-led May

Day parades),[87] celebrated the average American worker and the notion of "the people" as an inclusive mix of all races, religions, and ethnicities.[88]

By welcoming different ethnic organizations into the annual May Day parade, the CP expressed its support for this broader Popular Front and voiced its recognition of America's social diversity. Yet, officially the party hoped to draw these groups into a coalition within the CP, partly through the organizing work of the IWO and mass demonstrations on May Day. Like the many strands of ribbon that hang from a maypole, the CP sought to wind these different national groups together around the central axis of its communist program to work for the ultimate realization of the new socialist order. Just as it strove for the solidarity of workers around the world, so, too, it worked for solidarity among the many ethnic and racial groups within the United States.

The CP also may have used these spectacles of American pluralism and democratic promise as a defensive tactic in reaction to accusations made from within the labor movement, which asserted that May 1 was inherently un-American. Even though the Popular Front May Day demonstrations represented a climax in both the size and the breadth of participation in the holiday, including more than a half million people in New York in the late 1930s, most political moderates and conservatives did not observe the day. This included many workers who, because of the CP's dominance over the holiday, thought it was irrelevant. Even for socialists, who hoped to maintain the vibrancy of May Day as an opportunity to express their radical American identities, the communist presence became too much to bear. They continued to challenge the integrity of the CP-led parades throughout this decade. Paradoxically, this critique that the communist May Day was un-American came right on the heels of the holiday's heyday in the United States. The struggle over May 1 within the left that occurred between 1939 and 1941 in many ways presaged the holiday's ultimate fate. After World War II, communists would try to resuscitate May Day and defend it as an American event, but most citizens, and eventually even the more progressive workers among them, would come to reject it as a foreign import from Moscow that served no useful or redeeming political or cultural purpose in the United States.

Such aspersions came not only from the traditional antiradical corners of the AFL and the mainstream press, but also now, in the late 1930s, from former supporters of the united-front movement.[89] Much of this nascent hostility toward May Day was really aimed at the CP, which had come to dominate the annual celebration, and that anger was in turn rooted in the shock of the Nazi-Soviet Pact, announced in August 1939. It was not just the Old Guard socialists who continued to criticize the CP and its May Day events. It was now the militants, who had once expressed support for a united front, who denounced the communists. While the Old Guard socialists may not have been surprised at Stalin's self-serving embrace of Hitler's offer of a ten-year nonaggression pact, the militants (and even some communists) were shocked and horrified by the implications of such a deal. The mere creation of the pact signaled an unprincipled about-face on the part of the Soviets, as they appeased those whom they had for so long declared their greatest enemy. But the diplomatic agreement with fascist Germany had at its core the understanding that neither side would interfere if the other engaged in warfare. Not only did this signal the Soviets' willingness to turn a blind eye to whatever madness Germany may have planned to unleash on the continent as it advanced its drive for territorial expansion, but it also convinced the SP that Stalin had imperialist designs of his own. He would play those out in the Baltic states in the months following the formation of the pact. Rather than standing firm against the spread of fascism across Europe, it seemed to many observers that the Soviets had actually aided and abetted its advance, while at the same time exposing their own imperialist intentions for the partition of Eastern Europe.[90]

For many socialists, especially those who were Jewish, there could be no rapprochement with American communists once they defended this nonaggression pact. Even the former militant Charles Zimmerman found the breach too great to cross. In 1940, he added his voice to the chorus of those criticizing not only the communists, but also the CP-dominated May Day holiday. Writing in the *New York Sun*, Zimmerman argued that the spring holiday had lost its relevance for American workers. This once ardent supporter of the event, even in its united-front manifestation, now insisted that May Day no longer represented any segment of the American labor movement.[91]

Although the CP harshly criticized him for these comments, Zimmerman was partly correct. Despite the party's efforts to organize May Day as a celebration of America's political heritage and democratic ethnic pluralism, after 1939, many laborers, including those like Zimmerman who had supported united action before, began to reject May 1 demonstrations. Communist domination of the holiday made it unbearable to those who disagreed with the party's politics and its newly found opposition to the war against fascism. To them, May Day appeared to have become a tool of Moscow. And even for many of those on the left, it had become "un-American." Looking back on her life as a labor organizer and CP member, Pauline Dougherty recognized this problem. She believed that American workers like herself, native-born Irish and Yankee workers, had by the early 1940s come to identify more comfortably with the September Labor Day holiday. Dougherty argued that she and others like her had come to see May Day as an alien import from Russia, even though it originated in the United States. The holiday's affiliation with communism, and with the immigrant and second-generation workers in the CP ranks, did more for many native-born workers to erase those American roots than the flags and floats of the Popular Front did to claim it.[92]

Immigrant union members, like those within the ILGWU and ACWA locals who had temporarily embraced the CP-dominated May Day events in the mid- to late 1930s, also gradually became frustrated with the party's control of the holiday and began to feel at odds with its purpose. This sense of alienation grew after August 1939 as the communists lost touch with the pulse of what remained of the Popular Front left. Soon after the announcement of the Nazi-Soviet Pact, the party fell in line behind Moscow's orders and quickly prioritized its antiwar agenda over the fight against fascism. "The Yanks Are Not Coming!" became the new rallying cry. Communists displayed the slogan on posters at the party's New York headquarters and shouted it out during their May Day parades. For many laborers, even for many of the most progressive among them, and for many radicals, too, such a move indicated that the CP had lost all moral authority.[93]

And so, by late 1939, many leaders and members of the ILGWU's most progressive locals, like Zimmerman's Local 22, were convinced that communists pursued political goals that were anathema to the interests of American workers.[94] Instead of pursuing a united front with the CPUSA, most ILGWU locals decided to hold their own May Day meetings and demonstrations where they could focus on issues of immediate concern, such as bringing an end to relief cuts.[95] Although the radical rank and file from within some locals protested the separate events and voiced their desire to have the International join in the united front with the CP, by 1940, Dubinsky and Zimmerman led most of the union away from the joint events, overseeing independent ILGWU May Day celebrations instead.[96]

Figure 5.6. After the declaration of the Nazi-Soviet Pact in August 1939, the CP re-versed its position in support for the war against fascism. Its new cry, "The Yanks Are Not Coming," became a central feature in the party's May Day parades as illus-trated in this image from the New Masses, *May 7, 1940. Courtesy of the Tamiment Library and Robert F. Wagner Labor Archives, New York University.*

Such independent events would gradually dwindle in size and signifi-cance during the 1940s as the SP faded from the nation's political land-scape.[97] That left the CP as the primary arbiter of May Day, a position it had fought for since the intense partisan contestation of the early 1930s. During the mid-1930s, many party members and supporters had sincerely expressed the harmony they believed existed between their radical politi-cal aspirations and their democratic and pluralist heritage as Americans. By the Popular Front years, the party oversaw such May Day celebra-tions at the moment they resonated most deeply with concerns and val-ues voiced elsewhere in America's New Deal political culture. After World War II, communists and their supporters would struggle to restore the holiday to the glory of those Popular Front days. But the CP's links to Moscow (also celebrated in the parades of the 1930s and made very clear in 1939) sowed the seeds for May Day's alienation in the land of its birth, making the holiday vulnerable to the anticommunist hysteria that would characterize the postwar period.

6

World War II and Public Redefinitions of Americanism

1941–1945

Although May Day had reached a climax in terms of its numerical strength and cultural resonance during the Popular Front years, it did not maintain that position for very long. From World War II through the early years of the Cold War, those radicals and progressives who continued to support May Day would face their most difficult challenges. The holiday went from attracting 700,000 participants and spectators in New York during the late 1930s to its essential disappearance by the late 1950s. But what made the challenges of these years more potent than those raised in earlier decades?

Part of the answer lies in the actions that American communists and workers took during World War II. The Communist Party USA's (CPUSA) suspension of traditional May Day activities during the war was one reason the party could never revive the holiday to its former glory. At the same time, many laborers, be they politically radical or not, found it necessary to look for different ways to define their identities as progressive American workers during this crisis. By creating other forums for expressing their unique sense of working-class Americanism in wartime, these workers began to undermine the vitality of the May 1 holiday in the United States. Alongside the explicitly laborite expressions of patriotic Americanism that workers created on Flag Day and Labor Day during the war years, there also emerged a new holiday: "I Am an American Day." Drawing supporters from a broad cross-section of the population, this event saw newly naturalized citizens pledge their allegiance to the United States in company with longtime residents who took pride in celebrating America's democratic heritage. As the nation focused on uniting against the fascist threat abroad to defend that democracy, public celebrations like Flag Day, Labor Day, and "I Am an American Day," supplanted the suspended May Day events. In addition, African Americans under the leadership of A. Philip Randolph pressed their fight for civil rights within the context of both the wartime "double victory" campaign and the ceremonial assertions of democracy made in the "I Am an American Day" events by organizing a "We Are Americans, Too!" movement. As the nation's political culture shifted to one that accommodated such progressive assertions of democracy and racial equality during the war, class-based expressions of dissent and the May Day celebrations where they were traditionally voiced were nowhere to be found. And so, even before the Cold War would present its own challenges to radicals and workers who wanted to maintain May Day, political and cultural changes that took place during World War II laid the groundwork for the holiday's eventual demise.

By calling for an end to May Day celebrations from 1942 through 1946, the Communist Party (CP) broke the continuity of what had been an annual ritual. It no longer coordinated large Popular Front May Day parades as it had done in New York City and Chicago during the late 1930s. On May 1, 1942, the CP instead sponsored indoor mass meetings in support of the war; in 1943, it joined in a huge prowar rally at Yankee Stadium.[1] The cessation of the grand May Day celebrations was meant to be temporary, so that party members' money and time would be focused on mobilizing the country for battle. The Communist Party's abandonment of May Day parades and strikes resulted, in part, from its decision to support the allied fight against fascism after the German invasion of the Soviet Union in June 1941.

The suspension of parades and strikes was also the result of the disruption that characterized the Communist Party during the latter years of the war. In 1944, Earl Browder broadened the CP's wartime Popular Front policy by calling for it to form an alliance with "progressive capitalists" and to operate as "a pressure group within the Democratic party." In May 1944, the CPUSA was dissolved as an independent party and reorganized itself as the Communist Political Association (CPA) to carry out Browder's vision. The CPA maintained the suspension of communist-dominated May Day events as part of its support for the war effort. By the spring of 1945, however, opposition from communist leaders abroad (the famous Duclos letter) led to a reversal of this policy. The CPUSA reconstituted itself with William Z. Foster at its head in 1946. That same year, Browder was expelled from the party.[2] Coming out of World War II, then,

Spring House Cleaning

Figure 6.1. *After the German invasion of the Soviet Union in June 1941, the CP changed position again and came out in strong support for the fight against fascism, as illustrated here in the cartoon, "Spring House Cleaning," from the* New Masses, *May 5, 1942. Courtesy of the Tamiment Library and Robert F. Wagner Labor Archives, New York University.*

the reanimated CP took up its older revolutionary position once again. In so doing, it also tried to rejuvenate May Day as a rallying point for a rekindled political left.[3] But once the war ended, the party would face the challenge of trying to bring back a celebration—and a political agenda— that even many American workers did not want to see revived.

The reasons for this opposition were rooted in workers' experiences during the war. Union members who had become unhappy with the communist-dominated May Day of the late 1930s, or who wanted to find different ways to demonstrate their support for the war effort, began to turn their attention to more popularly accepted American holidays. In the early 1940s, locals within the Chicago Federation of Labor (CFL) and the International Ladies' Garment Workers' Union (ILGWU), and even the Transport Workers Union (TWU) Local 100, gave their support to reinvigorated Flag Day and Labor Day events. Many of TWU 100's leaders, including its president, Michael Quill, were communists or communist sympathizers, yet this did not stop the union from supporting these patriotic wartime events.[4] TWU membership support for the Flag Day and Labor Day events of 1942 indicated the genuine patriotism of the rank-and-file members, most of whom were not communists.[5] Support for such celebrations also demonstrated one of the ways laborers created a distinct sense of working-class Americanism during the war. In these gatherings they expressed both union militancy and national pride.[6]

Such labor patriotism was evident in the support that the CFL and TWU gave to the special wartime Flag Day parades of 1942. Both unions joined with the American Legion (which had many posts composed of trade union members) and other fraternal organizations to stage grand parades on Flag Day in Chicago and New York.[7] They combined their efforts with those of local public officials in response to President Roosevelt's call for such festivities to celebrate the twenty-seven countries then allied in the fight against fascism. Parades, mass meetings, religious services, and radio broadcasts took place around the nation and around the world.[8] As the Defense Committee of the CFL argued, the parades held in New York and Chicago were intended to show support "to our armed forces everywhere, to our Commander-in-Chief and to all our soldiers in the factories who are working harder than ever to turn out the tools for victory." The committee clearly recognized how workers were integral to the war effort in their capacity as producers of much-needed wartime materiel. But it also acknowledged the importance to the war effort of the patriotic display itself. The Flag Day parade would "bring new life everywhere," the

CFL committee argued, and would "renew our courage and determination to fight to the bitter end for an all-out victory against the enemies of mankind, the axis powers."[9]

Through their participation in the Flag Day parade of 1942, workers ritually linked themselves to the broader war effort and to this wider demonstration of allied unity and power. In New York, where TWU Local 100 joined in the parade, an estimated 500,000 people marched before 2.5 million spectators.[10] The transport workers gathered at Thirtieth Street, west of Eighth Avenue at 1 P.M. Carrying their union banners, they joined the parade, marching up Fifth Avenue to Seventy-second Street.[11] With the thousands of other participants, they passed by the reviewing stand that had been erected on the steps of the New York Public Library at Forty-second Street. As they walked, they were showered with tickertape cast down by spectators in the surrounding tall buildings.

The millions of spectators who lined the avenue saw the transport workers and many other delegations of laborers, "in their work clothes and uniform hats and with the tools of their trade in their hands." They also saw 300 floats go past, some depicting the ravages of war, others showcasing the allied nations and their united strength in opposing Hitler. And finally, they witnessed the long, precise lines of troops from the United States Army marching up the street. Those gathered to view the celebration that day might even have caught a glimpse of the forty fighter planes that roared overhead in a well-timed fly-over. As the *New York Times* described, it was "not only a thrilling sight, but also an impressive demonstration of American military and industrial might, and of the bonds of mutual loyalty and assistance among the nations of America, Europe, and Asia that are linked together to save civilization from the Axis aggressors."[12]

Members of TWU Local 100 in New York, and those unions affiliated with the CFL that turned out to march in Chicago, enthusiastically embraced this spirit of wartime patriotism. In these Flag Day parades they celebrated their unique contribution as workers on the home front (who were supplying and supporting the fight against fascism) as a central part of their public identity.[13] Similar expressions of working-class Americanism could be glimpsed in the plans for the wartime Labor Day parade that CFL leaders promoted in 1942. Riding high on the success of the June Flag Day demonstrations, the federation's officers hoped to stage a great parade of unions on Labor Day that September to reignite the worker's holiday and reinforce the legitimacy of the American Federation of Labor (AFL).

As editorials in the *New York Times* described it, by the mid-1930s, Labor Day had clearly become "a day when the majority of Americans think not so much of labor as of leisure." It had become "part of a three-day weekend" that marked the "termination of the Summer season."[14] Prioritizing leisure over demonstrations of labor's strength and solidarity was not new to the 1930s, of course. Labor leaders like Fitzpatrick had been struggling to stage successful union marches on Labor Day since the late 1900s and 1910s, when the temptations of competing popular entertainments began to rival the more regimented and expensive labor parades.[15] Although some of the newer industrial unions of the young Congress of Industrial Organizations (CIO) in San Francisco took the opportunity to demonstrate their solidarity on Labor Day in 1937 and 1938, the holiday still failed to inspire massive displays of union power around the country.[16]

Delegates from the craft unions that made up the CFL recognized this erosion of the holiday's original significance, even among their own rank-and-file membership. To counter this waning spirit, representatives from the Painters Union Local 180 and the Building Trades Council in Chicago sponsored resolutions at the CFL's regular meeting in June 1941. They called for the CFL to organize "a Parade and Patriotic Rally" on Labor Day, in which "every craft [would] be represented."[17] The motive for this celebration was rooted in the desire to express a sense of labor patriotism similar to that found in the June Flag Day parade. In a letter sent to the secretaries of the federation's locals, the CFL leadership argued that the September event would be a "gigantic demonstration of Union Labor's patriotism, unity and strength."[18] The importance of reclaiming the holiday for organized labor was thus a significant part of the federation's agenda.

Union members, like delegate Arthur Wallace of the Painters Union, who issued the resolution, also wanted to use the day to assert the authority both of their local craft unions and of their regional and national labor federations. In defending his resolution, Wallace argued that "it was more important than ever for the AFL to do everything possible to demonstrate that it is the only real and outstanding labor movement in the country."[19] For Wallace, and those in Chicago's other craft unions who backed his resolution, it was "more important than ever" to assert the authority of their parent federation, the AFL, because of the gains that militant industrial unions within the young Congress of Industrial Organizations had made since its formation as an independent body in May 1938.[20] Those new unions were succeeding in organizing the heavy industries of steel and meatpacking in Chicago, and their members had taken to demonstrating their pride and strength each May Day.[21] AFL officials disdained the CIO not only because of its ties to communist organizers and CP-led May Day events, but also because they considered it a dual union that disrupted the unity of the organized labor movement.[22] By 1941, it was clear that this industrial union movement was neither going to collapse nor give up its autonomy to the AFL. Part of Wallace's desire to revive Labor Day, then, was to use it to demonstrate the continued strength and vigor of the AFL's craft unions, despite the growing organization of his city's industrial sector under the leadership of the rival CIO. The federation's support for Labor Day (and for the wartime patriotism expressed on Flag Day) was of value in and of itself to labor leaders like Wallace, but it was also important as the trappings through which the AFL sought to become the dominant representative of the American labor movement against the competition of communist organizers and the CIO.

Fitzpatrick and other CFL leaders echoed this need to defend the significance of organized labor, and the AFL in particular, both to the wider public and to their own union members. They noted in their letter to the locals' secretaries how "the younger generation, now in the rank and file of our local unions, has never had the opportunity to demonstrate what the trade union movement has taught them."[23] The wartime context exacerbated this reality. Millions of new workers had entered the workforce during the war, and many of them had no experience with unions.[24] Fitzpatrick and his fellow CFL leaders argued that these younger members had to realize that the union was about more than the "benefits they received from their membership." They wanted them to understand that being in a craft union was also about demonstrating their accomplishments and strength as an organized movement, so that they could secure and extend the benefits that their forebears had won for them. By reclaiming Labor Day as a celebration of the worker, these leaders hoped that the CFL's members would share in the "same spirit and enthusiasm as those who started [their] great labor movement."[25]

In addition to this concern for organized labor's strength, union leaders sought to revive Labor Day to express their national loyalty and support for the war. The CFL's call for the grand parade in 1942 echoed this mix of union pride and patriotism on the part of those who saw themselves both as workers who were participants in an organized labor movement and as Americans in a time of war. The federation planned a massive parade for September 7, to be followed by a rally at Soldier Field. Union leaders hoped that the display would "actively demonstrate that [union members] are behind our people fighting in the front lines for America."²⁶ Although Fitzpatrick invited several important local and national officials, including Mayor Edward Kelly, AFL President William Green, and President Franklin Roosevelt, he turned down Kelly's offer to have troops from the Second Army join the line of march. While Fitzpatrick wanted to organize a display of American patriotism, he intended to keep the focus of the parade on labor alone because he wanted to use the day "for the revitalization of Labor's interest in Labor Day."²⁷

Despite the hopes of Fitzpatrick, Nockels, Wallace, and other leaders of the CFL and its constituent unions, the 1942 Labor Day parade and rally in Chicago never took place. After all the work they put into organizing the day during the final months of that summer, the leaders did not get the members' support, forcing them to cancel the program. The Chicago Teachers Union and the city's United Brick and Clay Workers expressed their regret but explained that their memberships were "scattered" during those final summer weeks, the teachers away on summer holiday and the bricklayers off on multiple job sites. Coordinating an impressive display for early September, their leaders argued, would be impossible.²⁸ Similarly, the Teamsters' Joint Council and the Hod Carriers' Joint Council had decided they could not turn out in time. And so Fitzpatrick felt he had no choice but to scrap the whole event.²⁹

This did not mean that workers did not find ways to define their labor patriotism—they just did so in a much less structured fashion than that planned by Fitzpatrick and the other CFL leaders. Although the Painters Union protested the cancellation of the citywide event, most workers seemed content to go their own way.³⁰ Some, like the members of the Teachers Union, enjoyed the last fruits of their summer break, while others, like those in the Chicago Trades and Construction Council, used the day to present a check for one hundred thousand dollars to the government for the war effort.³¹ Individual unions continued to observe Labor Day in their own way during the war years, often linking their activities to the fight against fascism. Although there would be no large, citywide displays of union strength in Chicago and New York, workers turned out either as individuals or with their locals on Labor Day to participate in bond drives and wartime parades, thereby linking their identity and interests to those of the nation during war.³²

One place where workers clearly made this public identification with the nation and its wartime efforts was in the "I Am an American Day" celebrations that were first observed in 1940. On May 3, 1940, under pressure from educational groups interested in fostering a better sense of citizenship among Americans, Congress designated that the third Sunday in May be a time to reflect on "our duties and responsibilities, as well as our good fortune, in being American."[33] President Roosevelt then issued a proclamation setting aside May 19, 1940, for the "recognition of all who, by coming of age, or naturalization, are attaining the status of citizenship." He called on Americans, especially new citizens, to pause on that day and reflect on the rights and duties "of all patriotic and home-loving Americans." Roosevelt asked them to "always think first of America and at the same time to think in terms of humanity." Assuring them that their new homeland would always be "a land of opportunity" and a source of "hope, liberty and justice," he requested these new citizens to "perform the high patriotic duty of supporting their government at all times in keeping with its principles, traditions and ideals as a democracy."[34] For Roosevelt, this annual focus on the figurative birth of new citizens would serve as a rallying point for national loyalty and unity. This was particularly important in a time when the native homes of many of these recent immigrants were being engulfed in the flames of war. Many of those immigrants believed it was important to "verify and clarify their status" as new Americans. Between 1941 and 1945, the number of people seeking naturalization increased dramatically. Many aliens (more than 112,000) gained their citizenship through service in the armed forces, but most (more than 1.5 million) were civilians who naturalized during the war.[35]

Beginning in 1940, Americans from all walks of life, including organized workers, answered Roosevelt's call and that of his successors by celebrating "I Am an American Day" in great outdoor meetings with mass recitations of the Pledge of Allegiance.[36] This new civic event became a focal point for the shaping of wartime, postwar, and Cold War Americanism. The gathering offered an opportunity for new citizens to consecrate (and for veteran citizens to reconsecrate) themselves to the democratic values of their nation at a time when those values seemed threatened initially by fascism and war, and later by communism.

The first "I Am an American Day" took place in May 1940 and consisted of the publication of Roosevelt's proclamation and that issued by Governor Lehman of New York, along with the delivery of sermons at various local churches on the themes of the rights and responsibilities of citizenship.[37] Not until later that year, at the New York World's Fair, did the event take on what would become its characteristic theatrical trappings. The National Conference of Christians and Jews sponsored this autumn American Day celebration and staged it on the fairgrounds on October 15.[38] It offered the public a special one-dollar combination ticket that would allow them entrance to the fair and to fourteen shows, including events intended to support the "American Day" theme.[39] Mayor La-Guardia extended his support, accepting an honorary chairmanship for the day's events.[40]

A mass recitation of the Pledge of Allegiance at noon was the focal point of the day. At that moment, "all activity throughout the grounds will cease while a voice sounding over the loudspeakers of the Fair's public address system will lead the visitors in the pledge."[41] This display of national loyalty was bracketed by parades staged at 10:30 A.M. and 12:15 P.M. More than 130,000 tickets were collected, as New Yorkers and out-of-town visitors flooded the sprawling fairgrounds in Flushing, Queens. Once the crowd had recited the pledge, Harvey Gibson, chairman of the World's Fair board, reminded them that the purpose of the day was to show the "greatness of democracy and the dignity of American life."[42]

Those who remained at the fair until the evening could see another version of this celebration of American democracy in the special pageant the ILGWU staged in the Court of Peace, a large open area located at the north end of the fairgrounds that was surrounded by the exhibits of various foreign countries, the large U.S. government building, and the "lagoon of nations" fountain.[43] In their pageant, "I Hear America Singing," 1,000 union members dramatized the history of the United States. They told a story based on Walt Whitman's poems, which had been set to music by George Kleinsinger, a jazz pianist and summer music director for several local New Deal Civilian Conservation Corps camps.[44] The ILGWU players brought to life episodes in America's past that spoke both to the development of the nation and to the expansion of liberty. The pastiche of dramatic moments from the country's history told a classic patriotic story of freedom, but with a laborite twist. It was a story of national liberation that coincided with the emancipation of the country's workers, ending in a celebration of the New Deal. According to the *New York Times*, the performance:

> showed the Civil War, the assassination of Lincoln, the building of the railroads, the coming of the immigrants, the rise of capitalism and the forming of the American Federation of Labor, the Triangle fire of 1911, the World War, the Sacco and Vanzetti case, the jazz age, the depression

and the NRA. It concluded with the entire cast with flags and banners facing the audience and standing in front of a large picture of President Roosevelt.[45]

The performers and their audience may have been swept up in the wartime fervor of the mass loyalty pledge earlier in the day, but here, during the performance of "Singing," they could define a more specific, social democratic reform version of American fealty and dignity. That rendition included references to labor's past tragedies and sacrifices, as well as its recent triumphs under the New Deal. Here, the story of the union movement was linked to that of the expansion of American freedom since the Civil War. The ILGWU players' final celebration of Roosevelt indicated where the workers pinned their hopes, both for the nation at war and for their union movement. As the hour-long performance concluded, the cast members, in song, urged the audience to "take off its coat, come out and vote 'the Franklin D. Roosevelt way.'"[46]

"I Hear America Singing" expressed the garment workers' support for FDR and the New Deal, which they and their leaders had solidified by October 1940. This position distinguished the ILGWU (which had returned to the AFL in June 1940) from John L. Lewis, head of the CIO, who gave his support to Wendell Willkie. It also further separated the garment workers from the CP, which opposed Roosevelt at this time.[47] In addition, there is evidence that the ILGWU's artistic team harbored deep anticommunist sentiment. Louis Schaffer, who staged "Singing," was known to be "bitterly anti-Communist," having fired members from the cast of the union's popular production of "Pins and Needles" (1937–1940) when he found out they were members of the CP.[48] In its pro–New Deal, pro-union celebration onstage, and with its anticommunist directors backstage, "Singing" added a distinctly noncommunist version of progressive working-class Americanism to the "I Am an American Day" events. It celebrated a democracy for all but communists.

In subsequent years, the "I Am an American Day" celebrations, held in May, took on many of the dramatic trappings that had been coordinated first during the special World's Fair events in October 1940. But over time, the political tone of the holiday changed. If there were room for the expression of progressive working-class Americanism in the ILGWU's pageant in October 1940, the "I Am an American Day" events staged in subsequent years promoted a classless vision of American identity. Centering on large outdoor meetings featuring prominent speakers and the mass

Pledge of Allegiance, the holiday fostered devotion to the nation above all else, thereby subsuming distinct class-based claims to power. Rather than the questioning of capitalism's structure that was inherent in socialist and communist May Day events, the "I Am an American Day" holiday sustained a progressive (and anticommunist) vision that heralded the value of democracy and the power of "the people."[49] But unlike the "American Day" of the early 1920s, which sought to narrow the definition of what it meant to be an American, this new celebration facilitated a paradigm of social unity and inclusion. Ethnic and racial pluralism were extolled, but within a ritual narrative of assimilation; America's greatly diverse population came together on this one day to pledge their allegiance to the nation. Just how that nation was conceived in these events would vary over time, and would become part of the larger process through which America's wartime, immediate postwar, and Cold War identity was culturally constructed.

In the early period of America's involvement in the war (first as an undeclared ally supplying Britain, then as a fighting partner after the attack on Pearl Harbor in December 1941), the "I Am an American Day" celebrations underscored the importance of national unity, yet also still embraced some of the progressive concerns found in the 1940 event. For the event's organizers, which generally included local government officials and leaders of religious and fraternal organizations, it was imperative that America's ethnically diverse population remain united and resolute in its fight against the axis powers. In New York, Mayor Fiorello LaGuardia, Roman Catholic Archbishop Francis Spellman, and Reform Rabbi Stephen Wise supported the overt demonstrations of loyalty to the American nation and the displays of devotion to American citizenship that the "I Am an American Day" celebrations provided, because they hoped that such a public event would sustain the unity needed in a time of war.[50]

As the fighting wore on, and it became clear that the American people were in the struggle for the duration, the "I Am an American Day" events held in New York, Chicago, and around the country sustained continued demonstrations of loyalty. They also provided a forum for the definition of postwar hopes and dreams.[51] This new focus could be heard in the speeches delivered at the celebrations held in New York in 1943 and 1944. In addition to calls for national unity and wartime loyalty, the speakers now implored Americans to prepare themselves for the problems that would arise in the postwar world. In 1943, Vice President Henry Wallace expressed a progressive vision for America's postwar role. In an address he delivered in New York that was heard by radio across the nation, he reminded listeners that Americanism stood for "the freedom and the welfare and the brotherhood of the plain people of the world, wherever they are." Wallace insisted that Americans would soon have the duty of ensuring that the peoples of war-torn Europe would not just be free of hunger and disease, but would share in the "ideals of democracy, peace, and tolerance." He implied that Americans, blessed with material abundance and political freedoms, were uniquely suited and obliged to play this role of global benefactor.[52]

In New York's 1944 "I Am an American Day" event, attended by an estimated 1.4 million people, speakers articulated similarly progressive visions for the nation and its future role in the world.[53] Brotherhood and the cooperation of nations were the watchwords of the day. Senator Robert Wagner gave the main address, in which he spoke of the brotherhood of man, the lessons of war, and the need to prevent future conflagrations through a postwar global organization of "peace-loving nations." He set out what he saw as America's new moral obligation, to be met not only with regard to its own people, but also to those around the world when he observed, "if our brothers are enslaved, our liberty is imperiled; if our brothers are hungry, our plenty is a myth; if our brothers are attacked, we are not safe." Wagner stopped just short of outlining a detailed program for implementing this vision of brotherly responsibility at home, citing a general need for the expansion of Social Security and educational opportunities and the construction of decent housing.[54] In this vision of postwar Americanism, the New Deal would be extended both at home and overseas. Episcopal Bishop William Manning, who spoke after Wagner, echoed this progressive global ambition, arguing for the creation of "a world in which men and women shall live free from fear and terror. . . . a world in which there shall be justice and fair dealing and brotherliness between men of all races and all colors, and in which the moral law of God shall rule."[55] For the time being, as the war still raged around the world, the "I Am an American Day" celebrations at home facilitated such progressive and democratic hopes.

Men and women of "all races and all colors" listened to Wagner and Manning when the two men spoke in Central Park. Pluralism was not only inherent in the progressive messages articulated on "I Am an American Day," the social profile of the participants and the crowd also suggested it. During the 1940 celebration, African-American ILGWU members performed a dance routine after their union staged its "I Hear America Singing" pageant.[56] And in subsequent years, Marian Anderson became a fixture on the "I Am an American Day" program in New York, where she sang "Ave Maria."[57] Kate Smith, who sang "God Bless America," often joined her. And, as suggested by the newspaper photos of the gatherings, women, both black and white, made up a sizable portion of those gathered at the rally.[58] The young holiday was, in this respect, a celebration of America's social diversity.

But the "I Am an American Day" holiday was a celebration that emphasized the *unity* of these diverse groups as Americans who came together as one to pledge their allegiance to the nation and the greater cause of winning the war; it was a wartime popular front against fascism. As part of the 1940 program, for example, the Rutgers University Glee Club sang "Ballad for Americans," the popular song that exalted the country's rich ethnic, racial, and religious mix. While radicals may have interpreted the lyrics of "Ballad" as refusing to propose a "single identification" for the Americans it celebrated, those lyrics were ambiguous enough to appeal to more politically moderate American liberals who championed "Ballad" as a celebration of the achievement of American freedom and the identification of its diverse ethnic population with a *united* American people. Communists played the song during the May Day parades of the Popular Front years, but so, too, did Republicans at their 1940 national convention and liberals during these wartime "I Am an American Day" events.[59]

Unlike earlier holiday gatherings, such as the Loyalty Day of the 1920s or Labor Day parades at the turn of the century, the new "I Am an American Day" events seemed to offer women in particular more opportunities to participate. This greater presence of women in public celebrations during the early 1940s may have resulted from the larger role they played in the public sphere as a result of the war. Six million women left the home for the paid workforce during the war, and some 300,000 joined the armed forces.[60] In an event designed to celebrate the American citizen, women, who were proving their mettle as such every day, could no longer be easily ignored. This was particularly true given the ethos of pluralism that pervaded the official rhetoric of the day, as Wallace, Wagner, and Manning espoused.

Yet, it was these *men* who spoke at the "I Am an American Day" events, not women. Kate Smith and Marian Anderson were welcome to provide the entertainment, but they were not there to comment on domestic or international events. No woman, not even Frances Perkins or Eleanor

Roosevelt, was given the rostrum. So although they may have come a long way in terms of their public presence at such events, women were still not fully equal actors to men in these forums. And, while women made up a sizable portion of the crowd, the press, at times, portrayed them as frivolous, flighty, and emotionally driven. When Frank Sinatra took the stage to sing at the event in 1943, the *New York Times* reported that "crowds of women, from grammar school to grandmother ages, surged down the aisles toward the platform," and that even once the police had stopped them from moving any closer, "squealing sounds continued until Mr. Sinatra cleared his throat to sing."[61] The greater visibility of women at the "I Am an American Day" celebration thus did not necessarily signal a significant change in their status, or in the popular perception of their status, as public actors.[62]

The same was true for African Americans. For many, this new holiday did not adequately address their fight for equality and their struggle against second-class citizenship. A. Philip Randolph, president of the Brotherhood of Sleeping Car Porters (BSCP) and head of the March on Washington Movement (MOWM), was a leading figure in the African-American community's national fight against segregation in the military, discrimination in employment (especially in government and defense-related jobs), and the persistence of Jim Crow. As the nation joined the fight against fascism abroad and denounced the horrors of Nazi racism, Randolph and other leading civil rights advocates called on America to be true to its values of equality and democracy at home: it must secure a "double victory." In 1943, Randolph coordinated a national conference to promote this campaign, naming it "We Are Americans, Too!"[63]

The conference was originally planned as the annual meeting of the March on Washington Movement. Civil rights activists had created the MOWM in 1941 to combat discrimination in government hiring. Randolph's threat of coordinating a march on Washington by several hundred thousand African Americans, including members of the BSCP, had pressured President Roosevelt into issuing Executive Order 8802, which created the Fair Employment Practices Committee (FEPC). Although this was a victory, segregation and discrimination in the military and in American society as a whole did not disappear, so Randolph kept the MOWM active after 1941 to continue the fight.[64]

Planning for the MOWM's 1943 meeting began in December 1942. At that point, the gathering was not referred to as the "We Are Americans, Too!" conference. Instead, the program was conceived under the much clumsier title of "Defeat Hitler, Mussolini and Hirohito by Enforcing and Observing the Constitution and Abolishing Jim Crow."[65] Although the original nomenclature was awkward, it did communicate the main thrust of the campaign: the domestic fight for equal rights was central to achieving victory abroad. Randolph understood this in terms of preserving the integrity of American democracy, and in terms of the very real effects that continued segregation and discrimination were having on African-American troops and war workers.[66] He insisted that "democracy must be saved in America to enable our nation to lead in the struggle for democracy all over the world. We cannot successfully win the world war and secure a just and durable peace unless we practice democracy at home."[67] Randolph's call for America to be true to its highest values by ending Jim Crow was both a principled and a practical demand.

His original plans called for a multiday conference in Chicago to be held in late May. On the final day of the conference, mass marches were to be held in cities around the nation, with their participants converging on city halls or state legislatures to demand an end to Jim Crow. Such action embodied the MOWM's commitment to "non-violent good will direct action."[68] In the midst of the war, such action would certainly draw attention to the cause, especially if hundreds of thousands of workers left their posts at the nation's wartime industrial machine to join one of the marches.

By January 1943, Randolph began to send letters to MOWM members and other leading civil rights advocates around the nation, seeking their support for the conference, which he now referred to as the "I Am an American, Too!" week. He may have initiated this name change partly for practical reasons, due to the clumsiness of the meeting's original title. Yet, given the popular presence of the "I Am an American Day" events in New York and Chicago at that time, Randolph most likely also wanted to invoke the themes of unity and patriotism associated with those celebrations. Such an invocation underscored the MOWM's loyalty to the nation during wartime ("I Am an American"). Yet, at the same time, it called attention to African Americans' sense of exclusion from full citizenship because of the persistence of Jim Crow ("I Am an American, TOO!"). African Americans might temporarily leave their wartime work posts to march for equal rights, but they did so as loyal and patriotic Americans who ultimately sought to strengthen both the country's moral fiber and its fighting morale. As Randolph explained to Mary McLeod Bethune, the purpose of the conference and the mass marches was to express the "collective will and determination of the Negro never to stop fighting during the war to win democracy abroad and to be free men at home."[69]

In January, after a written exchange with William Y. Bell, Jr., executive secretary of the Atlanta Urban League, Randolph agreed to change the name of the gathering one final time, from "I Am an American, Too!" to "We Are Americans, Too!" Bell argued that by using the term "We," the MOWM could "develop more group consciousness."[70] Randolph agreed, noting that he thought Bell's "suggestion of *WE* instead of *I* gives it strength. The 'we-ness' is always stronger than the 'I-ness' and I shall follow your suggestion."[71] In another move that was both practical and symbolic, Randolph decided to shift the dates of the meeting from late May until early July. To avoid having the "We Are Americans, Too!" conference conflict with the NAACP's gathering in June, and to afford the MOWM enough time to coordinate its meeting, Randolph rescheduled the conference for June 30 through July 4. It would thus also end "on the symbolic day of July Fourth."[72]

Just as was true for the popular "I Am an American Day" events of the early 1940s, the wartime context informed the rhetoric and focus of the "We Are Americans, Too!" conference. Rather than emphasizing the need for unity, however, the MOWM gathering stressed the need to save democracy. In the conference program, Randolph and E. Pauline Myers, MOWM national executive secretary, invoked the nationalist touchstones of Thomas Jefferson and the Declaration of Independence in calling for this crusade. "Now, more than any previous time in our history," they argued, "the tenets of democracy, as expressed in this Document, are important living things for Americans." Randolph and Myers continued, noting how "with the forces of hate and destruction unloosed upon the world, it is essential that we Americans should stand and fight for the principles and philosophy of government which have been handed down through the years by the Father of Democracy." They saw the world now divided in a war between "the forces of freedom and the forces of slavery—democracy on the one hand and fascism on the other." Lest they be "untrue to the spirit of the Founding Fathers," Randolph and Myers believed that it was their duty, and that of all Americans, to make sure the nation would "come out of this war with a new and greater freedom for all."[73]

This sense of urgency informed the crusade to expand democracy at home. But it also underscored Randolph and Myers' argument, echoed in the resolutions passed at the MOWM conference, that this crusade was indivisibly linked to a global struggle for freedom. The two leaders insisted that "the problem of the Negro in the United States is no longer a purely domestic question but has world significance." Not only was the problem "integrated with the larger strategy of defeating the Axis," as the MOWM had been arguing for, but it also was linked to much larger global changes. Randolph and Myers asserted that African Americans "have become the barometer of democracy to the colored peoples of the world: Africa, India, China, Latin America, and the West Indies, all look to the United States." They argued that the persistence of Jim Crow "suggests to [those people of color around the world] the kind of 'democracy' which would dominate the post war period should certain fascist-minded elements in this country have their way." Thus, the fight for equality and democracy at home was "tied up with the fate of the democratic way of life" and was "the most important social issue of today."[74]

The "We Are Americans, Too!" program supported this integration of national and international concerns. The delegates passed resolutions calling for the end to the poll tax, white primaries, discrimination in hiring, and segregation in the armed forces, as well as resolutions expressing support for the independence of India and the West Indies.[75] Panels focused on "The Future of the FEPC" and programs to abolish Jim Crow, along with the role of "The Negro in Peace and Postwar Planning—Africa, The Caribbean, The United States."[76] Just as Henry Wallace and Robert Wagner addressed the desire for unity in wartime and voiced the hope that America would be a progressive leader in the postwar world, Randolph and those African Americans gathered at the "We Are Americans, Too!" conference brought attention to their wartime concerns for equality and offered a different vision of postwar liberation. Even though on the closing day of the conference the marches were not held across the country as originally planned, Randolph proclaimed the gathering in Chicago a success.[77] It drew national attention to the struggle for civil rights, and reinforced the commitment within the African-American community to the double victory campaign.

Randolph's and the MOWM's definition of Americanism emphasized racial equality and a vibrant democracy both at home and around the world. It existed in the nation's public culture alongside the patriotic expressions of national unity found in the "I Am an American Day" events of the early 1940s, and the working-class Americanism created in wartime Flag Day and Labor Day parades. Nowhere to be found in these years were the more radical variants of Americanism that socialists and communists had traditionally voiced on May Day. The Communist Party's decision to suspend May Day demonstrations during the war rendered that holiday tradition dormant from 1941 until 1945. This did not mean that there could not be any expressions of dissent in the nation's public culture. The "We Are Americans, Too!" conference suggests that such protest was still possible, albeit now with race instead of class as its main focus. During the war, Americans created other forums in which to define their understandings of themselves as citizens. That included American laborers, who constructed a militant, yet patriotic, version of working-class Americanism. Whether or not they, or anyone else in the United States, would feel the need to revive May Day once the struggle against fascism came to an end remained to be seen.

7

May Day Becomes
America's Forgotten Holiday
1946–1960

Beginning in 1947 and continuing through the early years of the Cold War, those who championed the revival of May Day would face some of their most difficult challenges. Although Communist Party (CP) members and their supporters had high hopes for the holiday's rebirth after World War II, they would soon witness May Day's rapid decline. An integral part of this story was the deepening division within the organized labor movement between its militant (but anticommunist) contingents and its left-led wing. Equally important to the fate of May Day during the late 1940s and 1950s were the actions of veterans' groups, religious organizations, and nonradical union members. Intending to supplant the leftist May Day celebrations, these groups staged competing parades on May 1, including a revived Loyalty Day, during which they forged a particularly aggressive definition of nationalism. Martial in tone, their expressions of Cold War nationalism assumed that America's role was one of defender of the free world, understood in overtly anticommunist and pro–free enterprise terms. Faced with the competition of these new Cold War celebrations, a political culture now dominated by an anticommunist consensus, a divided labor movement, and a fading radical party base, May Day celebrations dwindled. The story of how Americans abandoned this radical holiday—then came to forget its history in the United States—became a part of the process through which political discourse in America dramatically narrowed in the two decades after World War II.

In part, this narrowing was due to the emergence of a new, Cold War Americanism, which would cast a chill over the nation's politics for decades. This unique expression of nationalism was created in public celebrations like "I Am an American Day." First observed in 1940, this holiday became popular during World War II as a celebration of the nation's unity in the face of fascist aggression. After the war, support for the annual celebration remained strong. Yet, its tone would change dramatically over the course of just a few years. The optimistic and progressive vision that Robert Wagner and Henry Wallace presented in 1944 did not last long. The signs of a more pessimistic, defensive Cold War Americanism were on the horizon, visible as early as the "I Am an American Day" gathering of 1946.

That year the main speaker in New York was Mayor William O'Dwyer, who warned his audience "against paying heed to foreign ideologies." Speaking on liberty, he cautioned that it "did not mean license," neither did it "encourage. . . . the fostering of strange ideologies contrary to our form of Government."[1] Although he did not identify a specific doctrine, the "strange ideologies" O'Dwyer referred to were most likely fascism and communism, the feared duo that the press and many politicians were then identifying together under the rubric of "totalitarianism."[2] The following year, O'Dwyer again expressed his concern, this time in even more strident tones, for the integrity and stability of America's political system. In his "I Am an American Day" proclamation, the mayor noted how the world was "beset by issues of gravest moment" and that on this special holiday, all Americans must "declare publicly their faith in the stability and permanence of the American form of government and its institutions."[3] Such language betrayed the growing anxieties of the early Cold War.[4]

This standoff between the United States and the Soviet Union had been developing in the aftermath of World War II. As America pursued its agenda of promoting democracy and free-market capitalism in Western Europe, and as the Soviet Union clung to its desire to expand its influence in Eastern Europe, the immediate post–World War II dream of "Big Three" unity quickly faded. By the time of the 1947 "I Am an American Day" event, the policy that would characterize America's position in the Cold War standoff had been defined. Just two months earlier, President Truman crystallized these emerging Cold War anxieties in his speech to Congress, where he outlined his vision for America in what he believed had become the new and dangerous global context of a divided world. Soviet communism had to be contained, he asserted, because it represented the forces of tyranny. It was a system based on "terror and oppression, a controlled press and radio, fixed elections, and the suppression of personal freedoms."[5] America, on the other hand, represented a way of life based on "representative government, free elections, guarantees of individual liberty, freedom of speech and religion, and freedom from political oppression."[6] In this speech the president articulated what has become known as the Truman Doctrine, asserting that it was the duty of the United States to "contain" Soviet communism in order to "support free peoples who are resisting attempted subjugation" and to assist them "to work out their own destinies in their own way."[7] Roosevelt, Wallace, and Wagner's vision of America leading the world in a brotherhood of mankind, their "social-democratic globalism," was no longer viable. Instead, there now was Cold War America's "nationalist globalism," a strident defense of democracy and free-market capitalism against the evils of communism.[8]

In 1949, this version of Americanism was clearly articulated by the two guest speakers at New York's "I Am an American Day" event, Federal Judge Samuel H. Kaufman and State Supreme Court Justice Ferdinand Pecora. After administering the oath of allegiance to the new citizens gathered in Central Park and leading the crowd in the pledge to the flag, the two men denounced the tyranny of communism as inimical to American democracy.[9] Kaufman sounded a more positive note, praising the "philosophy of democracy" as a "most vital and living force."[10] Pecora contrasted that democracy with the Soviet system, in which "the individual. . . . must serve the state in obedience to the arbitrary will of its self-constituted head." In totalitarian countries like the Soviet Union, he declared, "the human spirit is brutally debased and the people are being deprived of spiritual guidance and comfort." According to Pecora, not only was political democracy quashed behind the Iron Curtain, but also religious freedom and the spirit of hope that all humans carry in their heart to survive in the temporal world.[11]

Pecora, Kaufman, and others delivered speeches like these in the context of mass patriotic rallies in New York's Central Park and Chicago's Soldier Field. Their words were also broadcast around the nation over the radio to millions of Americans. Such oratory helped transform "I Am an American Day" into a forum where individuals could participate in the construction of a new nationalism. While Americans did not have access to the classified NSC-68 report that outlined the nation's Cold War foreign policy of containment and permanent military readiness, and while most did not follow the policy debates in Congress closely, millions could participate in the construction of their nation's emerging Cold War consensus in the public meeting places of their cities. At these annual "I Am an American Day" events, they heard the argument for defending freedom over tyranny, first aimed at the fascist menace during World War II, then, beginning in 1947, against the new bogey of totalitarianism. By turning out in the hundreds of thousands to hear such speeches and to pledge their allegiance to the flag, Americans demonstrated their patriotism, even as they contributed to the construction of a newly imagined nation: America as the leader and defender of the free world standing against the threat of communism.[12]

Among the Americans assembled at these annual rallies were thousands of workers, some in delegations from their labor unions like Bakers Local 17 and Transport Workers Union (TWU) Local 100.[13] Others participated in veterans' groups or fraternal organizations.[14] Many workers became more comfortable with the version of Americanism expressed in the "I Am an American Day" celebrations than with the radical Americanism voiced during May Day events. The nationalism that participants in the wartime Flag Day and Labor Day events and the postwar "I Am an American Day" rallies constructed advanced the belief that America was the leader of the free world, and had to remain such if the nation's democracy and the world's peace were to be sustained. This construction was not a simple process, nor was it limited to the forum of urban popular political culture.[15] But in that arena, average citizens, including many workers, could participate in the process of defining what it meant to be an American and what America meant as a nation. In so doing, they left no room for May Day. Celebrated chiefly by communists and left-led unions, the May 1 holiday would be difficult to sustain in the context of this new Cold War Americanism.[16]

Although the CP and some of its allied unions managed to revive May Day in 1946, staging an impressive parade of approximately 150,000 people in New York, the holiday's postwar renaissance was short-lived.[17] After the dismantling of the Communist Political Association and the ouster of Earl Browder in 1946, the reconstituted CPUSA retreated into a revolutionary orthodoxy that made united-front activity difficult.[18] At the same time, the currents of the early Cold War were already running swiftly through American politics. May Day and the radical left, which had become the holiday's custodian, suffered not only under the political pressures of the Second Red Scare, but also from the challenge of rival demonstrations staged by self-defined patriotic organizations. In addition to the "I Am an American Day" rallies sponsored by local political and religious leaders, there were now revived Loyalty Day parades sponsored by the Veterans of Foreign Wars (VFW) and "Union Square, USA" gatherings staged by New York's Fourteenth Street Association. The VFW purposefully coordinated Loyalty Day parades on May 1 to rout the political radicals from the streets, while the latter group sponsored patriotic rallies in Union Square to prevent communists and socialists from gathering there to celebrate May Day, as they had for decades. Striking at the heart of the radicals' celebratory calendar, May 1, and at its iconic public meeting place, Union Square, the VFW and the Fourteenth Street Association sought to eradicate the last vestiges of political radicalism from the one place it had made its greatest public showing: New York City.

The Veterans of Foreign Wars was the first group to challenge directly the CP-dominated May Day parade by organizing Loyalty Day demonstrations in the late 1940s and early 1950s.[19] Support for a nationwide celebration was first voiced in 1946, when Post 1059 of Queens County, New York, submitted a resolution at the VFW's annual "encampment." It called for "all VFW units [to] hold Loyalty Day Rallies on April 30 each year to combat rallies held annually on May 1 by communistic and unpatriotic groups and organizations."[20] The resolution was approved, and in subsequent years, VFW posts across the country organized large Loyalty Day parades, which gained widespread government support and press attention. Some of the biggest demonstrations took place in New York.

The Loyalty Day parades held in New York during the late 1940s and early 1950s contributed to the contemporary construction of a Cold War anticommunist consensus. The processions were overseen and approved by political officials who had come to disdain the presence of radicals in America. In 1948, for example, Mayor William O'Dwyer, an honorary chairman of the day's events, stood at the parade's reviewing stand, where he was joined by U.S. Attorney General Thomas Clark. At the time, Clark was coordinating the prosecution of eleven national Communist Party leaders who, under the 1940 Smith Act, had been charged with conspiracy to advocate revolution by violence.[21] By 1948, neither O'Dwyer nor Clark looked kindly on the radicals' May Day celebrations, and both eagerly took part in these competing Loyalty Day events. In so doing, they gave their imprimatur to the self-defined patriotic parade.

In subsequent years, the VFW members who marched past the reviewing stand were joined by other veterans' organizations (including the American Legion and the Catholic and Jewish War Veterans), youth

Figure 7.1. Members of the John Birch Society marching in a Loyalty Day parade in 1967. Communist Party of the United States Photographs Collection, Tamiment Library, New York University.

organizations such as the Boy Scouts, and contingents from local Catholic schools. After its formation in 1958, the John Birch Society also came out on Loyalty Day and continued to observe the holiday well into the 1960s.[22] As socially and politically conservative organizations, these groups came together on May 1 to assert a specifically anticommunist version of patriotism. The *New York Times* reported the events favorably, highlighting the number of marchers that turned out. It compared the growing size of the Loyalty Day parade to the flagging May Day demonstrations, interpreting the difference as proof of New Yorkers' steadfast rejection of communism.[23] In 1946, for example, the newspaper boasted that Loyalty Day had produced 750,000 spectators compared with May Day's 50,000. This led the city's VFW commander to assert that his troops had "walked them [communists] off the streets."[24]

By the early 1950s, the VFW led such demonstrations throughout the country, from Brooklyn and Jersey City to Sacramento and Glendale.[25] Through the melding of patriotic displays with a specific and strong anticommunist focus (i.e., the goal of "marching" the communists off the streets on May 1), these Loyalty Day parades both embodied and articulated the new popular Cold War Americanism that also was being created in the "I Am an American Day" celebrations. Yet, the Loyalty Day events, organized by and including thousands of military veterans, produced a more overt demonstration of the martial and masculine elements of this Cold War Americanism. These features were visible not only in the presence of the military veterans, National Guard troops and tanks, and active-duty soldiers on parade, but also in the special visit General Douglas MacArthur made to New York in 1951. MacArthur's appearance, along with that of rescued prisoners of war, took place at the height of the Korean conflict. It reminded spectators of the bloody battle against communism that was being waged on the other side of the globe. The celebration of General MacArthur as an anticommunist hero reinforced the martial nature of the new Cold War American identity that was on display in the Loyalty Day parade.[26]

The public denunciation of communism that was so central to this holiday welcomed legions of Catholics, including Francis Cardinal Spellman, the Knights of Columbus, and ranks of Catholic schoolchildren, into both the Loyalty Day parades and the emerging Cold War consensus of which they were a part.[27] Although the Catholic Church had long opposed communism because of its rejection of God and private property and its acceptance of revolutionary violence, the Church's hostility took on a new focus during the Cold War when it experienced repression under communist regimes in Eastern Europe. Marshal Josip Tito's sentencing of Aloysius Stepinac, the archbishop of Zagreb, to a sixteen-year jail term in 1946, and the 1948 arrest of Joseph Cardinal Mindszenty in Budapest became new rallying points in the Church's fight against communism.[28] During the 1949 Loyalty Day parade, a Hungarian contingent carried a crepe-draped portrait of Mindszenty in protest of the humiliation and abuse he had suffered at the hands of the communist secret police.[29] In addition to such Catholic anticommunist demonstrations in Loyalty Day parades, Francis Cardinal Spellman pointed out the fate of Mindszenty and Stepinac when he denounced communism from his pulpit during the late 1940s. In so doing, he, along with the Catholics who marched in the Loyalty Day parades, contributed to the nation's Cold War anticommunist consensus. That consensus included both a strong sense of loyalty to the United States and an equally strong opposition to communism, seen as anathema to the democracy and religious freedom inherent in the American way of life.

American Protestants and Jews also joined in the anticommunist consensus of these years. Leading Protestant evangelicals, like Billy Graham, incorporated anticommunism into their religious teachings, thereby reinforcing the Cold War belief of a world divided, not only between communism and democracy, but also between godless communism and Christianity. Americans seemed to embrace this religious identification for their nation: the 1950s saw both an increase in churchgoing and the introduction of the phrase "under God" into the Pledge of Allegiance.[30] For both Reform and Conservative Jews, taking up the anticommunist crusade had more to do with a desire to continue their assimilation into mainstream white American culture, as well as their identification of communism with the evils of anti-Semitism in the Soviet system. The purging of communists from the membership rolls of both the American Jewish Committee and the American Jewish Congress in 1949 and 1950, Rabbi Stephen Wise's participation in "I Am an American Day" celebrations, and the presence of Jewish war veterans in the Loyalty Day parades exemplify this strong anticommunist posture.[31]

In addition to the male participants in these Jewish and Catholic groups, many women were among those who demonstrated against communism in the Loyalty Day parades. Some belonged to the different religious and ethnic organizations that marched, while others came out to pledge their fealty to democracy and freedom among the ranks of military auxiliary units.[32] Women workers also joined in the demonstration, creating some of the parades' more amusing displays. In 1949, telephone operators carried a large banner that read, "We Don't Like Stalin's Party Line." In 1950, their sign read, "The Kremlin Has the Wrong Number."[33]

Unlike the Loyalty Day parades of the 1920s, which were exclusively male, these Cold War displays welcomed women into the ranks. Even though there were still expressions of more traditional gender roles, including the naming of a Loyalty Day "Queen" (in 1950, it was Ethel Merman, who rode through the parade in the back of a red convertible),[34] the parades of the 1950s gave women like the telephone operators space to assert their support for Cold War Americanism. In the nation's fight against the communist enemy, women filled a number of roles. Their presence in the Loyalty Day parade as military veterans and workers on the one hand, and as members of ethnic and religious organizations on the other, expressed the tension between the more public presence women had attained since World War II and the continued pull of the private sphere. That pull would strengthen as the Cold War deepened and reinforced Americans' desire for the domestic ideal: a family-centered culture in which the home was a refuge from the terror of the atomic bomb, the stresses of the corporate world, and the decadence of radical cosmopolitanism.[35] During the late 1940s and early 1950s, women asserted their right to venture into the public arena, yet did so by marching behind their men, in support of militant assertions of defensive Cold War nationalism.

By rejecting this narrow definition of nationalism and by asserting the American roots of the May 1 holiday, the Communist Party tried to defend May Day against the competition from Loyalty Day. Editorials and special articles in the *Daily Worker* touted how "Americans gave it to the world," celebrating the origins of May Day in the nation's nineteenth-century labor movement.[36] A group of participants in the 1947 May Day parade even marched in 1880s period dress, carrying signs with slogans from the first demonstration of 1886 to underscore the day's American origins.[37] The communists also rejected the VFW's assertions that it was "marching them off the streets," arguing that the "crowds [sic] cheers answer labor haters." The CP insisted that 70,000-80,000 people participated in the May Day parade, despite the lower count offered by the VFW and the police. The *New York Times* reported that only 30,000 people marched in the May Day parade, with approximately 110,000 spectators, compared to the 750,000 people it reported coming out for Loyalty Day the year before.[38] But the party charged that the police, who provided the estimates, had purposefully inflated the Loyalty Day numbers to make the communists look bad in comparison.[39] Insisting that the patriotic organizations were holding a "warmongers' parade" that was likely to lead the country "down the German path" of militarism and fascism, the CP rejected Loyalty Day's claim to the streets.[40] Instead, it clung to the hope that May Day would once again regain its former glory.[41]

Despite these attempts to defend the legitimacy of May Day, its supporters could not restore to it the influence it had wielded during its heyday in the 1930s, when it had sustained up to 250,000 participants. Not only did the holiday's organizers now have to contend with the opposition of the VFW and its affiliated groups, but after 1953, they also had to struggle with legal challenges that suspended their parades. Once the state firmly sided with May Day's detractors, communists and fellow travelers who wanted to maintain their tradition of marching on May 1 would find their attempts to do so stymied at every turn. The police commissioner's decision to deny the United Front May Day Committee its usual parade permit in 1953, a decision backed by the mayor and one that would be repeated in subsequent years, demonstrated how much the political climate in the city had changed from the early 1930s.[42] In those years, when the socialists and communists vied over access to Union Square, Mayor LaGuardia had appointed an independent committee to settle the dispute and find a way to satisfy both groups, which were considered valid political parties, albeit radical and marginal ones. By the early 1950s, during the height of the Red Scare, no such accommodation was offered by the state.

Instead, Mayor Vincent Impellitteri took up the concerns of veterans' groups and business associations in the city and denounced the May Day parade, arguing in late April 1953 that he would be "'very happy' if the permit [that had been granted to the organizing committee] would be revoked."[43] The controversy surrounding the permit issue had begun a few months earlier, when on January 31 the New York County chapter of Catholic War Veterans filed a petition asking the city council to forbid May Day celebrants from marching down Eighth Avenue and to require them instead to walk down Twelfth Avenue, "'or on some similar route far removed from the heart and center of the city.'" The veterans adopted this resolution, their commanding officer argued, "'because of persecution of Christian and Jewish peoples being conducted behind the Iron Curtain, the same Communist criminals who are murdering boys from New York City in Korea every day.'" Given this state of events, the Catholic veterans believed that it was inappropriate to have communists marching down the "heart and center" of their city on May 1.[44]

They were joined in their opposition to the presence of May Day revelers on Eighth Avenue by the West Side Association of Commerce Inc., which also filed an objection. Both petitions found their way to the State Supreme Court by late April when Mayor Impellitteri voiced his opposition to the parade. Going beyond the demands of the veterans, who merely wanted to shift the location of the parade, Impellitteri opened up the discourse to a broader condemnation of May Day and its supporters, arguing that because the Federal Subversive Activities Control Board had recently declared the Communist Party a "'subsidiary and puppet'" of the Soviet Union, its supporters and their holiday had no place on his city's streets. "'Now, with American boys dying in Korea because of Communist aggression,'" he asserted, "'these people just don't belong.'"[45]

Even the police commissioner, George P. Monaghan, agreed, explaining that *he* never authorized the permit, but that while he was away on vacation, the acting commissioner had granted it to the May Day Committee. Upon his return to New York in late April, when the controversy was heating up and the case was pending before the court, Monaghan publicly sided with the mayor and the petitioners in their opposition to the May Day parade. He told the *New York Times* that, "'In these times, when we are at war with the Communists, it would be in poor taste to have avowed enemies parading, ranting and shouting their venom against us."[46] City officials did not see the May 1 holiday as a long-standing American tradition, but rather had come to embrace the perspective of its detractors: May Day, it seemed to men like Impellitteri and Monaghan, had become an outlet for "ranting and shouting" puppets of Moscow.

On April 24, the State Supreme Court ruled on the petition to compel the withdrawal of the original permit, regardless of how it was originally issued. Citing a 1914 administrative code, the court revoked the permit on the grounds that the police commissioner's office "is prohibited from issuing a permit for a parade in a congested area unless the marchers had paraded for a period of ten years prior to July 7, 1914."[47] Because the organizers of May Day in 1953 could not point to a clear organizational link between their committee and the groups that had coordinated May Day parades before 1914, they could not counter the ruling. By using the 1914 code, the court was able to achieve the revocation of the permit while avoiding any direct political commentary on the nature of the parade or its supporters. Procedure, not politics, was cited to block the radicals from marching. Although Leon Straus, chairman of the United May Day parade committee, vowed that his group would try to find an area of the city that was not "congested" in an effort to get around this technical obstacle, he soon found that he would have to go through Monaghan to get the new permit.[48] Given the police commissioner's opinion of the radical holiday, his refusal to grant that permission is not surprising.

But in explaining his refusal to issue a new permit to Straus' group, Monaghan, unlike the court, did not hold back from employing politicized rhetoric. Although he, too, cited the technicality of an administrative code, he justified the use of that code through highly politically charged language. Monaghan noted how as police commissioner he was authorized to refuse to grant a permit "where he has good reason to believe that the proposed procession, parade or race will be disorderly in character or tend to disturb the public peace." Given that the United May Day committee had been listed by the attorney general as a subversive organization, just like the CP; given the current context of the Korean War and the deep animosity against communists felt among the general public; and given that the 1952 May Day parade had been met with a mob throwing eggs, tomatoes, and stones, Monaghan argued that he truly believed any demonstration by the radicals in the city could spark disorder, which he was duty bound to prevent. He essentially blamed May Day supporters for the violence that their opponents had meted out against them. And rather than seeking to protect the radicals, Monaghan sided with their conservative detractors and used the city code to deny them their right to free speech. He portrayed the city as a tinderbox and the May Day revelers as the match that could strike a conflagration when he described the "fever-pitched emotions and tensions among the people of our city against communism."[49] In concluding his justification for denying the parade permit, Monaghan echoed Impellitteri's concerns about the contemporary Cold War climate. The commissioner dramatically asserted that he would "not subject the people of this city to the sight of the red flag of communism while the red blood of our American boys is spilling in Korea."[50]

Marginalized within city politics, and facing open hostility from veterans' organizations, business groups, the police commissioner, and even the mayor, the CP and its United May Day committee were powerless to protest. The party could not mobilize as it had done during the permit disputes of the early 1930s, but remained limited to leveling verbal criticism within its press.[51] Instead of the large parade it hoped to organize on May 1, communists and fellow travelers had to be content to coordinate annual meetings in Union Square.[52] But, by 1954, the CP found it difficult to organize even these meetings. Mayor Robert F. Wagner's new administration maintained Impellitteri's opposition to the communist demonstrators, denying their request for a parade permit and limiting their gathering in the square to a ninety-minute meeting scheduled from 6:30 to 8 P.M.[53]

The May Day rally was pushed to this limited evening time slot because the influential Fourteenth Street Association had secured permission from the city to hold its own events in Union Square during the day. Created during the 1920s, this association of local merchants worked to improve conditions in the Fourteenth Street and Sixth Avenue area neighborhood by working with police to reduce the presence of panhandlers, to improve street lighting, and to introduce parking meters to boost sales at local retail shops. By the early 1950s, the association was led by its chairman, Leonard Jan Mitchell, owner of Lüchow's restaurant.[54] While the VFW marginalized and eventually helped eliminate communist parades on May 1, the Fourteenth Street Association undermined the radicals' claim to what had been their traditional gathering place. Not only had Union Square been the historic location for May Day rallies since the turn of the century, but it also had housed nearby the headquarters of many unions, including the ILGWU, and the Communist and Socialist parties. To prevent Communist Party members and their union supporters from gathering here on May 1 would be a significant blow to the radicals' confidence and would challenge their claim to dominate this part of the city. It would be a struggle over who would get to decide how to use and define the character of the city's public space. Members of the association, who were merchants from the surrounding neighborhood, sought "to establish 'a monopoly of Union Square by loyal American citizens, thus making the historic site unavailable for the rabble-rousing elements.'"[55] To bring about this "rededication of Union Square to Americanism,"[56] these supporters of anticommunist American nationalism would deny the space to radicals by staging a hostile takeover.

Along with their family and friends, members of the association gathered there on May 1 at 10 A.M. for a "six-hour patriotic demonstration," which included musical reviews and speeches for the adults and games for the children. "To indicate disapproval of previous left-wing demonstrations," the venue was temporarily renamed "Union Square USA."[57] Through such symbolic action, the Fourteenth Street Association sought to purge the communists from the city and reclaim the ground on which they stood. In place of the radical demonstrations that had once taken place in Union Square, anticommunist merchants created a celebration that heralded America as the leader of the "free world," the ultimate defender of individual freedom and unfettered capitalism. These businessmen legitimized their bourgeois values by ceremonially linking them to Cold War definitions of patriotism in the public square.

The efforts of groups like the Fourteenth Street Association and the VFW also suggest how Americans fashioned the local experience of the Cold War and Red Scare of late 1940s and 1950s. Here, at the grassroots level of America's public culture, average citizens constructed a new Cold War nationalism. Such nationalism was narrowly focused on an overtly anticommunist defense of political and economic freedom. As suggested by the thrust of the Loyalty Day events, it also tended to be martial and masculine in tone. Americans thus experienced the domestic Cold War not just in the well-known anticommunist crusades of Attorney General Clark, Senator Joseph McCarthy, and the House Un-American Activities Committee.[58] By staging parades and gatherings to eradicate the radicals' holiday, the VFW and Fourteenth Street Association actively contributed to Cold War anticommunist fervor. In chasing communists and communist sympathizers from public places, veterans, businessmen, and those New Yorkers who supported them, proclaimed and defended a new Cold War vision of Americanism. That vision undermined both the May Day holiday (including its memory as an American event) and the ability of political radicals to claim and define urban public space.

The rising tide of anticommunist sentiment that shaped this new Cold War vision of Americanism was not the only explanation for May Day's eroding support. Beyond the VFW and Fourteenth Street Association opposition to the May 1 holiday there was, among those who had been its most ardent supporters, a growing wariness about the usefulness of the day. Many radical and progressive workers found it increasingly difficult to sustain the holiday during the early Cold War. Over time, even some of the most left-leaning unions came to reject the radical holiday. Such was the case with District 65 of the Retail, Wholesale and Department Store Union and several locals within the Bakery, Confectionery and Tobacco Workers International Union in New York. Once such unions abandoned the holiday, there was little hope left for May Day's survival in America.

In the emerging Cold War climate, workers in these left-leaning unions started to quarrel among themselves as they questioned the integrity and usefulness of May Day. Many became fearful of the repercussions of being associated so closely with the Communist Party. Others pondered the utility of a holiday that had become linked not only to the CPUSA, but also to the global communist movement. Workers hashed out these concerns during debates on the floor of their annual conventions during the late 1940s and early 1950s. The records of these meetings reveal both the last attempts of more radical workers to defend May Day and the gradual erosion of union members' support for the holiday by the early 1950s.

In April 1946, members raised many of these issues in a lengthy discussion that took place during District 65's General Council meeting. After one report on May Day that detailed the union's plans to participate in that year's parade, Frank Boyle, a member from the needle processing section, expressed his displeasure. Arguing that May Day was not an American holiday but rather one that "dates back to the history of Europe," Boyle questioned why 65 had to participate in the event. He noted how his shop did not get the day off, and that if his members wanted to join the parade, they would lose pay. In Boyle's mind, May Day was a waste of time and money and served no discernible purpose.[59]

In response, a number of Boyle's fellow union members defended May Day, citing its American origins and its importance as a demonstration of labor solidarity. Sol Molofsky, 65's recreation director, first recalled the history of May Day in America dating back to 1886. He asserted that he planned to march in his army uniform as a veteran in the 1946 May 1 parade despite the headlines in the press that claimed, "it is undemocratic to come out and demonstrate on May Day." Speaking more to the criticisms of those outside the union, Molofsky refused to be intimidated by red-baiters. He insisted:

> I have the right to demonstrate for the things that I need to live in peace and security in America and May Day, 1946, is going to see a lot of guys doing the same thing and I am going to get my uniform to march in that May Day parade. No matter what they tell you, every time we have done things decent and good for us, we have been called red and all kinds of names, bolsheviks, etc., but we are determined to keep our eye on the ball and this May Day should see a good outpouring of our workers.[60]

With Molofsky's closing words, the union hall erupted in applause. After things quieted down, Jack Case from general processing explained that even though workers in his shop did not have May Day as a paid holiday in their contract, they had voted to take a half day off anyway. He noted how they "went down to the boss's office and told him that at 12:15 Wednesday the shop is going out." Case argued that for those in his shop, May Day provided an opportunity, in a time of cuts in overtime wages, for them to "demonstrate to our boss our willingness to fight the cuts."[61] Iris Wilson from garment supplies echoed this defense of May Day's purpose, noting that the sixty people from her shop who planned to march were doing so "to show what we want and what we intend to get and that is why we are marching on May Day."[62] And finally, Bruno Zelinsky issued a passionate defense of the holiday, calling it a distinctly American event that had meaning and significance for workers in the United States:

> Most labor people know that May Day started in America. European countries followed suit years later and not before us in America. . . . Therefore I think that we should study more about these May Day parades and labor history and make sure that we know before we can accuse ourselves and our labor of following some foreign ideology or stuff like that. I think that May Day is our day and we have to point out to the wealthy people in America that we are united and we will stop them from exploiting us.[63]

Zelinsky was not the only member of District 65 to insist that May Day was both an American and a union tradition.[64] Organizer Kenneth Sherbell echoed this sentiment in the union's May Day report in 1947. He noted how the holiday gave District 65 "an opportunity to show the world, by banners, placards, floats and displays and by our physical presence, who we are, the kind of work we do and to proclaim our aims and objectives." Sherbell recalled how his union had used May Day to "launch the two greatest organization drives. . . . the drive for 10,000 members by 1941 and the great '7 in 7' drive for 7,000 new members in 7 months."

Yet, despite this record, he acknowledged how among some of the union's members, "certain objections are generally raised in connection with our participation in the May Day parade," most notably "that May Day is a foreign importation." After debunking this myth, Sherbell exposed the second major objection raised by those who were wary of the union's endorsement of May Day: "that it leaves us open to the charge of being a Red Union and thereby hurts our efforts to organize." Dismissing this criticism by reminding his readers that the May 1 parades have historically aided in union organizing, he cynically asked, "does anyone have the illusion that we will stop being called Red if we do not endorse May Day?" Answering his own question, Sherbell argued that, "we will be called Red so long as we continue to be an honest, democratic organization and continue to fight for high wages, security and a better life."[65] In Sherbell's mind, the union was better off standing firm in its commitments to militant organizing and the May Day holiday, both of which, as he explained, long had gone hand in hand.

By 1947, this left-leaning union's assertion of May Day's American and union credentials was becoming more strident and defensive. Sherbell and other union supporters of May Day not only had to deal with their fellow workers' growing wariness of the holiday's usefulness. Now they also had to contest several external challenges to both May Day and organized labor. This was a dual struggle. First, there was growing anticommunist sentiment in the nation that was fostered not only in Truman's foreign policy statements, but also during events like "I Am an American Day" and Loyalty Day. Then, there was the conservative backlash against New Deal labor concessions led by red-baiting businessmen and Republican politicians, who had secured the passage of the Taft-Hartley Act. Staunchly supported by the National Association of Manufacturers, this law was intended to undermine the prolabor provisions of the Wagner Act. It instituted a ban on so-called unfair labor union practices to balance out the restrictions placed on employers' management tactics under Wagner.

Included among the unfair labor union practices that the Taft-Hartley Act banned were the closed shop, jurisdictional strikes, secondary boycotts, and union political campaign contributions. In addition, unions now could be subject to damage suits for breach of contract and foremen and supervisors were prohibited from joining unions. Most ominously for the nation's progressive unions, Section 9(h) of the new law required union officers to sign affidavits confirming that they were not members of the Communist Party or any communist organization.[66] If union leaders refused to sign the affidavits, their union would lose access to the National Labor Relations Board (NLRB). This included participation in NLRB elections, which gave unions the legal recognition to act as the sole bargaining agent for workers in a given shop. While the National Association of Manufacturers had lobbied hard for this law and celebrated its passage, the American Federation of Labor (AFL) and the Congress of Industrial Organizations (CIO) decried Taft-Hartley as a "slave labor bill."

Consequently, it became increasingly difficult for progressive unions with ties to the CP to sustain their unity and integrity. Much more than social ostracism was now at risk for turning out with the communists on May 1. District 65 maintained its commitment to May Day from 1948 to 1950, but only under considerable stress.[67] Union members were aware of the growing opposition they faced in their efforts to secure the integrity of organized labor and demonstrate its strength each May 1. During a General Council meeting in April 1948, for example, delegate Medlin from the cosmetics division acknowledged that they were to "have quite a bit of rivalry on May First" from the VFW, which planned to "march down Fifth Avenue at the same hour." Medlin recognized these Loyalty Day plans for what they were: "an attempt to sabotage our efforts for a great turnout." He thus called on his fellow unionists to "meet this challenge with at least seven or eight thousand 65'ers in the biggest turnout in the history of the union."[68]

Despite the opposition from the VFW, District 65 managed to stage a fairly impressive parade that year. Union members coordinated nine full divisions, totaling more than 3,000 marchers, carried dozens of placards, staged a number of floats, and spent more than two thousand dollars in the production of their displays.[69] Led by a color guard of seven men and one woman, union members followed behind eight American flags, carrying banners that proclaimed 65 to be their "fighting union." Despite

Figure 7.2. Despite increasing popular opposition to May Day during the Cold War, New York's District 65 continued to march in the annual parade. Here, the union's special Color Guard contributed to its display of patriotic union militancy on May Day in 1948. United Automobile Workers, District 65 Photographs Collection, Robert F. Wagner Labor Archives, New York University.

this show of patriotic union militancy, it was not the 8,000-member-strong turnout Medlin had hoped for. Perhaps the VFW's "attempt to sabotage" the union and May Day was a success? The intensifying Cold War climate had begun to chill the enthusiasm of District 65's rank and file.

David Livingston, chairman of the union's General Council, had warned that the current hostile climate, which now included the pressures of Taft-Hartley, would undermine the vitality of May Day and threaten the freedom of unions to participate. For Livingston, the political repercussions of such repression were enormous. May Day provided an opportunity for him to speak out against what he believed was wrong in "the way things are going." The problem, Livingston argued, was not merely the issues he wished to protest ("the way things were going"), but also the reactionary politics that accompanied such issues. Livingston was disturbed by the widening of the Second Red Scare, of which Section 9(h) of Taft-Hartley was a part. He cited the nation's House Un-American Activities Committee's support for the creation of a list of subversive "un-American" organizations, and he alluded to the increasing use of the Smith Act, under which eleven Communist Party leaders were being investigated for conspiring to

overthrow the U.S. government.[70] Believing that such episodes were por-
tents of a dangerous trend in the nation, Livingston explained to his fellow 65'ers that under such a law, "anybody or any organization who by any
method tries to change our government is now subversive." The repercussions of the creeping politics of reaction were frightening, he believed, and
impinged not just on his ability to express his dissent each May Day, but
also on his very identity as a dissenter. Somberly, he noted how "the day
when it is illegal for us to fight for a better world, the day when we can't
have Communist thoughts, if you please, that is the day when this country
as we know it will cease to exist. It is only a short step from there to concentration camps."[71] Speaking only three years after the end of the war in
Europe, Livingston evoked memories of the Holocaust that were still fresh
in the popular imagination. For progressives like Livingston, one of the
main lessons drawn from the war and the revelation of Nazi horrors was
the dangers of unchecked state power and mass politics. Along with others on the left, he had come to fear the damage that could be wrought by
stifling dissent in the name of national unity.[72]

*Figure 7.3. In this 1948 May Day parade in New York, District 65's banner proclaim-
ing it to be a "fighting union" reinforced the message of patriotic union militancy.
United Automobile Workers, District 65 Photographs Collection, Robert F. Wagner
Labor Archives, New York University.*

The stakes were high for the union, and especially for its more radical dissenters. In 1949, union leaders again called for a great turnout on May Day, arguing that "our employers and their big brothers of Big Business. . . . can't scare us. . . . we're sticking to our union by the biggest turnout ever."[73] Yet, once again, the level of participation was disappointing.[74] Even when the Cold War issues that were undermining May Day were criticized in the holiday's displays (in 1950, for example, District 65 highlighted "the demand for the repeal of the Taft-Hartley Law. . . . for an end to witch-hunts, [and] for the preservation of the Bill of Rights for all Americans"[75]), they still contributed to the holiday's decline. No matter how much union leaders and active union members denounced the effects of the repressive Cold War climate, by the early 1950s it clearly had begun to erode the rank and file's enthusiasm for May Day.

This was certainly the case in some locals within the Bakery, Confectionery and Tobacco Workers International Union in New York. Bakers Union Local 17 of Woodside had been a loyal supporter of May Day since the 1930s.[76] By 1947, however, things had changed. When the union's May Day parade committee made its report to the membership at the General Meeting in April, "a motion was made to participate in the May day [sic] parade by a vote and was defeated."[77] Because the minutes do not include a transcript of any debate that may have taken place before the vote, it is unclear why the bakers had now decided to withdraw their support for the holiday. However, additional evidence from the minutes suggests that the union members had come to reject the radical politics associated with May Day in favor of the Cold War Americanism that was emerging in the city's "I Am an American Day" and Loyalty Day events. In April 1948, Local 17's Executive Board accepted an invitation from the mayor's office to participate in the "American Day" celebration. It did the same in 1949 and agreed to join in the VFW's Loyalty Day parade.[78] In subsequent years, the union donated money to the local VFW, indicating sympathy for the veteran's organization and its more conservative agenda.[79]

Taking a stand against May Day and its radical political ties did not, of course, mean that these locals were less militant in their workplace demands.[80] Although District 65's David Livingston and other supporters of May Day initially believed that the annual radical day of protest was necessary to maintain union integrity and strength, many union leaders believed the opposite. As the Cold War and Red Scare heated up, such leaders recognized that any ties to communism, even if that meant marching alongside party members in the same parade, had become too

much of a liability. It left them and their organizations open to red bait-
ing by employers and (after the passage of the McCarran Internal Security
Act in 1950) to investigation by the attorney general for subversive activities.[81] Such penalties intensified the challenges that union leaders already
faced under the 1947 Taft-Hartley Law, which required them to sign noncommunist affidavits or risk their union's access to NLRB certification.
Widespread purges of communists from the ranks of individual unions
and from the CIO in 1949 were one of the significant results of this new
political reality.[82]

These pressures also influenced workers to abandon May Day. The constraints led the Cake Bakers Local 51 of Manhattan to support a motion
banning its participation in May Day parades. The membership voted for
the measure during a meeting in April 1950,[83] thus following the lead of
the New York State Federation of Labor and other central AFL bodies,
which had "banned members and affiliated groups from participating in
May Day Parades as detrimental to the cause of the AFL and all organized
labor."[84]

Such bans made it difficult for radical workers to participate in May
Day parades and maintain their union membership. Even if their union
no longer officially endorsed the holiday, some more politically progressive members still hoped to be able to march on their own. For Jack Tassara and Isidor Friedman of Local 51, such hopes were soon dashed. After
marching in the May Day parade in 1951, both men were expelled from
their union. After finding that the men had violated the union's ruling
from April 25, 1950, which had banned members from participating in the
May Day parade, the Executive Board of Local 51 decided to oust Tassara
and Friedman during its June 21 meeting.[85]

Tassara appealed the decision during the union's regular membership
meeting on June 26, but "on motion a vote was taken to sustain the decision of the Executive Board." It was a close vote, but the majority of the
members agreed with their leaders, who defended the expulsion as a necessary penalty for the violation of a democratically imposed restriction.
To be responsive to those members who sympathized with Tassara's situation, the board recommended that he be suspended from "all union rights
and privileges except for work for a period of five years," rather than be
expelled permanently. This motion was "overwhelmingly carried."[86]

Friedman did not fare so well. At the June 26 meeting, he protested
his expulsion by reading from a prepared statement. Claiming that he
"didn't know it was wrong to march in the May Day parade," he asserted

his standing as a good member of the union and presented a "statement of good conduct signed by 60 members in the Berke Cake Co.," where he worked. But Friedman did not stop at this defense. Instead, he launched into a protest of the current national political climate, citing the ugly riot at Peekskill[87] as an example of the violence and intolerance that had pervaded the nation. He concluded his appeal by making "scornful remarks concerning Bro. Irving Shapiro who saw him parading."

Friedman's approach did not sit well with many of his fellow unionists, nor was the Executive Board impressed. It rejected Friedman's claim that he did not know about the May Day ban, reminding him and all those assembled at the June 26 meeting that "Friedman had been warned not to participate in communist activities or sympathizer groups after he had attended a communist inspired peace rally in Chicago and permitted his photograph to appear in the press with his name as a member of Local 51." Friedman had not simply violated the union's rules; he had also embarrassed, and potentially undermined, the union by his rogue political activities. In addition, rather than expressing contrition during his appeal, he went on the offensive and spouted a radical political agenda before the board. Not surprisingly, the membership "voted overwhelmingly to sustain the action of the Executive Board and expel him from membership."[88]

Given the intense anticommunist sentiment that existed both within and outside the labor movement, by 1951, even District 65 could no longer sustain its support for May Day. That year, the General Council decided that, because "there exists division in various areas [of the union] over the parade," District 65 would "not officially endorse the parade but refer the communication [from the United May Day Committee] for consideration to each area and local."[89] It would still be possible for the locals affiliated with District 65 to stage their own displays in the May Day parade, but there would be no demonstration of the union as a whole.

In the meantime, the McCarran Committee's ongoing investigation of District 65's leadership had worn the union down, and pushed it to reverse its long-standing resistance to signing the Taft-Hartley noncommunist affidavits. According to the convention proceedings, by 1950, the union's membership, "while recognizing the viciousness of the Taft-Hartley law, decided that the best interests of the Union could be served by compliance and directed the officers of our Union to file the noncommunist affidavits as required by Section 9H of the law."[90] Yet, as union leader Samuel Neuberger later noted, this did not stop the government from pressuring the union. Even such "compliance was not enough for these reactionary congressmen and employers [who] wanted to destroy our union." According to Neuberger, "newspapers and government officials threatened [District 65's leadership with] persecutions [sic] for perjury." The investigations into the union continued to drag on for years. David Livingston and other union leaders, for example, were subpoenaed to testify before the McCarran Committee in 1952, distracting them from their work in building up and maintaining the union.[91] This harassment of the union's leadership undermined the strength and integrity of District 65, and fueled the wariness many of its members felt toward cooperating with communists on May Day. As was the case with the bakery union locals, once the membership decided to turn its back on the radical holiday, they could not be forced to support it.

Instead, by the 1950s, more and more unions that had once supported May Day came to abandon it. Most other unions had already long ceased celebrating the radical holiday, focusing instead on the September Labor Day. For many of these workers, the abandonment of May Day began during World War II, when they had participated in the special wartime Labor Day and Flag Day events and "I Am an American Day" demonstrations. Like that vibrant new holiday, the revived Labor Day events continued well into the postwar period. But if supporters of "I Am an American Day" came to voice a universal notion of Cold War Americanism, the September holiday allowed for a consumerist working-class articulation of Cold War Americanism. Unionists tapped into the heritage of Labor Day as *labor's day* to voice their concerns as workers. And they did so in what had become a changed cultural and political landscape—one transformed by the Cold War. At once adopting and adding to the language of the nation's Cold War anticommunist sentiment, these unionists wedded their defense of organized labor to the sanctity of free labor and a superior American standard of living. They contrasted both the blessings of free labor and the bounty of American consumer culture with the tyranny and deprivation they believed were inherent in communism.

During New York's 1959 Labor Day parade, leaders and members of TWU Local 100 spoke in this new language. That year more than 122,000 workers from the TWU, the ILGWU, and other unions marched under the banner of "A Strong Free Labor Movement Means a Strong Free America." TWU leaders had issued handbills to their membership announcing the event, in which they asserted that Labor Day was "the American working man's national holiday," and called on the rank and file to "demonstrate

workers' contribution to American living." This would be a patriotic celebration of the American worker and of his centrality in sustaining a
"strong free America."[92]

Yet, in making this nationalist connection, union leaders also hoped
that the Labor Day display would lend support to the TWU's ongoing
struggle with the Transit Authority for a better contract. TWU President
Matthew Guinan intended the Labor Day parade to be more than just a
celebration of free labor. He wanted to use this uniquely American day
to advance the cause of his union. Guinan called on his section officers
to rally the membership on Labor Day in a demonstration of TWU's
strength and in support of its "counteroffensive" against "the anti-labor
politicking in Washington."[93]

In response, TWU workers presented themselves as both patriotic
Americans and as American workers who deserved a share of the abundance that they helped produce for the nation under its free system. In
the 1959 Labor Day parade, union members symbolically linked their demands to what had become a source of pride during the Cold War: the
advanced standard of living that constituted the "American way of life."
Union members marched behind banners that read, "Strong Militant
Unionism Means: Better Vacations," "Strong Militant Unionism Means:
Better Pensions," "30-Hour Work Week," and "Better Sick Leave Benefits,"
in a parade their leaders touted as a "Mammoth March to Help Workers
to a Better Life."[94]

The TWU workers hoped that their demonstration would convince
employers of their right for a better life. They made their appeal as loyal
Americans who turned out on the "American workingman's national holiday," not on what they believed was the foreign and communist-dominated May Day. Yet, they also made their appeal as laborers. Harkening
back to traditional late-nineteenth-century Labor Day parades, TWU
members demonstrated their labor pride by "depict[ing] their own activities." They conducted "floats of subway cars, trolleys, double-decker buses
and other transit vehicles to show changes in the industry over 50 years."
Other union members tapped into this traditional method of demonstrating craft pride as well. Local 51 of the Bakery, Confectionery and Tobacco
Workers, for example, showed off a massive cake during the parade.[95]
Workers once again presented themselves as the axis of society, but here,
during the Labor Day demonstrations of the 1950s, they did so to demand
the continued integrity of their unions and to assert their right to share in
their nation's rising standard of living.

Workers pursued this dual agenda by merging two historical styles of working-class self-expression and deploying them to new ends in the Cold War context of the 1950s. In their Labor Day parades workers used the more traditional celebration of craft identity (reenactments of work on floats, displays of wares made by workers' calloused hands) to voice a more modern demand to share fully in the nation's growing consumer culture (via better wages and benefits). The former style (the expressions of craft pride) dates back to parades held in the late eighteenth century. Its revival here in the 1950s indicates a sense of continuity in the public memory of unionized workers; there was a rich expressive tradition that they could and did draw from to stage their public display of labor pride. And that pride indicated a renewed union militancy, at once politically "safer" and distinct from the radical militancy that communists expressed on May Day. The latter demand (for full participation in the nation's consumer culture) was made first by the workers, union and nonunion alike, who chose to absent themselves from Labor Day parades and enjoy their three-day weekend at amusement parks, movie theaters, and other venues that characterized American popular consumer culture in the 1900s and 1910s. This was very different from the shape the consumerist concern took in the 1950s, when workers voiced it from *within* the Labor Day parades as *part of* their union demands. The idea of a consumer class consciousness was still there, as it had been first developed in the early decades of the twentieth century,[96] but it now took on a unionist face, especially as it was expressed through the more traditional celebration-of-craft style. So while the demand for better wages and benefits made during the 1950s Labor Day parades was not completely new, there was a significant difference in the way workers presented and understood that claim.

Workers now brought those demands to bear in the new political context of the Cold War, where they could claim their right to share fully in an *American* way of life that stood in contrast to the deprivations of the Soviet system. The Cold War increased the purchase of their demands, while it shifted the focus of their concerns from the shop floor to increased purchasing power. The politics of the Cold War and the Red Scare also pushed workers and their union leaders into championing this new focus. As Lizabeth Cohen has noted, "in the wake of the 1946 strikes and the restrictions imposed by Taft-Hartley a year later, labor leaders reoriented their bargaining objectives away from demanding a greater say in shop floor operation and company decision-making from employers and more extensive social provision from government toward maximizing workers' purchasing power."[97] The 1950s Labor Day demonstrations suggest that many rank-and-file union members had come to embrace this perspective as well. In those parades they constructed a uniquely American working-class identity for themselves as they voiced their determination to share fully in their nation's growing consumer culture. In articulating this distinctly working-class version of Cold War Americanism, these unionists had little use for May Day, which they had come to see as an un-American Soviet import.

The few radicals who held on during the 1950s and tried to organize small May Day meetings wherever they could were marginalized within the dominant American Cold War political culture. Now when they attempted to take to the streets, they became targets of verbal abuse and physical attack, often enduring rotten eggs and ripe tomatoes.[98] In addition, these stalwart radicals also became targets of the federal government's crackdown on "subversive activities."[99] As a result of these pressures and the collapse of the Communist Party in the United States, by 1960, very few people remained to sustain America's May Day tradition. In fact, by 1956, there were very few CP members and supporters left to be affected by such federal government harassment. Membership in the party had dropped from its high of 85,000 to approximately 5,000 nationwide. Much of this decline can be attributed to the hostile atmosphere of the Cold War, but the numbers declined even further after the Khrushchev revelations of February 1956.[100] Disillusionment over Soviet admissions concerning Stalin's reign of terror led many party faithful to leave the ranks, and to abandon the holiday that had been a central part of their collective self-identification for decades.[101] Whereas the political persecution of the first Red Scare had intensified the commitment of many radicals to the cause and did not preclude the reemergence of May Day in the 1930s, that of the Second Red Scare was accompanied by a conglomeration of factors that would finally undermine the holiday. Not only did the anticommunist crusade alienate the party from the unions (at the same moment organized labor sought a less confrontational posture in the postwar boom economy), but the internal collapse of the communist movement in America after 1956 also doomed it—and May Day—to oblivion in the United States.[102]

By 1960, the holiday that had represented the aspirations of those who embraced radical politics was now all but abandoned in America.[103] May Day had become so strongly identified with the Soviet Union and global communism that it had been rendered useless as a vehicle for democratic protest in the United States. Even after the Second Red Scare of the late 1940s and early 1950s had passed, the May 1 holiday could not be revived to its former glory. May Day lost its wider audience, as the class divisions that were laid bare during the Great Depression seemed to fade in a postwar wave of consumption. The old radical and working-class holiday, born in the streets of Chicago and New York in the movement for the eight-hour day and expanded into an annual protest for the end of capitalism, rang hollow in a land of uneasy peace and unusual plenty.

One of the most significant reasons why large-scale May Day celebrations in America effectively ceased by 1960 was that radical and progressive workers had abandoned the holiday. Beginning during World War II, many laborers defined their own versions of working-class Americanism that had no room for communism or other forms of political radicalism. They turned out to contribute to the expression of a new Cold War nationalism in Loyalty Day parades and "I Am an American Day" mass meetings during the late 1940s and 1950s. At the same time, especially after the passage of the Taft-Hartley Act in 1947, many progressive unions purged their ranks of communists, whom they considered political liabilities. Other unions initially struggled to maintain their support for May Day, claiming its heritage as a product of the American labor movement and celebrating its uniqueness as a place to make progressive demands important to labor. This defense of May Day became increasingly difficult, however, as opponents of the holiday, like the VFW, continued to insist that it was a Soviet import, at a time when Moscow had become America's greatest enemy. Consequently, it became increasingly untenable for workers to make use of such an event for political gain in the United States. As the holiday gradually became more of a liability than an asset, even those unions that had supported it for decades came to reject May Day.

At the same time that May Day celebrations were fading from the urban landscape, the holiday's history was popularly rewritten so that its American past was conveniently erased. Once the manifestations of Red Scare persecutions routed the holiday's traditional guardians from their posts by the late 1950s, the discourse surrounding May Day came under the control of its detractors. While individuals like Sol Molofsky and Bruno Zelinsky would know and remember May Day's long history in the United States, their memories would not receive a public hearing. Their reminiscences remained in their hearts and hidden in their union's records. Most Americans never heard Molofsky's and Zelinsky's defenses of

May Day's American roots and political relevance. They had access instead to the assertions of those whose organizations could command both the city's streets and the front pages of major newspapers each May 1. Those May Day detractors ignored the fact that the American labor movement had created the day in 1886 and disregarded the holiday's rich history in the United States. Following the lead of the VFW, the Fourteenth Street Association, and even members of progressive unions, most Americans now understood May Day to be a Soviet import, produced and directed by the Communist Party in Moscow.[104]

In the process of this revision of its history, May Day became Cold War America's forgotten holiday. In the creation of a new Cold War American nationalism, visible in the 1950s Loyalty Day and "I Am an American Day" celebrations, the real history of May Day had no place. If, as Matthew Dennis asserts in his study of American holidays, "purposeful remembering requires purposeful forgetting, as collective pasts are assembled through an editing process that leaves much on the cutting room floor," then May Day had to be forgotten in order to prioritize the emerging popular understanding of America as the leader of the free world, a nation that stood against the Soviet communist monolith.[105]

This popular forgetting of May Day's history in America, along with its dwindling celebration in the United States, contributed to and exemplified the narrowing of the nation's political discourse that had unfolded from the end of World War II through the Cold War. May Day, a holiday that saw workers and radicals call for economic justice and equality, was easily (and dare one say, necessarily?) forgotten in a nation that came to prioritize its role as the defender of the free world (and of free enterprise) against collectivist communism. While other forms of dissent were still possible, and moved to the fore of the nation's political discourse, the class-based concerns of the Old Left and its labor allies as they had existed before the war were marginalized.[106]

Those who voiced other forms of protest, like the defense of African-American civil rights, were able to make the new Cold War consensus work in their favor, drawing attention to the hypocrisy of continued racial inequality in a nation that proclaimed itself to be the leader of the free world. These race reformers could thus advance their agenda in the postwar years.[107] This was more difficult for American workers. Many labor leaders were able to adapt their demands to fit the new boundaries of acceptable political discourse, but in so doing, they had to give up their more far-reaching objectives. During a time when the sanctity of private property was linked so centrally to the nation's identity at home, and when America was rising up against the enemy of collectivist communism around the globe, labor leaders found it almost impossible to demand a say in the process of production. Workers revived Labor Day during the 1950s, defining in those celebrations a distinct working-class variety of Cold War Americanism. Most workers believed in the new identity they constructed for themselves, but they really had no other discourse with which to speak publicly. They could celebrate their pride as workers, but they did so in a clear demonstration of their loyalty as Americans. By the late 1950s, workers had no outlet for truly radical dissent, including the questioning of the very foundations of capitalism. May Day, the ideal vehicle for such discourse, was no longer viable in the United States.

Instead, workers displayed their fealty to the nation on a distinctly American Labor Day and asserted their value as workers who helped sustain the country's booming free-enterprise economy. Speaking the language of this new Cold War Americanism, workers redefined the meaning of class by eroding traditional class markers. Laborers were not celebrated solely as producers, who deserved an equal share in the fruits of their labor under the guiding logic of the labor theory of value. Instead, they celebrated themselves as Americans, who as the engine of the nation's economic growth deserved a share of the consumer dream that had become known as the "American way of life." What made this assertion distinct from organized labor's calls earlier in the century for a "living wage," was that it took priority over questions of workplace control. And that happened because of the narrowing effect of the Cold War consensus, which made it practically impossible to question the underlying structure of the nation's economic system. Those unions that tried to do so, like the left-led United Electrical Workers, were marginalized, even within the organized labor movement.[108] Other laborers, like urban social workers, rejected their identity as laborers outright and instead, "rushed to join the would-be universal white 'middle-class' bandwagon" of the postwar years." As Daniel Walkowitz has argued, such a choice further undermined the viability of a serious class-based critique for American workers. He notes how "the diminution of a class 'other' meant that, when confronted with economic anxieties that accompanied 'downsizing' and the globalization of work, they could blame only racial others—blacks, Mexicans, Haitians, and so forth—or themselves,"[109] not the broader capitalism system within which they struggled.

Part of the reason for this was that in many sectors of the nation's public culture during the late 1940s and 1950s, including the "I Am an

American Day" and Loyalty Day demonstrations, American nationalism was defined with a distinctly *classless* accent. It is therefore tempting to argue that within the articulation of Cold War Americanism, questions of class were subsumed as the more pressing concerns of individual rights were prioritized and as a generic middle-class identity was embraced by more and more Americans. As May Day disappeared, so, too, did an awareness and concern over class differences. Both could be said to have been forgotten in the postwar boom and in the Cold War sanctification of free enterprise. In this estimation, class would be the baby that was tossed out with the bathwater of May Day. However, as the revived Labor Day demonstrations suggest, questions of class did not disappear. American workers just continued to define those questions within the framework of an evolving nationalism. Granted they had to work on much narrower terrain than at any time in the past century, because the longtime foil of May Day and its radical dissenting rejection of the capitalist system was no more. But workers did struggle to maintain the integrity of organized labor. With their left flank effectively dissolved, however, it would be a different—and a difficult—fight. Questions of equality and justice would be voiced under the rubric of the struggle for human and civil rights. Many unions would find new momentum by working within this rights-based approach during the 1960s and 1970s.[110] The fundamental questioning of the capitalist system and the inequities that it created, however, has remained a problematic and unpopular endeavor.

Conclusion

By the early 1960s, May Day had essentially disappeared from urban America. Radicals no longer marched through the streets of New York City and Chicago on May 1 as they had done since the 1880s. What public gatherings they managed to host during the 1960s and 1970s generally consisted of only a few hundred participants, a pale comparison to the great mass meetings of the 1930s, when a half million people turned out. Thanks to the efforts of the Veterans of Foreign Wars, the Fourteenth Street Association, and the American Federation of Labor (AFL), most Americans thought of May Day as a foreign affair celebrated only by workers and communists in the Soviet Union and behind the Iron Curtain. Yet, May Day had functioned as a foil in the creation of American nationalism for so many decades. Now that it was gone, what difference did it make? What effect did its absence have on the shape of American nationalism? What were the consequences of May Day's decline for political discourse in the United States? And why should we recall the holiday's history when it eventually waned to insignificance here?

The process of forgetting May Day helped birth the new Cold War Americanism that dominated the nation's political culture from 1947 through the 1960s. In opposition to this holiday, Americans sustained an anticommunist consensus and extolled the promise of democracy and the free market during Loyalty Day, "I Am an American Day," and even Labor Day celebrations. In these ways, the marginalizing of May Day became central to the construction of a new form of popular American nationalism. After 1960, once May Day parades diminished so that they no longer remained a point of contrast against which to define loyal Americanism at home, the holiday continued to cast a shadow from overseas; political radicalism and its greatest holiday still existed in other nations around the world. At the precise moment when Americans redefined their nationalism on a global stage, May Day became increasingly identified as a foreign event. It still functioned as a foil to Americanism, but it was now fully identified with the communist enemy in the Soviet Union, China, Eastern Europe, and throughout Latin America: an enemy Americans opposed as they laid claim to their identity as the defenders of the free world.

As Americans came to see the struggle against political radicalism as something external to the nation, they shifted their focus from the "social question" of class, which had been at the core of May Day celebrations for decades. Intrinsic to the Cold War Americanism that they now embraced was a sense of classlessness. Since by the mid-1950s some 60 percent of the population enjoyed a middle-class standard of living for the first time—including workers who benefited from the extensive benefits and cost-of-living adjustments that their unions secured for them—many Americans believed that the old problems of class had been answered in the postwar boom and the Treaty of Detroit.[1] Inherent in this Americanism was a belief that class divisions no longer existed in the United States, and that even to engage in a discussion of such concerns was un-American. This outlook presumed that such problems belonged to Europe, or some other faraway place. Such attitudes perpetuated the forgetting of May Day's history in the United States, and fostered the disbelief that such an event could have originated here. And that process, in turn, significantly narrowed the range of political discourse in the United States.[2] Cold War Americanism sustained an exceptionalist nationalism in which class differences were believed to have eroded under the benevolent wave of postwar democratic capitalist expansion.

But such perceptions belied reality. Class divisions did not disappear during the Cold War. Many workers in the nation's basic industries, who were protected by large industrial unions and benefited from the "Great Bargain" of the postwar years, may have been better able to enjoy the fruits of the nation's affluence, but not all workers were so fortunate. There were still many people—male and female, black and white—who struggled to organize unions, to have them recognized, and to use them to obtain the most basic workplace protections during the postwar years.[3] Yet, somehow most Americans, then and now, have considered these struggles to be peripheral to the perceived norm of America's affluence, stability, and equality. Attempts to protest otherwise have remained at the margins of the nation's political discourse.

Even when the federal government advanced major new policies to address the persistence of poverty amid the plenty and to build a "Great Society" during the mid-1960s, the prevailing assumptions driving such policy did not question the legitimacy of the capitalist system. This policy focus resulted, of course, from much deeper changes that had taken place in the nation's political economy since World War II,[4] changes that dovetailed with the creation of Cold War Americanism in the nation's popular culture. In the arenas of political economy and popular culture, postwar American liberals celebrated the vitality and transformative power of capitalism as natural and necessary to the nation's future. There was very little room in American political culture to question either the nature of capitalism itself or the redistribution of economic growth, as happened in many radical corners since the emergence of industrial capitalism in the late nineteenth century, and by more mainstream political thinkers during the New Deal. Instead, the focus was on finding ways of continuing to expand the pie after the war and to assist the disadvantaged on a personal level by providing them with the skills they would need to lift themselves out of poverty.[5] There was little sympathy for pursuing broader economic change or for challenging the systemic causes of inequality. That kind of political discourse, which May Day's supporters had voiced for so long, was now no longer viable.

By the early 1960s, then, such probing criticism was no longer part of the debate over the nature of the nation. Instead, the thorny questions surrounding the persistence of racial discrimination had moved to the forefront of the discussion. This process, which had begun at least as early as World War II, continued into the early Cold War. The modern civil rights movement and the wave of dissent that characterized the New Left energized this different focus.

The demand for racial equality and the denunciation of the war in Vietnam became central features in the small May Day meetings held in Union Square from 1960 until the mid-1970s. The number of participants ranged from a maximum of 2,500 in 1961 to a low of 300 in 1971.[6] While economic demands were also made at these functions, such as calls for medical insurance for the elderly and unemployment relief, the chief concerns were the promotion of African-American civil rights, bringing an end to the Cold War, and until 1972, the withdrawal of American troops from Vietnam.[7] These dwindling May Day gatherings tapped into the concerns of the New Left and into the broader ethos of the rights revolutions then sweeping the nation. Because of that, the supporters of these small May Day events did not prioritize a purely class-based critique. And even when such class-based concerns were raised, they remained on the fringe of this now most marginalized of public events. Because the Cold War context cast the May 1 holiday as a decidedly un-American affair, these

Figure C.1. Young anti-war protestors in New York on May Day 1969. Communist Party of the United States Photographs Collection, Tamiment Library, New York University.

radical supporters were unable to host the large-scale, multicity May Day assemblages of the past. They could not effectively promote their alternative political messages within the nation's narrowing political discourse.

The broader rights revolutions of the 1960s and 1970s that existed apart from May Day and dominated the discourse of dissent in those years sought to achieve deep-seated systemic change both in law and in social attitudes.[8] To do this, leaders of these struggles emphasized *individual* freedom as the philosophical, moral, and legal justification for their fight.[9] These revolutions were responsible for the dramatic advances in African-American civil rights and women's and gay liberation in the latter half of the twentieth century. The importance of these achievements cannot be underestimated. These advances also indicate how at the same time that the nation's political discourse was narrowing in terms of the consciousness of class, it was expanding to accommodate the demands of those who asserted their equal rights as individual citizens.[10]

Yet, even while Americans struggled for those rights, the parameters of American political discourse never really provided sufficient space for the radical, class-based discussions that had characterized the old May

Day celebrations. When those in the civil rights movement tried to focus their energies on the underlying problem of economic inequality,
they could not get very far. Even Martin Luther King, Jr. was unable to
push the agenda of his Poor People's Campaign much beyond its earliest
planning stage. He faced dissent within the civil rights movement from
those who questioned the wisdom of tackling the "oppression of class and
caste," and from those eager to employ more violent tactics. Before King
had a chance to deal with these obstacles, he was assassinated, shot down
just after taking the first public step in his new campaign by siding with
striking sanitation workers in Memphis.[11]

After the Cold War ended, the individualist thrust of the rights revolution remained the defining characteristic of dissent in America. Interestingly, what few May Day gatherings took place in the United States during
the late 1980s and 1990s reflected this shift from the class-based concerns
of the Old Left to the more personal, self-oriented politics of the late
twentieth century. In 1995, for example, a small group of self-proclaimed
anarchists gathered on the corner of Ninth Street and Avenue C in New
York, where they ate roast pig, drank beer, and smoked marijuana. One
of the participants, Jerry Levy, an adjunct professor at LaGuardia Community College, told reporters that the purpose of their gathering was to
protest police harassment in the neighborhood. One block east of this pig
and pot fest, a separate crowd thronged Tompkins Square Park to hear
punk bands play. That gathering was "organized by squatters on Thirteenth Street, who were fighting eviction from the city."[12]

In Washington Square Park in the West Village, May Day gatherings
also took place during the 1990s that included public pot smoking. In 1998,
those supporting what had become known as J-Day (Joint Day) tried to
hold a march in the park but were pushed out by a larger city-sponsored
event for local families. In this neighborhood, May Day had been a rallying point since the late 1970s for those who wished to indulge publicly
in personal drug use and to call for its legalization. It had become a part
of the hip, countercultural tone of the square. By the late 1990s, however,
that changed as Mayor Rudolph Giuliani's administration cracked down
on such demonstrations and replaced them with child-friendly events
that included "mimes, face-painters, and ponies."[13] May Day had briefly
become the focal point for a larger debate about identity and the use of
urban space, but it was one that was now wrapped up in the cultural politics of recreation and personal freedom, not a critique of capitalism that
called for economic justice.

As a labor and radical holiday concerned with promoting such justice, May Day had essentially disappeared in the United States during the late twentieth century. Even when immigrants and their supporters staged widespread demonstrations in protest of U.S. immigration policy on May 1, 2006, most American observers did not grasp the significance of the date. And if they did, they assumed that May Day was chosen because of its reputation as an international workers' day. Most participants and observers understood the call for immigrant solidarity, to be shown through demonstrations and a one-day boycott of the economy, to have its radical political roots in labor and socialist traditions found abroad. In truth, many of the thousands of workers who turned out on May 1, 2006, did bring that radical critique with them from Mexico or Latin America; such an analysis had long been absent in the United States. So, despite the brief renaissance of the holiday here, most people did not recognize its American roots. Those had been forgotten; May Day and its radical, class-based critique were now experienced solely as an imported tradition.

Aside from this brief revival in 2006, May Day has essentially disappeared in the United States and its long history here has been forgotten. Yet, it is important for a number of reasons to recall that history. On the most basic level, it reminds us that class has been a driving force behind American politics for much of the nation's past. Moreover, it illustrates the reactionary nature of much of American nationalism as it has been created since the mid-nineteenth century. The history of May Day reveals how, alongside that reactionary nationalism, radicals and workers constructed many creative alternatives. They offered different definitions of Americanism from which modern-day dissenters may or may not wish to draw in their struggles against inequality and injustice. May Day's American past also reveals one way many Americans achieved a balance between what might appear as irreconcilable political identities, considering themselves true Americans while at the same time espousing radical anarchist, socialist, or communist ideals.

As this study has shown, May Day was central not only to the lives of the political radicals who created and sustained it for more than sixty years, but also to the contours of American nationalism that were defined alongside and in reaction to it. From the 1880s to the 1960s, through their annual May Day celebrations anarchists, socialists, and communists presented themselves as radical Americans, offering different visions for the nation's future. For most, the purpose was to compel America's dominant democratic capitalist order to become more just. The different radical visions they forwarded included an idealized romantic transnationalism, an international socialism, a domestic social democracy, and a communist commonwealth that embraced ethnic pluralism. Although these systems did not take root in America, that they were advocated each May Day showed the process through which those unsatisfied with the status quo constructed alternative possibilities. The history of May Day illuminates these competing definitions of Americanism, and thus provides a significant chapter in the story of that period's nationalist imaginings.

During the 1890s, while politically moderate trade unionists in the AFL increasingly gave their support to the September Labor Day holiday, anarchists and socialists embraced the radical implications of May Day as the harbinger of the international socialist order that they hoped to realize. By the turn of the twentieth century, the young Socialist Party forged broad working-class coalitions and organized large-scale parades with up to 60,000 participants. Many of the unionists who joined in these parades did so to demonstrate their own identities as proud workers, like the Jewish bakers in 1911, and may not necessarily have shared in the socialists' revolutionary visions. In their May Day demonstrations, Socialist Party members vigorously defended their right to carry the American flag alongside the red flag as socialist Americans, who believed that the promise of democracy inherent in their nation's political system would only be fulfilled through the creation of a socialist commonwealth. Despite the best efforts of Socialist Party leaders to identify with America's democratic heritage, their May Day parades and mass meetings became targets of both political persecution and vigilante violence during the first Red Scare. Both conservative and progressive groups created new events to supplant the radical May 1 displays during the 1920s, including American Day, Loyalty Day, and National Child Health Day. Even within organized labor there was a continued movement away from the observation of May Day during the first decades of the twentieth century, as the leadership in the AFL supported Labor Day instead.

Within the context of the Great Depression of the 1930s, socialists and communists were able to revive their outdoor May Day parades and mass meetings, and the holiday reached its climax in numerical strength and cultural relevance. But because the Communist Party came to dominate the celebration in this decade, May Day would wane once again, as the accusation of its having been a foreign-controlled event found traction, first among anticommunists on the left and later, during the Cold

War, within a wider American public. In this Cold War climate, and reeling from the witch hunts of the Second Red Scare, those communists and progressive unionists who tried to maintain May Day's presence in the United States, like District 65, found it increasingly difficult. Not only did they confront dwindling support for the parades among their own ranks, but they also had to contend with the effectiveness of their opponents' campaign to define May Day as an un-American, Soviet import. Consequently, as May Day essentially disappeared from the streets of America, so its history disappeared from the nation's popular memory. The holiday's detractors, including military veterans, religious and community groups, and certain labor unions, dominated city streets with Loyalty Day and "I Am an American Day" celebrations that helped forge a new Cold War Americanism characterized by militant anticommunist and pro–free market sympathies. Those detractors captured the front pages of the major newspapers to promote this new Americanism, while they cast May Day as a foreign-inspired rally supported only by puppets of Moscow.

Although May Day's history in America has been forgotten as a result, it is a history with much to teach us. The different political identifications that radicals created for themselves and the nation each May 1 were articulated within the context of a broader American political culture. That creation existed as a type of cultural dialogue, often expressed in terms of protest with mainstream definitions of Americanism. Although the period from the 1880s to the 1920s has been correctly characterized as having housed the creation of a reinvigorated nationalism that was politically and socially exclusive,[14] the radical definitions of Americanism that were constructed on May Day during these years suggested alternative political possibilities. They were alternatives, including a range of approaches to socialism, anarchism, or trade unionism, that the growing immigrant and working-class communities sought as they confronted the consequences of industrialization. Such radical definitions of Americanism also speak to the malleability of American nationalism as a cultural construction that citizens shaped and reshaped over time.

Although the alternative radical Americanisms created on May Day always existed on the edges of American political culture, they found a home there, and during the 1930s even thrived, in part because that culture had just enough room to facilitate their construction. This remained true until the Cold War tightened the boundaries of that culture, pushing the radical elements beyond the pale. While protest and dissent have remained possible within American political culture, their economic focus has been limited. Such protest has not included a questioning of the nation's capitalist economy, nor have American dissenters been able to capture and redefine the core symbols of the nation.[15] The implications of this weakness for the political left in the latter half of the twentieth century have been profound. To be both a patriotic and a dissenting American has remained a formidable challenge.

Notes

NOTES TO THE INTRODUCTION

1. *New York Times*, May 2, 2006, p. A1.
2. Ibid., p. A18.
3. Ibid.
4. Ibid.
5. In general, the news coverage and commentary on the day did not mention any link to May Day. If there were a mentioning of the implications of the May 1 date, it was a negative reference to the holiday's foreign and socialist history. For examples of those who denounced May 1 as foreign and socialist, see Lou Dobbs, "Dobbs: Radical groups taking control of immigrant movement," CNN.com, http://www.cnn.com/2006/US/05/01/dobbs.immigrationprotests/index.html; and Leslie Sanchez's comments in "Part 2: Analysts Debate Immigration Protests," PBS Newshour transcript, May 1, 2006, "Immigrants Protest Across U.S.," www.pbs.org/newshour/bb/law/jan-june06/migrants_05-01.html. For examples of where there was no mentioning of May Day at all, see www.msnbc.com/id/12578901; www.cbsnews.com/stories/2006/04/27/politics/main/1550032.shtml; and www.latimes.com/news/local/la-050106immig_lat,0,6938733.story?coll=la-home-headlines. In 2007, protestors staged demonstrations around the country again, but the number of participants was much smaller due to disagreement among those who supported immigrant rights over how to proceed after the 2006 protests. Fear of arrest also kept many at home, especially after the extensive raids that had been carried out in immigrant neighborhoods in early 2007. See *New York Times*, "Protestors Press for Path to Citizenship," May 1, 2007. Although the *Los Angeles Times* acknowledged that Chicago was the "home of the original May 1 International Workers' Day more than a century ago," it mistakenly characterized that first May Day as "international," which, in 1886, it was not. See http://www.latimes.com/news/local/la-me-march2may02,0,3947088.story?coll=la-home-headlines.
6. See Ellen M. Litwicki, *America's Public Holidays, 1865–1920* (Washington, D.C.: Smithsonian Institution Press, 2000), especially 9–49; Kirk Savage, "The Politics of Memory: Black Emancipation and the Civil War Monument," in *Commemorations: The Politics of National Identity*, ed. John R. Gillis (Princeton, N.J.:

Princeton University Press, 1994), 127–149; and Richard J. Ellis, *To the Flag: The Unlikely History of the Pledge of Allegiance* (Lawrence: University Press of Kansas, 2005).

7. Litwicki, *America's Public Holidays*, 174–223. Ellis, *To the Flag*, 50–80.

8. I agree with Linda Gordon's conception of the term "identity" as something that is both constructed and yet has its own power to influence. See Linda Gordon, "Moralizing Doesn't Help," *International Labor and Working-Class History* 67 (Spring 2005): 31–32.

9. There have been some investigations into the history of May Day in America, but these are more limited in their scope and purpose. See Litwicki, *America's Public Holidays*, 70–112; Michael Denning, *The Cultural Front: The Laboring of American Culture in the Twentieth Century* (New York: Verso, 1997), xvi and 53–114; and Philip Foner, *May Day: A Short History of the International Workers' Holiday, 1886–1986* (New York: International Publishers, 1986). See also Andrea Panaccione, ed., *May Day Celebration* (Venice: Marsilio Editori, 1988) and Andrea Panaccione, ed., *The Memory of May Day: An Iconographic History of the Origins and Implanting of a Workers' Holiday* (Venice: Marsilio Editori, 1989), which have limited material on May Day in the United States.

10. Gary Gerstle and Nan Enstad have both demonstrated how an appreciation of the material context for cultural practices is necessary to their historical understanding, including the role that constructed class-based concerns and contested political beliefs play when they change over time. See Gary Gerstle, *Working-Class Americanism: The Politics of Labor in a Textile City, 1914–1960* (Princeton, N.J.: Princeton University Press, 2002); and Nan Enstad, *Ladies of Labor, Girls of Adventure: Working Women, Popular Culture, and Labor Politics at the Turn of the Twentieth Century* (New York: Columbia University Press, 1999).

11. Gerstle, *Working-Class Americanism*, xiv–xv.

12. Marcel van der Linden, "Transnationalizing American Labor History," *Journal of American History* 86:3 (December 1991): 1078–1092.

13. Thomas Bender, ed., *Rethinking American History in a Global Age* (Berkeley: University of California Press, 2002), 12 and 8.

14. See, for example, Stanley Aronowitz, *The Death and Rebirth of the American Left* (New York: Routledge, 1986); John P. Diggins, *The American Left in the Twentieth Century* (New York: Harcourt Brace Jovanovich, 1973); Ira Kipnis, *The American Socialist Movement, 1897–1912* (New York: Monthly Review Press, 1952); Aileen Kraditor, *The Radical Persuasion, 1890–1917: Aspects of the Intellectual History and the Historiography of Three American Radical Organizations* (Baton Rouge: Louisiana State University Press, 1981); and Michael Kazin, "The Agony and Romance of the American Left," *American Historical Review* 100:5 (December 1995): 1488–1512.

15. Eric Foner, "Presidential Address: American Freedom in a Global Age," *American Historical Review* 106:1 (February 2001): 1–16. The history of this

nationalism has recently begun to be explored for what it was: a social and cultural construction that changed over time. Historians who have carried out such investigations have incorporated the insights of Benedict Anderson's work on the cultural definition of "imagined communities" to discuss the formation of this sense of nationhood during certain annual holiday celebrations. Benedict Anderson, *Imagined Communities: Reflections on the Origin and Spread of Nationalism* (London: Verso, 1983; rev. ed., New York: Verso, 1991). Significant works have been produced that address this process for the Revolutionary and early national periods. See, for example, Simon Newman, *Parades and the Politics of the Street: Festive Culture in the Early American Republic* (Philadelphia: University of Pennsylvania Press, 1997); and David Waldstreicher, *In the Midst of Perpetual Fetes: The Making of American Nationalism, 1776–1820* (Chapel Hill: University of North Carolina Press, 1997). Other studies have tackled part of the period under consideration in this book, most noteworthy Ellen Litwicki's study of late-nineteenth- and early-twentieth-century public holidays and Richard Ellis' history of the Pledge of Allegiance (Litwicki, *America's Public Holidays*; Ellis, *To the Flag*). Approaching the process from the other side of the political divide, Ellis observes the construction of nationalism through a lens similar to that which I will use in this study of May Day: seeing that construction as one that is both a positive assertion of certain ideals and a negation of concepts (and people) deemed a threat.

16. I have adopted the concepts "official" and "vernacular" cultures rather liberally from John Bodnar's discussion of their role in the construction of public memory. See John Bodnar, *Remaking America: Public Memory, Commemoration, and Patriotism in the Twentieth Century* (Princeton, N.J.: Princeton University Press, 1992).

17. According to newspaper coverage in the *New York Times*, the *Daily Worker*, *The People*, and the *New York Call*, May 1 was celebrated in similar, if smaller, parades and meetings in other cities around the nation.

18. Geneviève Fabre and Jürgen Heideking, "Introduction," in *Celebrating Ethnicity and Nation: American Festive Culture from the Revolution to the Early Twentieth Century*, ed. Jürgen Heideking, Geneviève Fabre and Kai Dreisbach (New York: Berghahn Books, 2001), 2–3.

19. Paul Cohen and Michael Kammen also have observed, albeit in different political and cultural contexts, this process of change in the meaning of the past as it relates to shifts in present values. See Paul Cohen, *History in Three Keys: The Boxers as Event, Experience, and Myth* (New York: Columbia University Press, 1997), 238; and Michael Kammen, *Mystic Chords of Memory: The Transformation of Tradition in American Culture* (New York: Vintage Books Edition, 1993), 162.

20. Simon Newman argues that the parades of the early national period constituted a "politics of the street" where most ordinary people experienced politics. *Parades and the Politics of the Street*, 3–10.

21. For parades as a form of popular communication, see Susan G. Davis, *Parades and Power: Street Theatre in Nineteenth-Century Philadelphia* (Philadelphia: Temple University Press, 1986), 3–5.

22. For a judicious study of the many currents of nativism in American history, see John Higham, *Strangers in the Land: Patterns of American Nativism, 1860–1925* (Westport, Conn.: Greenwood Press,1963; New York: Atheneum, 1973).

23. This is not to say that women were not present at civic celebrations since the early national period, but that their presence was limited to supporting roles as the virtuous wives or mothers of the nation's male citizens (hence the flag presentations). At times, especially during the more radical Democratic Republican celebrations of the French Revolution, women took on more active roles to claim positions indicative of citizenship, but these specific episodes were contested and short-lived. See, for example, Newman, *Parades and the Politics of the Street*, 106–107, 128–130, and 154–157.

24. See, for example, Annelise Orleck, *Common Sense and a Little Fire: Women and Working-Class Politics in the United States, 1900–1965* (Chapel Hill: University of North Carolina Press, 1995); Nan Enstad, *Ladies of Labor, Girls of Adventure: Working Women, Popular Culture, and Labor Politics at the Turn of the Twentieth Century* (New York: Columbia University Press, 1999); and Mari Jo Buhle, *Women and American Socialism, 1870–1920* (Urbana and Chicago: University of Illinois Press, 1981).

25. For example, by 1935 black membership in the Communist Party stood at only approximately 2,300 *nationally*. See Mark Solomon, *The Cry Was Unity: Communists and African Americans, 1917–1936* (Jackson: University of Mississippi Press, 1998), 96–100, 138, 169, and 230.

26. My research resonates with the conclusions of historians who have recently argued for a more balanced approach to understanding this dual nature of the party. See, for example, Randi Storch, "'The Realities of the Situation': Revolutionary Discipline and Everyday Political Life in Chicago's Communist Party, 1928–1935," *Labor: Studies in Working-Class Histories of the Americas* 1:3 (Fall 2004): 19–44; Gerald Zahavi, "Passionate Commitments: Race, Sex, and Communism in Schenectady General Electric, 1932–1954," *Journal of American History* 83:2 (September 1996): 514–548; and James R. Barrett, *William Z. Foster and the Tragedy of American Radicalism* (Urbana and Chicago: University of Illinois Press, 1999).

NOTES TO CHAPTER 1

1. David R. Roediger and Philip S. Foner, *Our Own Time: A History of American Labor and the Working Day* (New York: Greenwood Press, 1989), 107. Stanley Nadel, "Those Who Would Be Free: The Eight-Hour Strikes of 1872," *Labor's Heritage* 2:2 (1990): 72.

2. "The May Day Demonstration of 1867 (*Illinois Staats-Zeitung* May 2 and 3, 1867)," in *German Workers in Chicago: A Documentary History of Working-Class Culture from 1850 to World War I,* ed. Hartmut Keil and John B. Jentz, trans. Burt Weinshanker (Chicago: University of Illinois Press, 1988), 254.

3. Ellen Litwicki refers to this celebration as the first May Day. Ellen M. Litwicki, *America's Public Holidays, 1865–1920* (Washington, D.C.: Smithsonian Institution Press, 2000), 75.

4. "The May Day Demonstration of 1867," 254.

5. Ibid., 254–255.

6. See, for example, Richard Platt, "An Account of the Federal Procession, etc. July 23, 1788," in *Interesting Documents,* ed. John S. Murphy (New York, 1819), 2–36; and Whitefield Bell, Jr., "The Federal Procession of 1788," *New York Historical Society Quarterly* 46 (January 1962): 4–40.

7. For the 1867 law and the ways employers flouted it, see Paul Kens, *Lochner v. New York: Economic Regulation on Trial* (Lawrence: University Press of Kansas, 1998), 20–21. See also James Green, *Death in the Haymarket: A Story of Chicago, the First Labor Movement, and the Bombing That Divided Gilded Age America* (New York: Pantheon, 2006), 31–33.

8. Roediger and Foner, *Our Own Time,* 5–15. See also Sean Wilentz, *Chants Democratic: New York City and the Rise of the American Working Class, 1788–1850* (New York: Oxford University Press, 1984); and Howard Rock, *Artisans of the New Republic: The Tradesmen of New York City in the Age of Jefferson* (New York: New York University Press, 1984).

9. Roediger and Foner, *Our Own Time,* 19, 39, 82, and 97–99. Melvin Dubofsky and Foster Rhea Dulles, *Labor in America: A History,* 5th ed. (Arlington Heights, Ill.: Harlan Davidson, 1993), 89–107. Litwicki, *America's Public Holidays,* 75.

10. Roediger and Foner, *Our Own Time,* 107.

11. Ibid., 73.

12. Ibid.

13. Ibid., 76–77.

14. Ronald Mendel, "Workers in Gilded Age New York and Brooklyn, 1886–1898" (Ph.D. diss., City University of New York, 1989), 26.

15. Bruce Nelson, *Beyond the Martyrs: A Social History of Chicago's Anarchists, 1870–1900* (New Brunswick, N.J.: Rutgers University Press, 1988), 15.

16. Ibid., 10.

17. Nelson, *Beyond the Martyrs,* 15. Mendel, "Workers," 8.

18. Albert Parsons, "Autobiography of Albert Parsons," 1–5, Albert Parsons Papers, 1887 February 17–November 8. Archives and Manuscript Division, Chicago History Museum (hereafter AMD, CHM). Parsons first moved from Texas to Philadelphia for a short time before heading to Chicago.

19. Donald L. Miller, *City of the Century: The Epic of Chicago and the Making of America* (New York: Simon and Schuster, 1996; Touchstone, 1997), 167–168.

William J. Adelman, *Haymarket Revisited* (Chicago: Illinois Labor Historical Society, 1986), 4. Parsons, 6–7.

20. Parsons, 7.

21. Ibid. Nelson, *Beyond the Martyrs*, 25.

22. Stan Nadel, "The German Immigrant Left in the United States," in *The Immigrant Left in the United States*, ed. Paul Buhle and Dan Georgakas (Albany: State University of New York Press, 1996), 44–62.

23. Nelson, *Beyond the Martyrs*, 128.

24. Ibid., 57–58.

25. Parsons, 8–9.

26. Miller, *City of the Century*, 471. Bruce Nelson's research shows that membership in the SLP in Chicago had declined to 100 members by 1886 while that of the anarchist International Working People's Association (IWPA) had reached a height of 2,800. Those who tended to flock to the IWPA instead of the SLP— "newer arrivals, less white collar, and more unskilled" workers—were increasing within the general population in the 1880s. Nelson, *Beyond the Martyrs*, 101.

27. Parsons, 22 1/2. Miller, *City of the Century*, 467.

28. Green, *Death in the Haymarket*, 129–131.

29. Parsons, 23.

30. Ibid., 36.

31. *The Alarm*, November 29, 1884, p. 1.

32. Adelman, *Haymarket Revisited*, 9. Green, *Death in the Haymarket*, 127–128.

33. Nick Salvatore, "Introduction," in Samuel Gompers, *Seventy Years of Life and Labor: An Autobiography*, ed. with Introduction by Nick Salvatore (Ithaca, N.Y.: ILR Press, 1984), xiv.

34. Nadel, "German Immigrant Left," 53–54.

35. Samuel Gompers, *Seventy Years of Life and Labor: An Autobiography*, ed. with Introduction by Nick Salvatore (Ithaca, N.Y.: ILR Press, 1984), 27.

36. Salvatore, "Introduction," xv.

37. Gompers, *Seventy Years*, 34.

38. Ibid.

39. Ibid., 32–33.

40. Ibid., 34–35.

41. Ibid., 35.

42. Mendel, "Workers," 156.

43. See Salvatore, "Introduction," xix–xxi and xxii–xxiii.

44. Gwendolyn Mink, *Old Labor and New Immigrants in American Political Development: Union, Party, and State, 1875–1920* (Ithaca, N.Y.: Cornell University Press, 1986), 45–112.

45. Salvatore, "Introduction," xxi.

46. Richard Jules Oestreicher, *Solidarity and Fragmentation: Working People and Class Consciousness in Detroit, 1875–1900* (Urbana: University of Illinois Press, 1986), 145.

47. Knights of Labor, *Record of the Proceedings of the Fifth Regular Session of the General Assembly, Held at Detroit, Michigan, September 6–10, 1881*, 269 and 288–289. Terence V. Powderly Papers, Microfilm edition, Reel 67. Emphasis added.

48. Ibid., 309 and 315.

49. Ibid., 269 and 309.

50. Terence V. Powderly, *Thirty Years of Labor: 1859 to 1889* (Columbus, Ohio: Excelsior Publishing House, 1889), 481.

51. Terence V. Powderly, "Address of the Grand Master Workman," in Knights of Labor, *Record of the Proceedings of the Fourth General Assembly*, 171. Terence V. Powderly Papers, Microfilm edition, Reel 67.

52. Gompers, *Seventy Years*, 95.

53. "Report of the Fourth Annual Session of the Federation of Organized Trades and Labor Unions of the United States and Canada, Chicago, Illinois, October 7, 8, 9, and 10, 1884," *Proceedings of the American Federation of Labor, 1881–1888* (Bloomington, Ill.: Pantagraph, 1905), 14.

54. Philip Hone, *The Diary of Philip Hone, 1828–1851: Volume I*, ed. Allan Nevins (New York: Dodd, Mead and Co., 1927), 157–158; George Templeton Strong, *The Diary of George Templeton Strong: Volume I*, ed. Allan Nevins and Milton Halsey Thomas (New York: Macmillan, 1952), 231–232; *Chicago Tribune*, May 1, 1890, p. 1; and *New York Times*, May 1, 1892.

55. David Glassberg, *American Historical Pageantry: The Uses of Tradition in the Early Twentieth Century* (Chapel Hill: University of North Carolina Press, 1990), 37 and 59.

56. Jack Goody, "Knots in May: Continuities, Contradictions and Change in European Rituals," in *Journal of Mediterranean Studies* 3:1 (1993): 30–31.

57. Glassberg, *American Historical Pageantry*, 32–40 and 52–67. For a full discussion of how traditional May spring rites informed nineteenth-century celebrations, see Donna Truglio Haverty-Stacke, "Constructing Radical America: A Cultural and Social History of May Day in New York City and Chicago, 1867–1960" (Ph.D. diss., Cornell University, 2003), 26–35.

58. "Report of the Fifth Annual Session of the Federation of Organized Trades and Labor Unions of the United States and Canada, Washington, D.C., December 8, 9, 10, and 11, 1885," *Proceedings of the American Federation of Labor, 1881–1888* (Bloomington, Ill.: Pantagraph, 1905), 9–11. The two dissenting delegates in the original vote were representatives from the Chicago Typographical Union and the CMIU from Albany. Yet, the Chicago Typographical Union was one of the 69 unions that returned a vote of approval of the FOTLU resolution when it was put

to the general membership. The rank and file overruled its delegate. See Entry for February 28, 1886, Minute Book, Volume 3, May 31, 1885–October 27, 1889, Chicago Typographical Union 16, General Minutes, 1885–1945, AMD, CHM.

59. Andrew Wender Cohen, *The Racketeer's Progress: Chicago and the Struggle for the Modern American Economy, 1900–1940* (New York: Cambridge University Press, 2004), 59, 71.

60. "Report of the Fifth Annual Session," *Proceedings,* 11–13.

61. Gompers, *Seventy Years,* 95.

62. *The Alarm,* August 8, 1885, p. 1. Emphasis original.

63. Ibid., September 5, 1885, p. 4.

64. David Montgomery, *The Fall of the House of Labor* (New York: Cambridge University Press, 1987; 1999 paperback), 196.

65. *The Alarm,* October 17, 1885, p. 1.

66. Ibid.

67. Ibid., January 23, 1886, p. 2.

68. Ibid., April 29, 1886, p. 1. Sidney Lens, "The Bomb at Haymarket," in *Haymarket Scrapbook,* ed. David Roediger and Franklin Rosemont (Chicago: C.H. Kerr Publishing Co., 1986), 14.

69. Gompers, *Seventy Years,* 96.

70. Paul Avrich, *The Haymarket Tragedy* (Princeton, N.J.: Princeton University Press, 1984), 186. Lens, "The Bomb," 14.

71. *Chicago Tribune,* May 2, 1886, p. 11.

72. Ibid.

73. Gompers, *Seventy Years,* 96.

74. "Report of the Sixth Annual Session of the Federation of Trades and Labor Unions of the United States and Canada, also the Proceedings of the First Annual Convention of the American Federation of Labor. Both Conventions Held at Columbus, Ohio, December 8–12, 1886," *Proceedings of the American Federation of Labor, 1881–1888* (Bloomington, Ill.: Pantagraph, 1905), 6.

75. Ibid.

76. Dubofsky and Dulles, *Labor in America,* 139.

77. "Report of the Sixth Annual Session," *Proceedings,* 6.

78. For example, in Washington, D.C., the Bricklayers' Unions, the Carpenters' Union, the Plasterers' Assembly and several other building trades from six Knights of Labor local assemblies struck. See *Chicago Daily Tribune,* May 1, 1886, p. 1.

79. Powderly, *Thirty Years of Labor,* 496–498.

80. Terence V. Powderly, "Address of the Grand Master Workman," *Record of the Proceedings of the Tenth Regular Session of the General Assembly, Held at Richmond, VA, October 4–20, 1886,* 39–40. Terence V. Powderly Papers, Microfilm edition, Reel 67.

81. Terence V. Powderly, *The Path I Trod: The Autobiography of Terence V. Powderly*, ed. Harry J. Carman, Henry David, and Paul N. Guthrie (New York: Columbia University Press, 1940), 104–106 and 142–144.

82. "Report of the Sixth Annual Session," *Proceedings*, 6.

83. See, for example, Henry David, *The History of the Haymarket Affair: A Study in the American Social-Revolutionary and Labor Movements* (New York: Russell & Russell, 1936); Paul Avrich, *The Haymarket Tragedy* (Princeton, N.J.: Princeton University Press, 1984); and Green, *Death in the Haymarket*.

84. Green, *Death in the Haymarket*, 270.

85. Nelson, *Beyond the Martyrs*, 194–200.

86. Parsons, 47–48.

87. Ibid., 46.

88. "Streets," *Supplement Part I. General Ordinances, 1887. Chicago Municipal Code* (Chicago, 1887), 101–102.

89. See, for example, *Chicago Tribune*, May 5, 1886, p. 1 and p. 2.

90. *The Alarm*, October 17, 1885, p. 1.

91. "'The First of May. The Anniversary of the Labor Movement. The History of the Development of the Labor Movement in Chicago' (*Vorbote*, May 4 and 18, 1887)," in *German Workers in Chicago*, 225.

92. Ibid., 224–226.

93. See Avrich, *The Haymarket Tragedy*, 300–308 and 343–354.

94. *The Alarm*, November 19, 1887, p. 1.

95. Ibid., November 10, 1888, p. 4.

96. *Chicago Daily Tribune*, May 1, 1892, p. 3.

97. Ibid., May 2, 1892, p. 1. The flag of the Debattir Club is now housed at the Chicago History Museum.

98. *Journal of the Knights of Labor*, May 12, 1892, p. 2.

99. Bruce Nelson discusses these differences, which predated the impact of Haymarket, in "'We Can't Get Them to Do Aggressive Work': Chicago's Anarchists and the Eight-Hour Movement," *International Labor and Working Class History* 29 (Spring 1986): 1–15.

100. See Entry for March 25, 1888, Minute Book, Volume 3, May 31, 1885–October 27, 1889, Chicago Typographical Union 16, General Minutes, 1885–1945, AMD, CHM.

101. Entry for August 7, 1887, Minute Book, Trades and Labor Assembly of Chicago, 1887–1889, AMD, CHM.

102. Gompers, *Seventy Years*, 97.

103. "Official Report of the Third Annual Convention of the American Federation of Labor. Held at St. Louis, Missouri. December 11, 12, 13, 14, 15, 1888," *Proceedings of the American Federation of Labor, 1881–1888* (Bloomington, Ill.: Pantagraph, 1905), 9–10.

104. For Washington's Birthday, see Matthew Dennis, *Red, White, and Blue Letter Days: An American Calendar* (Ithaca, N.Y.: Cornell University Press, 2002), 204–206.

105. Beginning in 1887, several states had declared the first Monday in September a holiday. The September Labor Day holiday became a national holiday in 1894. See discussion on Labor Day in chapters 2 and 3; and "Labor Day—Its Birth and Significance," *American Federationist* (October 1897), 183.

106. "Official Report of the Third Annual Convention," *Proceedings*, 24–26.

107. Dennis, *Red, White, and Blue Letter Days*, 203–209. Michael Kammen, *Mystic Chords of Memory: The Transformation of Tradition in American Culture* (New York: Random House, 1991; New York: Vintage, 1993), 106–109, 179–181, 219–220, 236–248, and 294–296.

108. Such expressions would boost the AFL's claim to responsible unionism, something it came to embrace in these years. See Mink, *Old Labor*, 164–167.

109. Gompers, *Seventy Years*, 97.

110. Mink, *Old Labor*, 45–112.

111. "Report of the Ninth Annual Convention of the American Federation of Labor, Held at Boston, Massachusetts. December 10, 11, 12, 13, 14, 1889," *Proceedings of the American Federation of Labor* (Bloomington, Ill.: Pantagraph, 1889), 14–15.

112. Terence V. Powderly, Correspondence to Terence V. Powderly from P. J. McGuire, with replies, 1886–1891. Terence V. Powderly Papers, Microfilm edition, Reels 16 and 27–31.

113. Knights of Labor, *Proceedings of the Thirteenth Regular Session of the General Assembly, Held at Atlanta, Georgia, 1889*, 34–36. Terence V. Powderly Papers, Microfilm edition, Reel 67.

114. Gompers, *Seventy Years*, 97. Entry for April 5, 1890, District Council Minutes, f. 15, February 16, 1889–December 6, 1890, Box 1, Series II, District Council of Chicago Minutes, Records of the United Brotherhood of Carpenters and Joiners of America, AMD, CHM. Entry for February 27, 1890, f. 13, December 26, 1889–April 30, 1890, Box 3, Series II, United Carpenters Council Minutes, Records of the United Brotherhood of Carpenters and Joiners of America, AMD, CHM.

115. *Chicago Daily Tribune*, May 2, 1890, p. 1. *New York Times*, May 2, 1890, p. 1.

116. "Report of the Proceedings of the Tenth Annual Convention of the American Federation of Labor. Held at Detroit, Michigan, December 8–13, 1890," *Proceedings of the American Federation of Labor* (Bloomington, Ill.: Pantagraph, 1890), 13.

117. Gompers, *Seventy Years*, 99.

118. This was a concern also shared by P. J. McGuire. See Hubert Perrier and Michel Cordillot, "The Origins of May Day: The American Connection," in *In*

the Shadow of the Statue of Liberty: Immigrants, Workers and Citizens in the American Republic, 1880–1920, ed. Marianne Debouzy (Saint-Denis: Presses Universitaires de Vincennes, 1988), 162–163.

119. Mink, *Old Labor,* 51–68.

120. Ibid., 164. Samuel Gompers to August Keufer, January 10, 1889. Gompers Letterbooks, Volume 3, Microfilm edition.

121. Gompers, *Seventy Years*, 98.

122. Perrier and Cordillot, "Origins of May Day," 165.

123. Ibid., 168.

124. Ibid., 167–168. "May Day," *American Federationist* 1:3 (May 1894): 52.

125. Perrier and Cordillot, "Origins of May Day," 169.

126. Ibid., 170.

127. Ibid., 171. Tensions reached a climax when Gompers refused to reissue a charter to the New York Central Labor Federation on the grounds that it was essentially an arm of the SLP, and therefore not a trade or labor organization but a political party, which was ineligible for an AFL charter. See Philip Taft Records, 1840–1976, f. 12, Box 3, "An Interesting Discussion at the Tenth Annual Convention," 6. Kheel Center for Labor-Management Documentation and Archives, M.P. Catherwood Library, Cornell University.

128. James R. Barrett, "Americanization from the Bottom Up: Immigration and the Remaking of the Working Class in the United States, 1880–1930," *Journal of American History* 79:3 (December 1992): 996–1020.

NOTES TO CHAPTER 2

1. "Report of the Proceedings of the Thirty-Third Annual Convention of the American Federation of Labor Held at Boston, Massachusetts November 9th to 23rd, Inclusive, 1903," *Proceedings of the American Federation of Labor* (Bloomington, Ill.: Pantagraph, 1905), 137.

2. See, for example, the discussion in chapter 1 of the 1892 May Day parade in Chicago. *Chicago Tribune*, May 2, 1892, p. 1.

3. For Italian immigration and population statistics, see Donald Tricarico, "Italians," *The Encyclopedia of New York City*, ed. Kenneth T. Jackson (New Haven, Conn.: Yale University Press, 1995), 605; and Humbert S. Nelli, "Italians in Urban America," *The Italian Experience in the United States*, ed. S.M. Tomasi and M.H. Engel (Staten Island, N.Y.: Center for Migration Studies, 1970), 77–81.

4. For the role of the "new" immigrants in May Day events, see Michael Kazin and Steven Ross, "America's Labor Day: The Dilemma of a Workers' Celebration," *Journal of American History* 78:4 (March 1992): 1305.

5. Rudolph Vecoli, "Primo Maggio: May Day Observances among Italian Immigrant Workers, 1890–1920," *Labor's Heritage* 7:4 (Spring 1996): 32.

6. Ibid. See also *The People*, April 24, 1898, p. 3, and April 23, 1899, p. 2.

7. Nunzio Pernicone, *Italian Anarchism, 1864–1892* (Princeton, N.J.: Princeton University Press, 1993), 261–272. Rudolph Vecoli, "The American Republic Viewed by the Italian Left," in *In the Shadow of the Statue of Liberty: Immigrants, Workers and Citizens in the American Republic, 1880–1920*, ed. Marianne Debouzy (Saint-Denis: Presses Universitaires de Vincennes, 1988), 27. Bruce Cartosio, "Sicilian Radicals in Two Worlds," *In the Shadow*, 119–120. Robert D'Attilio, "'Primo Maggio': Haymarket as Seen by Italian Anarchists in America," in *Haymarket Scrapbook*, ed. David Roediger and Franklin Rosemont (Chicago: C.H. Kerr Publishing Co., 1986), 229.

8. Paul Avrich, *Sacco and Vanzetti: The Anarchist Background* (Princeton, N.J.: Princeton University Press, 1991), 46–47.

9. Pietro Gori, "Primo Maggio," in *Bozzetti Sociale*, vol. 7, *Opere*, 2d ed. (La Spezia: Crono-Tipico, 1921), 106–135.

10. Rudolph Vecoli, "Primo Maggio," in *May Day Celebration*, ed. Andrea Panaccione (Venice: Marsilio Editori, 1988), 60.

11. Avrich, *Sacco and Vanzetti*, 56.

12. D'Attilio, "Primo Maggio," 229. Gori, "Primo Maggio," *Bozzetti*, 110–111.

13. Gori, "Primo Maggio," *Bozzetti*, 110–111.

14. Ibid., 114–135.

15. Donna R. Gabaccia and Fraser M. Ottanelli, "Introduction," *Italian Workers of the World: Labor Migration and the Formation of Multiethnic States*, ed. Donna R. Gabaccia and Fraser M. Ottanelli (Urbana: University of Illinois Press, 2001), 7.

16. Elisabetta Vezzosi, "Radical Ethnic Brokers: Immigrant Socialist Leaders in the United States between Ethnic Community and the Larger Society," trans. Michael Rocke, *Italian Workers of the World: Labor Migration and the Formation of Multiethnic States*, ed. Donna R. Gabaccia and Fraser M. Ottanelli (Urbana: University of Illinois Press, 2001), 121–122.

17. Pietro Gori, "The First of May," trans. Robert D'Attilio, *Haymarket Scrapbook*, 230. D'Attilio, "Primo Maggio," 229.

18. Pietro Gori, "Primo Maggio," in *Scritti Scelti*, Vol. II (Imola: Cooperative Tipografica Editrice, 1968), 324–325. Vecoli, "The American Republic," 27.

19. To achieve this international solidarity, socialists and anarcho-syndicalists (like Carlo Tresca) favored the organization of workers in unions and political parties, while anarcho-communists (like Luigi Galleani) rejected any type of organization and supported instead the direct action of the vanguard. See Vecoli, "Primo Maggio," *May Day Celebration*, 65; and Avrich, *Sacco and Vanzetti*, 52.

20. Edmond Taylor, "May Day," *Horizon* 14:2 (1972): 28.

21. See Figure 2.1, Walter Crane, "International Solidarity of Labor," 1889, in *Cartoons for the Cause 1886–1896* (London: Twentieth Century Press, 1907), 9. Art and Architecture Collection, Miriam and Ira D. Wallach Division of Art, Prints and Photographs, New York Public Library, Astor, Lenox, and Tilden Foundations.

22. *The People*, May 3, 1891, p. 1, and May 8, 1898, p. 1.

23. Ibid., May 3, 1891, p. 1.

24. Ibid. Emphasis added.

25. Frank Girard, *The Socialist Labor Party, 1876–1991: A Short History* (Philadelphia: Livra Books, 1991), 19–21.

26. See, for example, *The People*, April 28, 1895, p. 3.

27. Entry for April 21, 1896, SLP Central Committee Minutes, NYC, in Socialist Minute Books, 1872–1907, Collection I, Socialist Collections on Microfilm, Reel 2630, held at Tamiment Library/Robert F. Wagner Labor Archives, Elmer Holmes Bobst Library, New York University Libraries, New York University (hereafter Tamiment).

28. Entry for May 1, 1895, SLP Kings County Committee Minutes, NYC, in Socialist Minute Books, 1872–1907, Collection I, Socialist Collection on Microfilm, Reel 2631, Tamiment.

29. Entry for February 26, 1898, SLP May Day Conferences, 1898, Collection I, Socialist Collections on Microfilm, Reel 2631, Tamiment.

30. Entry for May 7, 1898, SLP May Day Conferences, 1898, Collection I, Socialist Collections on Microfilm, Reel 2631, Tamiment. Entry for April 11, 1899, SLP May Day Conferences, 1899, Collection I, Socialist Collections on Microfilm, Reel 2631, Tamiment. Entries for April 18, 1900, April 25, 1900, and April 27, 1900, SLP May Day Conferences, 1900, Collection I, Socialist Collections on Microfilm, Reel 2631, Tamiment.

31. See, for example, *The People*, May 3, 1891, p. 1; May 8, 1892, p. 1; May 7, 1893, p. 1; and May 5, 1895, p. 4.

32. Entry for February 24, 1902, SLP City Executive Committee, NYC, in Socialist Minute Books, 1872–1907, Collection I, Socialist Collection on Microfilm, Reel 2631, Tamiment.

33. Entry for February 26, 1898, SLP May Day Conferences, 1898, Collection I, Socialist Collections on Microfilm, Reel 2631, Tamiment.

34. Entry for March 19, 1898, SLP May Day Conferences, 1898, Collection I, Socialist Collections on Microfilm, Reel 2631, Tamiment.

35. Entry for April 2, 1898, SLP May Day Conferences, 1898, Collection I, Socialist Collections on Microfilm, Reel 2631, Tamiment.

36. Ellen M. Litwicki, *America's Public Holidays, 1865–1920* (Washington, D.C.: Smithsonian Institution Press, 2000), 151–155. Matthew Dennis, *Red, White, and Blue Letter Days: An American Calendar* (Ithaca, N.Y.: Cornell University Press, 2002), 205–207. Scot M. Guenter, *The American Flag, 1777–1924: Cultural Shifts from Creation to Codification* (Rutherford, N.J.: Fairleigh Dickinson University Press, 1990), 23, 161–178, and 183.

37. Litwicki, *America's Public Holidays*, 175–180. Guenter, *The American Flag*, 23 and 183. Concern for the fate of the nation and the state of urban order also stemmed from the perceived threat of new immigrants that constituted a "race-

conscious nativism." Richard J. Ellis, *To the Flag: The Unlikely History of the Pledge of Allegiance* (Lawrence: University Press of Kansas, 2005), 1–54.

38. *The People*, May 8, 1898, p. 1 and p. 2.

39. *New York Times*, September 19, 1897, p. IW2.

40. Ibid., May 1, 1898, p. 9.

41. Ibid.

42. *Proceedings of the Tenth National Convention of the Socialist Labor Party. Held in New York City June 2 to June 8, 1900* (New York: New York Labor News Co., 1901), 16–17.

43. *The People*, May 7, 1893, p. 1. *New York Times*, May 2, 1895, p. 7.

44. See, for example, Ellen M. Litwicki, "'Our Hearts Burn with Ardent Love for Two Countries': Ethnicity and Assimilation at Chicago Holiday Celebrations, 1867–1918," *Journal of American Ethnic History* 19:3 (Spring 2000): 3–34; Timothy Meagher, "'Why Should We Care for a Little Trouble or a Walk Through the Mud': St. Patrick's and Columbus Day Parades in Worcester, Massachusetts, 1845–1915," *New England Quarterly* 58:1 (March 1985): 5–25; Bénédicte Deschamps, "Italian-Americans and Columbus Day: A Quest for Consensus Between National and Group Identities, 1840–1910," in *Celebrating Ethnicity and Nation: American Festive Culture from the Revolution to the Early Twentieth Century*, ed. Jürgen Heideking, Geneviève Fabre, and Kai Dreisbach (New York: Berghahn Books, 2001), 124–139.

45. I share James Barrett's understanding of "Americanization from the bottom up." See James Barrett, "Americanization from the Bottom Up: Immigrations and the Remaking of the Working Class in the United States, 1880–1930," *Journal of American History* 79:3 (December 1992), 997.

46. Mary P. Ryan, *Civic Wars: Democracy and Public Life in the American City during the Nineteenth Century* (Berkeley: University of California Press, 1997), 248. David Glassberg, *American Historical Pageantry: The Uses of Tradition in the Early Twentieth Century* (Chapel Hill: University of North Carolina Press, 1990), 18.

47. Nan Enstad, *Ladies of Labor, Girls of Adventure: Working Women, Popular Culture, and Labor Politics at the Turn of the Twentieth Century* (New York: Columbia University Press, 1999). Annelise Orleck, *Common Sense and a Little Fire: Women and Working-Class Politics in the United States, 1900–1965* (Chapel Hill: University of North Carolina Press, 1995).

48. Craig Heron and Steve Penfold, *The Workers' Festival: A History of Labour Day in Canada* (Toronto: University of Toronto, 2005), 16 and 23. Diane Winston, *Red Hot and Righteous: The Urban Religion of the Salvation Army* (Cambridge: Harvard University Press, 1999), 76–85.

49. *The People*, May 5, 1895, p. 1.

50. Entry for January 15, 1898, SLP May Day Conferences, 1898, Collection I, Socialist Collections on Microfilm, Reel 2631, Tamiment. The Frauenverein was joined by the Frauen and Madchen Club and Branch 13 Working Women's Society.

51. *The People*, May 8, 1898, p. 1.

52. Mari Jo Buhle, *Women and American Socialism, 1870–1920* (Chicago: University of Illinois Press, 1981), 73–74.

53. *New York Times*, May 2, 1895, p. 7. The mainstream press noted their presence but seemed more disturbed by the women's affiliation with the socialist cause (and their donning of "red sashes") than by their public participation.

54. Ibid., 2–94.

55. Aileen Kraditor, *The Radical Persuasion, 1890–1917: Aspects of the Intellectual History and the Historiography of Three American Radical Organizations* (Baton Rouge: Louisiana State University Press, 1981), 185.

56. Entry for April 1, 1899, SLP May Day Conferences, 1899, Collection I, Socialist Collections on Microfilm, Reel 2631, Tamiment.

57. Buhle, *Women and American Socialism*, 19 and 26–28.

58. *The People*, May 7, 1899, p. 1.

59. See Figure 2.2: "May Day 1896" from *The People*, May 3, 1896, p. 1. Negative 80119d. Courtesy of the New-York Historical Society.

60. Ibid.

61. See discussion in chapter 1.

62. "Report of the Proceedings of the Fifteenth Annual Convention of the American Federation of Labor Held at New York, N.Y., December 9th to 17th, Inclusive, 1895," *Proceedings of the American Federation of Labor* (Bloomington, Ill.: Pantagraph, 1905), 30; "Report of the Proceedings of the Sixteenth Annual Convention of the American Federation of Labor Held at Cincinnati, Ohio, December 14 to 21, Inclusive, 1896," *Proceedings of the American Federation of Labor* (Bloomington, Ill.: Pantagraph, 1905), 63–64; "Report of the Proceedings of the Seventeenth Annual Convention of the American Federation of Labor, Held at Nashville, Tennessee December 13th to 21st, Inclusive, 1897," *Proceedings of the American Federation of Labor* (Bloomington, Ill.: Pantagraph, 1905), 19; "Report of the Proceedings of the Eighteenth Annual Convention of the American Federation of Labor Held at Kansas City, Missouri, December 12th to 20th, Inclusive, 1898," *Proceedings of the American Federation of Labor* (Bloomington, Ill.: Pantagraph, 1905), 122; and "Report of the Proceedings of the Twentieth Annual Convention of the American Federation of Labor Held at Louisville, Kentucky, December 6th to 15th, Inclusive, 1900," *Proceedings of the American Federation of Labor* (Bloomington, Ill.: Pantagraph, 1905), 19 and 68–69.

63. *American Federationist* 4:3 (May 1897): 52.

64. Ibid., 1:3 (May 1894): 51.

65. "Report of the Proceedings of the Thirty-Third Annual Convention of the American Federation of Labor Held at Boston, Massachusetts, November 9th to 23rd, Inclusive, 1903," *Proceedings of the American Federation of Labor* (Bloomington, Ill.: Pantagraph, 1905), 137 and 188.

66. Nick Salvatore, *Eugene V. Debs: Citizen and Socialist* (Chicago: University of Illinois Press, 1982), 200–201.

67. Nick Salvatore, "Introduction," in Samuel Gompers, *Seventy Years of Life and Labor: An Autobiography*, ed. with Introduction by Nick Salvatore (Ithaca, N.Y.: ILR Press, 1984), xxviii. See also Gwendolyn Mink, *Old Labor and New Immigrants in American Political Development: Union, Party, and State, 1875–1920* (Ithaca, N.Y.: Cornell University Press, 1986), 45–68.

68. Shelton Stromquist, "The Crisis of 1894 and the Legacies of Producerism," in *The Pullman Strike and the Crisis of the 1890s: Essays on Labor and Politics*, ed. Richard Schneirov, Shelton Stromquist and Nick Salvatore (Chicago: University of Illinois Press, 1999), 181.

69. Melvyn Dubofsky and Foster Rhea Dulles, *Labor in America: A History* (Wheeling, Ill.: Harlan Davidson, 2004), 184.

70. Stromquist, "The Crisis of 1894," 182. Re. the AFL's embrace of "industrial government" and its relationship to the National Civic Federation, see Mink, *Old Labor*, 161–182.

71. "Report of the Proceedings of the Thirty-Third Annual Convention of the American Federation of Labor," *Proceedings*, 137.

72. Richard P. Hunt, "The First Labor Day," *American Heritage* 33:5 (1982): 110.

73. Ibid., 111–112.

74. Jonathan Grossman, "Who Is the Father of Labor Day?" *Labor History* 14:4 (1973): 621–622.

75. Theodore F. Watts, *The First Labor Day Parade, Tuesday, September 5, 1882: Media Mirrors to Labor's Icons* (Silver Spring, Md.: Phoenix Rising, 1983), 51.

76. Hunt, "The First Labor Day," 112. Kazin and Ross, "America's Labor Day," 1303. Grossman, "Who Is the Father," 621–622.

77. On Cummings' background as a printer, see Kazin and Ross, "America's Labor Day," 1302.

78. Such concern did not stop Cleveland from calling up federal troops to break the Pullman boycott on July 3. See Salvatore, *Debs*, 130–132.

79. Mink, *Old Labor*, 130.

80. Ibid., 130–131.

81. P. J. McGuire claimed paternity in the *American Federationist* 4:8 (October 1897): 183, an assertion that has since been disputed. See George Pearlman, Typescripts and Research Materials, 1891–1975, Kheel Center for Labor-Management Documentation and Archives, M.P. Catherwood Library, Cornell University (hereafter Kheel). See also Grossman, "Who Is the Father," 612–623.

82. *American Federationist* 3:4 (June 1896): 68.

83. *American Federationist* 4:7 (September 1897): 156. Kazin and Ross, "America's Labor Day," 1296.

84. *American Federationist* 6:6 (August 1899): 128–129, and 10:10 (September 1903): 831. Similar demonstrations took place in Canada during these same years,

as craft workers there won statutory recognition of Labor Day from the Canadian Parliament in 1894. Although Labor Day set American workers apart from their European comrades who adhered to May Day alone, the Canadian example demonstrates that the U.S. experience was not completely exceptional. Like the Canadian version, American Labor Day had a distinctly nationalist focus. See Heron and Penfold, *The Workers' Festival*, 1–104.

85. Entry for May 6, 1888, Minute Book, Trades and Labor Assembly of Chicago, 1887–1889, Archives and Manuscript Division, Chicago History Museum (hereafter AMD, CHM). Entry for May 31, 1891, Minute Book, Volume 4, November 25, 1889–March 26, 1893, Chicago Typographical Union 16, General Minutes, 1885–1945, AMD, CHM.

86. See, for example, Whitefield Bell, Jr., "The Federal Processions of 1788," *New York Historical Society Quarterly* 46 (January 1962); 4–40; and Cadwallader Colden, *Memoir Prepared at the Request of a Committee of the Common Council of the City of New York and Presented to the Mayor of the City at the Celebration of the Completion of the New York Canals* (New York, 1825).

87. "The May Day Demonstration of 1867 (*Illinois Staats-Zeitung* May 2 and 3, 1867)," in *German Workers in Chicago: A Documentary History of Working-Class Culture from 1850 to World War I*, ed. Hartmut Keil and John B. Jentz, trans. Burt Weinshanker (Chicago: University of Illinois Press, 1988), 255.

88. Entry for July 8, 1899, District Council Minutes, f. 8, May 13, 1899–December 2, 1899, Box 1, Series II, District Council of Chicago, Records of United Brotherhood of Carpenters and Joiners of America (hereafter Records of UBCJA), AMD, CHM. Entry for July 20, 1888, United Carpenters Council Minutes, f. 8, April 27, 1888–August 17, 1888, Box 3, United Carpenters Council Minutes, 1887–1891, Records of UBCJA, AMD, CHM. Entry for August 30, 1888, UBCJ Local 1 Minutes, f. 4, January 5, 1888–February 15, 1889, Box 5, Local 1 Minutes, 1888–1894, Records of the UBCJA, AMD, CHM. Entry for August 16, 1889, UBCJ Local 1 Minutes, f. 6, July 19, 1889–February 7, 1890, Box 5, Local 1 Minutes, 1888–1894, Records of UBCJA, AMD, CHM. Entry for August 7, 1901, UBCJ Local 1 Minutes, f. 2, June 19, 1901–December 18, 1901, Box 7, Local 1 Minutes 1900–1904, Records of UBCJA, AMD, CHM.

89. See Figure 2.3: "Men Marching down West Jackson Boulevard in a Labor Day Parade," DN-0002298, Chicago Daily News negative collection, Chicago History Museum.

90. Harry R. Rubenstein, "With Hammer in Hand: Working-Class Occupational Portraits," in *American Artisans: Crafting Social Identity, 1750–1850*, ed. Howard Rock, Paul A. Gilje, and Robert Asher (Baltimore: Johns Hopkins University Press, 1995), 177–244.

91. *New York Times*, September 4, 1894, p. 9.

92. This was particularly true for the movement's regional and national leadership. See Stromquist, "The Crisis of 1894," 194–197.

93. Entry for August 10, 1888, United Carpenters Council Minutes, f. 7, July 26, 1887–January 6, 1888, Box 3, UCC Minutes, 1887–1891, Records of the UBCJA, AMD, CHM.

94. Entry for September 15, 1894, District Council Minutes, f. 2, August 11, 1894–December 29, 1894, Box 2, District Council Minutes, 1894–1903, Records of the UBCJA, AMD, CHM.

95. *American Federationist* 3:8 (October 1896): 171.

96. Entry for August 7, 1887, Minute Book, Trades and Labor Assembly of Chicago, 1887–1889, AMD, CHM.

97. Litwicki, *America's Public Holidays*, 83.

98. See, for example, *New York Times*, September 2, 1890, p. 8, and September 8, 1891, p. 3.

99. Re. the display of red flags on Labor Day, see *New York Times*, September 8, 1891, p. 3; September 5, 1893, p. 1; and September 3, 1895, p. 1.

100. Entry for August 14, 1892, Minutes of the Chicago Typographical Union 16, Volume 4: November 25, 1889–March 26, 1893, p. 390, Records of the Chicago Typographical Union 16, AMD, CHM. "The Labor Day Parade of 1903 (*Chicagoer Arbeiter Zeitung*, September 8, 1903)," in *German Workers in Chicago*, 259–263. In 1903 women made up 3.5 percent of the paraders.

NOTES TO CHAPTER 3

1. *New York Call*, May 2, 1916, p. 1.

2. Ibid., April 30, 1916, p. 1.

3. See Figure 3.1: "Garment Workers Parading on May Day, New York, New York, 1916," LC-USZ62-41871, George Grantham Bain Collection, Prints and Photographs Division, Library of Congress (hereafter Bain, PPD, LC).

4. Such attention to fashion (here, in the form of decorative flowers) may also have been one way they constructed their own version of working-class "ladyhood." See Nan Enstad, *Ladies of Labor, Girls of Adventure: Working Women, Popular Culture, and Labor Politics at the Turn of the Twentieth Century* (New York: Columbia University Press, 1999), 2–14 and 49–82.

5. *New York Times*, September 5, 1911, p. 18.

6. Annelise Orleck, *Common Sense and a Little Fire: Women and Working-Class Politics in the United States, 1900–1965* (Chapel Hill: University of North Carolina Press, 1995), 32–62.

7. Richard P. Hunt, "The First Labor Day," *American Heritage* 33:5 (1982): 110–112.

8. Theodore F. Watts, *The First Labor Day Parade, Tuesday, September 5, 1882: Media Mirrors to Labor's Icons* (Silver Spring, Md.: Phoenix Rising, 1983), 57–62.

9. "Proceedings of DA 16 Knights of Labor held at Wilkes-Barre, PA, April 28–29, 1890," 6–7; "Proceedings of DA 16 held at Scranton, July 28th and 29th

1890," 6; and "Proceedings of DA 16 held at Olyphant, PA, April 25–26, 1892," 7. Terence V. Powderly Papers, Microfilm edition, Reel 66.

10. *New York Times*, September 1, 1890, p. 2; September 8, 1891, p. 3; September 6, 1892, p. 9; September 5, 1893, p. 8; September 4, 1894, p. 9; and September 3, 1895, p. 9.

11. Entry for September 9, 1906, Volume 8, Minutes of Regular Meetings, May 1906–September 1909, Minutes, New York Typographical Society 6 Records, Manuscripts and Archives Division, New York Public Library, Astor, Lenox, and Tilden Foundations, New York (hereafter MAD, NYPL).

12. Entry for August 4, 1907, Volume 8, Minutes of Regular Meeting, May 1906–September 1909, Minutes, New York Typographical Society 6 Records, MAD, NYPL. Entry for August 7, 1910, Volume 9, Minutes of Regular Meeting, October 1909–October 1917, Minutes, New York Typographical Society 6 Records, MAD, NYPL. Entry for August 10, 1913, Volume 9, Minutes of Regular Meeting, October 1909–October 1917, Minutes, New York Typographical Society 6 Records, MAD, NYPL.

13. Entry for August 4, 1907, Volume 8, Minutes of Regular Meeting, May 1906–September 1909, Minutes, New York Typographical Society 6 Records, MAD, NYPL.

14. Entry for August 2, 1908, Minutes October 6, 1907–September 6, 1908, Chicago Federation of Labor, Minutes, Microfilm, Reel 2, Archives and Manuscript Division, Chicago History Museum (hereafter AMD, CHM).

15. Ibid.

16. "Notice! Central Trades and Labor Council Picnic," in "1912—Labor and Laboring Classes," Broadside Collection, Prints and Photographs Division, Chicago History Museum (hereafter PAP, CHM).

17. David Nasaw, *Going Out: The Rise and Fall of Public Amusements* (New York: Basic Books, 1993). Roy Rosenzweig, *Eight Hours for What We Will: Workers and Leisure in an Industrial City, 1870–1920* (New York: Cambridge University Press, 1983), 171–221. Michael Kammen, *American Culture, American Tastes: Social Change and the 20th Century* (New York: Basic Books, 1999), 76–83.

18. A similar dynamic took place in Canada. See Craig Heron and David Penfold, *The Workers' Festival: A History of Labour Day in Canada* (Toronto: University of Toronto Press, 2005), 115–141.

19. Michael Kazin and Steven Ross, "America's Labor Day: The Dilemma of a Workers' Celebration," *Journal of American History* (March 1992): 1307.

20. Entry for August 4, 1907, Volume 8, Minutes of Regular Meeting, May 1906–September 1909, Minutes, New York Typographical Society 6 Records, MAD, NYPL.

21. Executive Board Report of June 18, 1916, Minutes October 3, 1915–September 3, 1916, Chicago Federation of Labor, Minutes, Reel 4, AMD, CHM.

22. Lawrence Glickman, *A Living Wage: American Workers and the Making of Consumer Society* (Ithaca, N.Y.: Cornell University Press, 1997), xiii–xiv and 4–7.

23. Ibid., 25 and 68.

24. For a discussion of leisure reform, see Francis G. Couvares, *The Remaking of Pittsburgh: Class and Culture in an Industrializing City, 1877–1919* (Albany: State University of New York Press, 1984), 96–119.

25. As Alex McCrossen demonstrates, Sabbatarians also worried about the deleterious effects of commercialized leisure in these decades, especially as they related to the definition of Sunday observances. Alex McCrossen, *Holy Day, Holiday: The American Sunday* (Ithaca, N.Y.: Cornell University Press, 2000), 51–64 and 91–99.

26. "Report of the Proceedings of the Thirty-Second Annual Convention of the American Federation of Labor, Held at Rochester, New York, November 11 to 23, Inclusive, 1912," *Proceedings of the American Federation of Labor* (Washington, D.C.: Law Reporter Printing Co., 1912), 31. "Report of the Proceedings of the Thirty-Third Annual Convention of the American Federation of Labor, Held at Atlanta, Georgia, November 13 to 25, Inclusive, 1911," *Proceedings of the American Federation of Labor* (Washington, D.C.: Law Reporter Printing Co., 1911), 78.

27. "Report of the Proceedings of the Thirty-Fourth Annual Convention of the American Federation of Labor, Held at Philadelphia, Pennsylvania, November 9 to 21, Inclusive, 1914," *Proceedings of the American Federation of Labor* (Washington, D.C.: Law Reporter Printing Co., 1914), 55. *American Federationist* 14:9 (September 1907): 669. Debates over the issue of working-class respectability were not unique to these different interpretations of early-twentieth-century Labor Day. See Alan Dawley and Paul Fawler, "Working-Class Culture and Politics in the Industrial Revolution: Sources of Loyalism and Rebellion," *Journal of Social History* 9:4 (June 1976): 466–480.

28. Entry for July 19, 1908, Minutes, October 6, 1907–September 6, 1908, Chicago Federation of Labor Minutes, Microfilm, Reel 2, CHM.

29. See Figure 3.2: "Groups of People and Horse-Drawn Carriages Going in Two Directions down Michigan Avenue in a Labor Day Parade," DN-002297, Chicago Daily News negative collection, CHM.

30. *American Federationist* 14:9 (September 1907): 668.

31. *New York Times*, September 8, 1908, p. 6.

32. *American Federationist* 14:9 (September 1907): 670.

33. "Report of the Proceedings of the Twenty-Ninth Annual Convention of the American Federation of Labor, Held at Toronto, Ontario, Canada, November 8 to 20, Inclusive, 1909," *Proceedings of the American Federation of Labor* (Washington, D.C.: Law Reporter Printing Co., 1909), 199–200 and 252.

34. Ken Fones-Wolf, *Trade Union Gospel: Christianity and Labor in Industrial Philadelphia, 1865–1915* (Philadelphia: Temple University Press, 1989), 146–153 and 165.

35. "Report of the Proceedings of the American Federation of Labor, Held at St. Louis, Missouri, November 14 to 26, Inclusive, 1910," *Proceedings of the*

American Federation of Labor (Washington, D.C.: Law Reporter Printing Co., 1910), 48–49.

36. Ellen M. Litwicki, *America's Public Holidays, 1865–1920* (Washington, D.C.: Smithsonian Institution Press, 2000), 174–190 and 223–226.

37. Workers also used the language of Americanism and the patriotism of wartime to demand the "de-Kaisering of industry" on the shop floor during the war. See Joseph A. McCartin, *Labor's Great War: The Struggle for Industrial Democracy and the Origins of Modern American Labor Relations, 1912–1921* (Chapel Hill: University of North Carolina Press, 1997), 95–116.

38. *The People*, May 9, 1908, p. 1. *New York Call*, April 29, 1916, p. 4. *Chicago Socialist*, April 26, 1902, p. 1, and April 29, 1911, p. 1.

39. *New York Call*, April 29, 1916, p. 4, and May 2, 1916, p. 1.

40. For a discussion of this schism and the emergence of the SP, see Nick Salvatore, *Eugene V. Debs: Citizen and Socialist* (Chicago: University of Illinois Press, 1982), 183–190.

41. For the venues, see *The People*, April 29, 1905, p. 1; April 12, 1907, p. 6; April 27, 1907, p. 5; and May 9, 1908, p. 1. For the number of participants, see *The People*, May 25, 1907, p. 5; May 13, 1911, p. 5; May 12, 1912, p. 1; and May 9, 1914, p. 1. In Manhattan, this turnout was approximately 0.13 percent of the population circa 1910; in Chicago, it was less than 0.1 percent.

42. *The People*, May 4, 1907, p. 1; May 9, 1908, p. 1; April 30, 1910, p. 6; May 9, 1914, p. 1; and April 10, 1915, p. 6. Sectarian feuds and battles over the IWW's organization led the SLP to disassociate itself from the new union by 1908. Instead, the party supported its own faction, the Detroit IWW.

43. Salvatore, *Eugene V. Debs*, 186–197.

44. *New York Call*, May 1, 1911, p. 5, and April 30, 1910, p. 8.

45. Ibid., April 30, 1910, p. 8; May 1, 1911, p. 5; and May 1, 1913, p. 6. *The Workers' Call*, May 5, 1900, p. 1. *Chicago Socialist*, April 29, 1903, p. 2, and May 2, 1907, p. 1. Entry for February 19, 1916, Socialist Party, Local New York, Convention Minutes, 16 January 1916–9 May 1916, Socialist Party Minutes, 1900–1936, Series VI:8, Socialist Collections at Tamiment Library, Microfilm, Reel 10, Tamiment Library/Robert F. Wagner Labor Archives, Elmer Holmes Bobst Library, New York University Libraries, New York University (hereafter Tamiment).

46. *New York Call*, April 29, 1911, p. 1.

47. Ibid., April 29, 1911, p. 1; May 2, 1911, p. 1 and p. 2; May 2, 1912, p. 1 and p. 2; May 1, 1914, p. 1 and p. 3; and May 2, 1914, p. 1 and p. 2.

48. Enstad, *Ladies of Labor*, 85–118. Orleck, *Common Sense*, 31–79.

49. *New York Call*, May 1, 1909, p. 1 and p. 2; May 3, 1909, p. 1; May 2, 1911, p. 1; May 2, 1912, p. 1 and p. 2; and May 2, 1913, p. 2. In Manhattan, the largest turnout for the parade (50,000) constituted approximately 2.14 percent of the total population of the borough (1912); in Chicago, the 10,000 people who came out in 1909 made up about 0.45 percent of the city's total population.

50. Ibid., May 1, 1909, p. 1 and p. 2.

51. *Chicago Socialist*, April 29, 1905, p. 3; April 28, 1906, p. 1; May 2, 1907, p. 1; April 27, 1910, p. 4; and May 3, 1910, p. 2.

52. Ibid., May 3, 1907, p. 1; May 1, 1909, p. 2; and May 3, 1910, p. 2.

53. *New York Call*, May 1, 1909, p. 1 and p. 2; May 3, 1909, p. 1; May 2, 1911, p. 1; May 2, 1912, p. 1 and p. 2; and May 2, 1913, p. 2.

54. On the socialist presence in Brownsville, see Wendell Pritchett, *Brownsville, Brooklyn: Blacks, Jews, and the Changing Face of the Ghetto* (Chicago: University of Chicago Press, 2002), 33–39.

55. *New York Call*, May 3, 1909, p. 1; April 30, 1910, p. 1; and May 11, 1911, p. 1.

56. Ibid.

57. Agreement with some of the SP's policies may help explain why certain unions had the funds and the desire to turn out for the parade on May Day, even if they did not do so on Labor Day. Since May Day was also known as a day of protest, unions may have decided to march on May 1 when they had certain grievances to voice.

58. *New York Call*, May 2, 1911, p. 1 and p. 2.

59. The bakers' "big loaf" (six feet long and three feet wide) was carried on a platform adorned with flowers and red ribbons in the 1908 and 1909 parade as well. See Figure 3.3: "Bakers and Big Loaf—Labor Parade, New York City, 5/1/09," LC-USZ62-23414, Bain, PPD, LC. See also "Loaf Bread in Socialist Parade 5/1/08," LC-B2-66-8; "Parades—1908. Loaf of Bread Carried in Socialist Parade, NY, May 1908," LC-B2-65-12; and "May Day 1909—Large Loaf,", in Lot 10876-1, Bain, PPD, LC. *New York Times*, May 2, 1909, p. 8.

60. Paul Kens, *Lochner v. New York: Economic Regulation on Trial* (Lawrence: University Press of Kansas, 1998), 7–13.

61. *New York Call*, May 2, 1912, p. 1.

62. See, for example, the Ladies Waist Makers, *New York Call*, May 2, 1911, p. 1; various trades in the uptown division, *New York Call*, May 2, 1912, p. 1; and the White Goods Workers, *New York Call*, May 2, 1913, p. 1 and p. 2, and April 30, 1916, p. 1.

63. Ibid., May 1, 1917, p. 14.

64. Ibid., May 2, 1913, p. 1 and p. 2.

65. Ibid., May 1, 1913, p. 6.

66. Mari Jo Buhle, *Women and American Socialism, 1870–1920* (Chicago: University of Illinois Press, 1981), 105–171 and 222.

67. *New York Call*, May 2, 1915, p. 1 and p. 2.

68. Buhle, *Women and American Socialism*, 233–235.

69. Orleck, *Common Sense*, 93.

70. *New York Call*, May 2, 1915, p. 1 and p. 2. Orleck, *Common Sense*, 75–79.

71. See Figure 3.4, women in the carriage of the Women's Auxiliary Typographical Union in the September 6, 1909, Labor Day parade, "Labor Day

'09," LC-USZ62-33530, Bain, PPD, LC; and Figure 3.5, women marching in the 1910 May Day parade, "Holidays—May Day (Labor Holiday)—1910," LC-USZZ62-50083, Bain, PPD, LC. See also Figure 3.1, women garment workers assemble for the 1916 May Day parade in New York, LC-B2-3832-14, Bain, PPD, LC.

72. Buhle, *Women and American Socialism*, 222. Orleck, *Common Sense*, 87–112.

73. Kenneth Teitelbaum, *"Schooling for Good Rebels": Socialist Education for Children in the United States, 1900–1920* (Philadelphia: Temple University Press, 1993), 1–10, 57–70, and 137–175. Julia L. Mickenberg, *Learning from the Left: Children's Literature, the Cold War, and Radical Politics in the United States* (New York: Oxford University Press, 2005), 53 and 58–59. Kenneth Teitelbaum, "Socialist Sunday Schools," *The Encyclopedia of the American Left*, ed. Mari Jo Buhle, Paul Buhle, and Dan Georgakas (New York: Garland Publishers, 1990), 723–724. Pritchett, *Brownsville, Brooklyn*, 35–36. Buhle, *Women and American Socialism*, 300.

74. *New York Call*, April 30, 1912, p. 1 and p. 2; May 2, 1912, p. 2; May 2, 1913, p. 2; April 30, 1914, p. 1; May 2, 1914, p. 2; April 29, 1915, p. 2; May 2, 1915, p. 1; and April 30 1916, p. 1.

75. Ibid., April 30, 1912, p. 1 and p. 2.

76. For the children's parade, see *New York Call*, May 2, 1912, p. 2. For the adult parade, see, for example, *New York Call*, May 3, 1909, p. 1; April 30, 1910, p. 1; and May 11, 1911, p. 1.

77. Ibid., May 2, 1915, p. 1.

78. Ibid., May 2, 1915, p. 2.

79. In his research on the Socialist Sunday schools, Kenneth Teitelbaum found that most former students enjoyed their participation in the schools, recalling that it was "a heck of a lot of fun" and "a great time" that they "really looked forward to." Yet, some described their school experiences as "hideous!" and something that was forced on them by their parents. Teitelbaum, *"Schooling for Good Rebels,"* 132–133.

80. *New York Call*, May 3, 1909, p. 1.

81. Ibid., May 2, 1914, p. 1 and p. 2.

82. Ibid., May 2, 1918, p. 4.

83. David I. Macleod, *The Age of the Child: Children in American 1890–1920* (New York: Twayne Publishers, 1998).

84. *New York Call*, May 2, 1913, p. 1 and p. 2.

85. Ibid., May 2, 1912, p. 2. See Figure 3.6: "Protest Against Child Labor in a Labor Parade," from the 1909 May Day parade, LC-USZ62-22198, Bain, PPD, LC.

86. *New York Call*, May 2, 1912, p. 1.

87. John T. McGreevy, *Parish Boundaries: The Catholic Encounter with Race in the Twentieth-Century Urban North* (Chicago: University of Chicago Press, 1996), 21–25. Robert Anthony Orsi, *Faith and Community in Italian Harlem, 1880–1950* (New Haven, Conn.: Yale University Press, 1985). Dominic Pacyga,

Polish Immigrants and Industrial Chicago: Workers on the South Side, 1880–1922 (Columbus: Ohio State University Press, 1991), 126–146.

88. *New York Call*, May 2, 1912, p. 2.

89. McGreevy, *Parish Boundaries*, 22–25.

90. *New York Times*, May 2, 1901, p. 7, and May 2, 1912, p. 2. See Figure 3.7: "Children on May Day in Central Park, New York," 1908, LC-B2-66-14, Bain, PPD, LC.

91. David Glassberg, *American Historical Pageantry: The Uses of Tradition in the Early Twentieth Century* (Chapel Hill: University of North Carolina Press, 1990), 53–65.

92. The schools were organized by language groups, including German, English and Finnish. See, for example, *New York Call*, April 30, 1914, p. 1.

93. Ibid., April 30, 1914, p. 1, and May 2, 1914, p. 1 and p. 2.

94. Ibid., May 1, 1912, p. 5.

95. Ibid.

96. Ibid., May 3, 1909, p. 2; May 2, 1912, p. 1; and May 2, 1914, p. 1. See also "Holidays—May Day (Labor Holiday)—1913," LC-USZ62-45803, Bain, PPD, LC.

97. *Chicago Socialist*, May 5, 1906, p. 1.

98. *Chicago Tribune*, May 2, 1892, p. 1.

99. "Display of Flags," Approved December 6, 1918, sec. 24, chap. 23, Addenda, in New York, N.Y., *New Code of Ordinances of the City of New York. Including the Sanitary Code, the Building Code and Park Regulations, Adopted June 20, 1919, with Addenda of All Amendments to January 1, 1919*, compiled by Arthur Cosby (New York: Banks Law Publishing Co., 1919), 602.

100. *New York Call*, May 3, 1909, p. 2.

101. Ibid.

102. Ibid.

103. Entry for April 18, 1910, Minutes of the City Executive Committee, 1906–1914, Series VI:5, Socialist Party Minutes, 1900–1936, Socialist Collection at Tamiment Library, Microfilm, Reel 9, Tamiment.

104. *New York Call*, May 2, 1912, p. 1.

105. Ibid.

106. Entry for May 3, 1912, Minutes of the May Day Demonstration Conference, Socialist Party Local New York, Letterbooks, 1907–1914, Series V:46, Socialist Collections in Tamiment Library, Microfilm, Reel 7, Tamiment.

107. May 1912, Resolution of the Executive Committee, Local New York, Socialist Party, Socialist Party Local New York, Letterbooks, 1907–1914, Series V: 46, Socialist Collections in Tamiment Library, Microfilm, Reel 7, Tamiment.

108. *Chicago Daily Socialist*, May 1, 1912, p. 6.

109. *New York Times*, May 2, 1912, p. 1.

110. Paul Avrich, *Sacco and Vanzetti: The Anarchist Background* (Princeton, N.J.: Princeton University Press, 1991), 97–100.

111. *New York Call*, May 2, 1916, p. 1. See Figure 3.8: "IWW at Mulberry Sq. 5/1/14," Lot 10876-4, Bain, PPD, LC.

112. Not surprisingly, Samuel Gompers was one of the more outspoken of those who would voice such opposition. He and the AFL's secretary, John Frey, led the attack against two resolutions brought to the floor of the federation's annual meeting in 1919 that called for the AFL to officially recognize May 1, not the first Monday in September, as Labor Day. Gompers and Frey defended the September Labor Day as the legitimate American holiday and denounced May Day as an event that had become too European and political for the AFL to embrace. The federation rejected both resolutions. See "Report of the Proceedings of the Thirty-Ninth Annual Convention of the American Federation of Labor, Held at Atlantic City, New Jersey, June 9 to 23, Inclusive, 1919," *Proceedings of the American Federation of Labor* (Washington, D.C.: Law Reporter Printing Co., 1919), 196, 210, and 331.

113. *New York Call*, May 2, 1915, p. 2, and May 2, 1916, p. 1.

NOTES TO CHAPTER 4

1. *New York Times*, May 2, 1925, p. 1.

2. Ibid.

3. Ibid.

4. *Daily Worker*, May 4, 1925, p. 1 and p. 2.

5. Ibid., p. 2.

6. Lynn Dumenil, *The Modern Temper: American Culture and Society in the 1920s* (New York: Hill and Wang, 1995), 203–247.

7. Richard Polenberg, *Fighting Faiths: The Abrams Case, the Supreme Court, and Free Speech* (Ithaca, N.Y.: Cornell University Press, 1987), 34.

8. Nick Salvatore, *Eugene V. Debs: Citizen and Socialist* (Chicago: University of Illinois Press, 1982), 319.

9. Paul Avrich, *Sacco and Vanzetti: The Anarchist Background* (Princeton, N.J.: Princeton University Press, 1991), 130–135 and 143.

10. Avrich, *Sacco and Vanzetti*, 174–176. Polenberg, *Fighting Faiths*, 170–178.

11. Avrich, *Sacco and Vanzetti*, 174–175.

12. In 1919, for example, five Socialist assemblymen were ejected from the New York State Legislature because of their party affiliation. Salvatore, *Eugene V. Debs*, 322. *New York Call*, May 1, 1920, p. 4.

13. *New York Call*, April 29, 1919, p. 1.

14. Debs did not serve his full term, but was released on December 25, 1921. See Salvatore, *Eugene V. Debs*, 294–296 and 328. O'Hare served fourteen months of her sentence. See Avrich, *Sacco and Vanzetti*, 114. Stokes did not serve her full term either. She won an overturn of her conviction in 1921. See Polenberg, *Fighting Faiths*, 85–86, and Mari Jo Buhle, "Stokes, Rose Pastor," *Encyclopedia of the*

American Left, ed. Mari Jo Buhle, Paul Buhle, and Dan Georgakas (Urbana and Chicago: University of Illinois Press, 1992), 750.

15. Department of Organization and Propaganda, Socialist Party of the United States, "International Labor Day—1919. Program for Your May 1st Meeting" (Chicago, 1919), sections 2, 3, and 5. Vertical File, "May Day (1918–24) GF," Tamiment Library/Robert F. Wagner Labor Archives, Elmer Holmes Bobst Library, New York University Libraries, New York University (hereafter VF, "May Day (1918–24) GF," Tamiment).

16. For example, Rose Pastor Stokes and many others sent May Day greetings to Debs when he was in jail. See letter from Theodore Debs to Stokes, May 16, 1919, Rose Pastor Stokes Papers, 1905–1933, in Socialist Collections in Tamiment, XIX, Microfilm, R2697. Tamiment Library/Robert F. Wagner Labor Archives, Elmer Holmes Bobst Library, New York University Libraries, New York University (hereafter Tamiment). Quote is from Kate Richards O'Hare. See letter from O'Hare to her family, May 3, 1919, letter number 3, Kate Richards O'Hare Papers, 1919–1920, Microfilm, R4245.

17. Department of Organization and Propaganda, SPUS, "International Labor Day—1919," VF, "May Day (1918–24) GF," Tamiment.

18. Department of Organization and Propaganda, SPUS, "International Labor Day—1919," section 13, Eugene Debs, "Speech by Eugene V. Debs"; section 3, William Kruse, "To the Youth of America"; and section 9, Irwin St. John Tucker, "Restore the Republic!" VF, "May Day (1918–24) GF," Tamiment.

19. Department of Organization and Propaganda, SPUS, "International Labor Day—1919," section 5, Rose Pastor Stokes, "May Day 1919: A Challenge and a Greeting," VF, "May Day (1918–24) GF," Tamiment.

20. *The People*, April 10, 1920, p. 1. *New York Call*, May 1, 1919, p. 12.

21. Department of Organization and Propaganda, SPUS, "International Labor Day—1919," section 7, J. Louis Engdahl, "May Day Greetings," VF, "May Day (1918–24) GF," Tamiment.

22. Polenberg, *Fighting Faiths*, 85.

23. *New York Call*, May 2, 1919, p. 2.

24. Ibid.

25. For parade permit denials and arrests for the distribution of socialist literature, see *New York Call*, April 29, 1920, p. 1; May 2, 1920, p. 2; May 1, 1921, p. 1 and p. 8; and May 2, 1921, p. 1. For the red flag ban in New York, see "Display of Flags," Approved December 6, 1918, sec. 24, chap. 23, Addenda, in New York, N.Y., *New Code of Ordinances of the City of New York. Including the Sanitary Code, the Building Code and Park Regulations, Adopted June 20, 1919, with Addenda of All Amendments to January 1, 1919*, compiled by Arthur Cosby (New York: Banks Law Publishing Co., 1919), 602.

26. *New York Call*, May 2, 1919, p. 3.

27. Ibid., p. 1 and p. 3.

28. Ibid., April 29, 1921, p. 1 and p. 2; April 30, 1921, p. 1; May 1, 1921, p. 2; April 29, 1922, p. 9; April 30, 1922, p. 3; and May 1, 1923, p. 1 and p. 2.

29. Ibid., April 29, 1921, p. 2; May 1, 1921, p. 2; May 2, 1921, p. 12; April 29, 1922, p. 3; May 2, 1922, p. 2; May 1, 1923, p. 1 and p. 2; and May 2, 1923, p. 2.

30. Fraser M. Ottanelli, *The Communist Party of the United States: From the Depression to World War II* (New Brunswick, N.J.: Rutgers University Press, 1991), 9–16. Kate Weigand, *Red Feminism: American Communism and the Making of Women's Liberation* (Baltimore: Johns Hopkins University Press, 2001), 16–17.

31. Figure 4.1, May Day issue cover, *New Masses*, May 1929. Courtesy of the Tamiment Library and Robert F. Wagner Labor Archives, New York University.

32. *Daily Worker*, April 26, 1924, p. 6, and April 28, 1927, p. 1.

33. Ibid., April 26, 1924, p. 6. On May Day and Russia, see also April 30, 1927, supplement p. 13.

34. Ibid., April 26, 1924, supplement p. 2.

35. American Defense Society, "Ten Proposals for Defense Action," November 1917, Box ADS Papers, 1916–1917, in American Defense Society Records, Manuscript Department, New-York Historical Society, courtesy of the New-York Historical Society (hereafter ADS Records, MD, N-YHS).

36. Typed statement of ADS proposals, no date, Box ADS Papers, 1916–1917, and *American Defense*, June 30, 1919, p. 1, Box ADS Papers, late 1918, ADS Records MD, N-YHS.

37. Letter from E. L. Harvey, Publicity Director of the National Security League to the Advertising Manager at AT&T, March 2, 1920, Box ADS Papers, 1919–1921, ADS Records, MD, N-YHS.

38. Minutes of the Annual Meeting of the American Defense Society, April 4, 1921, in a letter from C. M. Penfield to Charles Davison, May 19, 1921, Box ADS Papers, 1920–May 1922, ADS Records, MD, N-YHS.

39. Letter from R. W. Hurd to Charles Davison, April 19, 1921, Box ADS Papers, 1920–May 1922, ADS Records, MD, N-YHS.

40. Program for "America Day Meeting Under the Auspices of the American Defense Society," May 1919, p. 10, Box ADS Papers, 1923–1926, ADS Records, MD, N-YHS. Note that in 1919, before Hurd's tenure as chairman, American Day was held on May 17. But the nativist purposes remained the same as when the day moved to May 1.

41. *New York Times*, May 18, 1919, p.16.

42. Program for "America Day Meeting Under the Auspices of the American Defense Society," May 1919, p. 8, Box ADS Papers, 1923–1926, ADS Records, MD, N-YHS.

43. *New York Times*, May 18, 1919, p. 16.

44. Program for "America Day Meeting Under the Auspices of the American Defense Society," May 1919, p. 12, Box ADS Papers, 1923–1926, ADS Records, MD, N-YHS.

45. Paul Harris, a lawyer in Chicago, founded the first Rotary Club as a businessmen's club. By 1912, the focus of what became a nationwide network of clubs had shifted to public service and volunteerism, including educational work with boys. See Arnold Oren, *The Golden Strand: An Informal History of the Rotary Club of Chicago* (Chicago: Quadrangle Books, 1966), 18–26, 119, 135, and 144.

46. The club's work among boys began as wartime service during the Great War. See, for example, *Spokes in the Wheel of the Rotary Club of New York* 5:7 (June 1918): 21.

47. *New York Times*, May 2, 1920, p. 1. Oren, *Golden Strand*, 135–137.

48. *New York Times*, May 2, 1920, p. 1.

49. *New York Call*, May 2, 1920, p. 6.

50. *New York Times*, May 2, 1920, p. 1.

51. Ibid.

52. Oren, *Golden Strand*, 135–136.

53. *New York Times*, May 2, 1923, p. 21.

54. Ibid., May 2, 1923, p. 21. Oren, *Golden Strand*, 136.

55. Ibid., May 1, 1921, p. 12.

56. Ibid., May 2, 1920, p. 1, and May 2, 1923, p. 21.

57. *New York Call*, May 2, 1929, p. 1.

58. These progressive elements of the Loyalty Day parade, along with the educational and recreational activities planned for the rest of Boys' Week, most likely explain the presence of the Henry Street Settlement House children in the events. See Lillian Wald, *Windows on Henry Street* (Boston: Little, Brown and Co., 1934), 25, 45–46, 144, 156–159, and 290–310.

59. BSA headquarters relied on wealthy donors, who provided the bulk of the organization's budget. Some of the top donors were Andrew Carnegie, John D. Rockefeller and Mrs. Russell Sage. David MacLeod, *Building Character in the American Boy: The Boy Scouts, YMCA and Their Forerunners* (Madison: University of Wisconsin Press, 1983), 151.

60. *Chicago Daily Socialist*, April 29, 1911, p. 7.

61. More than 50,000 American soldiers died in six months of fighting. See Jennifer D. Keene, "Americans as Warriors: 'Doughboys' in Battle during the First World War," in *OAH Magazine of History* 17:1 (October 2002): 15.

62. Michael Kimmel, *Manhood in America: A Cultural History* (New York: Free Press, 1996), 82–89 and 9–10.

63. On Armistice Day, see Matthew Dennis, *Red, White, and Blue Letter Days: An American Calendar* (Ithaca, N.Y.: Cornell University Press, 2002), 235. On antiradical vigilante violence associated with the American Legion on Armistice Day, see the discussion of their attack on the IWW in Centralia in 1919 in William Pencak, *For God and Country: The American Legion, 1919–1941* (Boston: Northeastern University Press), 151–152.

64. The Boy Scouts' loyalty oath taken to parents and the country, its military-style organization and discipline, controlled outdoor physical excursions, and community service projects satisfied the middle-class parent's need to raise obedient, disciplined, strong, and patriotic boys. See MacLeod, *Building Character*, 171–187.

65. See the example of Kulke's raids above, and *New York Call*, May 2, 1919, p. 3. Evidence that there were those within the working-class who embraced a conservative version of patriotism, which included a disdain for all things "foreign," can be found in the Lynds' discussion of working-class participation in the Klan. See Robert S. Lynd and Helen Merrell Lynd, *Middletown: A Study in American Culture* (New York: Harcourt, Brace and World, 1929), 481–484.

66. *New York Call*, May 1, 1921, p. 7.

67. Women were often relegated to the sidelines during civic events, especially during the nineteenth century. See, for example, Mary P. Ryan, *Civic Wars: Democracy and Public Life in the American City during the Nineteenth Century* (Berkeley: University of California Press, 1997), 248; and David Glassberg, *American Historical Pageantry: The Uses of Tradition in the Early Twentieth Century* (Chapel Hill: University of North Carolina Press, 1990), 18.

68. *New York Times*, May 1, 1921, p. 12.

69. Oren, *Golden Strand*, 136–137. In Chicago, the Rotary organized Boys' Week into the 1960s. According to Oren, the Loyalty Day parade was suspended because there were too many boys who were interested in joining and it became too difficult to organize.

70. See, for example, the rally of the Brooklyn Citizen's Patriotic May Day Celebration Committee in Prospect Park on May 1, 1926 (*New York Times*, May 3, 1926, p. 12); and the VFW's parade on May Day, "in patriotic demonstration against Communism," in 1930 (*New York Times*, May 3, 1930, p. 2).

71. Herbert Hoover, *The Memoirs of Herbert Hoover: The Cabinet and the Presidency, 1920–1933*, vol. 2 (New York: Macmillan, 1952), 31–32.

72. MacLeod, *The Age of the Child: Children in America, 1890–1920* (New York: Macmillan, 1998), 35–38 and 49–51. On his advice to Hoover, see Katherine Glover, *The Story of May Day, 1924–1928* (New York: American Child Health Association, 1928), 1.

73. Glover, *The Story of May Day*, 2.

74. Letter from Herbert Hoover to President Calvin Coolidge, February 18, 1924, in Glover, *The Story of May Day*, 23–24.

75. Hoover, *Memoirs*, vol. 2, 98.

76. Root lost sight in one eye in 1922. After an operation saved some of the sight in her other eye, she raised close to five million dollars to establish the Wilmer Ophthalmological Institute at Johns Hopkins. Stephen Hess, *America's Political Dynasties* (Garden City, N.Y.: Doubleday and Co., 1966), 267–268. Glover, *The Story of May Day*, 8.

77. May spring pageants, maypole dances, and special crafts were already familiar to teachers and students. See Alice Maude Kellogg, *Primary Recitations* (Philadelphia: Penn Publishing Co., 1925), 16, 21, and 44; Alice Maude Kellogg, *Spring and Summer School Celebrations* (Philadelphia: Penn Publishing Co., 1923), 65–90; Catherine Snodgrass, *Springtime: A May Day Pageant* (New York: A.S. Barnes and Co., 1924). The new messages of health and hygiene were added to these familiar activities. See, for example, the photos between pages 44 and 45 in Glover, *The Story of May Day*, and Grace T. Hallock, ed., *May Day Festival Book, 1927* (New York: American Child Health Association, 1927).

78. Glover, *The Story of May Day*, 3–4.

79. Ibid., 13 and 15.

80. Ibid., 81.

81. Hoover, *Memoirs*, vol. 2, 99.

82. Samuel Gompers, Press Release for Information and Publicity Service, AFL, March 25, 1924, in The American Federation of Labor Records: The Samuel Gompers Era, Microfilm edition, 5632, Reel 118.

83. "Report of the Proceedings of the Forty-Seventh Annual Convention of the American Federation of Labor, Held at Los Angeles, California, October 3 to 14, Inclusive, 1927," *Proceedings of the American Federation of Labor* (Washington, D.C.: Law Reporter Printing Co., 1927), 94.

84. Ibid.

85. U.S. Congress, House, Committee on Education, *Child Health Day: Hearing before the Committee on Education* (17th Cong., 1st Sess., April 13 and 29, 1928), 1.

86. Ibid.

87. Ibid.

88. This was known as Senate Resolution 89. In the House it was identified as House Joint Resolution 184. See U.S. Congress, House, Committee on Education, *Child Health Day: Hearing before the Committee on Education* (17th Cong., 1st Sess., April 13 and 29, 1928), 1.

89. Ibid., 2–3 and 4–5.

90. Ibid., 19.

91. Ibid., 31.

92. Ibid.

93. "Congressional Joint Resolution, Designating May 1 as Child Health Day," in Glover, *The Story of May Day*, 28.

94. Calvin Coolidge, "President's Proclamation—1928," in Glover, *The Story of May Day*, 27.

95. ACHA, *American Child Health Association, Teamwork for Child Health* (New York: ACHA, 1929), 12–21.

96. Ibid., 31–39 and 67–68.

97. ACHA, *American Child Health Association, Celebrating May Day in 1929* (New York: ACHA, 1929), 13–15.

98. The influence of the present on the way individuals, groups, and societies recall the past has been addressed in the recent literature on historical memory. See, for example, Paul Cohen, *History in Three Keys: The Boxers as Event, Experience, and Myth* (New York: Columbia University Press, 1997), 238; Michael Kammen, *Mystic Chords of Memory: The Transformation of Tradition in American Culture* (New York: Vintage Books Edition, 1993), 162; and John R. Gillis, "Memory and Identity: The History of a Relationship," *Commemorations: The Politics of National Identity*, ed. John R. Gillis (Princeton, N.J.: Princeton University Press, 1994), 3.

99. "Report of the Proceedings of the Forty-Eighth Annual Convention of the American Federation of Labor, Held at New Orleans, Louisiana, November 19 to 28, Inclusive, 1928," *Proceedings of the American Federation of Labor* (Washington, D.C.: Law Reporter Printing Co., 1928), 84.

100. *Daily Worker*, April 30, 1927, p. 4.

101. Ibid., April 26, 1929, p. 6.

102. Ibid.

103. Ibid., April 23, 1932, p. 4.

104. Fraser M. Ottanelli, *The Communist Party of the United States: From the Depression to World War II* (New Brunswick, N.J.: Rutgers University Press, 1991), 15–16, 18–19, and 47.

105. Ottanelli, *The Communist Party*, 20–37. Christine Ellis, "People Who Cannot Be Bought," in *Rank and File: Personal Histories by Working-Class Organizers*, ed. Alice Lynd and Staughton Lynd (Boston: Beacon Press, 1973), 26.

106. Randi Storch, "'The Realities of the Situation': Revolutionary Discipline and Everyday Political Life in Chicago's Communist Party, 1928–1935," *Labor: Studies in Working-Class History of the Americas* 1:3 (2004): 21.

107. The IWO was a benevolent organization, made up of several language fraternal associations, founded in 1930 by members of the CP and the Jewish Workmen's Circle. See Ottanelli, *The Communist Party*, 125–126; and Max Bedact, "IWO: Ten Years of Our Order, 1930–1940," in *The Fraternal Outlook* (June–July 1940): 10–14. Julia L. Mickenberg explores the genre of "proletarian children's literature" that the IWO and Young Pioneers circulated during the late 1920s and early 1930s in her work, *Learning from the Left: Children's Literature, the Cold War, and Radical Politics in the United States* (New York: Oxford University Press, 2006), 52–53.

108. Sam Pevzner, "The Gang Learns About May Day," in *Ten Plays for Boys and Girls*, ed. Ben Blake (IWO, 1935), 24–34. IWO Publications, Box 48, International Workers Order Records, Kheel Center for Labor-Management Documentation and Archives, M.P. Catherwood Library, Cornell University (hereafter Kheel).

109. Ben Blake, "Introduction," in *Ten Plays for Boys and Girls*, ed. Ben Blake (IWO, 1935), 7–8. IWO Publications, Box 48, International Workers Order Records, Kheel.

110. Pevzner, "The Gang," 24–28.

111. Ibid., 31–32.

112. Ibid, 33.

113. Ibid., 33–34.

114. In terms of "proletarian children's literature" of the day, Julia Mickenberg has observed how "boy protagonists far outnumber girls in the literature." Mickenberg, *Learning from the Left*, 72–73.

115. See Figure 4.2, a William Gropper cartoon that depicts a brawny male carrying a flag in May Day parade. *New Masses*, May 4, 1937, p. 10. Courtesy of the Tamiment Library and Robert F. Wagner Labor Archives, New York University. See also the many illustrations in the May Day issues of the *Daily Worker* that celebrated either the scrappy male worker (shown out demonstrating on May Day) or the exaggerated brawny male figure (usually confronting a "fat capitalist" character): *Daily Worker*, April 29, 1930, p. 6; May 1, 1931, p. 2; April 22, 1932, p. 4; and April 28, 1934, p.13. These images are contradicted by the photographs of actual May Day parades, which included women in prominent positions. See, for example, *Daily Worker*, May 3, 1933, p. 6. The image of the brawny workman was also used in socialist literature: see the covers of the *Young Socialist Magazine* for May 1919, April 1919, May 1918, and May 1917.

116. See chapter 3.

117. See, for example, Abridged Minutes, National Executive Committee Meeting, April 15 and 16, 1933, p. 7, YPSL, Series II, Youth and YPSL Papers, Socialist Party Records, Microfilm, Reel 81; and Thesis and Resolutions for the Seventh National Convention of the Communist Party of the USA, Central Committee Plenum, March 31–April 4, 1930, Series 6:15, CPUSA Convention Proceedings, 1921–1972, Earl Browder Papers, Microfilm, Reel 7.

118. Paul C. Mishler, *Raising Reds: The Young Pioneers, Radical Summer Camps, and Communist Political Culture in the United States* (New York: Columbia University Press, 1999), 42.

119. On the persistence of local ethnic-based neighborhood institutions in the 1920s, see also Lizabeth Cohen, *Making a New Deal: Industrial Workers in Chicago, 1919—1939* (New York: Cambridge University Press, 1990), 53–97.

120. Mishler, *Raising Reds*, 44.

121. In 1929, approximately 1,000 Pioneers walked out of school to join in the parade; three were arrested for distributing leaflets: *Daily Worker*, May 3, 1929, p. 1 and p. 5. In 1930, approximately eighty Pioneers were arrested on May Day and in the days immediately following for handing out party leaflets: *Daily Worker*, May 3, 1930, p. 1.

122. *Daily Worker*, May 3, 1926, p. 1 and p. 3.

123. *New York Times*, May 2, 1927, p. 2.

124. *Daily Worker*, April 26, 1930, p. 6.

125. See, for example, *New York Times*, May 2, 1930, p. 20. That year some fifty arrests were made.

126. Fannia Cohn, "Pioneer Youth of America," reprinted from *American Federationist*, September 1925, in Fannia Cohn Papers, Microfilm, Reel 12, Manuscripts and Archives Division, New York Public Library, Astor, Lenox, and Tilden Foundations, New York (hereafter MAD, NYPL).

127. The YPSL of Chicago was established first, gaining the official support of the SP in 1912. The YPSL became a national organization by 1915.

128. Letter to YPSL of Greater New York from Executive Secretary Morris Novick, April 28, 1923, in Youth and YPSL Papers, Series II, Socialist Party of America Papers, Microfilm, Reel 81. Addition to Report of Bronx YPSL, April 27, 1927, in Youth and YPSL Papers, Series II, Socialist Party of America Papers, Microfilm, Reel 81.

129. This reinforces Mishler's conclusions. See Mishler, *Raising Reds*, 42.

130. Peggy Dennis, *The Autobiography of an American Communist: A Personal View of a Political Life, 1925–1975* (Westport, Conn.: Lawrence Hill & Co., 1977), 20.

131. Ibid., 21.

132. Robert Schrank, *Wasn't That a Time? Growing Up Radical and Red in America* (Cambridge: MIT Press, 1998), 28.

133. Ibid., 49.

134. Ibid., 28.

135. Ibid.

136. Ruth Pinkson, "The Life and Times of an Elderly Red Diaper Baby," in *Red Diapers: Growing Up in the Communist Left*, ed. Judy Kaplan and Linn Shapiro (Urbana and Chicago: University of Illinois Press, 1998), 232.

137. Ibid.

138. Schrank, *Wasn't It a Time?*, 82–87.

139. Ibid., 126.

140. Ottanelli, *The Communist Party of the United States*, 48.

141. Joe Preisen, quoted in Vivian Gornick, *The Romance of American Communism* (New York: Basic Books, 1977), 45.

142. See, for example, Judy Kaplan and Linn Shapiro, eds., *Red Diaper Babies: Growing Up in the Communist Left* (Chicago and Urbana: University of Illinois Press, 1998).

143. Karl Millens, quoted in Vivian Gornick, *The Romance of American Communism* (New York: Basic Books, 1977), 148.

144. For example, Mario, Robert Schrank's working-class friend, who is Italian and a Roman Catholic, had ties to ethnic and religious associations in his neighborhood that also taught him hostility to socialism and communism. See, Schrank *Wasn't It a Time?*, 87.

NOTES TO CHAPTER 5

1. CP membership rose to 19,000 in 1933, 27,000 in 1935, and 65,000 by the late 1930s. See Fraser M. Ottanelli, *The Communist Party of the United States: From the Depression to World War II* (New Brunswick, N.J.: Rutgers University Press, 1991), 43–44. The SP bounced back to a membership of 16,000 by 1932, but because of a schism in the mid-1930s, its support never rose above 20,000 again. See Nick Salvatore, *Eugene V. Debs: Citizen and Socialist* (Chicago: University of Illinois Press, 1982), 336.

2. *The Socialist Call*, April 27, 1935, p. 1.

3. See, for example, *The Socialist Call*, April 27, 1935, p. 9; April 27, 1935, p. 13; and May 1, 1935, special May Day supplement, p. 2.

4. See, for example, *Daily Worker*, April 29, 1930, p. 2; May 2, 1930, p. 1; April 19, 1932, p. 1; and April 20, 1932, p. 4.

5. Figure 5.1, May Day issue cover, *New Masses*, May 1930. Courtesy of the Tamiment Library and Robert F. Wagner Labor Archives, New York University. On May Day in 1932, the Friends of the Soviet Union, an organization affiliated with the CPUSA, sponsored a delegation of American workers on a trip to Moscow. It was hoped that the delegates would see "exactly what is going on in the Workers' Fatherland," and take that information back to the United States. See Friends of the Soviet Union, May First Delegation Campaign, 1932, Correspondence and Publications, Communist Party of the United States of America, Files of the Communist Party of the USA in the Comintern Archives, Microform 515, Reel 234, Delo. 3027, Tamiment Library/Robert F. Wagner Labor Archives, Elmer Holmes Bobst Library, New York University Libraries, New York University (hereafter CPUSA, Comintern Files, Tamiment).

6. M. Epstein, "May Day, 1934" (New York: Communist Party, New York District, 1934), 5–9 and 16–18. *Daily Worker*, April 21, 1931, p. 1; April 29, 1931, p. 1; April 20, 1932, p. 1; and April 27, 1933, p. 1 and p. 2.

7. See discussion in chapter 4.

8. "Results of the Presidential Election and Tasks of the Communist Party of the USA," Draft for the Bureau of the Anglo-American Leader Secretariat, October 10, 1933; and "The Operation of the Manifesto of the ECCI on the United Front in the U.S.A.," July 3, 1933, in CPUSA, Comintern Files, Reel 237, Delo. 3083, Tamiment.

9. "Results of the Presidential Election and Tasks of the Communist Party of the USA," in CPUSA, Comintern Files, Reel 237, Delo. 3083, p. 69, Tamiment.

10. As early as 1933 Mike Gold called for the unity of all antifascists, while the Socialist Student League for Industrial Democracy and the Communist National Student League cooperated in a joint antiwar rally. See Ottanelli, *The Communist Party*, 57–65.

11. V. R. Berghahn, *Modern Germany: Society, Economy and Politics in the Twentieth Century*, 2d ed. (New York: Cambridge University Press, 1987), 129–131.

12. "Communist Party Proposes United Action," March 30, 1933, in *A Documentary History of the Communist Party of the United States. Volume II: Unite and Fight*, ed. Bernard K. Johnpoll (Westport, Conn.: Greenwood Press, 1994), 341–347. United Front May Day Committee, "All Out May First," 1933, CPUSA flyer, in CPUSA, New York, Vertical File Collection, Tamiment.

13. Letter from Earl Browder to the National Executive Committee of the Socialist Party of America, September 14, 1934, Correspondence, 1929–1967, Subseries A: SPA, Series II: Organizational Files, 1904–1967, Normal Thomas Papers, Microfilm edition, Reel 54, Manuscripts and Archives Division, New York Public Library, Astor, Lenox, and Tilden Foundations, New York (hereafter MAD, NYPL).

14. United Front May Day Conference, "May Day Plan of Action for Affiliated Organizations," April 13, 1935, CPUSA, NY, 1935, Vertical File Collection, Tamiment.

15. May Day United Front Conference, Draft Program of Action, 1934, CPUSA, Comintern Files, Microfilm 515, Reel 287, Delo. 3710, Tamiment.

16. *Daily Worker*, April 5, 1934, p. 2; April 12, 1935, p. 1; and April 26, 1935, p. 1.

17. Robert D. Parmet, *The Master of Seventh Avenue: David Dubinsky and the American Labor Movement* (New York: New York University Press, 2005), 119–120 and 182. Florence Rossi, March 17, 1982, Box 2, 1U2V, OH002, Oral History of the American Left, Tamiment.

18. Open Letter "To All Members of the Young People's Socialist League and the Socialist Party," 1933, in Series II, Youth and YPSL Papers, 1915–1963, Socialist Party of America Papers, Microfilm, Reel R2070.

19. For a complete discussion of the 1934 Union Square permit fight, see Donna Truglio Haverty-Stacke, "Constructing Radical America: A Cultural and Social History of May Day in New York City and Chicago, 1867–1945," (Ph.D. diss., Cornell University, 2003), 278–284.

20. *Chicago Daily Tribune*, May 1, 1933, p. 1.

21. Ibid.

22. Ibid., p. 2.

23. Ibid.

24. James Green, "Remembering Haymarket: Chicago's Labor Martyrs and Their Legacy," in *Taking History to Heart: The Power of the Past in Building Social Movements* (Amherst: University of Massachusetts Press, 2000), 130 and 137. James Green, *Death in the Haymarket: A Story of Chicago, the First Labor Movement and the Bombing That Divided Gilded Age America* (New York: Pantheon, 2006), 301–320.

25. The sixth went off at a Teamsters meeting in Lake Forest and the seventh struck an affiliate of the Borden Company in Chicago. *Chicago Daily Tribune*, May 2, 1933, p. 1 and p. 6, and May 3, 1933, pp.1–2.

26. Ibid., May 3, 1933, pp. 1–2, and May 14, 1933, p. 3. The Chicago Teamsters consisted of independent locals that had broken away from the International Brotherhood of Teamsters and the AFL in 1905, after the major strike that took place in the city that year. It was a militant union of some 13,000 members, who refused to transport nonunion goods into or throughout Chicago. Andrew Wender Cohen, *The Racketeer's Progress: Chicago and the Struggle for the Modern Economy, 1900–1940* (New York: Cambridge University Press, 2004), 118, 212–213, and 284.

27. *Chicago Tribune*, May 1, 1933, p. 1 and p. 2; and *Daily Worker*, April 17, 1934, p. 1, and April 18, 1934, p.1.

28. *Daily Worker*, April 5, 1935, pp. 1, 2, and 3; April 17, 1935, p. 1; April 26, 1935, p. 1; and April 29, 1935, p. 1. A similar struggle took place in 1936. Ibid., April 3, 1936, p. 1.

29. Ibid., May 2, 1934, p. 1. IWO, "Manual for Builders," f. 4, Box 27: JPFO records in IWO Records, Kheel Center for Labor-Management Documentation and Archives, M.P. Catherwood Library, Cornell University (hereafter Kheel).

30. *Daily Worker*, May 3, 1935, p. 1. See, for example, *Daily Worker*, April 13, 1934, p. 1 (Steel and Metal Workers Industrial Union; Left Wing Group of ILGWU); April 27, 1934, p. 1 (Local 499 Painters and Decorators Union); April 30, 1934, p. 1 (four locals from AFL-affiliated Bakers Union); and April 6, 1935, p. 1 (Painters' and Paperhangers' Local 121; United Textile Workers Union; Carpenters' Union Local 2090; ILGWU Local 20).

31. By 1935 black membership in the party stood at only approximately 2,300 nationally. Mark Solomon, *The Cry Was Unity: Communists and African Americans, 1917–1936* (Jackson: University of Mississippi Press, 1998), 96–100, 138, 169, and 230. For the participating African-American dominated organizations, see, for example, *Daily Worker*, April 26, 1930, p. 4 (American Negro Labor Congress; Food Workers Union); April 29, 1932, p. 1 (Cafeteria, Restaurant and Hotel Workers Union; League of Struggle for Negro Rights); and April 30, 1933, p. 2 (Unemployed Councils from Harlem).

32. Melvyn Dubofsky and Foster Rhea Dulles, *Labor in America: A History* (Wheeling, Ill.: Harlan Davidson, 2004), 280–283.

33. Ottanelli, *The Communist Party*, 137–142. Lizabeth Cohen, *Making a New Deal: Industrial Workers in Chicago, 1919–1939* (New York: Cambridge University Press, 1990), 310–313. Local 5 would be expelled from the AFL in 1940. See Daniel Walkowitz, *Working with Class: Social Workers and the Politics of Middle-Class Identity* (Chapel Hill: University of North Carolina Press, 1999), 215.

34. Van Gosse, "'To Organize in Every Neighborhood, in Every Home': The Gender Politics of American Communists between the Wars," *Radical History Review* 50 (1991): 109–142. For examples of party members organizing the unemployed, see also Christine Ellis, "People Who Cannot Be Bought," in *Rank and File: Personal Histories by Working-Class Organizers*, ed. Alice Lynd and

Staughton Lynd (Boston: Beacon Press, 1973), 26–33. On neighborhood work, see also CPUSA, Cook County Council, "Cook County Campaigner," 1:1 (May 1939), f. 515, o. 1, Delo. 4085, CPUSA, Files of the CPUSA in the Comintern Archives, R-7548, Reel 307, Tamiment.

35. See, for example, the line of march for the 1935 May Day parade in *Daily Worker*, April 23, 1935, p. 3.

36. For a brief biography of Divine, see "Father Divine," in *The African-American Century: How Black Americans Have Shaped Our Country*, ed. Henry Louis Gates, Jr., and Cornel West (New York: Free Press, 2000), 122–125.

37. Max Zaritsky, quoted in a news release, May 28, 1929, in f. Union Affairs and Correspondence 1920s, Box 1 Unions Affairs (Cloth Hat, Cap, and Millinery Workers International Union), Max Zaritsky Papers, Tamiment.

38. Louis Nelson, "United Front from Above," in f. 3 Communist Party, 1935–1949, Box 2: ILGWU Local 155 Knitgoods Workers' NYC Manager's Records, Louis Nelson, 1933–1968, Kheel.

39. Provisional May Day Committee, "To All Organizations of Labor!" 1936, in f. 8, May Day Committee, 1932–33 and 1939, Box 4: ILGWU Broadsides, Kheel. Despite his general distrust of the CP, Randolph briefly cooperated with communists in their united front against fascism and their work in support of black civil rights beginning in 1936 as leader of the National Negro Congress. See Paula F. Pfeffer, *A. Philip Randolph, Pioneer of the Civil Rights Movement* (Baton Rouge: Louisiana State University Press, 1990), 34–40.

40. Provisional May Day Committee, "To All Organizations of Labor!" 1936, in f. 8, May Day Committee, 1932–1933 and 1939, Box 4: ILGWU Broadsides, Kheel.

41. Minutes of the Executive Board, Dressmakers Local 22 ILGWU, March 31, 1936, p. 430, and April 11, 1936, p. 434, Volume 6, January 1, 1936–December 31, 1936, Box 1: Executive Board Minutes, 1934–1942, ILGWU Local 22 Dressmakers Union Records, Kheel.

42. Knitgoods Workers United May Day Initiative Committee, Invitation to United May Day Meeting, in f. 3 Communist Party, 1935–1949, Box 2: ILGWU Local 155 Knitgoods Workers' NYC Manager's Records, Louis Nelson, 1933–1968, Kheel.

43. Letter from David Dubinsky to Charles Zimmerman, March 25, 1936, f. 8b, May 1, 1936–1948, Box 326: Correspondence, President, June 1932–June 1936, David Dubinsky Papers, ILGWU Records, Kheel.

44. For examples of earlier versions of Zimmerman's dissent, see Parmet, *Master of Seventh Avenue*, 100–103; on the militants and Old Guard in the SP, see Parmet, 118–120 and 129.

45. Open letter to ILGWU membership from David Dubinsky, a one-page flyer reproduced in English, Italian, and Yiddish, f. 8b, May 1, 1936–1948, Box 326: Correspondence, President, June 1932–June 1936, David Dubinsky Papers, ILGWU Records, Kheel.

46. Dubinsky expressed these fears in a letter to Harry Laidler, Executive Director of the League for Industrial Democracy. Laidler's reply in a letter from April 23, 1936, insisted that the push for the united May Day came from within the ILGWU (in Locals 22, 117, and 119), and not from the CP. See letter to Dubinsky from Laidler, April 23, 1936, f. 8b, May 1, 1936–1948, Box 326: Correspondence, President, June 1932–June 1936, David Dubinsky Papers, ILGWU Records, Kheel. Laidler discussed Dubinsky's fears that the CP and militants were revolting against his leadership in the unions in a letter to Norman Thomas April 28, 1936, in Correspondence, January 1936–October 1936, Series I: General Correspondence, Norman Thomas Papers, Microfilm edition, Reel 6, MAD, NYPL.

47. Harvey Klehr, *The Heyday of American Communism: The Depression Decade* (New York: Basic Books, 1984), 7–8. Ottanelli, *The Communist Party*, 13–14.

48. Letter from Norman Thomas to Luigi Antonini, April 8, 1936, in Correspondence, January 1936–October 1936, Series I: General Correspondence, Norman Thomas Papers, Microfilm edition, Reel 6, MAD, NYPL.

49. Letter from Norman Thomas to Provisional Committee for May Day Conference, April 3, 1936, and letter from Thomas to United Labor May Day Committee, April 21, 1936, in Correspondence January 1936–October 1936, Series I: General Correspondence, Norman Thomas Papers, Microfilm edition, Reel 6, MAD, NYPL.

50. Letter from the Executive Secretary, Cook County SP, to Emil Arnold, Painters Union 275, March 2, 1936, in Series III: State and Local Records, Illinois, Socialist Party of America Papers, Microfilm, Reel 2085, Tamiment.

51. "The United Front in the USA: The Arguments of the Socialist Party Against It, and the Answer of the CP USA," CPUSA, Comintern Files, Reel 301, Delo. 3958, pp. 17–31, Tamiment.

52. "May Day Preparations," in Report of Cook County Executive Committee, March 16, 1936, p. 3, in Series III: State and Local Records, Illinois, Socialist Party of America Papers, Microfilm, Reel 2085, Tamiment.

53. Press release quoting letter from Harry Laidler in response to Louis Waldman, 1936, in Series III: State and Local Records, New York, Socialist Party of America Papers, Microfilm, Reel 2091, Tamiment. The conflict over joining a united May Day demonstration was just one of many reasons for this split.

54. *Daily Worker*, May 2, 1936, p. 1; *The Socialist Call*, May 2, 1936, p. 3, and May 8, 1937, p. 3.

55. Letter from Elmer Johnson, Cook County Secretary, CPUSA, District 8, to SP Cook County, March 10, 1937, in Series III: State and Local Records, Illinois, Socialist Party of America Papers, Microfilm, Reel R2086, Tamiment.

56. In 1936, many of these so-called Trotskyists entered the SP en masse after the Socialist's right wing broke away. They became especially influential in the YPSL. See Klehr, *The Heyday*, 318.

57. Letter from S.R. Shapira to James Oneal, May 5, 1937, in f. 1937, Box 1: Correspondence, James Oneal Papers, Tamiment.

58. Richard Wright, "Richard Wright," in *The God That Failed: Six Studies in Communism*, ed. Richard Crossman (London: Right Book Club, 1950), 121–162.

59. Ibid., 164.

60. Ibid., 164–165.

61. Ibid., 165.

62. Ibid.

63. Ibid., 121–162.

64. Wendell Carroll, November 30, 1983, Box 1, U2D, OH002, Oral History of the American Left, Tamiment.

65. Letter to David Dubinsky penciled on the back of the open letter to members 1936 from L. Barkin, in f. 8b, May 1, 1936–1948, Box 326, in Correspondence, President, June 1932–June 1936, David Dubinsky Papers, ILGWU Records, Kheel.

66. These communists, radical reformers, and left-leaning unionists also continued to challenge the remnants of antiradical Americanism found on the political right and in the small Loyalty Day gatherings that the VFW sponsored in this decade. The VFW held small Loyalty Day parades and mass meetings during the 1930s, which sometimes conflicted with SP and CP plans to use Union Square. See, for example, *Daily Worker* May 1, 1931, p. 4, and April 4, 1934, p. 2.

67. Local 9 of the ILGWU, for example, voted to join with the united parade in 1938. See *Daily Worker*, April 28, 1938, p. 1. For the other unions and organizations, see *Daily Worker*, April 25, 1938, p. 4, and April 27, 1938. See also, Figure 5.2: "May Day 1936, Number 11, DC 9 Painters Union, AFL," Tamiment Library, New York University. Photograph by John Albok.

68. For example, in 1938, 200,000 marched in New York and 50,000 in Chicago (*Daily Worker*, May 1, 1938, p. 1; May 2, 1938, p. 1). In 1939, 200,000 marched in New York, with a half million lining the sidewalks, and 70,000 paraded in Chicago (*Daily Worker*, May 2, 1939, p. 1 and p. 4). In 1940, 90,000 marched in New York (*Daily Worker*, May 2, 1940, p. 1), and in 1941, 75,000 paraded and 250,000 lined the streets (*Daily Worker*, May 2, 1941, p. 1).

69. See Figure 5.3: "May Day 1937, Teachers Union Local 5, AFL," Tamiment Library, New York University. Photograph by Daniel Nilva.

70. Ottanelli, *The Communist Party*, 128.

71. See chapters 2, 3, and 4.

72. See Ottanelli, *The Communist Party*, 122–123; *Daily Worker*, May 2, 1936, p. 1; and "May Day Guide: Suggestions to Socialists," 1936, in Series III: State and Local Files, New York, Socialist Party of America Papers, Microfilm, Reel R2091, Tamiment.

73. Michael Denning, *The Cultural Front: The Laboring of American Culture in the Twentieth Century* (New York: Verso, 1996), 4.

74. Earl Browder, general secretary, "Report to the Tenth National Convention of the Communist Party of the USA on Behalf of the Central Committee,"

delivered on Saturday, May 28, 1938, at Carnegie Hall, New York, in Series 6:15, CPUSA Convention Proceedings, 1921–1972, Earl Browder Papers, Microfilm, Reel 2499.

75. Peter V. Cacchione, James W. Ford, and Israel Amter made this argument in a debate between the CP and the American Legion in 1938. See *The American Legion and the Communist Party Discuss Democracy: A Debate* (New York: Workers Library Publishers, 1938).

76. Albok, a Hungarian immigrant, arrived in New York in 1921 and set up a tailor shop on Madison Avenue in 1923. John Albok, NP-63 Collection, Tamiment.

77. "May 1, 1938. March from Union Square": photographic negative numbers 1, 4, 5, 6, 8, 11, 12, and 32, f. "May Day 1938," in John Albok, NP-63 Collection, Tamiment. See also John Albok, "May Day 1938," VHS Tape 35, Hour 16. 16:23:36 American flag carried near start of parade; 16:24:40 man carries Am. flag near start of huge IWO contingent; 16:25:12 man dressed as Jefferson on a passing float. Tamiment/Wagner Moving Picture Collection, Tamiment.

78. See Figure 5.4: "May 1, 1938, Number 1, March from Union Square," Tamiment Library, New York University. Photograph by John Albok. Although he focuses on Germany, Gottfried Korff's discussion of the "militant clenched fist" as a sign of workers' solidarity for the political left is insightful. Gottfried Korff, "From Brotherly Handshake to Militant Clenched Fist: On Political Metaphors for the Workers' Hand," *International Labor and Working-Class History* 42 (Fall 1992): 70–81.

79. *The American Legion and the Communist Party Discuss Democracy: A Debate* (New York: Workers Library Publishers, 1938).

80. *Daily Worker*, May 1, 1937, part 2, p. 2

81. Ottanelli, *The Communist Party*, 125–126. Fred Blair, July 26, 1983, Box 1, U2C, OH 002, Oral History of the American Left, Tamiment.

82. General Secretary Max Bedact's Report to the General Executive Board of the IWO, March 1939, f. 6, Box 1: IWO Records, Kheel. Closing Remarks by Max Bedact, IWO General Council Session, November 24–26, 1944, f. 11, Box 1: IWO Records, Kheel.

83. See, for example, the delegation from the Ukrainian Section, IWO in the 1938 May Day parade in Figure 5.5: "May 1, 1938. March from Union Square, Ukrainian IWO," Tamiment Library, New York University. Photograph by John Albok.

84. *Daily Worker*, May 1, 1939, p. 2.

85. Terry Martin, "The Origins of Soviet Ethnic Cleansing," *Journal of Modern History* 70:4 (December 1998): 813–861.

86. Terry Martin, *The Affirmative Action Empire: Nations and Nationalism in the Soviet Union, 1923–1939* (Ithaca, N.Y.: Cornell University Press, 2001), 1–26 and 312–343.

87. Michael Denning argues that the song became the "unofficial anthem" of the Popular Front movement because it celebrated both the *promise* of American democracy that had yet to be fulfilled and the nation's social pluralism. See, Denning, *The Cultural Front*, 115 and 128.

88. This brief discussion of 1930s Popular Front culture is intended to express the broad outlines of this aspect of 1930s culture. For a deeper discussion of the complex and varied trends of 1930s American culture, see Denning, *The Cultural Front*, and Warren Susman, "The Culture of the Thirties," in *Culture as History: The Transformation of American Society in the Twentieth Century* (New York: Pantheon, 1984), 150–183.

89. For examples from the mainstream press during the 1930s, see *New York Times*, May 2, 1931, p. 4; May 2, 1933, p. 1 and p. 3; May 2, 1934, p. 1; and May 2, 1936, p. 1; and *Chicago Tribune*, May 1, 1933, p. 1 and photos on p. 32; May 1, 1934, p. 12; May 2, 1935, p. 6; and May 2, 1938, p. 2. For the AFL, see "Report of the Proceedings of the Fifty-Fourth Annual Convention of the American Federation of Labor Held at San Francisco, California, October 1 to 12, Inclusive, 1934," *Proceedings of the American Federation of Labor* (Washington, D.C.: Law Reporter Printing Co., 1934), 372–375; "Report of the Proceedings of the Fifty-Fifth Annual Convention of the American Federation of Labor Held at Atlantic City, New Jersey, October 7 to 19, Inclusive, 1935," *Proceedings of the American Federation of Labor* (Washington, D.C.: Law Reporter Printing Co., 1935), 317–321; and "Report of the Proceedings of the Fifty-Sixth Annual Convention of the American Federation of Labor Held at Tampa, Florida, November 16 to 27, Inclusive, 1936," *Proceedings of the American Federation of Labor* (Washington, D.C.: Law Reporter Printing Co., 1936), 618–628.

90. On the details of the pact, see Gerhard L. Weinberg, *Hitler's Foreign Policy: The Road to World War II, 1933–1939* (New York: Enigma, 2005), 906–911.

91. Zimmerman's comments in the *Sun* were reproduced in *Daily Worker*, April 28, 1940, p. 1.

92. Pauline Dougherty, January 1982, Box 1, U2G, OH 002, Oral History of the American Left, Tamiment.

93. Ottanelli, *The Communist Party*, 182. Wendell Carroll, November 30, 1983, Box 1, U2D, OH002, Tamiment.

94. Dubinsky had long held this belief. See David Dubinsky, "May Day Address at Polo Grounds," May 1, 1936, and "Greeting by David Dubinsky, President, International Ladies' Garment Workers' Union, Randall's Island Stadium, May 1, 1937," in f. 6 and 8, respectively, Box 399: David Dubinsky Correspondence, President June 1932–June 1966, ILGWU Records, Kheel.

95. "Program, May Day Festival 1938, Hippodrome Opera Company," and May Day Committee for Locals of the ILGWU, Press Release, April 25, 1939, f. 5 May Day Celebrations 1930s–1940s, Box 25: Charles Zimmerman Records,

Secretary-Manager, Dressmakers' Union Local 22, 1919 and 1933–1958, ILGWU Records, Kheel.

96. "An Open Letter to the Executive Board, Local 22, ILGWU," 1938, f. 5 May Day Celebrations 1930s–1940s, Box 25: Charles Zimmerman Records, Secretary-Manager, Dressmakers' Union Local 22, 1919 and 1933–1958, ILGWU Records, Kheel.

97. Instead of the grand parades of 20,000 or 50,000 it organized in the early 1930s, the SP held private May Day dinners for several hundred members in 1941 and 1942. See Letter from Irving Barshop, SP, to Martin Feldman, Local 132, April 18, 1941, Series III: State and Local Files, New York, Socialist Party of America Records, Microfilm edition, Reel 2091, Tamiment. *The Socialist Call*, April 25, 1942, p. 8.

NOTES TO CHAPTER 6

1. *Daily Worker*, May 2, 1942, p. 1 and p. 5, and May 3, 1943, p.1.

2. James R. Barrett, *William Z. Foster and the Tragedy of American Radicalism* (Chicago: University of Illinois Press, 1999), 212–232. Joshua Freeman, *In Transit: The Transport Workers Union in New York City, 1933–1966* (New York: Oxford University Press, 1989), 274–275.

3. See chapter 7 for a full discussion of these postwar events.

4. Although he supported the CP, Quill was equally, if not more, dedicated to his union, which he recognized as the base of his power and influence in New York. See Harvey A. Levenstein, *Communism, Anticommunism, and the CIO* (Westport, Conn.: Greenwood Press, 1981), 58–59; and Freeman, *In Transit*, 55–57.

5. By 1942, even those who may have been party members following the party line would have backed the war effort. See Freeman, *In Transit*, 158–161.

6. Gary Gerstle discusses other examples of working-class patriotism during the war in "The Working Class Goes to War," in *The War in American Culture: Society and Consciousness During World War II*, ed. Lewis A. Erenberg and Susan E. Hirsch (Chicago: University of Chicago Press, 1996), 105–127.

7. Re. trade union posts within the American Legion, see "Report of Meeting 10/24/39, 59th Annual Convention of AFL," f. 2-9, Box 27, CFL-John Fitzpatrick Papers, Archives and Manuscript Division, Chicago History Museum (hereafter AMD, CHM). Freeman, *In Transit*, 30.

8. *New York Times*, June 14, 1942, p. 37. In addition to the parades in Chicago and New York, celebrations were staged around the country and around the world. See *New York Times*, June 11, 1942, p. 14; June 15. 1942, p. 1; and June 7, 1942, p. 16.

9. "Report of Defense Committee to CFL," June 7, 1942, f. 3-11, Box 28, CFL-John Fitzpatrick Papers, AMD, CHM.

10. Minutes from TWU Local 100 Meeting, June 8, 1942, f. 2, Box 1, Records of TWU Local 100 (New York City), 1931–1978, Wagner 234, Tamiment Library/

Robert F. Wagner Labor Archives, Elmer Holmes Bobst Library, New York University Libraries, New York University (hereafter TWU 100, Wagner 234, Tamiment). *New York Times*, June 14, 1942, p. 1 and p. 38. By the time of the attack on Pearl Harbor in December 1941, TWU leadership "had already adopted an interventionist stand." As Joshua Freeman argues, union *members* also came to support the war, but for a "variety of reasons" ranging from a Popular Front sense of antifascism to more traditional, nationalist motives. See Freeman, *In Transit*, 228–229.

11. Minutes from TWU Local 100 Meeting, June 8, 1942, f. 2, Box 1, Records of TWU 100, Wagner 234, Tamiment.

12. *New York Times*, June 14, 1942, p. 38.

13. *Federation News*, June 13, 1942, pp. 2–3, f. 5-12, Box 30, CFL-John Fitzpatrick Papers, AMD, CHM. The presence of these more traditional strains of patriotism within the CFL did not signal any loss of union militancy. While John Fitzpatrick encouraged his Federation to cooperate with the American Legion in its celebration of American democracy in the 1939 "Stand By America!" event, he and the CFL's secretary, Edward Nockels, drew the line when it came to allying their organization with known union-busters. Nockels, for example, protested the *Chicago Tribune*'s listing the American Vigilent [sic] Intelligence Federation as a patriotic society, arguing that this organization, led by Harry A. Jung, was really a "labor-baiting, strike-breaking detective agency and anti-Semitic outfit." For "Stand By America Day," see Letter from Arthur E. Canty to John Fitzpatrick, and flyer advertising "Stand By America!" rally, May 17, 1939, f. 3-1, Box 28, CFL-John Fitzpatrick Papers, AMD, CHM. For Nockels' denunciation of Jung's organization, see Letter from E. N. Nockels to Robert McCormick, February 6, 1936, f. 3-2, Box 28, CFL-John Fitzpatrick Papers, AMD, CHM.

14. *New York Times*, September 2, 1935, p. 16.

15. See chapter 3 for a discussion of these struggles.

16. *New York Times*, September 6, 1937, p. 14, and September 6, 1938, p. 7.

17. *Federation News*, June 13, p. 3, f. 5-12, Box 30, CFL-John Fitzpatrick Papers, AMD, CHM.

18. Letter from John Fitzpatrick, Joseph D. Kennan, A. W. Wallace, and Charles A. Noble to Secretaries of Local Unions in Chicago and Vicinity, June 18, 1942, f. 5-12, Box 30, CFL-John Fitzpatrick Papers, AMD, CHM.

19. *Federation News*, June 13, p. 3, f. 5-12, Box 30, CFL-John Fitzpatrick Papers, AMD, CHM.

20. For a brief history of the emergence of the CIO, see Melvyn Dubofsky and Foster Rhea Dulles, *Labor in America: A History* (Wheeling, Ill.: Harlan Davidson, 2004), 280–283.

21. See, for example, the presence of SWOC and the Packinghouse Workers Organizing Committee in the 1938 May Day parade: *Daily Worker*, April 25, 1938, p. 4. The CFL had repeatedly rejected appeals from the CP's May Day Committee

for a united-front May Day. During these same years, the CP used the May Day demonstrations as rallying points for its work in organizing the meatpacking and steel industries in Chicago. See, for example, *Daily Worker*, April 5, 1935, p. 3; April 12, 1935, p. 3; April 6, 1935, p. 8; April 3, 1937, p. 1; and April 25, 1938, p. 4.

22. Relations between the AFL and the CIO were still quite strained in 1941. For the AFL's opposition to communism and its red-baiting of the CIO, see Levenstein, *Communism*, 104–109. For the AFL's attempts to preserve and defend the "craft alternative" to union organizing against the industrial model of the CIO, see Nelson Lichtenstein, *State of the Union: A Century of American Labor* (Princeton, N.J.: Princeton University Press, 2002), 63–71.

23. Letter from John Fitzpatrick, Joseph D. Kennan, A. W. Wallace, and Charles A. Noble to Secretaries of Local Unions in Chicago and Vicinity, June 18, 1942, f. 5-12, Box 30, CFL-John Fitzpatrick Papers, AMD, CHM.

24. Nelson Lichtenstein, *The Most Dangerous Man in Detroit: Walter Reuther and the Fate of American Labor* (New York: Basic Books, 1995), 202.

25. Letter from John Fitzpatrick, Joseph D. Kennan, A. W. Wallace, and Charles A. Noble to Secretaries of Local Unions in Chicago and Vicinity, June 18, 1942, f. 5-12, Box 30, CFL-John Fitzpatrick Papers, AMD, CHM.

26. Letter from Arthur W. Wallace to Charles Noble, July 8, 1942, f. 5-12, Box 30, CFL-John Fitzpatrick Papers, AMD, CHM.

27. Letter from John Fitzpatrick to FDR, June 22, 1942, Letter from John Fitzpatrick to Henry Morgenthau, June 22, 1942, Letter from John Fitzpatrick to William Green, June 22, 1942, Letter from Edwin M. Watson to Fitzpatrick, June 24, 1942, and Letter from William Green to Fitzpatrick, June 26, 1942, f. 5-12, Box 30, CFL-John Fitzpatrick Papers, AMD, CHM. President Roosevelt could not attend the event. William Green did not commit to attending either, citing his need to consider all the other Labor Day invitations he had received that year.

28. Letter from Ira S. Turley to Charles Noble, July 22, 1942, and Letter from Oscar Erhardt to John Fitzpatrick, July 21, 1942, f. 5-12, Box 30, CFL-John Fitzpatrick Papers, AMD, CHM.

29. Letter from John Fitzpatrick to all AFL Local Unions of Chicago and Vicinity, August 3, 1942, f. 5-12, Box 30, CFL-John Fitzpatrick Papers, AMD, CHM.

30. Letter from Jens Koller to Joseph Kennan, August 12, 1942, f. 5-12, Box 30, CFL-John Fitzpatrick Papers, AMD, CHM.

31. Letter from Fitzpatrick and Kennan to AFL Locals of Chicago, August 3, 1942, f. 5-12, Box 30, CFL-John Fitzpatrick Papers, AMD, CHM.

32. See, for example, the participation of the ACWA in the 1943 Bond Drive in New York: *New York Times*, September 7, 1943, p. 25.

33. *New York Times*, May 19, 1940, p. 74. Franklin L. Burdette, "Education for Citizenship," *Public Opinion Quarterly* 6 (1942): 269–277.

34. FDR's letter reprinted in *New York Times*, May 20, 1940, p. 6.

35. Reed Ueda, "The Changing Path to Citizenship: Ethnicity and Natu-ralization during World War II," in *The War in American Culture: Society and Consciousness during World War II*, ed. Lewis A. Erenberg and Susan E. Hirsch (Chicago: University of Chicago Press, 1996), 202–203. Ueda notes how "the pas-sage of the Smith Act in 1940, which required all aliens to be registered and fin-gerprinted and widened the grounds for deportation, may well have raised their [the immigrants'] concern over their status."

36. "I Am an American Day" celebrations were held in New York until 1967, but they never approached the same scale as those staged during the 1940s and 1950s. In 1963, for example, only approximately 30,000 people turned out in Central Park, the largest gathering for that decade. *New York Times*, May 27, 1963, p. 47.

37. *New York Times*, May 4, 1940, p. 19; May 16, 1940, p. 14; and May 18, 1940, pp. 18–19.

38. October 15 was a day before draft registration was to begin. The selection of this day for the patriotic celebration may have been intended to increase sup-port for this military buildup. See *New York Times*, September 27, 1940, p. 31.

39. *New York Times*, September 27, 1940, p. 31, and October 15, 1940, p. 28. Regular admission to the World's Fair cost 75 cents for adults and 25 cents for children. The additional price for "I Am an American Day" admission was to cover the expense of arranging the parades, pageant, and mass meeting. It also functioned as a fundraiser for the church sponsors (they would keep 5 percent of the ticket sales).

40. *New York Times,* September 29, 1940, p. 36.

41. Ibid., October 15, 1940, p. 28.

42. Ibid., October 16, 1940, p. 23.

43. See the map drawn by H. W. Arnold and Amy W. Wells reproduced in the frontispiece of Richard Wurts et al., *The New York World's Fair 1939/1940 in 155 Photographs* (New York: Dover, 1977).

44. "The Composer," in George Kleinsinger, *I Hear America Singing: A Can-tata Based on the Poems of Walt Whitman* (New York: Edward B. Marks Music Corp., 1941).

45. *New York Times*, October 6, 1940, p. 47. Kleinsinger's score clearly formed the basis for the pageant, but the references to the AFL, the Triangle Fire, Sacco and Vanzetti and the NRA do not appear in the original score. These themes must have been introduced by the ILGWU producers. See Kleinsinger, *I Hear America Singing*.

46. *New York Times*, October 6, 1940, p. 47.

47. Robert D. Parmet, *The Master of Seventh Avenue: David Dubinsky and the American Labor Movement* (New York: New York University Press, 2005), 182–187.

48. Michael Denning, *The Cultural Front: The Laboring of American Culture in the Twentieth Century* (New York: Verso, 1998), 306–307.

49. In his study of the Progressives, Shelton Stromquist explores the history of the movement's failure to recognize "the reality of class-constituted power and the possibility of political mobilization around class interests," and argues that liberals (as the intellectual and ideological descendants of the Progressives) adopted this failure later in the twentieth century. See Shelton Stromquist, *Re-Inventing "The People": The Progressive Movement, the Class Problem, and the Origins of Modern Liberalism* (Urbana: University of Illinois Press, 2006), 11. One could argue that the liberals who supported "I Am an American Day" fell into this category.

50. *New York Times*, April 30, 1941, p. 7; April 27, 1941, p. 27; May 4, 1941, p. 20; and May 18, 1942, p. 1.

51. Ibid., May 22, 1944, p. 7.

52. Ibid., May 17, 1943, p. 1 and p. 3. John Fousek has described Wallace as the "leading exponent of social-democratic globalism, advocating what many viewed as a global New Deal." John Fousek, *To Lead the Free World: American Nationalism and the Cultural Roots of the Cold War* (Chapel Hill: University of North Carolina Press, 2000), 56 and 89.

53. *New York Times*, May 22, 1944, p. 1

54. Ibid., May 22, 1944, p. 1 and p. 7.

55. Ibid.

56. Ibid., October 16, 1940, p. 23, and October 6, 1940, p. 47.

57. Ibid., May 18, 1941, p. 36; May 19, 1941, p. 3; May 18, 1942, p. 8; and May 21, 1945, p. 2.

58. *New York Times*, May 5, 1941, p. 12; May 18, 1941, p. 36; May 19, 1941, p. 3; May 18, 1942, p. 8; May 22, 1944, p. 7; and May 21, 1945, p. 2.

59. Denning, *The Cultural Front*, 115 and 128. Stephen Frug, "A Ballad's Ballad: The Divergent Reception of *Ballad for Americans*," unpublished seminar paper, Cornell University, 1999.

60. William H. Chafe, *The Unfinished Journey: America Since World War II* (New York: Oxford University Press, 1995), 11–17.

61. *New York Times*, May 17, 1943, p. 3.

62. The effects of World War II on traditional understandings of gender roles in American society were limited. While the war opened up opportunities for a restructuring of those understandings, it did not result in radical change. During and after the war, most men and women perpetuated the primacy of marriage and childbearing for women. See Elaine Tyler May, "Rosie the Riveter Gets Married," in *The War in American Culture: Society and Consciousness during World War II*, ed. Lewis A. Erenberg and Susan E. Hirsch (Chicago: University of Chicago Press, 1996), 128–143.

63. "Call to We-Are-Americans-Too-Conference," 1943, Papers of A. Philip Randolph, Microfilm edition, Reel 22, Schomberg Center for Research in Black Culture, New York Public Library, New York (hereafter APR, Schomberg).

64. Paula F. Pfeffer, *A. Philip Randolph, Pioneer of the Civil Rights Movement* (Baton Rouge: Louisiana State University Press, 1990), 50–53.

65. "Randolph Suggests 'I Am an American, Too' Week," Press Release, December 30, 1942, APR, Reel 22, Schomberg.

66. Letter from A. Philip Randolph to Francis Biddle, August 9, 1943, APR, Reel 20, Schomberg.

67. "Call to We-Are-Americans-Too Conference," 1943, APR, Reel 22, Schomberg.

68. "Randolph Suggests 'I Am an American, Too' Week," Press Release, December 30, 1942, APR, Reel 22, Schomberg. "Randolph Tells Technique of Civil Disobedience," June 26, 1943, APR, Reel 35, Schomberg.

69. Letter from A. Philip Randolph to Mary McLeod Bethune, March 3, 1943, APR, Reel 20, Schomberg.

70. Letter from William Y. Bell, Jr., to Randolph, January 14, 1943, APR, Reel 20, Schomberg.

71. Letter from Randolph to William Y. Bell, Jr., Exec. Sec. Atlanta Urban League, January 22, 1943, APR, Reel 20, Schomberg.

72. Letter from Randolph to Charles Wesley Burton, Business Director, MOWM, Chicago Division, March 29, 1943, APR, Reel 20, Schomberg.

73. Letter from Randolph and Myers to Delegates, Members, and Friends, June 30, 1943, in "We Are Americans, Too!" Conference Program, APR, Reel 22, Schomberg.

74. Ibid.

75. "Report on the Committee on Resolutions to the 'We Are Americans-Too' Conference," APR, Reel 22, Schomberg.

76. "We Are Americans, Too!" Conference Program, July 1–4, 1943, APR, Reel 22, Schomberg.

77. The conference decided to cancel the planned marches, in part because of the recent race riots in Detroit. Delegates did not want to inflame racial tensions further by organizing their protest march. *New York Times*, July 4, 1943, p. 12. *Washington Post*, July 6, 1943, clipping in scrapbook, APR, Reel 35, Schomberg.

NOTES TO CHAPTER 7

1. *New York Times*, May 20, 1946, p. 4.

2. At this time, in 1946, O'Dwyer still had strong ties to the American Labor Party (ALP) and communists within its ranks. His denunciation of dangerous ideologies most likely referred to what many feared at the time: the threat

of totalitarian dictatorship as embodied in the recently defeated Hitler and the growing aggression of Stalin. Re. O'Dwyer's ties to the ALP, see Joshua B. Freeman, *Working-Class New York: Life and Labor Since World War II* (New York: New Press, 2000), 57.

3. *New York Times*, April 20, 1947, p. 4.

4. As Joshua Freeman notes, by 1949, O'Dwyer "had thoroughly distanced himself from the Left" as the Cold War heated up. Freeman, *Working Class New York*, 80–81.

5. Harry S. Truman, "The Truman Doctrine," in *Great Issues in American History: From Reconstruction to the Present Day, 1864–1981*, ed. Richard Hofstadter and Beatrice K. Hofstadter (New York: Vintage, 1982), 405–406. William H. Chafe, *The Unfinished Journey: America Since World War II* (New York: Oxford University Press, 1995), 67.

6. Truman, 405.

7. Ibid., 406.

8. John Fousek, *To Lead the Free World: American Nationalism and the Cultural Roots of the Cold War* (Chapel Hill: University of North Carolina Press, 2000), 7–15, 103–129, and 187–191.

9. *New York Times*, May 16, 1949, p. 3.

10. From May 31 to July 7, 1949, Samuel H. Kaufman also presided over the first trial of Alger Hiss, which ended in a deadlocked jury. The local conservative dailies and many Republican politicians then criticized Kaufman as favoring the defense and derided him as being soft on communism. Allen Weinstein, *Perjury: The Hiss-Chambers Case* (New York: Knopf, 1978), 412–413 and 466–469.

11. *New York Times,* May 16, 1949, p. 3.

12. Most years the numbers ranged from 150,000 to 300,000, but in 1949 an estimated 1.25 million people turned out in New York. *New York Times*, May 16, 1949, p. 3.

13. While many of its leaders may have had ties to the CP, most of TWU Local 100's membership did not, nor did they believe that their leaders were communist, because men like Michael Quill, Austin Hogan, Douglas MacMahon, and John Santo did not make such links public before 1948. See Joshua B. Freeman, *In Transit: The Transport Workers Union in New York City, 1933–1966* (New York: Oxford University Press, 1989), 74–75. By 1948, even Quill openly broke away from the CP. He then purged Local 100 (and later of the International) of leaders who maintained ties to the communists. Freeman, *In Transit*, 296–314.

14. *New York Times*, May 22, 1944, p. 7. See also Executive Board Minutes from April 14, 1948, Bakers Union Local 17, Box 4, f. 3, Bakery, Confectionery and Tobacco Workers International Union, AFL-CIO, Local 3 Records, 1902–1993, Wagner 135, Tamiment Library/Robert F. Wagner Labor Archives, Elmer Holmes Bobst Library, New York University (hereafter Bakery, Wagner 135, Tamiment). Letter from Mayor Wagner to Matthew Guinan, President TWU

Local 100, dated August 20, 1954, Box 2, f. 14, Records of TWU Local 100 (New York City); Transport Workers Union of America, Records of Locals, 1931–1978, Wagner 234, Tamiment Library/Robert F. Wagner Labor Archives, Elmer Holmes Bobst Library, New York University (hereafter TWU 100, Wagner 234, Tamiment).

15. President Truman articulated this charge and challenge for the nation in his speech before Congress in March 1947, where he laid out the foreign policy doctrine that took his name.

16. Socialists and their allied unions still celebrated May Day too, but they did so in smaller indoor meetings or dinners during which party leaders, like Norman Thomas, denounced the totalitarianism of the CP. See, for example, *New York Times*, May 1, 1946, p. 27; March 13, 1947, p. 54; May 2, 1947, p. 5; May 1, 1948, p. 5; and May 2, 1948, p. 33.

17. Howard Fast, *Being Red* (Boston: Houghton Mifflin, 1990), 142.

18. James R. Barrett, *William Z. Foster and the Tragedy of American Radicalism* (Chicago: University of Illinois Press, 1999), 212–232; and Fraser M. Ottanelli, *The Communist Party of the United States: From the Depression to World War II* (New Brunswick, N.J.: Rutgers University Press, 1991), 215.

19. Richard M. Fried, *The Russians Are Coming! The Russians Are Coming! Pageantry and Patriotism in Cold-War America* (New York: Oxford University Press, 1998), 52.

20. *Proceedings of the Veterans of Foreign Wars of the United States, Department of New York, for the Year 1945–1946. Twenty-Seventh Annual Encampment. Held at Brooklyn, N.Y. July 3, 4, 5, 6, 1946*, ed. Frederic J. Brack (Albany: Williams Press), 114.

21. Fried, *The Russians Are Coming!*, 54. Stephen J. Whitfield, *The Culture of the Cold War* (London: Johns Hopkins University Press, 1991), 46–49. Martin Bauml Duberman, *Paul Robeson* (New York: Knopf, 1988), 379.

22. See Figure 7.1, Loyalty Day Parade, 1967, from f. "May Day, 1967" Box 170, NP223, Communist Party of the United States Photographs Collection, Tamiment Library, New York University.

23. Fried, *The Russians are Coming!*, 55.

24. Fried, *The Russians are Coming!*, 56. See also *New York Times*, May 2, 1946, p. 1.

25. *VFW Magazine* (June 1951): 13–18.

26. President Truman had relieved MacArthur of his duties as commander-in-chief of the United Nation's forces in Korea on April 3, 1951, for insubordination. The VFW welcomed him as an anticommunist hero at its Loyalty Day parade on April 28. Herbert Malloy Mason, Jr., *VFW: Our First Century* (Lenexa, Kans.: Addax Publishing Group, 1999), 120.

27. Eric Jarvis, "Joining the Cold War Consensus: American Catholics and the Budapest Trial of Cardinal Mindszenty," Session 1, American Catholic Historical

Association, American Historical Association Annual Meeting, Chicago, Illinois, January 3, 2003.

28. Whitfield, *Culture of the Cold War*, 95.

29. *New York Times*, May 1, 1949, p. 1. The secret police had "stripped [Mindszenty] of his clothes and had the cardinal dressed in the costume of a clown, while the jailers and other secret police officers shouted obscenities at him." They later beat him "until he fainted." See Whitfield, *Culture of the Cold War*, 95.

30. Whitfield, *Culture of the Cold War*, 77–91.

31. Marc Dollinger, *Quest for Inclusion: Jews and Liberalism in Modern America* (Princeton, N.J.: Princeton University Press, 2000), 129–143. This also may have indicated a deepening divide within America's Jewish community broadly defined, as many secular Jews still supported the political left, be they members of the Communist Party, fellow travelers, or liberal Democrats.

32. *New York Times*, May 2, 1948, p. 3, and May 1, 1949, p. 1.

33. Ibid., May 1, 1949, p. 1, and April 30, 1950, p. 1.

34. Ibid., April 30, 1950, p. 1.

35. Elaine Tyler May, "Cold War-Warm Hearth: Politics and the Family in Postwar America," in *The Rise and Fall of the New Deal Order 1930–1980*, ed. Steve Fraser and Gary Gerstle (Princeton, N.J.: Princeton University Press, 1989), 153–181.

36. *Daily Worker*, May 2, 1948, sec. 2, p. 2; May 1, 1954, p. 3; May 1, 1957, p. 7; and May 3, 1959, p. 12.

37. Ibid., May 2, 1947, p. 3.

38. *New York Times*, May 2, 1947, p. 9, and May 2, 1946, p. 1.

39. *Daily Worker*, May 2, 1947, p. 3, and May 3, 1948, p. 4.

40. Ibid., May 3, 1948, p. 9, and May 2, 1949, p. 3.

41. Ibid., May 2, 1951, p. 6.

42. *New York Times*, May 1, 1953, p. 3, and *Daily Worker*, May 1, 1953, p. 1.

43. *New York Times*, April 22, 1953, p. 18.

44. Ibid., February 1, 1953, p. 28.

45. Ibid., April 22, 1953, p. 28.

46. Ibid., April 24, 1953, p. 13.

47. Ibid., April 25, 1953, p. 8.

48. Ibid.

49. Ibid., Text of Monaghan Statement, April 29, 1953, p. 11.

50. Ibid.

51. *Daily Worker*, May 1, 1953, p. 1.

52. Ibid., May 4, 1953, p. 3; May 3, 1954, p. 1 and p. 8; May 2, 1955, p.8; and May 1, 1956, p. 1 and p. 8.

53. *New York Times*, April 16, 1954, p. 13.

54. Ibid., July 8, 1923, p. 14; January 3, 1926, p. RE4; and November 29, 1952, p. 19.

55. Ibid., March 14, 1954, p. 58.

56. Ibid., May 2, 1954, p. 52

57. Ibid.

58. For Clark, McCarthy and HUAC, see Whitfield, *Culture of the Cold War,* 9–12, 16, 29, 37–42, and 47–51.

59. Frank Boyle, District 65 General Council Meeting Proceedings, April 29, 1946, p. 2, Box 2, f. 3, District 65, General Membership Mtgs. Minutes, Box 1, f. 2, United Automobile, Aircraft, and Automobile Workers of America, District 65 Records, 1933–1992, Wagner 006, Tamiment (hereafter District 65, Wagner 006, Tamiment).

60. Sol Molofsky, District 65 General Council Meeting Proceedings, April 29, 1946, pp. 2–4, Box 2, f. 3, District 65, Wagner 006, Tamiment.

61. Jack Case, District 65 General Council Meeting Proceedings, April 29, 1946, pp. 4–5, Box 2, f. 3, District 65, Wagner 006, Tamiment.

62. Iris Wilson, District 65 General Council Meeting Proceedings, April 29, 1946, p. 5, Box 2, f. 3, District 65, Wagner 006, Tamiment.

63. Bruno Zelinsky, District 65 General Council Meeting Proceedings, April 29, 1946, p. 6, Box 2, f. 3, District 65, Wagner 006, Tamiment.

64. These sentiments were not unique to District 65. See Bakery, April 17, 1948, Box 1, f. 11, Local 1 Membership Minutes, Bakery, Wagner 135, Tamiment.

65. Kenneth Sherbell, "May Day Report," March 29, 1947, District 65 General Council Minutes, Box 2, f. 2, District 65, Wagner 006, Tamiment.

66. Melvyn Dubofsky and Foster Rhea Dulles, *Labor in America: A History* (Wheeling, Ill.: Harlan Davidson, 2004), 337; James R. Green, *The World of the Worker: Labor in Twentieth-Century America* (Chicago: University of Illinois Press, 1998), 198–199.

67. In 1948, 65 disaffiliated from the Retail, Wholesale and Department Store Union (RWDSU) and the CIO after the RWDSU's international executive board mandated all locals to comply with 9(h) and suspended local officers who refused. See Freeman, *Working-Class New York,* 78.

68. Medlin, District 65, Proceedings of the General Council Meeting, April 26, 1948, pp. 49–50, Box 2, f. 12, District 65, Wagner 006, Tamiment.

69. "Estimates on May Day" and "Budget for May Day," Box 67 f. 16 (May Day 1948), District 65, Wagner 006, Tamiment.

70. From February until October 1949, eleven leaders of the Communist Party were tried and convicted in New York for violating Section 11 of the Smith Act (its conspiracy provision). Overall, by the mid-1950s, "one hundred and twenty-six Party leaders were eventually indicted (under the Smith Act), of whom ninety-three were convicted." Whitfield, *Culture of the Cold War,* 48–49.

71. David Livingston, District 65, Proceedings of the General Council Meeting, April 26, 1948, pp. 54–58, Box 2, f. 12, District 65, Wagner 006, Tamiment.

72. Alan Brinkley, "World War II and American Liberalism," in *The War in American Culture: Society and Consciousness during World War II*, ed. Lewis A. Erenberg and Susan D. Hirsch (Chicago: University of Chicago Press, 1996), 320–322.

73. Irving Baldinger, May Day Report, Minutes of 10th General Council, April 25, 1949, District 65, Wagner 006, Tamiment.

74. *Daily Worker* claimed a total of 75,000 marchers from all organizations (May 2, 1949, p. 1). District 65 had distributed 3,000 buttons to participating members that year. Minutes of the 10th General Council, April 25, 1949, Box 2, f.16, District 65, Wagner 006, Tamiment. Neither figure approached the numbers that turned out during May Day's heyday during the late 1930s.

75. Kenneth Sherbell, May Day Report, Minutes of the General Council Meeting, March 27, 1950, Box 3, R-5506, District 65, Wagner 006, Microfilm version, Tamiment.

76. Minutes from April 6, 1938, April 14, 1938, April 28, 1938, March 16, 1939, April 13, 1939, April 20, 1939, and April 27, 1939, Local 1 Executive Board Minutes, Box 1 (Local 1 and Old Local 3) f. 5, Bakery, Wagner 135, Tamiment. Minutes from April 9, 1938, April 27, 1938, April 15, 1939, April 26, 1939, Local 17 Executive Board Minutes, Box 4 (Local 17) f. 1, Bakery, Wagner 135, Tamiment.

77. Minutes from the General Meeting, April 19, 1947, Box 4, f. 3, Local 17 Minutes, Bakery, Wagner 135, Tamiment.

78. Minutes from the Executive Board Meeting, April 14, 1938, April 28, 1948, March 30, 1949, and May 4, 1949, Box 4, f. 3 Local 17 Minutes, Bakery, Wagner 135, Tamiment.

79. Minutes from the Executive Board Meeting, March 28, 1951, September 12, 1951, March 5, 1952, September 10, 1952, Box 4, f. 3, Local 17 Minutes, Bakery, Wagner 135, Tamiment.

80. While some historians have argued that worker militancy declined in the postwar years, to be "replaced by routinized bargaining," Joshua Freeman finds that "transport workers did not become less militant over time, nor were rank-and-file dissidents necessarily more radical than union bureaucrats." He does, however, note that "while transit workers were highly combative in the postwar era, their struggles were narrower and had less lasting impact than their earlier collective activity." Freeman, *In Transit*, 330–331.

81. The McCarran Act (which Congress passed over President Truman's veto) "required communists to register with the government, revoked passports of those suspected of communist sympathy, and established provisions for setting up concentration camps for subversives in the event of a national emergency." Chafe, *The Unfinished Journey*, 105.

82. By 1949, the delegates to the CIO's annual convention voted to ban members of the Communist Party from serving on the CIO's Executive Board, and "gave the purified Executive Board the power to expel, by a two-thirds vote,

any affiliate whose policies and activities were 'consistently directed towards the achievement of the program and purposes of the Communist Party, any fascist organization, or other totalitarian movement, rather than the objectives and policies set forward in the constitution of the CIO.'" Harvey L. Levenstein, *Communism, Anticommunism, and the CIO* (Westport, Conn.: Greenwood Press, 1981), 299. Over the next two years, eleven unions were purged, costing the CIO 900,000 members. See Green, *The World of the Worker,* 201.

83. Minutes from Regular Membership Meeting, April 25, 1950, Box 5, f. 4 Local 51 Minutes, Bakery, Wagner 006, Tamiment.

84. Minutes from Regular Membership Meeting, June 26, 1951, Box 5, f. 5 Local 51 Minutes, Bakery, Wagner 135, Tamiment.

85. Minutes from June 26, 1951, Regular Membership Meeting, Box 5, f. 5 Local 51 Minutes, Bakery, Wagner 135, Tamiment.

86. Ibid.

87. On the Peekskill riot, see Duberman, *Paul Robeson,* 363–380.

88. Minutes from June 26, 1951, Regular Membership Meeting, Box 5, f. 5 Local 51 Minutes, Bakery, Wagner 135, Tamiment.

89. Minutes of the 7th General Council, April 4, 1951, p. 2, Box 3, f. 4, R-5506, District 65, Wagner 006, Microfilm version, Tamiment.

90. Samuel Neuberger, McCarran Committee Report, General Council Minutes, March 12, 1952, Box 3, f. 6, District 65, Wagner 006, Tamiment.

91. Ibid.

92. Clipping from the *Wall Street Journal,* f. 17 Labor Day Parade, 1959–1963, Box 28, Series I, TWU 100, Wagner 234, Tamiment.

93. Letter from Matthew Guinan to All Section Officers, July 23, 1959, Box 28, f. 17, TWU 100, Wagner 234, Tamiment. The union was also fighting for a better contract and against the "challenge of increased automation": see handbills, "To All TWU Members: Labor Day Is Our Day" and "To All Members of Local 100: March with TWU," Box 28, f. 17, TWU 100, Wagner 234, Tamiment.

94. Mimeograph of Labor Day costs and banners by locals, and small advertising card "Come see the Labor Day Parade," TWU 100, Box 28, f. 17, TWU 100, Wagner 234, Tamiment.

95. Clipping from the *Daily News,* July 31, 1959, TWU Local 100, Box 28, f. 17, TWU 100, Wagner 234, Tamiment. Minutes of Executive Board, September 1, 1959, Local 51 Cake Bakers Union, Box 5, f. 9, Bakery, Wagner 135, Tamiment.

96. For the development of this consumer class consciousness on Labor Day outside of the parades, see the discussion in chapter 3.

97. Lizabeth Cohen, *A Consumer's Republic: The Politics of Mass Consumption in Postwar America* (New York: Vintage, 2003), 153–154.

98. *New York Times,* May 2, 1952, p. 4. *Daily Worker,* May 5, 1952, p. 2.

99. In 1956, the U.S. Subversive Activities Control Board investigated the United May Day Committee (UMDC), a CP front group led by Louis Weinstock,

and required it to register with the attorney general. These proceedings distracted those like Weinstock from focusing their full attention on organizing the annual May Day parade, and drew the UMDC into the orbit of federal observation and suspicion, thus further alienating it from most workers. See U.S. Subversive Activities Control Board, Docket 111-53. Herbert Brownell, Jr., Attorney General of the United States, Petitioner, v. United May Day Committee, Respondent (Washington, D.C.: Government Printing Office, 1956), 1–2 and 4–57.

100. Khrushchev criticized Stalin and his regime of "suspicion, fear, and terror" in a speech before the 20th Congress of the Communist Party in February 1956. He also acknowledged the purges of 1936–1938. The speech was made public in the United States in April 1956. See James R. Barrett, *William Z. Foster and the Tragedy of American Radicalism* (Urbana and Chicago: University of Illinois Press, 1999), 252–257.

101. Whitfield, *Culture of the Cold War*, 50; Ottanelli, *The Communist Party*, 216. Yet, not all party members left, even after 1956. Some, like Gil Green and Israel Amter, remained loyal to the end. See Letters from Gil Green to Lillian Green, March 20, 1956, and June 12, 1956, Box 3, f. 2 and 3, Gil Green Papers, Tamiment. Israel and Sadie Amter, Autobiographical Typescript, pp. 224–225, Tamiment.

102. In 1959, for example, only a few thousand gathered in Union Square. *Daily Worker*, May 10, 1959, p. 5.

103. Remnants of the CP and other left-wing political groups would continue to stage gatherings on May 1 well into the 1990s, but these were generally small affairs that attracted, at most, perhaps 1,000 people. See discussion of post-1960 May Day in the Conclusion. See also Photos of May Day gatherings from 1960–1999, Box 170, f. May Day 1960–f. May Day 1999, Daily Worker/Daily World Photo Collection, CPUSA Collection, Tamiment Library, New York University.

104. See, for example, *New York Times*, May 3, 1953, p. E8.

105. Matthew Dennis, *Red, White, and Blue Letter Days: An American Calendar* (Ithaca, N.Y.: Cornell University Press, 2002), 7.

106. John Fousek notes how, "in the Cold War, 'free enterprise' was increasingly accepted as the most fundamental, most American form of freedom." As a result, the challenges that labor leaders, like Walter Reuther, tried to pose to "economic injustice could not strike the same nationalist chords as the NAACP's challenge to racial injustice." See Fousek, *To Lead the Free World*, 161.

107. Jonathan Rosenberg, *How Far the Promised Land? World Affairs and the American Civil Rights Movement from the First World War to Vietnam* (Princeton, N.J.: Princeton University Press, 2006), 185–213. Fousek, *To Lead the Free World*, 12–13, 83–87, 136, 140–147, 159, and 161.

108. The UE was expelled from the CIO in 1949. Fousek, *To Lead the Free World*, 148–149.

109. Daniel J. Walkowitz, *Working with Class: Social Workers and the Politics of Middle-Class Identity* (Chapel Hill: University of North Carolina Press, 1999), 290.

110. The United Farm Workers, the American Federation of State and County Municipal Employees, and other unions have followed this path since the 1960s. See Green, *World of the Worker*, 234–248; and Nelson Lichtenstein, *State of the Union: A Century of American Labor* (Princeton, N.J.: Princeton University Press, 2002), 178–211.

NOTES TO THE CONCLUSION

1. As one historian has noted, "as a result of the postwar boom, nearly 60 percent of American people had achieved a 'middle-class' standard of living by the mid-1950s." See William H. Chafe, *The Unfinished Journey: America Since World War II* (New York: Oxford University Press, 1995), 112. The expansion of this middle-class standard of living was made possible in large part by union efforts to secure higher wages and benefits. See, for example, Joshua Freeman's discussion of municipal unionism during the 1960s and 1970s. Joshua B. Freeman, *Working-Class New York: Life and Labor Since World War II* (New York: New Press, 2000), 201–214. One of the first, and biggest, contracts to secure such wage increases and benefits, including a cost of living adjustment, *while at the same time giving up the demand for a say in the process of production*, was the five-year contract secured between the UAW and GM in 1950. It has become known as the Treaty of Detroit, and served as the model for most major union contracts by the 1960s. See Nelson Lichtenstein, *State of the Union: A Century of American Labor* (Princeton, N.J.: Princeton University Press, 2002), 123.

2. In discussing some of the factors that contributed to the "virtual disappearance of the notion of a working class" in America by the late 1990s, Joshua B. Freeman notes how "for decades there had been a national predilection to spurn the language of class." See Freeman, *Working-Class New York*, 327.

3. These included migrant farm workers, service sector workers, sanitation and other public sector workers. See Freeman, *Working-Class New York*, 201–214; Lichtenstein, *State of the Union*, 178–211; Melvyn Dubofsky and Foster Rhea Dulles, *Labor in America: A History* (Wheeling, Ill.: Harlan Davidson, 2004), 391–393.

4. Alan Brinkley, "The New Deal and the Idea of the State," in *The Rise and Fall of the New Deal Order, 1930–1980*, ed. Steve Fraser and Gary Gerstle (Princeton, N.J.: Princeton University Press, 1989), 84–121 and especially 109.

5. Eric Foner, *The Story of American Freedom* (New York: W.W. Norton & Co., 1998), 285.

6. *New York Times*, May 3, 1960, p.11; March 3, 1961, p. 19; May 2, 1961, p. 14; May 2, 1962, p. 2; May 2, 1963, p. 3; May 2, 1964, p. 2; May 2, 1968, p. 43; and May 2, 1971, p. 69.

7. May Day photographs, Box 170, folders, May Day 1960–May Day 1980, NP 223, CPUSA Photographs Collection, Tamiment Library, New York University. See Figure C1, Antiwar Protestors, May Day 1969, Box 170, f. May Day 1969, NP 223, CPUSA Photographs Collection, Tamiment Library, New York University.

8. Foner, *American Freedom,* 288.

9. Ibid., 275–305.

10. Ibid., 275–305. Lichtenstein, *State of the Union,* 171–177 and 191–196.

11. Lichtenstein, *State of the Union,* 199. Chafe, *The Unfinished Journey,* 365–367. Shelton Stromquist comes to a similar conclusion about modern liberals' failure to acknowledge the importance of class, but his argument focuses on the roots of that weakness in the history of the Progressive movement. See Shelton Stromquist, *Reinventing the People: The Progressive Movement, the Class Problem, and the Origins of Modern Liberalism* (Urbana: University of Illinois Press, 2006).

12. *New York Times,* May 7, 1995, p. CY6.

13. Ibid., May 3, 1998, p. 45.

14. See, for example, Ellen M. Litwicki, *America's Public Holidays, 1865–1920* (Washington, D.C.: Smithsonian Institution Press, 2000), 9–49.

15. See Gary Gerstle, *Working-Class Americanism: The Politics of Labor in a Textile City, 1914–1960* (Princeton, N.J.: Princeton University Press, 2002), 334–335.

Index

Page numbers in *italics* refer to illustrations

About the Author

DONNA T. HAVERTY-STACKE is Assistant Professor of History at Hunter College, City University of New York, where she teaches courses in U.S. cultural, urban, and labor history.